An Outline History

of

AMERICAN DRAMA

Joseph Jefferson III as Rip Van Winkle

(From the collection of the author)

An Outline History
of
AMERICAN DRAMA

by
Walter J. Meserve

Feedback Theatrebooks & Prospero Press

Manufactured in the United States of America.

Feedback Theatrebooks & Prospero Press
305 Madison Avenue Suite 1146
New York, New York 10165

Post Office Box 174, Naskeag Point Road
Brooklin, Maine 04616

ISBN 0-937657-18-2

Table of Contents

Preface
(1994)

More than thirty years ago when I wrote the Preface to the first edition of this book, I thought of it as preparation for a more thorough history to come -- a history of several volumes. I still have that objective. Other scholarly endeavors and teaching assignments, however, intruded into my academic life, and I am now only halfway through my project. I published *An Emerging Entertainment: the Drama of the American People to 1828* in 1977 and *Heralds of Promise: the Drama of the American People During the Age of Jackson, 1829-1849* in 1986. By some arithmetic progression *Echoes of the Public Voice: the Drama of the American People from 1850 to 1890* should appear in 1995, and it may. Three more volumes will complete the project I imagined more than thirty years ago.

Renewal is always healthy, and it seems appropriate to give this preparatory *Outline* a lively update. I know considerably more about American drama now than I did in 1964, and I have tried to incorporate that knowledge -- particularly pertinent to the eighteenth and nineteenth centuries -- along with helpful dates and the reevaluation of playwrights and plays that the passage of time has made possible. I have also added a new final chapter, bringing the story of playwrights, plays, theatres and dramatic criticism up to the present.

There have been exciting changes brought to the study of American drama over the past thirty years -- more emphasis on the subject in colleges and universities, and scores of books and articles. But some of the observations I made in my 1965 Preface surprisingly still hold true. No scholar has yet analyzed the progress of American drama throughout its 300-year history or tried to impose any critical order on its development. Only two books consider the broad scope of American drama -- Garff Wilson's *Three Hundred Years of American Drama and Theatre*, 1973, and *American Drama*, Volume VIII of the *Revels History of the Drama in English*, 1977, by Travis Bogard, Richard Moody and me -- and these studies place equal emphasis upon drama and theatre. The challenge for all scholars of American dramatic literature is still before us!

W.J.M.

Preface
(1965)

American drama is a most neglected part of the study of American literature. Nearly a third of a century has passed since anyone has attempted an historical assessment of American drama, and no scholar has discussed the developing movements of American drama or tried to impose any critical order upon the 300 years which separate contemporary drama from the first play written by a Colonist in English and performed in America. No one need argue that the literary value of American drama during its first 200 years is very slight. That goes without saying. But as an index to an active society, as a background for modern American drama, and for the literary value of many plays, a study of American drama has its value as well as being a more significant and closely related part of American letters than is usually imagined. It is the purpose of this outline to present the many developing trends in American drama with the supporting detail and critical observations which will make this material meaningful to the student, the scholar, and the casual reader of American plays.

To make this material meaningful I have discussed each topic in terms of its historical development, the achievements of particular dramatists, and the contribution of particular plays. In all instances the plots of important plays are summarized and the titles of relatively significant plays are listed. Because most plays and playwrights suggest more than a single point of view, however, authors and their plays are frequently treated or mentioned under more than one heading. To show the closeness and interdependence of American drama, theatre, and criticism, each chapter relates the progress of dramatic criticism and the achievements of the theatre to a developing American drama. Using information that has not been available to previous historians of American drama (the product of recent research and scholarship) and approaching the subject from the point of view of trends, ideas, and the contributions of particular plays rather than from a chronological discussion of important dramatists, this outline history provides a new and basic approach for a more appreciative understanding of American drama.

W.J.M.

Chapter One

The Beginnings of American Drama

"The first efforts at dramatic literature in this country were wild," wrote William Dunlap in *A History of the American Theatre* (1832). American plays were "the essays of youth, not sufficiently instructed in anything, and deficient in literary education, and though received favorably . . . both the dramatist and the people they addressed had not yet sufficiently matured their notions of the result of the great political changes which had taken place to know how far to assert independence in literature or government or how far to imitate their European ancestors." Like much of what Dunlap wrote in his history, these generalizations require thoughtful skepticism. "Wild," for example, may not be the best word to describe some of the dull contributions to Colonial theatre; a number of Dunlap's hopeful playwrights, it should be noted, were among the educated elite; and certainly, few of their efforts were "received favorably." Dunlap's final point, however, reveals the perception for which he deserves his esteemed reputation in the history of American drama and theatre.

Paralleling social and political attitudes which divided the early colonists, literature, particularly dramatic literature, developed along partisan lines. Much depends, therefore, upon an understanding of the people who wrote these plays: men and women of the theatre or of the library! Within this division of endeavor -- which fostered an unhealthy antagonism until modern times -- some playwrights insisted upon imitating the fashions and traditions of English and European drama in both form and idea while others emphasized distinctively American concepts. All showed the diversity of objectives that characterize American drama from its beginnings until the present day.

If early attempts at dramatic literature were wild, one could surely describe the beginnings of an American theatre as stormy. Performances of plays were opposed by local groups of self-appointed guardians of the rights of others, by Colonial governments and by certain religious sects. Bankruptcy was a common hazzard for theatre managers. Playwrights were constantly subjected to abuse by theatre managers, actors and a public that by and large still preferred the arts and entertainment of the "Mother Country."

It is not strange that good native drama before 1800 was rare. The middle-class tastes which dominated the popular theatre did not appeal to an artistic temperament; and the lack of protection by a copyright law discouraged many would-be playwrights with literary skills who also were apprehensive of Anglophile public tastes and lacked an entreé to the theatre world. Plays, therefore, perhaps by default, were written mainly by opportunists, political or theatrical. The results -- propaganda plays, poetic tragedies and comedies imitative of the English -- were produced, if at all, in a secondary position. The major theatre fare consisted of pirated English and European plays, adaptations, translations and the classics. Occasionally, in healthy contrast, American originality appeared in the stage Yankee and in plays with native themes. By 1800, although conditions in the theatre remained chaotic, a drama which could be called American was slowly forming.

I. COLONIAL THEATRE AND DRAMA

Primitive peoples have always enjoyed celebrating the changes in nature as they affect the life cycle, and the celebrations and ceremonies of the American Indians might be considered the first forms of drama to appear in North America. It has also been argued that certain late seventeenth- and early eighteenth-century treaty ceremonies involving Indians and the White Man should be considered among the beginnings of American drama. The settlers, however, needed their own form of amusement; and the raw material for their theatre was the life they led. They fought with the Indians for their lives, strove for fortune in the new plantations of the South or argued with their neighbors about religion in New England and politics in New York. Their experiences provided material for some plays; playwrights also turned to the familiar themes of English and European drama. Whichever impulse excited them, the newcomers early felt the need for drama. And they soon began to satisfy that need.

A. Drama in the Colonies: First Performances

What makes a drama distinctly American is a moot point -- open to geographical, linguistic and political discussion. Early drama in the Colonies may be called "American" only because the term is a convenience. The land itself had been claimed by the French, the Spanish, the English and the Indians. The people were as varied as could be imagined -- in language, politics, economics, religion, customs and so on -- and could be related only by the fact that they shared the same New World. But the Colonies of England became the United States of America on a specific date. Before then plays were written and performed, and this drama developed without great attention to this "specific date" at a pace consistent with the demands and permissiveness of society. It could not have been otherwise, and it is that development that will be described in this study.

1.   THE FIRST AMERICAN PLAY

The history of drama is the history of people, and the people who settled America were a diverse group, speaking and writing in different languages. Perhaps the earliest theatrical activity took place at a Spanish mission on or about June 24, 1567, in Tequesta, Florida, where, according to Francisco de Villareal, a lay brother, two comedies were performed.   One, he wrote to his superior, dealt with the war between the flesh and the devil. Both may have been traditional church plays, or they may have been written for the occasion. Historians may never know.

During the conquest by the King of Spain of the territory of New Mexico in 1598-99, Captain Marcos Farfán de los Godos wrote an original comedy which was performed in the spring of 1598 near what is now the city of El Paso, Texas. The subject was "the conquest of New Mexico" and, like the comedy in Tequesta, was written to please the soldiers.   The third possibly "first" play, a masque written by Marc Lescarbot, a Frenchman, was performed on November 14, 1606, at Port

Royal, Acadia [Nova Scotia]. Celebrating the return to the Habitation of the Sieur de Poutrincourt from a voyage down the coast, *Le Theatre de Neptune en La Nouvelle-France* was a comical expression by Lescarbot and others during a period of hard times. It was soon published in France but did not receive an English translation until 1927.

2. EARLY AMERICAN PLAYS ON STAGE

(a) *Ye Bare and Ye Cubb* (1665) by Cornelius Watkinson, Philip Howard and William Darby

Having performed their play on August 27, 1665, in Accomac County on the Eastern Shore of Virginia, the author-actors were informed on by Edward Martin and summoned by the King's attorney who told them to appear appropriately dressed on November 16, 1665, at court, where they would act out their play. Of the three, only Darby, who apparently argued their case, was arrested. At the hearing, however, the judge found the players "not guilty of fault" and ordered Martin to pay all court costs.

(b) Other Plays Written and Performed

About the turn of the century (1699-1702), Richard Hunter successfully petitioned John Nanfan, the Acting Governor of New York, for permission to present plays in New York City, although it is uncertain whether or not he made use of his license. Indicative of theatre activity in the South was a recital in 1702 by students of William and Mary College of a "pastoral colloquy." The following year, 1703, Anthony Aston (1682-1749?), a wandering English actor, wrote in his journal: "We arrived in Charles-Town, full of Lice, Shame, Poverty, Nakedness and Hunger. I turned player and poet and wrote one Play on the Subject of the country." Whatever its merits, Aston's play was not preserved.

3.   FIRST PLAY PRINTED IN AMERICA: *ANDROBOROS* (1714) BY ROBERT HUNTER (d. 1734)

(Plot) The play opens in the Senate, where the Senators are portrayed as a ridiculous group who praise Androboros (whose name means man-eater) for courage and prudence he has not shown and rail violently against the Keeper, Governor Hunter.

In Act II the Senate dissolves itself to become a Consistory, and the play becomes a bitter attack on the clergy. The farcical hero, Androboros, is the object of blatant satire in Act III. Stupidly believing in his own deification, he is shown to be so ethereal that some cannot see and others cannot hear him, although most people can smell him. The play ends as all, including Androboros, who is hardly a man-eater, are trapped by the Keeper.

(Discussion) *Androboros*, by Robert Hunter, Governor of New York and New Jersey from 1710 to 1719, is now preserved at the Huntington Library in California. From its formal dedication through its three acts -- The Senate, The Consistory, The Apotheosis -- the play is an occasionally witty but rowdy attack on the Provincial Council, the church government and Lieutenant Governor Nicholson as Androboros. Although the construction of *Androboros* is rough and unfinished, the play has both a theatrical quality and a literary pretense which lend it some distinction. Moreover, its satire is pungent and devastating.

B. Actors and Acting Companies in the Colonies

During much of the early eighteenth century, the actor in England experienced hard times. The drama of the Restoration (1660-1700) had been witty and brilliant but a bit too vulgar for the tastes of the rising middle class. Jeremy Collier's attack on the theatre, *Short View of the Immorality and Profaneness of the English Stage* (1698), clearly indicated the change that was coming. Playwrights like William Congreve left the stage. Moralists, humanitarians and sentimentalists took their places, with the result that theatre attendance dropped sharply. Probably the Colonies suggested an opportunity to some actors. At any rate, a number of them, though certainly not the best of England's performers, came individually and in companies to the New World, sometimes via Jamaica, and found both opportunity and adversity.

1. PROBLEMS OF ACTORS IN AMERICA

Had actors thought to consider the kinds of people who had come to America -- a large number of whom were of the same middle class which was changing the English theatre -- they might have foreseen some of their problems. But actors are traditionally optimistic, and in a special prologue introducing the first performance of the first professional company to come to America (Williamsburg, Virginia, September 15, 1752), their faith was expressed:

> Haste, to Virginia's Plains, my sons, repair,
> The Goddess said, Go confident to find
> An audience sensible, polite and kind.

The players were soon to find, however, limited quantities of all three desirable qualities in the attitudes of some of the Colonial Fathers and the people.

(a)   Opposition by Religious Groups
One problem that had bothered actors since Tertullian (c. 200 A.D.) and that became crucial for the actor in Colonial America was the antagonism of the small but strict religious sects. New England, and Boston in particular, long retained a reputation for severity toward the theatre, and Pennsylvania was little more hospitable. In the Penn Colony (1681), three groups -- the Quakers, the Germans and the Scotch-Irish -- opposed theatres and helped pass laws prohibiting their activity.

(b)   Opposition by Governments
Reflecting the attitude of the people, governing officers and legislatures opposed theatrical ventures. On May 6, 1709, the Governor's Council of New York passed a law forbidding "play-acting and prize fighting." Following a minor riot caused by a 1750 performance in Boston, the Council and Legislature acted to prohibit all stage plays which, it was felt, tended "to increase immorality, impiety and a contempt for religion." Not until 1793, after the Selectmen of Boston had thoroughly considered the matter, was the law repealed. A Pennsylvania act of 1779 (repealed in 1789) declared all theatrical performances illegal. As war with England became imminent, the Continental Congress itself decided that amusements were not in keeping with the spirit of solemnity enveloping the Colonies, and on October 20, 1774, issued an interdict against "exhibition of shews, plays, and other

expensive diversions and entertainments." On October 16, 1778, a more severe interdict declared that government employees "who shall act, promote, encourage, or attend such plays" would lose their jobs.

(c)   Actors' Response to Opposition

Such discouraging opposition taxed the inventive resources and finesse of the Colonial actors and acting companies. Lewis Hallam, manager of the first theatre company to appear in Virginia, prepared for his visit to New York in 1753 with a long ad in the New York *Mercury* extolling the virtues of his actors. Occasionally, managers and actors defended their art in prologues to plays:

> Much has been said at this unlucky time,
> To prove the treading of the stage a crime.
>   . . . .
> Yet wise men own, a play well chose may teach
> Such useful moral truths as churchmen preach.

At other times an actor might hide behind a subterfuge of evasive words, by proposing a "Histrionic Academy," or naming a theatre the Boston Museum, or performing *Othello* as a "Series of Moral Dialogues in five parts depicting the evil effects of Jealousy and other Bad Passions and Proving that Happiness can only Spring from the Pursuit of Virtue." Mainly, the actors in the Colonies met their problems with fortitude, ingenuity and moderate success.

2.   EARLY THEATRES AND ACTING COMPANIES IN THE COLONIES

Information about early theatres in the Colonies is very sketchy. Anthony Aston is known to have performed in Charleston, South Carolina, in 1703 and the following winter spent his time in New York "acting, writing, courting." It is quite clear, too, that the first theatre was contracted for on July 11, 1716, in Williamsburg, Virginia. In 1723, a band of players visited Philadelphia, bowed to Quaker resentment of plays and performed outside the city limits. In New York, the New Theatre opened on December 6, 1732, with a performance of George Farquhar's *The Recruiting Officer* (1706). In 1735 at

Charleston, Thomas Otway's *The Orphan* (1680) was performed in a courtroom before an enthusiastic audience, and on February 12, 1736, the "New Theatre in Dock Street" was opened. Plays were also produced occasionally in Williamsburg during the next several years, and theatres continued to be built throughout the century.

Murray and Kean Acting Company: Professional Theatre
Not until August, 1749, when a company of actors headed by Walter Murray and Thomas Kean acted plays in a warehouse on Water Street, Philadelphia, did America at last have the beginnings of professional theatre.   From March 5, 1750, until July 8, 1751, the Murray and Kean Company performed once or twice a week in New York in a Nassau Street building. Their next stop was Williamsburg, where in October, 1751, they opened a new theatre with Shakespeare's *Richard III*. Robert Upton, advance man for Lewis Hallam, deserted his employer and joined Murray-Kean in the spring of 1751.   His later attempt to establish his own company in New York was not successful.

3.   A COMPANY OF COMEDIANS FROM LONDON:
      LEWIS HALLAM

Records show that Murray and Kean's "Virginia Company" continued playing for nearly twenty years. Most significantly, however, it had stimulated an interest in the theatre, thus creating an advantage for Lewis Hallam's Company of Comedians, which opened at Williamsburg on September 15, 1752, with *The Merchant of Venice*. Newly arrived from London, experienced and competent, the company performed its opening bill "before a numerous and polite audience with great applause" (*Virginia Gazette*, September 22, 1752). In June, 1753, Hallam left Williamsburg and, after periodic difficulties with church and government groups, produced plays in New York, Philadelphia and South Carolina. His next stop was Jamaica -- perhaps to avoid the plague, perhaps to recoup losses in a colony that boasted some wealth. There, Lewis Hallam died and the company disbanded. But a tradition of theatre in America had been well begun.

4. DAVID DOUGLASS (c.. 1720-1786)

In 1758, David Douglass, a successful actor and manager of a theatre company in the West Indies, married Lewis Hallam's widow, reorganized the Hallam company with Mrs. Douglass as the star, and her son, young Lewis Hallam, as the leading man -- and went to New York. Faced with opposition from the authorities, Douglass, with typical resourcefulness, disassociated himself from plays, declaring his interest solely in "Dissertations on Subjects, Moral, Instructive, and Entertaining," and was allowed to open with Nicholas Rowe's *Jane Shore* (1713) on December 28, 1758. He played in a temporary theatre on Cruger's Wharf until February 7, 1759, when his permit expired and the company left for Philadelphia, where, in spite of opposition by religious groups, he was allowed to open a new theatre on Society Hill. After a successful season there and some time in Maryland and Williamsburg, Douglass invaded New England during the late summer of 1761. Never without some religious or government opposition, Douglass nonetheless became sufficiently encouraged during the early 1760s to build temporary theatres in Annapolis, Maryland; Newport, Rhode Island; and New York City. During these years, anti-British feeling persuaded him to call his players the "American Company."

No figure in the American theatre before the Revolution compares with David Douglass. His company enjoyed notable seasons; his success in overcoming objections to plays was remarkable; as a performer, he was always well received; as a builder of theatres, he had no equal during his lifetime. He should also be remembered for his Southwark Theatre in Philadelphia -- the first permanent theatre in America, where, in 1767, he produced the first play written by an American and presented on an American stage by professional actors: *The Prince of Parthia.*

C. Drama in the Colonies

While theatres were being built and acting companies were performing in many Colonial towns, plays written by Americans were few and disappointing. Beginning a tradition which lasted for more than one hundred years in America, players and managers took their repertories mainly from the popular successes of England and the Continent. Perhaps both actors and managers wrote plays before 1767, but their work was inconsequential.

1. FARCES AND DIALOGUES

Fifty years after *Androboros*, an anonymous wit created *The Paxton Boys* (1764), an unfocussed satire based on events in western Pennsylvania involving the Paxton Boys and the responses of factions in the government of the Colony. A number of dialogues already existed, such as "Dialogue Between Christ, Youth and the Devil" (published anonymously in 1735) and John Checkley's "Dialogue Between a Minister and an Honest Country-Man, Concerning Election and Predestination" (1741).

2. THE PRINCE OF PARTHIA (1759?) BY THOMAS GODFREY (1736-1763): FIRST PLAY WRITTEN BY AN AMERICAN AND PERFORMED IN AMERICA BY PROFESSIONAL ACTORS

Thomas Godfrey is described by John Galt (*The Life and Studies of Benjamin West, Esq.*) as "having given the most promising indications of an elegant genius for pathetic and descriptive poetry." That promise never materialized, however, and except for one venture in heroic tragedy, he is inconsequential in a history of literature. *The Prince of Parthia*, a tragedy in five acts probably written in 1759, was published in 1765 by Nathaniel Evans, a friend of the poet. Douglass' presentation on April 24, 1767, was not repeated. Not until March 26, 1915, when the tragedy was produced by the Zelosophic Society of the University of Pennsylvania, was the play revived.

(Plot) The play tells the story of a good but weak king, Artabanus, and his three sons -- Arsaces, in whom "ev'ry virtue meets"; Vardanes, a man of pride, ambition and "canker'd heart"; and Gotarzes, the youngest son, a "glorious youth." As prizes from his victorious battle, Arsaces brings home Evanthe and Bethas. Not realizing that King Artabanus wants Evanthe for himself, Arsaces chooses her as his reward for victory. Vardanes, plotting to overthrow the Empire, excites the anger and jealousy of the king, who orders the arrest of Arsaces but is himself killed by Vardanes' henchmen to avenge personal insults. Meanwhile, Vardanes has attacked the city and is defeated only after Arsaces, freed by Gotarzes, turns the tide of the battle. Mistakenly told of Arsaces' death, Evanthe takes poison, living only long enough to bid goodbye to Arsaces, who then kills himself, leaving Gotarzes to bring order to the city.

(Discussion)   Unfortunately, *The Prince of Parthia*, the first American play, is imitative in both style and theme of English models. Shakespeare is a rich source: the rescue of a man from drowning, dreams of destruction (*Julius Caesar*); the king's wish to retire, numerous storms (*King Lear*); the ghost (*Hamlet*); the heroine's self-administered poision and the hero's subsequent suicide (*Romeo and Juliet*). A number of these devices typical of Shakespeare, however, were also conventions of much of Tudor and Stuart drama. Imitation of heroic tragedy and the excessive sentiment and rhetoric of the early eighteenth century are also clearly discernible. In the classical tradition of the heroic, Godfrey made frequent mention of the gods and the fates; the heroine's confidant watches the battle action and erroneously describes the death of the hero. The hero is superhuman in the Marlovian tradition. Major themes of love and honor are exploited in the heroic fashion, complementing the almost unbearably excessive speech of the hero.

Yet *The Prince of Parthia* has some creditable qualities: a theme of love and honor, a relatively straightforward plot, clearly accomplished exposition and action frequently motivated by the characters and structured toward a logical and unified conclusion. The modern reader, unfortunately, bored by excessively displayed emotion and exhausted by the unity of action, is also numbed by the moral (love versus honor) and political (democracy versus tyranny) themes forced upon the playwrights of the era. The most difficult part of the play to enjoy -- the poetry -- remains, except in a few passages, uninspired.

3.   **OTHER EARLY COLONIAL DRAMA**

Among existing plays, *The Disappointment* is interesting for the controversy it caused, and *Ponteach* has some dramatic value as well as an American theme. *The Conquest of Canada;*

or, the Siege of Quebec by George Cockings (d. 1802) was published in late 1772 and produced by David Douglass early the next year at the Southwark Theatre in Philadelphia. Called a "historical tragedy," this play is a forced and sentimental tribute to General Wolfe and his exploits during the battle for Quebec.

(a)   *The Disappointment; or, the Force of Credulity* (1767)
       by Thomas Forrest

(Plot) As they discuss hidden treasures, Hum, Parchment and Quadrant discover that they have lost some valuable papers. A fourth man, Raccoon, finds the papers, and demands and is given a part interest in the treasure, which turns out to be worthless. The whole affair has been a hoax. Songs and a moral discourse enliven the entertainment, as do numerous coarse suggestions, particularly in Act II. In 1796, a second edition included satirical references to the President and the Congress.

(Discussion) Only by chance was the first play written by an American and produced in America a tragedy rather than a comedy. Early in 1767 -- the same year *The Prince of Parthia* was produced -- the American Company had put into rehearsal *The Disappointment*, a comic opera in three acts by Colonel Thomas Forrest (published in New York, 1767, under the pseudonym of Andrew Barton). Based on a trick Forrest had played on an old Dutchman who was searching for buried treasure, the play ridiculed the idea that Blackbeard the Pirate had buried any of his treasures on the banks of the Delaware River. Despite some interesting Scottish and Irish elements, the play is both crude in dramatic structure and coarse in subject matter. When the people actually involved in the hoax complained, it was decided that the play was "unfit for the stage," which brought an abrupt halt to rehearsals and the hasty substitution of *The Prince of Parthia*.

(b)   *Ponteach; or, the Savages of America* (1766)
       by Robert Rogers (1731-1795)

(Plot) Cheated frequently by the trappers and the English soldiers, Ponteach and his sons, Philip and Chekitan, plot their revenge. Only the Mohawk chief Hendrick refuses to cooperate, and Philip is chosen to convince Hendrick that he must fight the English. Ambitious and unscrupulous, Philip plans to provoke Hendrick by killing his daughter, Monelia (whom Chekitan loves), and blaming the British for the deed. When Chekitan discovers that Philip has murdered Monelia, he kills him and takes his own life. Ponteach is left to grieve for his sons. At the end, the British are victorious, but Ponteach retains his pride:

> British may boast, the gods may have their will,
> Ponteach I am, and shall be Ponteach still.

(Discussion) The first play to treat a native subject at all seriously, *Ponteach* by Major Robert Rogers was published in London in 1766 but not acted in America before the Revolution. In his 1914 edition of *Ponteach,* Allan Nevins questioned Rogers' authorship, but Rogers seems to have been mainly responsible for the play if not its sole author. London critics in 1766 accepted the play as Rogers' work but had little good to say for it. Concentrating on the cruel treatment of the Indians, the play is called a tragedy and presents a tragic-heroic figure in Ponteach. Some picturesque nature images and a few strong and dignified speeches by Ponteach distinguish the play, but like many early plays, it suffers from stilted language, amateurish polemics, a mixed style (mainly prose, with short passages in blank verse) and too numerous changes of scene.

(c)   *The Trial of Atticus Before Justice Beau for a Rape*
       (pub. 1771), anonymous
Consistent with earlier satiric farces, *The Trial of Atticus* is a rambling and episodic condemnation of a broad segment of Colonial society. In eight scenes, the author attacks lawyers, judges, the clergy, gossips, teachers, innkeepers and more, while the anti-hero upsets the judicial system by refusing to confess.

4.   COLLEGE DRAMA IN THE COLONIES

Although in the cities the drama suffered frequent attacks by religious groups and political parties, within the colleges of Colonial America it found some security. Writing of a production of *The Masque of Alfred,* produced at the College of

Philadelphia in 1756-57, Provost William Smith noted that the students had "from time to time delivered proper Speeches and acted Parts of our best dramatic Pieces before large Audiences with great Applause" (*Pennsylvania Gazette,* January 20, 27 and February 3, 10, 1757). In 1771, students at the College of New Jersey produced "The Rising Glory of America," a dialogue by Philip Freneau, America's best-known poet of the Revolution, and H. H. Brackenridge, playwright and author of *Modern Chivalry,* one of America's earliest novels.

II. DRAMA DURING THE REVOLUTION AND THE POST-REVOLUTIONARY PERIOD TO 1800

Almost as soon as the theatre in America had become reasonably well established, a crisis occurred -- the War for Independence.   Anticipating the serious situation, the Continental Congress in 1774 recommended that all public entertainments be suppressed. Thus began an eight-year period during which the stage was mainly controlled by the British military, who performed some of the best plays of England and the Continent and entertained not just soldiers but great numbers of Colonists.   Mainly, the actors were British soldiers and women who had, as Arthur Hornblow, historian of the American stage, wrote, "followed the drum," but some were members of Douglass' disbanded American Company.

American drama, on the other hand, was perhaps given additional impetus by the war years.   With the spirit of nationalism, Americans found a new *raison d'etre* for the drama.   Plays became a prominent part of the "War of the Belles-Lettres," so aptly described by Vernon L. Parrington in *Main Currents in American Thought.* By the time the theatres were reopened after the war, American drama had launched a modest but definite beginning. A variety of aspects of American life appeared -- moral lessons and dramatized political issues, social farces which often featured the native Yankee character or the Negro and commented on society in America, national plays by the score, plays imitative of English drama -- in general, a reflection of the times. By the turn of the century,

America had a serious dramatist and student of the theatre in William Dunlap, and its first effective writer of comedy in Royall Tyler.

A. Plays Reflecting Patriot Views

Long before the battles at Lexington and Bunker Hill, the contest between Whig and Tory, Patriot and Loyalist, was being waged in literary circles. In the drama, the mode was satiric farce, and what playwrights lacked in theatrical skills they made up for with partisan fervor. Frank and even libelous, only a few of these frequently anonymous satires have been preserved. Written in haste and for a particular purpose by men and women of little dramatic talent, the plays have been forgotten except as examples of the drama of the Revolution.

1. MRS. MERCY OTIS WARREN (1728-1814): PARTISAN SATIRIST

Sister of James Otis, the patriot statesman, wife of James Warren, once President of the Provincial Congress, and close friend of John and Abigail Adams, Mrs. Warren was well equipped to satirize the social as well as the political issues of the times. Essentially a gadfly of the war, harrassing the enemy with bitter satire and poignant observations on liberty and patriotism, Mrs. Warren responded to the events that she observed. Always a lady of culture, and a member of the literati, she inserted in her pamphlet plays the conventional sentiment and moral strictures of the day along with interesting biographical, social and political comment. In spite of occasional theatrical effectiveness, however, she was clearly amateurish and lacked any real dramatic talent. Her published poems are also undistinguished, but her three-volume *History of the Rise, Progress, and Termination of the American Revolution* (1805) has value for historians. It is ironic that she remains best known for her farces, clearly reflections of her serious opinions yet probably written more as an emotional outlet than for literary acclaim.

(a) *The Adulateur* (1773)
(Plot) The scene is Servia: Brutus and Cassius are attempting to inspire the people to patriotic action. When it is reported

that the soldiers of Rapatio have attacked the citizens in "promiscuous slaughter," Brutus urges a revolution, and angry citizens appear before Rapatio, who alternately blames the Patriots for whatever wrongs exist and threatens economic revenge. The climax shows a pathetic picture of a frightened Rapatio but a distinct hope for national freedom as Brutus weeps for his country.

(Discussion) In weak blank verse, Mrs. Warren's first play is a "tragedy" in five acts, a bitter comment on conditions in New England during the immediate pre-Revolution days. Servia is New England; the "promiscuous slaughter," the Boston Massacre; the "great hall," Boston's Faneuil Hall. As usual in the satires of Mrs. Warren and other writers of this period, the characters in *The Adulateur* are actual people thinly disguised: Brutus (James Otis), Rapatio (Governor Thomas Hutchinson, the last royal governor of Massachusetts), Cassius (Samuel Adams), Hazelrod (Peter Oliver, Chief Justice of Massachusetts).

(b) *The Group* (1775)
(Plot) As the play begins, the audience sees a swarm of Harpies led by Massachusettensis (Daniel Leonard, a Tory) in the form of a basilisk: "The whole supported by a mighty army and navy, from Blunderland [England] for the laudable purpose of enslaving its best friends." One by one, members of the Group comment on their acts of villany and rationalize their betrayal of the Patriot cause. After only momentary concern for Hell and retribution, the Group decides that for fame and personal gain they can forego conscience and moral living.

(Discussion) The most incisive and perhaps the most important of Mrs. Warren's plays, this polemical farce in two acts enjoyed a patriot theme which made it quite popular reading. The Loyalist Group -- a Council appointed by the King rather than elected by the Assembly, thus abrogating the Charter of Massachusetts -- is composed of "selfish venal men," as their names suggest: Hateall (Timothy Ruggles), Humbug (John Erving), Spendall (William Pepperell). Obviously, the play is meaningless without an understanding of the situation in Massachusetts at that time when England's actions (the Stamp

Act, the Intolerable Acts, the Sugar Act, the Townshend Acts) toward the American Colonists were felt to be unbearable by the Sons of Liberty and other patriots.

(c) Other Plays

The Defeat (1773) shows Rapatio defeated by Patriots who fight for freedom -- to assemble, have a free press and govern themselves. In 1790, Mrs. Warren published two dull didactic tragedies in verse: *The Sack of Rome* and *The Ladies of Castile*. "Debilitated by the habits of every species of luxury," she wrote in the Preface to *The Sack of Rome*, "man has sunk to his lowest depravity and wants a lesson in morality, valour, and virtue." In Rome, the Emperor's passion for another man's wife drives him to rape her before he is killed when an invading army sacks Rome. Innocent victims of the battle are the Emperor's daughter and the young soldier whom she loves. *The Ladies of Castile* describes Spain's last heroic struggle for liberty before the establishment of despotism by the family of Ferdinand. Both plays show Mrs. Warren's concern for freedom -- from England's social as well as political control.

(d) Plays Attributed to Mrs. Warren

The Blockheads; or, The Affrighted Officers (1776)
This three-act farce is frequently attributed to Mrs. Warren, although A. H. Quinn, quite correctly, denied her authorship on the basis of the play's crudity of thought and language. As a satire, however, it uses some of the same characters that had appeared in her plays. Concerned with General Howe's unsuccessful attempt to subdue the Americans at Dorchester Heights, the play satirizes the quarrels among the English, their doubts about their own cause and their cowardice. Subtlety is completely lacking, and vulgarity dominates many scenes. The play ends with a popular flag-waving technique which was not known to be used by Mrs. Warren: "And let's conclude with huzzahs for America."

An interesting note to this play was the situation which supposedly stimulated its composition. During a performance in Boston (Jan. 8, 1776) of *The Blockade of Boston*, attributed to General Burgoyne, an English soldier dashed on stage to shout that the rebels were attacking Bunker Hill. It took a moment for the audience to realize that this was not part of the play. Known to detest Burgoyne, Mrs. Warren may have written *The Blockheads* as a response to his farce.

The Motley Assembly (1779)
This one-act farce ridicules the Massachusetts Assembly or legislative body. Once a simple diversion and entertainment for young ladies, the Assembly has a new significance; and politically vacillilating fathers now refuse to allow their daughters to attend a Whig assembly for fear the British may return to Boston. The play shows a disdain, typical of Mrs. Warren, for those who felt that they could not maintain their social standing and also support the Revolution. Awkward and slight, and with some crude language, the play has wit and in its best lines can be favorably compared to Royall Tyler's *The Contrast*.

2.   HUGH HENRY BRACKENRIDGE (1748-1816): WAR OF THE BELLES-LETTRES

Although his reputation in the history of American literature rests quite appropriately on his authorship of the early picaresque and satirical novel *Modern Chivalry*, Brackenridge also contributed two plays to the Whig-Tory "War of the Belles-Lettres." "The subject is not love," he wrote of his plays, "but valour. I meddle not with any of the effeminating passions but consecrate my muse to the great themes of patriotic virtue, bravery and heroism." With the combination of sentiment and nationalism which these words suggest, he did not create a drama of great importance. Only in comparison with contemporaries, who lacked his literary facility, was he outstanding. Although not a poet of consequence, his plays display passages of dignified blank verse and a sense of humanity which make his work significant at this early time. As in *The Rising Glory of America* (written with Philip Freneau), the plot of *The Battle of Bunkers-Hill* is carried on largely by conversation which can rarely be considered dramatic. Essentially, there is too much exposition and exhortation and too little action. *The Death of General Montgomery* is more effective as drama and as a pointed attempt to help the Colonial cause. Presumably, neither play was acted professionally.

(a) *The Battle of Bunkers-Hill* **(1776)**
In five short acts, this patriotic effusion in blank verse praises
the courage of the American leaders and their men. The
English generals (Gage, Howe, Burgoyne) and the American
generals (Warren, Putnam, Gardner) explain their positions
and exhort their men to greater efforts before the battle in
which the British are repulsed, Warren is killed and Gardner
wounded. With the final American retreat, the English honor
their enemies. An epilogue is followed by an ode, a speech by
George Washington and a song in praise of American efforts.

(b) *The Death of General Montgomery* **(1777)**
Mainly a patriotic play built around a recognized hero, *The
Death of General Montgomery* dramatizes the attack on the
fortress of Quebec. Disaster is foreshadowed throughout, but
the death of General Montgomery is shown only in a tribute by
Aaron Burr. Ever a patriot, Brackenridge managed to reproach
the King, Parliament and the English General Carleton.

3. POLITICAL FARCE-MELODRAMA:
**   *THE FALL OF BRITISH TYRANNY* (1776)**

Suggestive of other partisan dramas and in itself an ambitious
attempt to dramatize the beginning war years, *The Fall of
British Tyranny; or, American Liberty Triumphant, the First
Campaign* by John Leacock (1729-1802) is described as "A Tragi-
Comedy of Five Acts as lately planned at the Royal Theatrum
Pandemonium, as St. James's. The Principal Place of Action is
America." Although the language of the Whig-Tory argument
is occasionally quite realistic and the plot idea of a scope
which suggests something more than the usual nationalistic
propaganda, the characters are caricatures, though identifiable, and the action is episodic and farcical. That there were
several editions of the play in 1776 suggests its popularity, and
it may have been produced in Philadelphia.

(Plot) Emphasizing the idea that the American Revolution
began in England's Parliament, the play begins with a vigorous
speech by Lord Paramount (Earl of Bute) proposing to
impoverish the Colonies through taxes, punitive legislative
acts and even military force. Opposed to Lord Paramount, are
Lord Wisdom, Lord Religion and Lord Justice (William Pitt,

the Bishop of St. Asaph and the Earl of Camden). In Boston, the English tyranny is deeply resented, and the British regulars are routed at Lexington and Concord by Colonial militia. Act V shows American prisoners of war joyous because they consider themselves victorious in battle, as Generals Washington, Putnam and Charles Lee pledge their support to the cause of liberty and their country.

B. Plays Reflecting Loyalist Views

The bitter, satirical and condemnatory views in Patriot plays were no more acrimonious than those presented in Loyalist plays. The intensity of the partisan views is, in fact, a major characteristic of these satires and farces. Extant Loyalist plays indicate that few opportunities were overlooked to belittle the motives and abilities of the Colonists. Slanderous remarks about the Patriot leaders were common. Truth was not important; propaganda for the cause was.

1. *THE AMERICANS ROUSED IN A CURE FOR THE SPLEEN, OR AMUSEMENT FOR A WINTER'S EVENING. BEING THE SUBSTANCE OF A CONVERSATION ON THE TIMES OVER A FRIENDLY TANKARD AND PIPE BETWEEN SHARP, A COUNTRY PARSON, BUMPER, A COUNTRY JUSTICE, FILLPOT, AN INNKEEPER, GRAVEAIRS, A DEACON, TRIM, A BARBER, BRIM, A QUAKER, PUFF, A LATE REPRE-SENTATIVE. TAKEN IN SHORTHAND BY SIR ROGER DE COVERLY* (1775), ATTRIBUTED TO JONATHAN SEWALL*

This bombast is typical of several existing Tory tracts in which the arguments from the British point of view are presented with wit and intelligence in contrast to the confusion and ignorance of those who espouse the Whig philosophy. When the Patriots were unsure of themselves, their vacillations became excellent material for Tory propaganda, and Jonathan Sewall (1728-1796) was a notorious Tory.

2. *THE BATTLE OF BROOKLYN, A FARCE IN TWO ACTS. AS IT WAS PERFORMED ON LONG ISLAND, ON TUESDAY, THE 27TH DAY OF AUGUST, 1776. BY THE REPRESENTA-TIVES OF THE TYRANTS OF AMERICA, ASSEMBLED AT PHILADELPHIA,* AUTHOR UNKNOWN

This episodic and libelous pamphlet appeared in two more editions in 1777. The action shows American General Stirling, badly frightened at the prospect of battle, trying to bolster his courage by drink; a young prositute tells of her experiences with Washington and Harrison; the Patriot chiefs, Washington and Putnam, reveal their cowardice.

Although history has shown that the Revolutionary leaders were woefully unwise in that battle, the harshness of the attack on the conduct of the Continental soldiers and the villification heaped upon Washington and his officers is unparalleled in other extant dramas of that time. Sketchy in its plot and scurrilous in its attack, this is clearly a drama, not a series of speeches, but it is, first of all, propaganda.

C. Nonpartisan Drama: Robert Munford (1737?-1783)

Most of the satires of the Revolution were strictly partisan, but one of the few playwrights who showed any detachment was Colonel Robert Munford, who fought for the Revolution. Presenting quite accurately the feelings of the majority of the people, who did not know what to do during the days of uncertainty early in the Revolution, Colonel Munford, landowner and politician, wrote *The Candidates* and *The Patriots*, published together in 1798.

Underrated as dramas, Munford's plays, both written during the 1770's, were the best in America prior to Tyler's *The Contrast* (1787). *The Candidates; or, the Humours of a Virginia Election* is a brief and light satire on elections. With scenes of farcical and racy humor interspersed with references to local events and election practices, the plot contrasts the candidacy of Mr. Wou'dbe with that of Sir John Toddy and Strutabout. *The Patriots*, a five-act comedy, mixes love and politics to attack the half-hearted and professed Patriots. In both plays the final acts are contrived and anecdotal.

D. Royall Tyler (1757-1826): The Beginnings of American Comedy

The first comedy and the first play on a native subject written by an American and produced by a professional company was

The Contrast by Royall Tyler. A Harvard College graduate in 1776, and a major in the Continental Army, Tyler was admitted to the bar in 1780. Returning to military duty during Shay's Rebellion (1787), he visited New York City and met Thomas Wignell, the leading comedian of the Old American Company. Later that year, on April 16, Wignell acted with personal success in *The Contrast* at the John Street Theatre. Tyler also wrote a novel, *The Algerine Captive* (1797), and many essays and verses and perhaps nine more plays or adaptations, only four of which have survived. His main career, however, was not in literature but in law, and he eventually became Chief Justice of the Supreme Court of Vermont (1807-13) and Professor of Jurisprudence at the University of Vermont (1711-14).

1.   *THE CONTRAST* (1787)

(Plot) With a slight plot involving love, filial obligation, intrigue and the follies of fashion, this play abounds in contrasts -- between ideas, lovers, servants, fashions and so on. While Charlotte and Letitia comment cleverly on men, themselves and their society, Maria Van Rough is being told that she must marry Dimple, whom she despises as a man "whose only virtue is a polished exterior." Colonel Manly, Charlotte's brother, is a dramatic contrast to Dimple, whose servant, Jessamy, toys with Manly's servant, Jonathan.   The main action of the play revolves around Dimple's personal problem: although engaged to Maria, he loves the person of Charlotte and the fortune of Letitia. To complicate matters, Manly has met, impressed and been impressed by Maria. In the final act, Dimple's duplicity is exposed; Manly will marry Maria; and Letitia and Charlotte have learned a moral lesson.

(Discussion) Not matched in America for wit and humor until A. C. M. Ritchie's *Fashion* in 1845, *The Contrast* has occasionally been revived in modern times, generally in university theatres, but in 1787 it played for only five performances. A contemporary critic found the dialogue in need of pruning, the sololiquies improbable and ridicule of Lord Chesterfield's letters imprudent.   Another reviewer, who signed himself "Candour" in the *Daily Advertiser*, April 18, 1787, was impressed: "It was certainly the production of a man of genius, and nothing can be more praiseworthy than the sentiments of the play throughout. They are the effusions of an honest patriot heart expressed with energy and eloquence." Although modern readers probably cannot approach this play in the spirit of "Candour" ("the contrast drawn between a gentleman, who has read Chesterfield and received the polish of Europe, and an unpolished, untraveled American"), they may find it sprightly, witty and still very funny.

In descriptive terms *The Contrast* is more a caricature of society than a social comedy. There is much farcical action. Jessamy is the traditional intriguer; Jonathan is the shrewd but naive country-bumpkin Yankee who became a major figure in American farce-comedy by the middle of the nineteenth century; Colonel Manly is the serious defender of honor and country -- a startling contrast to Charlotte, the witty and indelicate flirt whose "head runs so upon beaux." Charlotte, however, establishes the pace of the play with her wit, while her lines express most of Tyler's satire upon fashion. What is scandal, she says "but amusing ourselves with the faults, foibles, follies, and reputations of our friends." Among the more humorous scenes are Jonathan's attendance at a play, *The School for Scandalization,* and Jessamy's lessons to Jonathan on how to court a girl with an object of "cherubim consequences."

The Contrast also has a liberal amount of sentiment, moralizing and nationalism -- necessary ingredients of the successful American play. The patriotism that the Prologue proclaims --

> EXULT each patriot heart! -- this night is shewn
> A piece which we may fairly call our own . . .

Colonel Manly exemplifies in every action. And the outcome of the play is a national triumph. The necessary moral sentiment of the play is clear in Maria's "filial obligation." There are particular morals to be drawn, too, in the actions of both Charlotte and Colonel Manly. That moralizing was required for Tyler's audience is evidenced by a Boston performance of the play in 1792 advertised as "A MORAL LECTURE in FIVE PARTS."

2. OTHER PLAYS

A month after *The Contrast* opened in 1787, another play by
Tyler, a comic opera called *May-Day in Town; or, New York in
an Uproar*, was performed at the John Street Theatre. Not
extant, the play failed, perhaps because, as a contemporary
critic suggested, the main female character was a scold whom
the New York women may have resented. Other titles include
The Mock Doctor (1796), *The Farm House* (1796) and *The
Georgia Spec* (1797).

Of the four plays by Tyler that are reprinted in *America's Lost
Plays*, Volume 15, three are sacred dramas in blank verse: *The
Origin of the Feast of Purim, Joseph and His Brethren* and *The
Judgment of Solomon*. The fourth, *The Island of Barrataria*, is
an amusing, satrical play based on parts of *Don Quixote*.

E. William Dunlap (1766-1839): Father of American Drama

William Dunlap was the first professional dramatist in
America. Although he must now be considered only a mediocre
playwright, his contribution of at least sixty plays (twenty-
nine either wholly or partly original), his tireless and
honorable work as a theatre manager and his reputation as the
author of the first history of the American theatre make him a
significant figure in the history of American drama. In 1833, a
critic for the New York *Mirror* (X, 266) wrote: "His numerous
pieces were almost invariably performed with applause; and
free as they are from false taste and extravagance, show the
power of fixing attention and exciting interest by legitimate
means -- of touching the true springs of mirth and pity and
terror." Later critics have pointed out that in large part
Dunlap gained his reputation by catering to popular tastes
with his melodramas.

Dunlap also brought respectability to a theatre badly in need
of this quality. A pioneer in an unproven field, with
remarkable industry and abilities superior to his
contemporaries, he created occasionally superior but often
uneven plays which, along with his abiding interest in drama,
secure his title as "Father of American Drama." The Dunlap

Society (established in 1885) has published many of his plays and promoted criticism of his works.

Born in Perth Amboy, New Jersey, of staunch Loyalist parents, William Dunlap enjoyed a fair education. After his family moved to New York City in 1777, he found great delight in watching the plays performed by the British soldiers at the John Street Theatre. Ten years later he wrote his first long play, *The Modest Soldier; or, Love in New York,* perhaps inspired by Royall Tyler's *The Contrast,* which had appeared that year, 1787. Lacking roles for important members of the American Company, Dunlap's play was not immediately produced, but he had begun his career as a dramatist.

1.   AS THEATRE MANAGER

In the spring of 1796, the younger Lewis Hallam and John Hodgkinson, partners in the Old American Company performing at the John Street Theatre in New York, persuaded Dunlap to buy into the management. According to the agreement, Dunlap, as manager, had the freedom to produce his own plays. Jealousy between Hallam and Hodgkinson, however, spoiled the bright future Dunlap might have imagined.

By spring of 1797, Hallam had left the management and Hodgkinson had taken part of the company to Boston, leaving Dunlap to supervise the building of the new Park Theatre -- a stone construction three stories high with a well-equipped stage, excellent scenery, and three tiers of boxes, a gallery and a pit, all colored in pink and gold -- which, opening on January 29, 1798, was in almost constant financial trouble. On April 27, 1798, Hodgkinson withdrew and Dunlap took over the company, with fears that he expressed in his *History* (II, 38):

> The opinion of the writer is . . . that he was not fitted for the arduous task. Had it been his lot to direct a theatre patronized by an enlightened government . . . he might have been entitled to the grateful remembrance of his fellow-men.

Dunlap never got his government-subsidized theatre; instead, an act of God harrassed him when a yellow fever epidemic in New York delayed his opening until December of that year.

On December 10, 1798, a week after the opening of the 1798-99 season, Dunlap produced with startling success his own adaptation of an English version of August von Kotzebue's *The Stranger*. Kotzebue (1761-1819), the most popular German dramatist of the eighteenth century, proved to have tremendous appeal for American middle-class audiences, and by the end of the 1800 season, Dunlap had produced nineteen of Kotzebue's plays, which had allowed him to star Hodgkinson and Thomas A. Cooper. This season and that of 1801 were his most successful. Then a series of incidents occurred: Cooper left for England; dramatic critics started writing, particularly Jonathan Oldstyle (Washington Irving), whose very first letter called attention to the absurdities and inadequacies of the Park Theatre productions; Mrs. Hodgkinson, one of the mainstays of the company, died; Hodgkinson left New York. The setbacks were too severe, and in February 1805 Dunlap declared bankruptcy and closed his theatre. It should be noted, however, that he left the theatre materially well furnished and well supplied with manuscripts and that his tour as theatre manager was not as dismal as the ending sounds.

In 1806 Dunlap tried theatre management once more, this time as assistant to Cooper, who reopened the Park (1806-1811) but without noticeable success. After a stint as traveling companion to the colorful and impressive but alcoholic English tragedian George Frederick Cooke, Dunlap gave up theatre management for good in 1812.

2.   AS PLAYWRIGHT

Without question, Dunlap was the premier dramatist of his time. Realizing that a dramatist had no chance of success without some claim on the theatre, he became a manager. Partially as a practical measure to facilitate success, and partially as a consequence of his pioneering nature, Dunlap wrote comedy, melodrama, farce, tragedy, propaganda drama, ballad-opera, adaptations and translations. Even compared with writers in Europe, where Kotzebue was being hailed as the German Shakespeare, and in England, where Richard Brinsley Sheridan was contenting himself with adaptations, Dunlap's work suggests historic importance. Although his numerous adaptations indicate a professional expediency, his best plays were those mainly original with him. On these plays -- *André, The Father, Leicester, The Italian Father* -- his reputation as a playwright rests.

A sensitive artist with imaginative ideas which he did not always follow, Dunlap showed an interest in literature which was not unswerving, a feeling for dramatic character and language and a love of the theatre. Perhaps his years in theatre management hurt him as a playwright, for after 1812 his plays are not effective; and except for his *History* he did little of note after the turn of the century. Yet for his time he was a major dramatist, and in any history is the principal figure in the establishment of an American drama.

(a)   Comedy: *The Father; or, American Shandyism* **(1788)**
(Plot)   After a Prologue praising the moral tendency of the stage in the New World, the action centers on Mrs. Racket. Tired of an indifferent and dissipating husband, she tries to excite him by pretending an affection for Captain Ranter. An unfortunate choice, Ranter is proved to be a thief through events involving Mrs. Racket's sister, and Mrs. Racket's reconciliation with her husband parallels the revelation of Ranter's villainy.

(Discussion) This second comedy by an American-born author to be performed on the professional stage (John Street Theatre, New York, September 7, 1789), *The Father* was, according to its author, "received with great applause by the citizens." Its run of four performances was considered a favorable reception. Generally modeled on Laurence Sterne's novel, *Tristram Shandy*, proposing to teach and to amuse, *The Father* has reasonably drawn characters and a "terseness and unstudied ease" in the dialogue, which a critic of the contemporary *American Quarterly Review* found indispensable to genuine comedy.   Printed in a revised version in 1806, the play presented more carefully developed characters and scenes and more moralizing.

(b) Romantic Tragedy:
The Fatal Deception; or, The Progress of Guilt **(1790)**
(Plot) Returning after a long absence at war, Lord Leicester
rescues Dudley Cecil from robbers before reaching Kenilworth,
where Matilda, his bride, has been living in adultery with
Henry, Dudley's younger brother. Frantic at Leicester's return,
Matilda urges Henry to kill her husband, but in the dark of
Leicester's room, Henry mistakes his victim and kills Dudley.
Meanwhile, Leicester, learning of Matilda's infidelity, vows
revenge, and Matilda goes mad, tries to poison Leicester and
stabs herself when she fails. Finally, Henry, feeling himself
"marked for destruction," refuses combat with the wronged
husband and dies willingly on the sword of Leicester, who
forgives the dying sinners.

(Discussion) Based on the story of Lord Leicester and Amy
Robsart, the play was produced in 1794 and later published in
1806 as *Leicester*. Although having a certain intensity and
force, *Leicester* is marred by loose construction, unrelieved
tragedy and weakly motivated action.   Dunlap, however,
deserves credit for seeing the dramatic potential of the
Kenilworth story, which provided the necessary sentiment as
well as a revenge theme and a mad scene.

(c) Historical Tragedy: *André* **(1798)**
(Plot) André, in prison awaiting execution, asks only that he be
shot rather than hanged. His friend, Captain Bland of the
American army, pleads with General Washington for André's
life. Refused, Bland tears the cockade from his helmet. (This
action was hissed by the first-night audience, and Dunlap cut
the scene.)   When Bland's mother asks that André be
exchanged for her husband, Colonel Bland, who is being held
by the British as a hostage for André, her plea is also refused
by Washington. Again, young Bland is incensed. Finally,
Honora, André's fiancée, comes to plead for her lover -- again in
vain. In the final act, Captain Bland, made to understand
reality, apologizes for his unsubordination; Honora becomes
insane; and André goes to his execution bravely.

(Discussion) *André*, first performed at the Park Theatre, New
York, March 30, 1798, is based on the capture and execution of

Major John André, the British messenger who, after meeting with Benedict Arnold, was captured and hanged by the Americans in 1780. Possibly because the event was too close, the play, Dunlap's best, was not a popular success, although it lasted for five performances. In 1803, Dunlap bowed to the popular demand for patriotic spectacles and rewrote *André* as *The Glory of Columbia -- Her Yeomanry.* Essentially the original concept of the play was destroyed, but the spectacle was successful on stage.

In spite of excessive romanticism and sentiment as well as the artificialities of language and action typical of the drama of that time, *André* has much that suggests excellence. It is not, however, Andre's courageous preparation for the kind of death that he must face (hanging) which is the central dramatic issue of the play. The major conflict lies within a country which must assert its rights at the same time that it maintains a strong sense of humanity. Facing the problem is Washington. Opposing him is Bland, a romantic and brash young man, fiercely loyal to André for once saving his life. But a country's honor must be triumphant, and as one might expect, nationalistic sentiment predominates. Within these two themes -- a country's maturity and the courage of a man facing death -- *André* is well unified and includes effective exposition and change of pace. Except for the women, the main characters are real and well drawn. Although weak in language and poetry, it is a meaningful play that can still be read with pleasure.

(d) Translations and Adaptations
Almost from the time he entered theatre management, Dunlap began to adapt and translate English and European plays. By the turn of the century, he was putting most of his energies into this work.

Plays of Kotzebue
After his success with *The Stranger,* Dunlap continued this interest in Kotzebue, translating and adapting, among others, *False Shame* (1799), which was extremely successful and supported the theatre during the season in which it was produced. The plot unfolds a conventional farce of lost

daughters and sisters, confused lovers and mistaken identities. The source of false shame of one character is a physical deformity; of another, poverty. At the final curtain, however, everyone is happy: married or reconciled, they join in singing "Joy, brightest spark from Heaven."

Concerning *The Stranger*, one critic wrote (*The New York Drama*, Volume I, 1876, footnote to the play):   "That interpretation of human passion cannot be wholly false, which awakens so many responses. The sentiment cannot be wholly mawkish or sickly, which, among various people and at various times, touches the deepest sensibilities of an audience." Critical opinions may have changed, but nineteenth-century audiences invariably enjoyed the play and did not question either the sentiment or the interpretation of life.

French Plays
Mainly interested in French melodramas, Dunlap borrowed widely: *The Voice of Nature* (1803), based on L. C. Caigniez's *Le Jugement de Salomon; The Wife of Two Husbands* (1804), from Pixerécourt's popular melodrama, *Le Femme à deux Maris;* and *Thirty Years; or, The Life of a Gamester* (1828), from *Trente Ans; ou, La Vie d'un Joueur* by Prosper Goubaux and Victor Ducange.

Produced first at the Bowery Theatre in New York, February 22, 1828, *Thirty Years* proved to be one of Dunlap's most successful melodramas. George St. Germain, a compulsive gambler controlled by a villain, steals, abuses his patient wife and finally commits murder before a spectacular but moral plot makes Germain a victim of his unhappy fate.

(e)   Other Plays
Darby's Return (1789), a brief comic sketch written for Thomas Wignell, is a gentle satire on a "gallant" soldier who returns to his village in Ireland and tells of his adventures in the United States. *Yankee Chronology; or, Huzza for the Constitution* (1812), a combination sketch and monologue, celebrates the beginning of the War of 1812 as Ben Bundle, an American sailor, describes the battle between the Constitution and the English Guerrière and sings a song, "Yankee Chronology," tracing the

Revolution from Lexington to Yorktown. The tremendous popularity of this patriotic but artless work suggests the popular standards of the day. *A Trip to Niagara* (1828) is mainly interesting for its diorama of eighteen scenes along the Hudson as a steamboat moves up the river from New York to Catskill Landing.

3. AS THEATRE HISTORIAN

A History of the American Theatre (1832), Dunlap's most significant contribution to American drama, consists mainly of an interesting narrative of personal observations on a growing theatre. Recent theatre historians have deplored its errors and misleading statements, but they still regard it as an invaluable historical source written in a frequently delightful fashion. Dunlap also wrote prefaces to his published plays and *Memoirs of the Life of George Frederick Cooke* (1813). Many of his ideas, such as federal support for the theatre and curtailment of the star system, have remained meaningful.

F. Post-Revolutionary Drama: Varied Directions

When the Revolution was over and the partisan farcical satires on events had disappeared, the theatre continued its role as a means of propaganda, entertainment and moral instruction. Numerous playwrights considered social and political issues. Others, inspired by the work of Tyler and Dunlap, wrote farce comedies and kept alive native character types. At the same time, the theatres continued to depend upon European dramatists. Translations and adaptations were constantly on the American stage, along with the pirated versions of current English successes and, of course, Shakespeare and the best of England's classical drama. Along with these popular trends, the practicing moralists were at work, and colleges were showing an increasing interest in drama.

1. NATIONALISTIC AND POLITICAL PLAYS

The tendency of playwrights during the Revolution to dramatize national issues and various attitudes toward political problems continued to be popular. Proud of their freedom, dramatists inserted nationalistic comments in almost everything they wrote, and the democratic spirit of the new country became a common theme.

(a) Nationalistic Spirit
Numerous plays, from farce to poetic tragedy, gained some popularity through their patriotic sentiment. *The Better Sort; or, A Girl of Spirit,* an anonymous "operatical, comical farce" published in 1789, satirizes the American fashion of naively accepting foreign ideas and develops a true champion of America as its heroine. *Americana; or, A New Tale of the Genii,* a patriotic spectacle dramatizing the bringing of the Genius of Liberty from England to America, was probably written during the Revolution but was not performed until 1798. Nationalistic feeling is strong in David Everett's (1770-1813) *Daranzel; or, The Persian Patriot* (1798), in which Daranzel successfully leads a fight for freedom similar to the American Revolution.

(b) Political Issues
Plays also emphasize or make passing comment on a variety of domestic problems which were also political issues -- the Constitution, money and speculation, taxation, the Whiskey Rebellion, education and other such subjects. *The Politician Outwitted* (1788) by Samuel Low (b. 1765) is a contentious defense of the new Constitution made memorable through the antics of a Yankee clown-type named Humphrey Cubb. *The Politician; or, The State of Things* (1798) by John Murdock (1748-1834) makes a strong plea for nationalism: "I trust the people will know how to prize their singular happy situation among the nations of the earth, and join heart and hand in supporting the tired patriot who is at the head of their national affairs." John Beete's *The Man of the Times; or, A Scarcity of Cash* (1797) combines sentiment with a satire on the tactics of money lenders during the Revolution.

(c) Patriot Leadership
Complementing those plays which comment on some aspect of the new nation or its policies were the plays which praise its leaders and suggest broader influences. Two of the best plays celebrating heroes or events are William Brown's *West Point Preserved* (1797) and *Bunker Hill; or, The Death of General*

Warren (1797) by John Daly Burk (1776?-1808), a major dramatist of this brief period. According to A. H. Quinn (*History of American Drama*), Burk's play was frequently revived as a Fourth of July spectacle, having, as it does, a realistic attack on the Hill in the last act. Another play, *Columbia and Britannia,* published in 1787 by "Philophron" and probably not produced, celebrates the international prestige of a country now reconciled with Britannia and accepted as an equal by both Britannia and Gallia.

(d) A National Affair: Barbary Coast Pirates

Before the turn of the century, America had enough problems to satisfy most of its politicians and its playwrights. Plays that mention foreign powers usually have a harsh word for England and a sympathy -- sometimes reluctant, especially from the Federalists -- for the French. The one external affair, however, which provided material for playwrights was the war with the Barbary Coast pirates. Although the fighting did not occur until 1801 when America's infant navy was sent to Tripoli, the North African states -- Morocco, Algeria, Tunis and Tripoli -- had for some time been making an effective income by plundering merchantmen that sailed into the Mediterranean. *Slaves in Barbary* (1797) by David Everett is concerned with that persecution, which aroused Americans to anger and indignation.

The most important American play dealing with the pirates is *Slaves in Algiers; or, A Struggle for Freedom* (1794) by Susanna H. Rowson (1762-1824), actress and playwright, but best known for her amazingly successful sentimental novel *Charlotte Temple* (1791). Concerned with the rescue of some Americans held prisoner by the pirates, the play, Mrs. Rowson's only extant drama, mixes an abundance of sentiment with the melodrama of captures, disguises and escapes.

2.   SOCIAL FARCE AND EARLY CHARACTER TYPES

Of her aims as a playwright, Mrs. Rowson wrote: "It has been my endeavor to place social virtues in the fairest point of view and hold up to merited contempt and ridicule their [the people's] vices." Her objectives, shown also in *The Female Patriot* (1795) and *Americans in England* (1797), were shared by

many: the stage became a place to improve manners and morals
and to castigate social foibles and vices; satire, the accepted
technique; sentiment, the means to please the middle-class
taste; and farce-comedy, the usual genre. Consequently, plays
were frequently a hodge-podge of social and political comment.

(a) Social and Political Themes

One of the more successful practitioners of the fusion of social
and political ideas was John Murdock, whose *The Triumphs of
Love; or, Happy Reconciliation* (1795) includes comment on
various topics of the day: Quakers, the Whiskey Rebellion, a
foreign-born character who loves America as a place of freedom
and opportunity, the problems of the Barbary pirates and
slavery. A critic described the play as having "sentiments that
do honor to the writer's heart, both as man and citizen."

(b) Varied Satire

Understandably, topics for comment or satire suggest the social
biases of the day. Attitudes toward Catholics are expressed in
the anonymous play, *The French Revolution* (1790), and in *A
New World Planted* (1802) by Joseph Croswell (1786-1857).
Jews are generally treated with disdain. Professional men are
sometimes satirized -- physicians, lawyers and the clergy.
Before the Revolution, lawyers were generally treated as
troublemakers.

(c) Character Types

Before 1800 the principal character types -- the Yankee, the
Indian, the Negro and the Irishman -- had been successfully
introduced to the stage. Although the Yankee was once
thought original with Tyler in *The Contrast*, a humorous New
England Yankee named Jonathan had previously appeared in
The Downfall of Justice (1777). *The Politician Outwitted*
includes the Yankee Humphrey Cubb, and *The Better Sort* has a
Yankee named Yorick. Indians were clearly featured in such
early theatricals as Lescabot's *The Theatre of Neptune*, but
Robert Rogers is credited with the first serious interest in the
Indian with *Ponteach; or, The Savages of America* (1766). Anne
Kemble Hatton wrote an opera in 1794 about *Tammany; or, The
Indian Chief*, and Joseph Croswell introduced Pocahontas to
the American theatre in *A New World Planted*. The comic

Negro appears in a number of plays, usually as a servant talking in dialect -- *The Fall of British Tyranny* (1776), *The Downfall of Justice* (1777), *Sans Souci* (1785) and probably first in Thomas Forrest's *The Disappointment* (1767). John Murdock, however, created a more individual Negro in *The Triumphs of Love* (1795) with Sambo, a simple, warmhearted, generous person. The stage Irishman, an adopted rather than a native son, appears in *The Disappointment, The Triumphs of Love* and John Minshull's *Rural Felicity* (1801). These several plays forged the models for the four character types which were to be enormously popular during the next fifty years.

3.   ROMANTIC TRAGEDY

The trend toward poetic tragedy, started by Thomas Godfrey and followed by William Dunlap, continued through the eighteenth century and later became the mark of the serious dramatist. Unfortunately, the writing of poetic dramas was not reserved for poets only, or even for those with dramatic talent. Illustrative of early poetic tragedies are *The Patriot Chief* (1784) by Peter Markoe (1752-1792) and *The Mercenary Match* (1784) by Barnabas Bidwell (1763-1833). A more interesting but less successful play in the theatre was John Daly Burk's *Female Patriotism; or, The Death of Joan D'Arc* (1798). A. H. Quinn called this play one of the "bright spots that reward the reader of our early drama." Generally unrelieved in their tragedy, frequently dull in plot and written in quite ordinary verse, the romantic tragedies are of interest to the historian of drama but are the least satisfying for the general reader.

4.   STRICTLY MORAL LESSONS

Playwrights well knew that the moral lesson in a play was extremely important, not only for the audiences of New England but throughout the New World. The anonymous author of *The Better Sort* clearly stated that the playwright's task was to improve morals:

> For this the comick muse first trod the stage;
> And scourg'd the vice and folly of the age,
> Manners and sometimes principles she mended,
> Took her task up where the preacher ended.

When Dunlap rewrote *The Father* and increased the moralizing in the play, he acted in direct response to the desires of his audiences. The romantic tragedies of the time, the sentimental comedies, even the satires -- all were written to create a moral effect. Sometimes the didacticism is so dominant that plot disappears and only dialogue remains. One of the largest collections of published dialogues is Charles Stearn's 540 pages of *Dramatic Dialogues for the Use of Schools* (1798).

5.   COLLEGE DRAMA

After the Revolution, college students continued to write and produce plays such as *The Mercenary Match* by Barnabus Bidwell, performed by Yale College students in 1784, and *The French Revolution*, written and produced by a student at Dartmouth College in 1790. Such activity was indicative of an interest which was to lie relatively fallow for over a hundred years before it became a meaningful part of America's theatre productivity.

III. THEATRE DURING THE REVOLUTION AND THE POST REVOLUTIONARY PERIOD TO 1800

During the last quarter of the eighteenth century, the American theatre renewed its struggle for acceptance. Seriously hampered during the war years, it now made distinct advances in building theatres and developing companies of actors. Theatre management continued to be a risky business. Theatre people, however, were optimistic even as the slackening of opposition by church and state seemed offset by growing harrassment from theatre critics.

A.   Theatre During the Revolution

Theatre during the Revolution was largely controlled by the British. General Burgoyne opened a Boston theatre in 1775; General Howe's so-called "strolling company" opened its season in Philadelphia on January 19, 1778. The center of British theatre activity, however, was New York, where each season until 1782 a number of the best plays of the time were produced -- including the first American performance of Sheridan's *The Rivals*. Congress did everything it could to discourage the acting of plays, but neither American soldiers nor citizens were cut off completely from the theatre. Soldiers at Valley Forge presented plays in the spring of 1778, and American forces opened the Southwark Theatre in Philadelphia later that year. Pennsylvania, Massachusetts and New York were reasonably severe in their enforcement of the law against enacting plays; but Maryland as a state did not abide by the Congressional interdicts concerning entertainment, and both Baltimore and Annapolis enjoyed plays during the late years of the war.

B.   Theatre from the Revolution to 1800

After the Revolution, the members of the American Company who had gone to Jamaica began to return, but without David Douglass, who had retired from the company and become a British judge in Jamaica. In 1782 John Henry was the first to use the theatres built by the Old American Company; the young Lewis Hallam arrived in 1784. By 1785 they had joined forces and settled in New York's John Street Theatre where, with Thomas Wignell, they began to dominate American theatre circles for the next several years. In 1791 Wignell left to form his own company, and John Hodgkinson took his place in the Old American Company. Not until Wignell returned from England with a larger and more talented company was the monolopy of the Old American Company broken. As the number of theatre companies increased, so did the need for theatres. Charleston began to build a theatre in 1792. Two years later, two famous theatres were opened: the Chestnut Street Theatre in Philadelphia and the Federal Street Theatre in Boston.

During these years many new and talented actors and actresses gained eminence on the American stage: Mrs. Oldmixon, Eliza Kemble Whitlock, Thomas A. Cooper and Joseph Jefferson I. The theatre also provided its usual abundance of exciting and sometimes scandalous events. In an extended feud between the management and the gallery hoodlums in Boston's Federal Street Theatre, "apples, stones or other missiles" were nightly hurled into the orchestra. The rebellion of actors against conditions in John L. Solee's French Theatre in Charleston was colorfully reported in the newspapers. Although this kind of news made the headlines, far more significant were the establishment of permanent theatres and the development of large companies of actors and actresses in America.

IV. SUMMARY

Although it was a policy of theatre managers during this time and for many years to come to laud foreign plays and to discourage American playwrights, plays written before the turn of the century reveal the distinct beginnings of an American drama. Many, of course, indicate little dramatic talent and were written more to criticize and to propagandize than to create a work of art, but the passion of some exhibited in these plays often strikes a spark of real life.

Because the Whig and Tory playwrights were much more interested in propaganda than in art, they became special pleaders whose characters said only what the author demanded. The play was a weapon: it had a distinct purpose and an episodic structure determined by that purpose. Today, such plays are mainly interesting as partisan social history and as caricature or panegyric -- having objectives similar to the satiric poetry of Philip Freneau and the essays of Thomas Paine. Although dramatically weak, many plays show enough passion, wit and ingenuity to make them quite readable.

In *The Contrast* by Royall Tyler lie the faint beginnings of social comedy in America. The plays of William Dunlap show the serious dramatist experimenting with the drama as his talent excites him and as expediency demands, and creating both in amount and in qualified excellence a noteworthy beginning for American drama. The creation of American character types was another step forward, while the numersous plays commenting on social foibles and political issues indicate the vitality of a growing drama.

Essentially, this was a weak period for English and European drama, and America adulterated her natural force by adapting and translating and imitating the romantic tragedies of England and the sentimental melodramas of France and Germany. But such was the fashion! It is with extreme care, certainly, that one commends the literary merit of more than a handful of these plays. Journalistic critics of the drama were just beginning to appear before the turn of the century, but they wrote primarily in terms of the plot, production and the accomplishments of the actors. More recent critics would perceive that in the drama before 1800 the foundations for the development of an American drama were being established.

SELECTED BIBLIOGRAPHY

Anderson, John. *The American Theater in New York.* New York: Dial Press, 1938.

Brown, Alice. *Mercy Warren.* New York: C. Scribner's Sons, 1896.

Brown, T. A. *A History of the New York Stage from the First Performance in 1732 to 1901.* 3 vols. New York: Dodd, Mead, and Co., 1903.

Coad, Oral S. *William Dunlap: A Study of His Life and Works.* New York: The Dunlap Society, 1917.

Dunlap, William. *A History of the American Theatre.* New York: J. and J. Harper, 1832.

Hartman, John Geoffrey. *The Development of American Social Comedy from 1787 to 1936.* Philadelphia: Univ. of Penn. Press, 1939.

Hewitt, Barnard. *Theatre U.S.A., 1665 to 1957.* New York: McGraw-Hill Book Co., 1959.

Hornblow, Arthur. *A History of the Theatre in America,* vol. I. Philadelphia: J. B. Lippincott Co., 1919.

Hughes, Glenn. *A History of the American Theatre, 1700-1950.* New York: S. French, 1951.

Ireland, Joseph N. *Records of the New York Stage from 1750 to 1860.* 2 vols. New York: T. H. Morrell, 1866-1867.

Mayorga, Margaret G. *A Short History of the American Drama.* New York: Dodd, Mead & Co., 1932.

Meserve, Walter J. *An Emerging Entertainment: The Drama of the American People to 1828.* Bloomington: Indiana Univ. Press, 1977.

Moses, Montrose J. *The American Dramatist.* Boston: Little, Brown, and Co., 1925.

Odell, George C. D. *Annals of the New York State.* 15 vols. New York: Columbia Univ. Press, 1927-49.

Pollock, Thomas C. *The Philadelphia Theatre in the Eighteenth Century.* Philadelphia: Univ. of Pennsylvania Press, 1933.

Quinn, Arthur Hobson. *A History of the American Drama from the Beginning to the Civil War.* New York: Appleton-Century-Crofts, Inc., 1943.

Rankin, Hugh F. *The Theater in Colonial America.* Chapel Hill: Univ. of North Carolina Press, 1965.

Wilson, Garff B. *Three Hundred Years of American Drama and Theatre.* Englewood Cliffs: Prentice-Hall, 1973.

Chapter Two

Drama of a New Nation, 1800-1865
A Period of Experimentation and Imitation

From the beginning of the century through the period of the Civil War, the progress of American drama was steady and scattered with impressive efforts but still discouraging for American dramatists. The theatre continued to expand amid difficulties. Various actors and actresses achieved reputations which gained applause in America and even in England, but such appreciation was most frequently excited by youthful exhuberance rather than mature excellence, although there were exceptions. Certainly the best remembered theatrical events of this period resulted more from the pains of growth than from superiority of performance. Between the actor or the manager and the playwright there was little sympathy and even less cooperation. On only a very few occasions did a high point in the history of American theatre and the appearance of a significant play in the history of American drama occur simultaneously. The influence of the actor (and the actor-manager) was supreme; the tastes of American audiences were no higher than usual; the dramatist remained insignificant. With their eyes on their fortunes, the actors and actor-managers tried to provide the theatregoers with both the sentiment they enjoyed and the English plays they thought it fashionable to applaud. At the same time the actor claimed the privilege of giving full vent to the declamatory style of acting then popular. A few actors specialized in the peculiarities of a single character, such as the stage Yankee.

American dramatists, meanwhile, were forced either to imitate the style of successful foreign plays or to write a play for a particular actor. In either instance their work was likely to become unintentionally philanthropic. With very little professional status and without protection of a copyright law -- not to mention the pirating techniques of that day -- a playwright could gain very little. In theatre programs the name of the playwright was frequently omitted, and the playwright's financial return was embarrassingly slight. The

American dramatist was truly at the mercy of managers, whose reasoning, if unethical, was at least understandable: Why pay Americans to write plays when we can get (i.e., steal) new plays from England for nothing?

In a preface to his play *Thérèse, the Orphan of Geneva* -- which was taken down in shorthand from the theatre pit and thus stolen by theatre managers in London -- John Howard Payne complained about the situation of the dramatist and the subsequent poor plight of dramatic literature in America. No doubt, he expressed the opinions of many. J. S. Jones, a prolific writer of farce-comedies, stated bluntly that there was no Standard American Drama because nobody would pay for it. Robert Montgomery Bird, a poet-dramatist, found it most disagreeable "to write for and be admired by groundlings! villains that will clap when you are most nonsensical and applaud you most heartily when you are most vulgar. . . ." Perhaps the time was not right for serious and creative dramatists. Certainly, with few exceptions -- and these, failures -- men and women with reputations in literature did not write for the stage. And it would be a long time before theatre managers would lament this condition.

From 1800 to 1865, only a handful of dramatists achieved anything approaching high literary quality. These dramatists were not frequently encouraged, nor was the literary value of their work appreciated. Professional dramatic criticism had just started before the turn of the century, and of the few attempts to establish purely theatrical magazines, none lasted more than a year or two. Washington Irving was an outstanding and delightful critic, and with tongue in cheek, his reviews suggest a perceptive attitude toward critics:

> The critics [Andrew Quoz explains to Jonathan Oldstyle] are the very pests of society; they rob the actor of his reputation, the public of their amusement; they open the eyes of their readers to a full perception of the faults of our performers; they reduce our feelings to a state of miserable refinement, and destroy entirely all the enjoyments in which our coarser sensations delighted.

Generally, critics throughout the century were notorious for their ignorance of drama as literature as well as of drama as a scenic and declamatory production. In America as in England, criticisms of the theatre were published in "Sporting and Theatrical" journals such as the New York *Clipper* and the New York *Illustrated Times*. The earliest theatrical newspaper was the New York *Dramatic News and Society Journal*, established in 1874. From the early 1830s on, the *Spirit of the Times* has been a major source for theatre and drama scholars.

Before the Civil War, the greatest opportunity for the aspiring dramatist lay in becoming an actor or actor-manager-dramatist, as did John Howard Payne, Dion Boucicault and John Brougham. Others wrote plays, became disenchanted and left the theatre -- as did Robert Montgomery Bird. Still others wrote the innumerable lesser plays for their own or another's acting. It seems to have been neither a very happy time for the serious American dramatist nor a very productive period for good American drama. Yet plays of merit were being written in America which revealed both hope and promise. Among these are Payne's *Brutus* and *Charles the Second,* James N. Barker's *Superstition,* Robert M. Bird's *The Broker of Bogota,* Anna C. M. Ritchie's *Fashion,* Nathaniel H. Bannister's *Gaulantus the Gaul* and Cornelius Mathews' *Witchcraft; or, The Martyrs of Salem.* George H. Boker's *Francesca da Rimini* is considered by many to be superior to any play written on either side of the Atlantic Ocean during this time. But, quite generally, drama in America was diverse and superficial.

At the close of the eighteenth century, the drama was established as a source of entertainment, a political weapon, a means of glorifying the nation and a teacher of moral behavior. These trends continued as playwrights experimented further with their material. As wars were fought and a self-conscious new nation became aware of the necessity of tradition, various aspects of America's past appeared on the stage -- all patriotically exalted. Those playwrights who wanted to write serious drama imitated the verse plays of England and with a few notable exceptions remained simply imitators. Native characters soon proved an effective source of comedy, and while the Negro became a minstrel as well as a serious character in plays, the stage Yankee as a comic character was expanded to provide a full evening's entertainment. As cities grew and social classes became distinguishable, the particular characteristics of these classes provided an object of ridicule in plays, and comedies of social caricature gained popular acclaim. In essence, American drama developed constantly, though slowly, and with significance in some areas, but it still revealed the divided interests of the country's playwrights: (1) struggling for existence and experimenting with native material, and (2) attempting to gain status by imitating the drama of England and Europe.

I. PLAYS FROM THE TOWN CRIER: NATIONALISM ON THE STAGE

In his *History* (I, 163-4) William Dunlap quoted James Kirke Paulding, American novelist and dramatist, on national drama:

> By a national drama, we mean, not merely a class of dramatic productions, written by Americans, but one appealing directly to the national feeling -- founded upon domestic incidents -- illustrating or satirizing domestic manners, and, above all, displaying a generous chivalry in the maintenance and vindication of those great and illustrious peculiarities of situation and character by which we are distinguished from all other nations.

If interpreted generously, Paulding's definition might include most of the plays discussed in this chapter, because the majority of dramas written during these years included references to some aspect of the manners, politics and character of the nation. By this same definition, however, national drama is limited to political incidents and historical events. Not only in the "coonskin cap" New Democracy of Andrew Jackson but also in the ultranationalistic ideas of John Quincy Adams' Puritan New England, the "feelings of national glory" and "love of country" were prominent. The drama, always dependent upon popular tastes, followed the nationalistic trend. Like the crier who heralded the news concerning the welfare of town and country, these plays commented on political events and lauded the honor of the new nation.

A. Political Events and Issues

The inclination of post-Revolutionary playwrights to comment on political events continued -- as it continues today. After the heated presidential campaign of 1800, for example, Thomas Jefferson defeated the incumbent, John Adams, and ended twelve years of Federalist rule. The following year, a play by J. H. Nichols celebrated Jefferson's inauguration: *Jefferson and Liberty; or, Celebration of the Fourth of March* (1801). Adams is ridiculed as the Duke of Braintree, and all are portrayed as corrupt until Jefferson gives his inaugural speech promising freedom and justice.

1.   REACTION TO PARTICULAR EVENTS

The purchase of Louisiana in 1803 inspired James Workman (d. 1832) to write a farce-comedy called *Liberty in Louisiana* (1804). James Nelson Barker's *The Embargo; or, What News?* (1808) supports Jefferson's highly controversial Embargo Act of 1807, which forbade the export of all goods from America. *Removing the Deposits* (1835) by Henry J. Finn (1790?-1840) refers to Andrew Jackson's decision in 1833 to deposit no more funds with Nicholas Biddle's Bank of the United States.

2.   BORDER DISPUTES

N. H. Bannister's *The Maine Question* (1839) is concerned with the boundary dispute involving some 12,000 square miles of wilderness claimed by both Maine and Canada. The Oregon Controversy of 1846 was dramatized that same year by Joseph M. Field (1810-1856) in *Oregon; or, The Disputed Territory,* a kind of masque with Oregon, Texas and California -- three territories wanted by President James K. Polk -- acting parts.

3.   THE POLITICIAN

Politicians appear in many plays. In the early 1820s, Seba Smith of the Portland, Maine, *Courier* created Major Jack Downing, a Yankee comic-critic of political issues and politicians who dressed in the clothes we now give to Uncle Sam. In 1834 an anonymous playwright put this Downeast Yankee's political arguments into a play, *Major Jack Downing; or, The Retired Politician. Whigs and Democrats; or, Love of*

No Politics (1839), attributed to J. E. Heath (1792-1862), and *The Politicians* (1840) by Cornelius Mathews (1817-1889) satirizes methods used in a rural election in Virginia and the evils of the local campaign, respectively.

B. Reflected Glory: America's Past

As a young country still not completely certain of the distinctive values of originality and imitation, America was cautiously impressed by the importance of traditions and the past in England.   On the other hand, strong feelings of nationalism prompted dramatists to exploit the few past events and the people of whom America could boast. The Revolution, of course, immediately offered itself as material, as did other military engagements, such as the battles with the Barbary Coast pirates, the War of 1812 and the Mexican War. Various activities of the Colonial Period were also dramatized. Generally, however, national plays are not among the best of this period, and only a relatively few plays have survived.

1.   PLAYS ABOUT THE COLONIAL PERIOD

Among the plays depicting Colonial times, Richard Penn Smith's historical melodrama *William Penn* (1829) dramatizes the title character's heroics in saving the life of the Indian chief Tammany.   George H. Miles' *DeSoto, the Hero of the Mississippi* (1852) combines an exploration theme with a Colonial setting.   James Nelson Barker's *Superstition* (1824) dramatizes New England intolerance and the incident of a Puritan leading the people against the Indians.   Most of the plays with Indian characters -- at least seventy-five written before the Civil War -- are set in Colonial times.

2.   PLAYS ABOUT THE REVOLUTION

By far the most stimulating period for early nineteenth-century American playwrights was that of the Revolution.   Heroes, battles, fashions of the time -- all appeared on the stage, in either original plays or adaptations of historical novels. Washington was most frequently used as a hero, but the treasonous act of Benedict Arnold was depicted in several plays in which Major André figured prominently.   Generally, the plays are unpretentious farce-melodramas.

(a)   *Putnam, the Iron Son of '76* (1844)
by Nathaniel H. Bannister (1813-1847)

Nathaniel H. Bannister, an accomplished actor-playwright whose brief career has been neglected by historians, had six of his numerous plays published and enjoyed an excellent reputation in theatres of the South and West. An experimenter and an imaginative writer, Bannister is best remembered for *Putnam*, a "national military drama," which eulogizes the career of General Israel Putnam and, with the feats of Black Vulture, a trained horse and perhaps the "real hero of the play," became a model for future equestrian spectacles on the American stage.

(b)   Battles of the Revolution

Certain battles of the Revolution and the general atmosphere of the times are reflected in numerous plays, such as *The Boston Tea Party of 1774* (1843) anon.; *The Cradle of Liberty; or, Boston in 1775* (1832) by S. E. Glover; and *A Tale of Lexington* (1822) by Samuel B. Judah.

(c)   Historical Novels of the Revolution Dramatized

Several contemporary historical novels were very successfully adapted to the stage. In 1856 Clifton W. Tayleure dramatized John P. Kennedy's popular novel, *Horseshoe Robinson*. Charles P. Clinch's *The Spy, a Tale of the Neutral Ground* (1822) is one of several adapations of James Fenimore Cooper's novels.

(d)   A Romance of the Revolution: *Love in '76* (1857)
by Oliver Bell Bunce (1828-1890)

Called the best of the Revolutionary plays by A. H. Quinn, *Love in '76* treats the love of Captain Armstrong of the American army for Rose Elsworth, daughter of a loyalist and sister of an officer in the English army. A lively comedy, it dramatizes a series of clashes of wit in which a clever woman snares the man she loves. With the help of disguises, the plot is effectively worked out, and the dialogue is humorous, witty and less stilted than that of other plays of the period.

3.   PLAYS ABOUT THE WAR WITH THE BARBARY STATES

For some reason the romance of pirates and the Mediterranean did not interest many playwrights. The best plays dealing with the Barbary pirates, Mrs. S. H. Rowson's *Slaves in Algiers*, was written before the fighting began -- at least before Jefferson dispatched the Navy in 1801. One of the better plays is James Ellison's *The American Captive; or, The Siege of Tripoli* (1811), revised by J. S. Jones under the title *The Usurper; or, Americans in Tripoli* (1841). The plays tells a story of romantic adventure, but nationalistic sentiment prevails as the playwright urges America to negotiate and asks for the freedom of the brave sons of America. Other Barbary States War plays include Maria H. Pinchney's colorful closet drama, *The Young Carolinians; or, Americans in Algiers* (1818), *The Siege of Tripoli* (1820) by Mordecai Noah and Jonathan S. Smith's extravagant work, *The Siege of Algiers; or, The Downfall of Hadgi-Ali-Bashaw, a Political, Historical and Sentimental Tragi-Comedy* (1823).

4.   PLAYS ABOUT THE WAR OF 1812

According to W. W. Clapp, Jr. (*A Record of the Boston Stage*, 1853, p. 134), "In the early days of the theatre, every public event of sufficient importance was immediately dramatized, and during the progress of the war [1812], the spirit was kept up by the frequent productions of pieces in honor of our naval victories." Spectacles on stage, of course, were well appreciated. Consequently, the capture of the *Macedonia* by the *United States* was celebrated in *The Return from a Cruise* (anonymous, 1812), and the victory of the *Constitution* over the *Guerriére* in William Dunlap's *Yankee Chronology* (1812).

(a) Plays by Richard Penn Smith (1799-1854)

The most significant of those playwrights who chose to dramatize the War of 1812 was Richard Penn Smith -- a member of the so-called Philadelphia school of dramatists. A lawyer by profession and a bit of a dilettante by choice, Smith became a competent craftsman of the drama in his best plays. (He wrote at least seventeen comedies, melodramas and tragedies, of which *Caius Marius*, 1831, is considered the best.) *The Eighth of January*, produced in Philadelphia on January 8,

1829, to celebrate the election of Andrew Jackson, dramatizes Jackson's victory over the British at New Orleans on January 8, 1815. Although poorly written, the play was successful -- obviously in consequence of the well-timed production. The momentous victory at Plattsburg when General McDonough's fleet defeated the English on September 1, 1814, was the basis of *The Triumph at Plattsburg* (1830). Smith, however, sacrificed historical accuracy in the play for the melodrama of fictional disguise, escape and pursuit.

(b) Battles of the War of 1812

Mordecai M. Noah (1785-1851), a distinctive leader in Jewish America, an occasional playwright and a firm friend of the drama in America, dramatized the Battle of Chippewa, July 5, 1814, in play called *She Would Be a Solider; or, The Plains of Chippewa* (1819). More romance than history, the play tells the story of Christine, who, to avoid an unwanted marriage and to find Lenox whom she loves, disguises herself as a man and enlists as a soldier, only to be discovered and condemned as a spy before she is finally saved -- by Lenox, of course. Other plays on the war include C. E. Grice's *The Battle of New Orleans* (1815), G. W. P. Custis' *The Eighth of January* (1831) and *North Point; or, Baltimore Defended* (1833) and Richard Emmons' *Tecumseh; or The Battle of the Thames* (1836).

5.   PLAYS ABOUT THE MEXICAN WAR

William Gilmore Simms' *Michael Bonham; or, The Fall of Bexar* (1852) dramatizes the life of a Charleston soldier who fought through the Texas skirmishes to the battle of the Alamo. According to A. H. Quinn, the only surviving play on the Mexican War is *The Battle of Buena Vista* (1858); other titles include *The Siege of Monterey, Our Flag is Nailed to the Mast* and *Victory Upon Victory*.

II. POETIC DRAMA:
THE SERIOUS DRAMATIST AT WORK

If serious and high dramatic purpose existed in American plays before the Civil War, it found expression in the poetic dramas. From Godfrey's *Prince of Parthia* (1765) to Boker's *Francesca da*

Rimini (1855), the development of poetic drama can be traced from its most imitative beginnings to the greatest height in romantic tragedy reached by an American in the nineteenth century.   Having literary aspirations, poetic dramatists followed the dictum of Horace -- to teach and to delight -- and if they stressed the first precept, they were only obeying the impulse of the age.   Their names -- James Nelson Barker, John Howard Payne, Nathaniel Parker Willis, Robert Montgomery Bird, Cornelius Mathews, George Henry Boker -- identify some of the most significant figures in American drama before the Civil War.   Their plays are among the best that America can offer for this century.

That period before the Civil War was a period of poetry and of romantic themes. An American literature was being created by Washington Irving, Nathaniel Hawthorne, Ralph Waldo Emerson, Henry Wadsworth Longfellow, James Fenimore Cooper, Edgar Allan Poe and Herman Melville, among others. Unlike other literary forms, however, which stressed independence from England, the drama generally accepted English leadership as the standard, and theatre managers and actors demanded it.   Attempting to follow the mood of the times, as well as to reach a meaningful success in their art, serious dramatists wrote poetic drama.

Considering all of the drama of this time, poetic plays by and large show the influence of foreign drama, while plays in prose tend to exploit the qualities that are distinctly American, although there are many poetic dramas with native themes. Historians of the drama have not agreed as to the value of poetic drama: A. H. Quinn organized a third of his history around the poetic dramatists; Montrose Moses seemed to feel that from the point of view of good theatre these writers were overrated. From a historical perspective of American drama and its accomplishments during the first sixty or more years of the nineteenth century, it can be shown that poetic plays fit into a significant niche.

Throughout the history of American drama, poetic plays have enjoyed a cyclical popularity. Prevalent during the early half of the nineteenth century, they all but disappeared during the realistic movement of the last part of the century. In the early years of the twentieth century, a half-dozen poet-dramatists wrote some effective plays, only to be overwhelmed by World War I. A few post-war dramatists -- notably Maxwell Anderson -- tried to express their ideas in poetry, and during the years following World War II a number of poets -- Archibald MacLeish and Robert Lowell among them -- wrote for the theatre with some success. More recently in America, the art of poetry has become obscured as the appreciation of precise language has declined.

A.   The Pattern of Poetic Drama

More than other dramatists, the writer of poetic plays had limited choices.   The audience, the actor and the theatre manager all made certain demands.   According to dramatic critic William Winter, the verse dramatist had to entertain and to instruct a dull multitude that "never felt anything 'til it was hit with a club." Hence, the subtleties of verse had little effect, and dramatic ironies were lost on the audience.   The actor, in turn, demanded speeches which would best adapt to a flamboyant delivery. Consequently, there emerged in America a poetic drama that, with foreign or native inspiration, followed certain patterns in plot, purpose, theme, setting and characters. The best plays, of course, in some ways defied the pattern and thereby gained, in part, their excellence.

1.   THE PLOT

Although a few poetic comedies were written, most of the poet-dramatists had pretentions toward tragedy and were influenced by: (1) the melodramatic romances of the French (Alexandre Dumas and Victor Hugo, particularly the latter's *Preface to Cromwell*); (2) the sentimental and humanitarian dramas of the German, Kotzebue; (3) the plays of Elizabethan England; and (4) the dramas of sensibility and domestic tragedy of eighteenth-century England.   Plots vary, some writers bowing more to one model than to another. The general tragic plot, however, became sufficiently familiar that *Portfolio* magazine in 1803, with some facetiousness and some truth, gave the following instructions to the writer of tragedy:

In order to make a strident, striking and poetic plot, the author must collect as many black-looking tragedies as his industry can discover; the older they are the better; interweaving and jumbling them together, so that it will be impossible to develop or understand them. After arranging the plot, the time must be laid in a century long since gone by, and the place in a remote kingdom and among grandees never heard of. Then for the sentiments; these you will find in the Bible, in moral treatises, in Addison's *Cato*, in Darwin's *Botanic Garden*, in a thousand well-known books and common-place works, where no one can suppose he has had the impudence to pick them up.

Montrose Moses, with reference to poetic plays, complained of the "second hand spirit" that pervaded American drama.

2.   THE SETTING

The historical setting of the poetic dramas provided the audiences with the pageantry and grandeur they enjoyed and with the moral instruction they demanded. In a prologue to James McHenry's *The Usurper* (1827), J. N. Barker wrote:

Our Poet's pencil paints the moral scene
Teaching what ought to be by what has been.

The majority of verse plays employed an ancient setting. Rome was a particular favorite, as seen in Payne's *Brutus* and Bird's *The Gladiator*. With its history of rebellion, war and tyranny, Rome could support a political theme in which the American attitude toward democracy and freedom could be readily understood. A medieval background was often employed for similar reasons. By writing of distant places and olden times, dramatists believed that they could infuse greater issues and more universal themes into their works. Some dramatists used native themes to advantage, but the setting was always from a past that could suggest grandeur as well as offer instruction.

3.   THE CHARACTERS

The best dramatists created characters of human dimensions, such as Ravensworth in Barker's *Superstition* and Lanciotto in Boker's *Francesca da Rimini*. Too frequently, however, the characters are not individuals but social types. Lacking a sense of greatness and showing little psychological insight on the part of the dramatist, these characters are more appropriate to melodrama than tragedy. The heroes are simply virtuous -- lovers, leaders, honorable men. Having no internal conflict, they have only to love the heroine, defeat the villain and speak moral platitudes. The villain is the hero's opposite -- evil, vicious, a scoffer at democracy, a man of unscrupulous ambition, sometimes ugly and physically deformed. Frequently, however, because of his greater imagination, he is the most interesting character in the play.

The women in these plays are of two distinct types. There is the angelic woman -- virtuous, modest, obedient, faithful, truthful, beautiful and emotionally cold. She is to be worshipped, not loved. Frequently, this woman is driven insane by the cruelties of a man's world. The more interesting and more realistic woman is the sinner, a woman destroyed by passion, which the virtuous heroine, of course, never feels.

4.   THE THEME

A major interest of plays early in the century, and of poetic drama in particular because it was the serious drama of the time, was moral instruction. In varying degrees plays became moral lectures: the poetry became sermonic, the characters personifications of vice and virtue to be punished and rewarded. Partially in response to demands for moral drama yet following the traditions of English tragedy, the verse dramatist dealt almost exclusively with themes that were considered universal: (1) freedom and patriotism, (2) romantic love, (3) marital infidelity and (4) parental tyranny and filial duty. A popular theme which combined public and domestic issues was the struggle of love with honor or duty.

5.   THE POETRY

The demands of theatre upon the poet-dramatist had a distinct effect upon the kind of poetry written, although, with the exception of a few, those who wrote poetic plays were not good poets. Speeches in regular, stilted and lifeless blank verse became rhetorical sermons rather than real speech. To most dramatists and, seemingly, to critics and managers, poetic speech meant exaggerated poetic diction with excessive use of abstract terms. Verbosity was common; imagery concerned with animals and mythology was elaborate. In *Caridorf* (1827), Bird exposed the common technique:

> Make thou no stops, no commas, no colons, nor periods; but between sentences draw thou a long dash, for this is significant of passion. Let there be breaks in the sentiment and style, the moderate complaining suddenly jumping into piteous ejaculations, with many an *O* and *Ah, Alas* and *Ah, me.* Then let the conclusion die away into a melancholy oath. . . .

There is, unfortunately, little to commend in the poetry of these plays. Few dramatists were capable of writing good poetic plays, but from these few there are surprising rewards.

B.   Foreign influences on Poetic Drama

As the patterns of poetic drama indicated, foreign influences on theme and technique were dominant in America. Of the many who wrote almost entirely of foreign scenes, three dramatists present sustained achievements -- John Howard Payne, Robert Montgomery Bird and George Henry Boker.

1.   JOHN HOWARD PAYNE (1791-1852)

As an actor and later as a dramatist, Payne was associated with the theatre for most of his life. Popular as a young actor in America, he went to England in 1813; but failing to impress the audiences, he left the stage and began a new career as a playwright. In February 1816 he started translating and adapting French plays for the management at the Drury Lane Theatre. Then, however, he decided to write a tragedy for the great English actor, Edmund Kean, *Brutus; or, The Fall of Tarquin,* which was produced with success in December of 1818 -- success for everyone, that is, but John Howard Payne. Accused of plagiarism and abused by Drury Lane management, he also suffered a disastrous season as manager of Sadler's Wells Theatre. Sent to debtors' prison, he wrote *Thérèse, The Orphan of Geneva* (1821), which bought him his freedom.

Before returning to America in 1832, Payne wrote several popular plays. Among these are *Clari; or, The Maid of Milan* (1823), which includes "Home, Sweet Home," the poetry for which Payne is best remembered, and *Charles the Second* (1824), the successful comedy which he wrote in collaboration with Washington Irving. Back in America, Payne was treated to benefit performances of his plays and toasted by a literary group in New York: "Our distinguished countryman -- John Howard Payne. The family of literature welcomes him to the home whose praises he has so sweetly sung." Although his plays were widely produced, he received little recompense for his work; and after an unsuccessful attempt to found a magazine and some bitter comments on the plight of the dramatist, he left the theatre. When he died in 1851, he was the United States Consul at Tunis.

Payne's place in the history of American drama is significant. He was the first American dramatist to establish a successful reputation abroad, and of the sixty or more plays attributed to him, several held the stage for many years, while his best efforts at comedy and tragedy are still worth consideration. In each of the following types of drama, he presented a contemporary achievement -- comedy, melodrama, opera -- and in *Brutus*, he set a trend in romantic tragedy. Although his genius was not for creating the original play, he did have remarkable talent for recognizing dramatic material and for extracting theatrical success from his sources. It should be remembered that at this time it was a great advertisement for a play to be the first English version of the latest French success. With his reputation abroad, his skillful use of dramatic materials and his two or three major achievements in drama, he carried on the spirit of American drama begun by William Dunlap.

Brutus; or, The Fall of Tarquin (1818)
(Plot) In Rome, Sextus Tarquin has seized the throne by murdering the father and brother of Lucius Junius, who now lives with the victors and feigns the "fool." Upset by a prophecy that "The race of Tarquin shall be kings, till a fool drive them hence, and set Rome free!" Tullia, Sextus' queen, suspects Lucius Junius and names him Brutus. Meanwhile, Titus,

Brutus' son, not recognizing the tyranny, has decided to marry Sextus' daughter, Tarquinia. Sextus, having heard Collatinus boast of Lucretia's faithfulness as a wife, rapes her and describes his feat to Brutus, who drops his mask of idiocy and uses Sextus' action and Lucretia's suicide to rally the Romans to fight. Tullia dies; Sextus Tarquin is stoned to death; and Titus, controlled by those who conspired against Brutus, must be condemned. Passing this sentence, Brutus cries, "Justice is satisfied, and Rome is free!" before he falls, a final victim.

(Discussion) First performed at London's Drury Lane Theatre on December 3, 1818, the play was indebted, Payne noted in his Preface, to "seven plays upon the subject of Brutus." Its two major themes, however, come from myth and history: (1) Brutus' use of Sextus Tarquin's rape of Lucrece to expel the Tarquins, and (2) Brutus' dramatic condemnation of his own son. The success of the play was immediate and lasting. Written for Edmund Kean, the play also appealed to the American actor Edwin Forrest, who was attracted by the strong role of Brutus and the artifical elegance, which occasionally exposes dignity and power in the blank verse.

2.   ROBERT MONTGOMERY BIRD (1806-1854)

A scholarly and versatile man but naive in money matters, Bird started a trend in American drama parallel with that developing in French drama and became the foremost writer of American romantic tragedy in the first half of the nineteenth century. Beginning his mature life as a physician, he found more satisfaction in a career in playwriting until his association with Edwin Forrest, the actor, proved unbearable. He then turned to politics, journalism and the writing of novels: *The Hawks of Hawk-Hollow* (1835) and *Nick of the Woods* (1837), among others.

When Bird began his literary career, the Romantic influence was being felt in American literature. Romanticism, a convenient term to describe some changes in literature that occurred particularly in the early nineteenth century, meant many things. It was the untamed and emotional attitude toward nature that distinguished Wordsworth's poetry. It was the emphasis on idealism and imagination that sparked the writings of Emerson and Thoreau; the interest in the Gothic that inspired Poe and Hawthorne; the sense of freedom, idealized individuals and a realistic attitude toward background and scene that marked the historical romances of James Fenimore Cooper, John P. Kennedy, James Kirke Paulding and William Gilmore Simms. Bird was a major force in bringing Romanticism to American drama.

Bird's relationship with Edwin Forrest was both his inspiration and his nemesis. In 1828, Forrest announced the first of nine playwriting contests through which he hoped to get new plays for himself and, perhaps, to inspire American-born dramatists. Four of the nine prize-winning plays were written by Bird and two of these -- *The Gladiator* and *The Broker of Bogota* -- became permanent plays in Forrest's repertoire. Having written plays from which Forrest reaped a fortune, Bird received only $1000 for each play. Arrangements were poor, misunderstandings grew, and Bird stopped writing for the stage in 1837. Thanks to Forrest's 1836 English tour, Bird was elected to the English Dramatic Author's Society; in 1853 *The Gladiator* reached its one-thousanth performance in the forty years Forrest kept it in the theatre.

Bird's particular skill in writing plays is not difficult to discover. The fact that he was able to write successfully for Forrest suggests three things: (1) that he had a keen instinct for the dramatic situation; (2) that he could create a well-developed hero; and (3) that he could write the kind of rhetorical and exclamatory poetic speech that fitted Forrest's robust style of acting. In describing his theory of dramatic composition, Bird noted that everything must lead toward the climax and stimulate interest in the hero -- the power of the story, the passion of the characters, the strength of their speech and interest in the events. Unlike Payne, Bird found his dramatic incidents and inspiration in history, to which he applied a dramatic imagination and his novelist's ability to tell an interesting story. *The Broker of Bogota* and *The Gladiator* are his best plays, both tragedies, the former better as literature. In all his plays the Romantic attitude is prominent.

The Gladiator (1831)

(Plot) Spartacus, a well-known Thracian gladiator captured by the Romans, refuses to fight Pharsarius until he is promised freedom for himself and his family. Just before the fight, Spartacus and Pharsarius discover that they are brothers; the gladiators then rush the Roman guards, winning a great battle. When the brothers argue over Spartacus' decision to return a captive to Rome, Pharsarius takes his followers into battle and is defeated. In the play's climax Spartacus, learning that his wife and child are dead, charges into battle to die like a gladiator.

(Discussion) Immediately successful, the play remained a favorite of Edwin Forrest, who performed the role of Spartacus for his debut in London on October 17, 1836. The critic of the London *Courier* was impressed: "America has at length vindicated her capability of producing a dramatist of the highest order, whose claims should be unequivocally acknowledged by the Mother Country." According to his custom, Bird took freely from history and added conflicts and the touch of humanity which make Spartacus a meaningful symbol of freedom. Into the most powerful tyranny the world has known, Bird brought Spartacus, a gladiator, who represents the value of individual man struggling against overwhelming force. The nobility of the theme is matched by Spartacus' deeds, for example, the powerful emotional climax of his call for the gladiators' revolt at the end of Act II:

> Death to the Roman fiends that make their mirth
> Out of the groans of bleeding misery!
> Ho, slaves, arise! it is your hour to kill!
> Kill and spare not -- for wrath and liberty!
> Freedom for bondmen -- freedom and revenge!

The Broker of Bogota (1834)

(Plot) Led into dissolute ways by Caberero, Ramon is disinherited by his father, Febro the broker, and, because he has no inheritance, is rejected by the father of Juana, his betrothed. Febro tries to bribe Caberero to leave the city, but Ramon, desperate for money, rebukes his father. When Febro is robbed by Caberero, evidence that he stole from himself for his own advantage is very convincing until Ramon, overwhelmed by remorse and persuaded by Juana, confesses his own and Caberero's guilt to the Viceroy, who frees Febro. Febro happily learns that the Viceroy's son is in love with his daughter and all seems well until Ramon jumps to his death and Febro falls lifeless to the floor.

(Discussion) True to his views on dramatic composition, Bird made all speeches, scenes and characters contribute to the interest in the main character. Baptista Febro, a good and noble man whose love goes beyond his middle-class morality, is both hero and victim. But because he is in no way responsible for such circumstantial misfortunes, the play is more melodramatic pathos than domestic tragedy. Opposing him is Caberero, a "devil-born destroyer of men's sons," whose greed and indifference to moral values in society provide the basic plot. The Viceroy states the theme and moral of the play: "The rigid sire and disobedient son."

3.   GEORGE HENRY BOKER (1823-1890)

Of the many poetic dramatists of this period, Boker is the only one with any substantive reputation as a poet. Although some of his plays were written after the Civil War, his best work, *Francesca da Rimini*, appeared in 1855 and is not only the best dramatic tragedy of the century but the last one of any consequence during this period when poetic drama was popular and serious dramatists used it consistently. With the emergence of local color fiction and the beginnings of Realism in literature, poetic drama was generally rejected by theatre managers as not in the public taste. Although Boker's lyric and narrative poetry concerned with the Civil War (*Poems of the War*, 1864) are some of the best of that period, his work did not reflect prevailing social, economic or literary changes. His romantic dramas written after the Civil War were seldom acted, and he remains a second-rate poet and a poetic dramatist whose work might as well have stopped in 1855. But not before! From Payne through Bird to Boker, American drama progressed from skillful fusion and imitation, to the creation of human characters in theatrically effective plays, to a work of both literary and dramatic merit.

While Boker also wrote poetic comedies, such as *The Widow's Marriage* (1852) it is only for his tragedies that he is distinguished among American dramatists. Actually, he fared much better than his contemporaries and, for his earlier work, earned a generous amount of money and fame. His particular forte was his ability to create effective blank verse and to write witty as well as empassioned dialogue. Unlike Bird, who satisfied the demands of starring actors by emphasizing a single hero in each play, Boker built several characters into strong, forceful individuals with inner conflicts. His climaxes, too, were not those of spectacle and bombast but of power and beauty. Although he wrote several plays (*Calaynos*, 1848; *Leonor de Guzman*, 1853; *Glaucus*, 1886) he remains recognized mainly for a single masterpiece -- *Francesca da Rimini* -- which was not successful on stage until Laurence Barrett revived it in 1882. In the 1850's the acting profession, tightly bound by the Star System, could not accommodate to the rich demands of Boker's imagination shown through a variety of characters in *Francesca da Rimini*.

Francesca da Rimina (1855)

(Plot) To cement relations between Ravenna and Rimini, a marriage of state has been arranged between Francesca, daughter of Guido da Polenta of Ravenna, and Lanciotto, the hunchback son of Malatesta da Verruchio of Rimini. Reluctantly, Lanciotto agrees and sends his brother, Paolo, to Ravenna for Francesca who, romantic and ingenuous, assumes that Paolo is Lanciotto and falls in love with him. Paolo finally confesses, but not until Francesca arrives in Rimini does she learn of Lanciotto's deformity. Hopeful of love, Lanciotto discovers otherwise with his wedding kiss and rushes off to war. Left behind, Paolo and Francesca find that they can contain their emotions no longer. When Pepe, the evil and vengeful court fool, overhears the lovers, he steals Paolo's dagger and happily goes to Lanciotto with a twisted tale. Unbelieving but enraged, Lanciotto kills Pepe and returns to the palace to face Paolo and Francesca, who readily admit their love and their sin. Compelled by his honor to kill them, Lanciotto ends his own life regretting his act and his destiny, realizing that he loved his brother more than honor.

(Discussion)   E. S. Bradley (*George Henry Boker: Poet and Patriot*, 1927) described *Francesca da Rimini* as "the greatest American romantic tragedy, and one of the greatest poetical tragedies in the language."   Rimini and Ravenna were both thirteenth-century city-states caught up in the struggle for power between the emperor and the pope. Into this scene Boker brought the traditional themes of love and honor, filial loyalty and the evil consequences of sin, whether born of political greed or individual passion. The story of Paolo and Francesca has been treated many times in literature, but Boker was the first to write a play in English on the subject.

In addition to its poetry, the most distinguished of any poetic drama of nineteenth-century America, the play derives considerable power from the insight which Boker brought to his characters.   Dramatically, he centered thoughtful attention on Lanciotto, whose physical ugliness is contrasted with the sensitivity of his soul. Francesca is a vital person whose experiences in love are reflected in the maturing of her attitude.   In Pepe, Boker found the ideal character whose warped humanity promotes the idea of a fateful as well as a personal tragedy. A clever fool who hides behind the coxcomb, an evil intriguer who enjoys inflicting unhappiness and lives for cruel revenge upon Lanciotto, Pepe foreshadows the action.

In pleasing contrast to most tragedies of this period, *Francesca da Rimini*, with its humor, ironies and diversified scenes, enjoys effective change of pace and relief from overwhelming tragedy. The beginning scene with the minstrel has a light and charming touch. And there is broad humor in Guido's teasing of his servant girl, and wit in Pepe's clever and ironic songs.

4.   THE PHILADELPHIA GROUP

Although Philadelphia had once been an unwelcoming place for actors and dramatists, by 1800 the Chestnut Street Theatre had been built and Thomas Wignell's acting company had been called the best in the country.   It is not surprising that Philadelphia should be the home of some of the better-known dramatists of the period, including Richard Penn Smith, Robert Montgomery Bird and Mordecai Noah.   Among others who wrote poetic plays were James McHenry (1785-1845) with his tragedy, *The Usurper* (1827), drawn from the druidical times; David Paul Brown (1795-1872), who wrote *Sertorius; or, The Roman Patriot* (1830), a play laid in Spain and dealing with the power of Sertorius, his victory over Pompey and his eventual death; and Robert T. Conrad (1810-1858), whose *Jack Cade* (1835), based on Wat Tyler's insurrection in England and the Kentish Rebellion of 1450, was, according to *The Dramatic Authors of America* (1845), "undoubtedly destined to rank among the very highest dramatic productions of our language."

5. THE NEW YORK-NEW ENGLAND GROUP

Although by the late 1820s, the Tremont Theatre and the Federal Theatre were bringing good plays to Boston, the city was still not a strong center of theatre activity.   New Englanders who were serious in their work, such as Nathaniel Parker Willis and Epes Sargent, went to New York. But there were others.   Henry W. Longfellow (1807-1882), poet and teacher, wrote *The Spanish Student* (1843), a "closet drama" concerned with the love of a student for a gypsy girl. Julia Ward Howe (1819-1910) wrote two poetic tragedies: *Leonora; or, The World's Own* (1857), which tells the story of Leonora's revenge upon the married Italian nobleman who seduced her; and *Hippolytus* (1864).   Frances Wright (1795-1852) came to New York to produce her tragedy *Altorf* (1819), named for William Tell's home and dramatizing in romantic fashion the activities of Tell. Cornelius Mathews, a New Yorker, had a prodigious career in literature as an essayist and critic.

(a) Nathaniel Parker Willis (1806-1867)
An essayist, poet, editor and playwright, Willis contributed in several ways to the growth of American literature, in sketches, such as *Pencillings by the Way* (1835), and in poetry. Although one of the most popular and best paid "magazinists" of mid-nineteenth-century America, he found little satisfaction in his intense if brief association with the theatre.   His first play, a blank-verse tragedy entitled *Bianca Visconti* (1837), set in Milan, involves intrigues of love and politics.

Tortesa the Usurer (1839)
(Plot) In Florence, Tortesa arranges to give certain lands to Count Falcone in return for his daughter, Isabella, in marriage.

But Tortesa really loves Zippa, a spirited lass who thinks herself in love with Angelo, a painter, who, in turn, shares a deep and secret love with Isabella. After much confusion, Tortesa is made to understand the situation, gives Isabella his blessing and the count his land and finds that Zippa will be happy to marry him.

(Discussion)   This play is one of the few acceptable verse comedies of the time. Edgar Allan Poe wrote in *Burton's Gentleman's Magazine* of August 1839 that its "merits are naturalness, truthfulness, and appropriateness upon all occasions of sentiment and language; a manly vigor and breadth in the conception of character." Owing debts to Shakespeare and romantic tradition, the comedy depends on character and various well-contrived scenes of sharp humor. Tortesa himself is a strange hero -- an object of both laughter and sympathy.

(b)   Epes Sargent (1813-1880)

A Boston journalist and a serious playwright who wrote for popular actors and actresses in the fashion of the day but without much success, Epes Sargent was responsible for two romantic tragedies in verse. Both illustrate the romantic theme of love versus honor or duty. *The Bride of Genoa* (1837, later published in *The New World,* 1842, as *The Genoese*) starred Josephine Clifton in the breeches role of a romantic hero who must free his future father-in-law from his problems, avenge his own father's murder, break the yoke of tyranny in Genoa and win the heroine. *Velasco* (1837), laid in eleventh-century Spain, also emphasizes honor before love and provided roles for Ellen Tree and James Murdock.

(c)   Cornelius Mathews (1817-1889)

Considered one of the most significant playwrights of his generation, Cornelius Mathews was also one of the bright young men of American letters during the 1840s in New York. When he died, the New York *Clipper* noted that he was sometimes called the "Father of American Drama." Editor, essayist and playwright, he wrote two plays with Colonial themes: *Jacob Leister* (1848), based on the life of a governor of New York, and *Withcraft; or, The Martyrs of Salem* (1846), which ranks among the best American plays written before the Civil War.

Dramatizing the terrors of the Salem witch hunts, Mathews exercised his belief that there was something special about America as a land of beauty and freedom where the brave-hearted must not succumb to corrupt authority. Among the many plays he claimed to have written are *False Pretenses; or, Both Sides of Good Society* (1855) and *Broadway and the Bowery* (1956).

6.   THE CHARLESTON AND SOUTHERN GROUP

Since pre-Revolution days, the theatre in Charleston, South Carolina had been active, and during the first part of the nineteenth century, a group of playwrights provided it with some interesting, though not outstanding, plays. Two of the more effective of these dramatists were John Blake White (1781-1859) with *Modern Honor* (1812) and *Foscari; or, The Venetian Exile* (1806) and Isaac Harby (1788-1828) with *The Gordian Knot* (1807) and *Alberti* (1819).

In other parts of the South active playwrights existed, but they usually moved north to produce their plays. *Irma; or, The Prediction* (1829), written by James M. Kennicott of New Orleans, presents a girl whose life is ruined by the prediction that she will be a murderess. Baltimore produced Nathaniel H. Bannister, who wrote several verse tragedies -- *Caius Silius; or, The Slave of Carthage* (1835), *Rathaimus the Roman* (1835) and *Gaulantus the Gaul* (1836), a distinctive work in the playwright's brief career.

C.   American Themes in Poetic Drama

Although poetic plays in America mainly exhibit the foreign scene, a few, most of them in weak verse, present nationalistic themes. The American Indian, for example, frequently stimulated playwrights to try their hand at poetry. John Augustus Stone's *Metamora* illustrates the genre. The best of the romantic tragedies written on an American theme, however, is J. N. Barker's *Superstition*.

JAMES NELSON BARKER (1784-1858)

Barker's major biographer, Paul H. Musser (*James Nelson Barker*, Philadelphia, 1929), mentions eleven plays, the best of which are *Tears and Smiles* (1807) and *How to Try a Lover* (1817), two comedies; a romantic tragedy in poetry, *Marmion; or, The Battle of Flodden Field* (1812); and the tragedy entitled *Superstition; or, The Fanatic Father* (1824). Writing only as an avocation, Barker showed his seriousness in his eleven critical articles on "The Drama" (appearing in the *Dramatic Press,* Philadelphia, December 18, 1816, to February 19, 1817), as well as in his own account of his work in William Dunlap's *History* (pp. 308-316). His main career, however, was in government administration, both local and federal.

From his writings it is clear that Barker was interested in America. Like Washington Irving, William Cullen Bryant, James Fenimore Cooper and Ralph Waldo Emerson, he regretted [in his Introduction to *Marmion,* 1812] the American "provincial sense of inferiority which still lingers among some, even of our highest-minded, with regard to the arts and refinements of society." His first completed play was *America,* a one-act masque (1805), "consisting of poetic dialogue, and sung by the genius of America, Science, Liberty, and attendant spirits." *The Indian Princess; or, La Belle Sauvage* (1808) was the first play about Indians to be acted in America. Barker's work, however, is most significant in suggesting the direction that American drama would take.

Superstition; or, The Fanatic Father (1824)
(Plot) Isabella and her son, Charles, are newcomers to New England. Returning to his village from college, Charles encounters The Unknown, in reality Isabella's father, one of the judges of Charles I. He also meets his sweetheart, Mary, the daughter of Ravensworth, the village clergyman, and protects her from the advances of George, light-hearted nephew of Sir Reginald Egerton who was sent by Charles II to find the regicide. In the village the Indians attack and are repulsed when The Unknown appears and rallies the villagers. Ravensworth, however, turns the villagers against Charles because of his familiarity with The Unknown, charges Charles and Isabella with sorcery and accuses Charles of murdering George and attempting to rape Mary. Protecting Mary, Charles refuses to plead and, at the frenzied insistence of Ravensworth, is executed. As The Unknown enters and is reunited with his

daughter, Isabella, who dies of shock, Mary breathes her last, raving of her love for Charles. Too late, Sir Reginald enters with a pardon for the regicide, The Unknown, and identifies Charles as the King's son.

(Discussion) The major theme revolves around New England intolerance activated by the superstitious mind. To this, Barker fused the incident in which the Puritan refugee Goff led the villagers against the Indians. Years later, Cooper was to employ the same story of the regicides of Charles I in *The Wept of Wish-Ton-Wish,* and Hawthorne would use the story of The Unknown in his short story, "The Gray Champion."

The characterization in *Superstition* gives it distinction -- particularly that of the villain Ravensworth, whose personality, fused with the widespread belief in witchcraft, makes the ending inevitable. A clergyman, he mistakes his own passions for the voice of God and enjoys a powerful influence over his people through his relentless revenge upon those who refuse to bow to his authority. Showing fiendish glee at the hero's destruction, Ravensworth, like Hawthorne's Chillingworth in *The Scarlet Letter,* is consumed by his own desire for revenge. A villain-hero, his intelligence, his eloquence, his beliefs and his passions make him clearly the most interesting person in the play.

In structure, the play shows the swift action and change of pace of the better romantic tragedies. Incidents vary from the meeting with The Unknown to the duel, to the Indian attack, to the trial, the execution and the pardon that comes too late. There is some wit and humor in the speeches of Sir Reginald and his nephew, and the poetry in the play generally aids its dramatic effectiveness.

III. AMERICAN CHARACTER TYPES: JONATHAN, SAMBO AND METAMORA

That spirit of the American Revolution which had fostered feelings of personal and national independence was intensified by the so-called "Second War of Independence," the War of 1812. At no time during the nineteenth century in America was the feeling of nationalism higher than in the period following that war. As the common man found his voice more powerful in politics through the election of men like Andrew Jackson and saw a measure of his individual accomplishments in building a new country, his pride became sensitive. He assumed an anti-foreign bigotry, particularly toward the Irish immigrants who came by the tens of thousands during the 1840s, and a few years later, he created an "American Party" with the slogan "Americans must rule America." This strong sense of Nationalism made itself felt -- significantly -- in literature and in the theatre.

It was in 1820 that the British critic Sydney Smith assured himself a place in histories of American literature with his rhetorical question: "In the four quarters of the globe who reads an American book or goes to an American play?" Unfortunately, the barb contained a bit of truth -- felt more poignantly in America than in Europe. Some in America tried to encourage the arts; others scornfully condemned them. One of the latter, John Neal, a Maine novelist with more rancor than humor in this instance, wrote in *Blackwood's Magazine,* XVI, 427 (October 1824); 567 (November 1824); XVII, 48 (January 1825):

> *Comedies* -- See *Drama.* No such thing in America. One Mr. White has written two or three; but we have never seen or read them. They are spoken well of -- in America. *Drama* -- Mr. Noah . . . has written some tolerable farces, and some intolerable popular entertainments. . . . The writers of America have no encouragement, whatever, to venture upon the drama. *Farces* -- About a dozen or twenty sober, childish, or disagreeable "entertainments" have been produced, in the United States of America -- by the natives -- within the memory of man, we believe -- under this title. . . .

More constructive critics, such as Washington Irving and Robert Montgomery Bird, wrote essays supporting the independence of American literature and arts from European models and describing values that would make American creations distinctive. Some nationalistic dramas reveal the same uniquely American approach that is seen in the historical novels of Cooper and James Kirke Paulding. But Sydney Smith's question was, perhaps, more stinulating that he realized. Intense nationalism in politics spilled over into literature until, in 1837, Ralph Waldo Emerson's address, "The American Scholar," became recognized as America's Declaration of Intellectual Independence. Individualism and self reliance were important for the nation as well as for the individual -- for literature and the arts as well as for politics. But the people had to be provided with a representative American -- a symbol of their distinctive qualities -- and Royall Tyler's Jonathan from *The Contrast* presented one solution to this problem.

American literature became identifiable only after writers had recognized the potential of American scenery, custom, character and ideas. In the drama, custom and character met in Jonathan, who was aided in his representation of America by other characters -- the Negro and the Indian. All enjoyed a certain similarity. Each was introduced into the drama before 1800, and each developed irregularly during the nineteenth century. And in a sense, they were bound together by a similar desire for freedom: the Yankee from the English, the Indian from the Yankees and the Negro from bondage.

Each of the three characters -- the Yankee, the Negro and the Indian -- reached a high point of popularity during the mid-nineteenth century and later became absorbed into the various social themes of modern drama. Jonathan of *The Contrast* developed from a greenhorn, whose credulity and prejudices made him an object of ridicule, to a shrewd hero, a witty storyteller whose clothes and language made him even more picturesque. The Negro, who had been a clownish servant, became both a minstrel character and a dramatic hero by mid-century. The Indian, primarily exploited as a major character from the beginning, continued in a primary role until John Brougham, momentarily, burlesqued him out of existence. It is significant that when the Indian left the stage the void was almost immediately filled by the backwoodsman, who became a new symbol of Nature's Nobleman and America's individual prowess.

A. The Yankee Character

The origins of the stage Yankee, the character that so impressed England that *Punch* cartoonists soon referred to America as "Master Jonathan," are not clear. He appeared in Tyler's *The Contrast,* but he had been seen on stage before this play. In part, his popularity resulted from the 1822-1823 visit to America of the English actor Charles Mathews, who, after his return to England, collaborated with Richard B. Peake to write *Jonathan in England* (1824). This play's success was so great that it inspired numerous actors in America to write or seek out Yankee plays. About the same time, the Yankee began to appear in humorous essays and poems. Seba Smith, publishing the stories of Major Jack Downing in the Portland, Maine *Courier,* was the first. Judge Halliburton's *Sam Slick* and James Russell Lowell's *Hosea Biglow Papers* soon followed.

Even before Mathews' visit, certain characteristics of the Yankee has been established. The preface to the 1815 edition of David Humphreys' play, *The Yankey in England,* comments:

> The Yankey is . . . made up of contrarities -- simplicity and cunning; inquisitive from nature and excessive curiosity, confirmed by habit; credulous, from inexperience and want of knowledge of the world; believing himself to be perfectly acquainted with whatever he partially knows; tenacious of prejudice; docile, when rightly managed; when otherwise treated, independent to obstinacy; easily betrayed into ridiculous mistakes; incapable of being overawed by external circumstances; suspicious, vigilant, and quick of perception, he is ever ready to parry or repel the attacks of raillery by retorts of rustic and sarcastic, if not of original and refined, wit and humour.

The beginnings had been made, and now patterns were being established. *The Contrast* produced the first widely imitated Yankee. Mathews interested the actors, while Seba Smith suggested the costume they might wear (very close to the traditional garb of the modern Uncle Sam). The humorous stories provided some of the personality quirks.

1.   THE YANKEE (c. 1800-c.1820)

Imitation of Tyler's Jonathan continued in a variety of plays. As the century progressed, the Yankee became a chief character in plays, and his personality became more fully developed. With the helpful and kindhearted hero of *Jonathan Postfree; or, The Honest Yankee* (1807) by Lazarus Beach and the New England peddler who likes the girls and sings "Yankee Doodle" in A. B. Lindsley's *Love and Friendship; or, Yankee Notions* (1809), the Yankee achieved more important billing in a single play. The most significant step, however, in the saga of the Yankee was David Humphreys' *Yankey in England* (1815), which includes a seven-page glossary "of words used in a peculiar sense in this Drama; pronounced with an accent or emphasis in certain districts; different from the modes generally followed by the inhabitants of the United States."

2.   THE POPULAR YANKEE AND HIS CREATORS

One of the best comic opera-dramas of the period featuring Yankee characters is *The Saw-Mill; or, A Yankee Trick* (1824) by Micah Hawkins (1777-1825). With *The Forest Rose* (1825) by Samuel Woodworth, the Yankee became a very successful stock character in comedy and farce. By the 1840s, he had attained a certain stability as well as his greatest height in popularity, although Yankee actors and plays were still applauded with enthusiasm into the 1860s. As the years passed, this romantic, homespun philosopher and honest purveyor of his own tastes and desires was occasionally joined by a Yankee Gal. More than a hundred Yankee plays were written during this period.

(a)   Samuel Woodworth (1785-1842):
The Forest Rose; or, American Farmers (1825)

(Plot) On an American farm everyone is in love: Harriet and William, Lydia and Blandford, Jonathan Ploughboy and Sallie. Into this network of romance comes Bellamy, an Englishman and a cad, whose lust for Harriet moves him to attempt her abduction. But he is tricked, and the veiled girl whom Bellamy has paid to have delivered to his sloop in the harbor turns out to be the Negro servant Rose, "the forest Rose." Finally, all are happy but Bellamy, who warns that he will get revenge when he publishes his *Three Months in America* -- a jibe at the practices of European visitors.

(Discussion)   Although Woodworth wrote other plays, his place in American drama is judged mainly by *The Forest Rose,* which not only helped establish the Yankee character but also achieved popular success on the American stage for forty years. Called a comedy with musical accompaniment, the play shows pretentions to literature in the introduction to Act I, which begins, "The overture expresses the various sounds which are heard at early dawn in the country. . . ." Although Jonathan Ploughboy is not the main character, much of the humor of the play comes from his shrewd talk, his inability to court the girls and his simplicity.

(b)   Joseph S. Jones (1809-1877): *The People's Lawyer* **(1839)**
A man of energy and imagination who also earned a medical degree from Harvard College, Jones was active in Boston theatre circles as playwright, stage manager and actor from the 1830s through the 1850s. The author of more Yankee plays than any other playwright -- perhaps as many as 150 farces and melodramas -- he was aware of the lack of copyright protection for the dramatist and objected to publishing his works. His few published plays include *The Green Mountain Boy* (1833), *The Carpenter of Rouen* (1837) and *The Surgeon of Paris* (1838). *The People's Lawyer,* a comedy in two acts, became popular for the Yankee character of Solon Shingle, who provides atmosphere, wit, humor and a Yankee twang but has little connection with the plot. Revised several times and even billed as *Solon Shingle,* the play is unexceptional in all but the character of the Yankee.

(Plot) Charles Otis, a clerk, is fired because he cannot accept dishonest practices. When the boss leaves, Solon Shingle enters, mischievously puts flour and lampblack on himself and accidentally fires a pistol he finds. At his home, Charles tries to help John, another clerk, who has stolen a watch; he even writes a confession for him, only to be arrested by the police who find both watch and confession on his person. In court, Solon Shingle is sworn in as a witness by mistake and talks on and on about his "apple sarse" being stolen. Then Robert

Howard, the People's Lawyer, enters, makes John confess and wins an acquittal for Charles.   Having previously rescued Charles' sister, Grace, from a drunken man and from Charles' lecherous boss, Howard is a true hero.   Solon Shingle simply talks, talks, talks.

(c)   Cornelius A. Logan (1806-1852):
       The Vermont Wool Dealer (1838)
An actor and a theatre manager, Logan was the first native-born playwright to write Yankee vehicles.   Generally, he wrote as the demands of the box office dictated.   *The Wag of Maine* (1834), revised as *Yankee Land,* featured a delightful Yankee called Lot Sap Sago.   Logan's most popular play, however, was a one-act farce entitled *The Vermont Wool Dealer.*   With its Yankee character, Deuteronomy Dutiful, its Irish choreboy and its Negro serving girl, it included most of the typical comedy characters.   Here the Yankee, a blunt, easygoing fellow, is the main character, and amid the usual physical action of farce, his humor dominates.

(d)   *The Yankee Pedler; or, Old Times in Virginia* (1836)
This play, evidently written by William Bayle Bernard (1807-1875) for George Handel "Yankee" Hill, exists in several versions, but it was always a favorite vehicle for Yankee actors.   Plots differ slightly, but the main character is Hiram Dodge, the "Yankee Pedler of Fancyware," a brash wit and an impatient lover.   Minstrel humor garnishes his speech, and his language sounds as colorful as his actions prove impertinent.   The play tells of his visit to the Fuller plantation in Virginia and his many problems in winning the love of Jerusha.

(e)   The Yankee Gal
Several plays include Yankee Gals -- Jedidah in *The Stage Struck Yankee,* Jerusha in *The Yankee Pedler* -- but only as minor characters.   Other plays feature this female version of the Yankee.   *The Yankee Housekeeper* (1857) was supposedly written particularly for William Florence and his wife, an American acting team.   Mrs. Florence played Peg Ann Mehitable Higginfluter, a maid-of-all-work from Maine who gets involved in all manner of love affairs and intrigues.   Her language, sauciness and vigor supplied the evening's enter-

tainment.   Mr. and Mrs. Barney Williams also frequently
starred in plays, such as *Irish Assurance and Yankee Modesty*
(1851) by James Pilgrim, in which Williams played the
Irishman and his wife the Yankee Gal.   Although never as
popular as the Yankee plays, these works add their peculiar
charm to the American Yankee caricature.

(f)   Other Yankee Plays

The list of Yankee plays is a long one -- E. H. Thompson's *Sam
Patch* (1839), O. E. Durivage's *The Stage Struck Yankee* (1840),
H. J. Conway's *Hiram Hireout* (1851) and *Major Jack Downing;
or, The Retired Politician* (anon., 1834).   Actually, the Yankee
went everywhere and did many things.   He was also much
imitated by the English playwrights.   For the late 1860s
Odells' *Annals of the New York Stage* lists the following plays
being produced: *The Yankee Jailer, The Yankee Inventor,
Yankee Courtship, The Yankee in Cuba, Yankee Duelists,
Yankee Tars in Scotland* and *The Fighting Yankee*.   It must be
admitted that playwrights were reluctant to abandon such a
stageworthy character.

3.   THE YANKEE ACTORS

A cult of Yankee actors, specializing in Yankee characters and
even offering prizes for Yankee plays, started in the 1820s,
stimulated by the success of Charles Mathews.   One of the first
was James H. Hackett (1800-1871), who in 1828 adapted George
Colman's *Who Wants a Guinea?*, changed the name of a
character from Solomon Gundy to Solomon Swap, a Yankee, and
retitled the piece *Jonathan in England* (1828), after Mathews'
successful play.   George Handel Hill (1809-1849), known as
"Yankee" Hill, was failing as an actor until he discovered the
Yankee characters, becoming to critics "the most authentic" of
all.   Other Yankee actors were John E. Owens (1823-1886), who
retitled Jones' play *Solon Shingle*; Joshua Silsbee (1813-1855);
and Dan Marble (1810-1849), who, according to Joseph Jefferson
(*Autobiography*, p. 20), dressed "much after the present
caricature of Uncle Sam, minus the stars but glorying in stripes."
While he lasted, the Yankee specialist was a strange
combination of actor, storyteller and musical comedy star.

B.   The Negro Character

During the first quarter of the century, the Negro continued to be portrayed as a clownish servant.   Then, as the Yankee became popular, the Negro character underwent a curious split and was exploited in two ways: in farce or social comedy, and in the minstrel show.   The servant Sambo became both Uncle Tom and Mr. Bones.   By the time of the Civil War, he had become a major character in American drama.

1.   THE NEGRO AMONG THE YANKEES

As the number of Yankee plays increased during this period, more Negro characters appeared, and the Negro was subjected to different approaches by playwrights. As a servant, a Negro was easily slipped into Yankee plays where his assumed social inferiority was exploited by the Yankee. The "Forest Rose" is used to play a trick on Bellamy, who is shocked to discover that the veiled girl with him is a Negro rather than the beloved Harriet. The same trick was used by Cornelius Logan in *The Vermont Wool Dealer*.   Playwrights made jokes about Negroes, and used Negroes to play jokes upon others.

In the few social comedies of this period, the Negro enjoyed higher social status and more character development but was still exploited for humor. Aunt Chloe in Mrs. Sidney Bateman's *Self* (1856), is a comparatively serious interpretation of the Negro. Zeke, from Mrs. Ritchie's *Fashion* (1845) illustrates a changing attitude toward the Negro as a character and as part of the play's structure. Zeke's speech indicates an acquaintance, though inadequate, with literate people, and he is not a stupid servant. In fact, he fulfills his part in the intrique of the play very well. It is interesting that the only person who treats him with disrespect is Adam Truman, the Yankee.

2.   THE NEGRO AS MINSTREL

The Negro as a featured actor in Ethiopian Opera and the minstrel show was first created through the imagination of one man, Thomas Dartmouth Rice (1806-1860), in 1828, and then expanded into a business in which, from the Virginia Minstrels (1842-1843) founded by Dan Emmett through 1870, hundreds of minstrel companies were formed. By the turn of the century the tenor of the minstrel show had changed: the spectacle had become more important than the Negro, and the minstrel show gradually disappeared from the professional stage.

3.   THE NEGRO AS HERO

There can be no question as to which American play best illustrates the Negro as hero -- *Uncle Tom's Cabin* (1852). Harriet Beecher Stowe's other novel concerned with the Negro in the South, *Dred* (1856), was presented in three different dramatizations, but none was successful on the American stage. Plays about the Civil War and slavery, however, were numerous: *Neighbor Jackwood* (1857) by J. T. Trowbridge; *The Escape; or, a Leap for Freedom* (1858) by William Wells Brown (1816?-1884), the first known American Negro to write a play about slavery; *Ossawattomie Brown* (1859) by Mrs. J. C. Swayze; and James McCabe's *The Guerillas* (1862), which first dramatized the problems of the freed slave and his reluctance to go north. Few major characters of these plays, however, were Negroes. After *Uncle Tom's Cabin,* the most successful play with a Negro theme was Boucicault's *The Octoroon.*

The Octoroon; or, Life in Louisiana (1859)
by Dion Boucicault (1820-1890)
(Plot)   George Peyton, returning to the heavily mortgaged Plantation Terrebonne which he has inherited from his uncle, Judge Peyton, becomes interested in the octoroon Zoe, his uncle's illegitimate daughter. The villain M'Closky, who finds that the judge never legalized Zoe's freedom, is also attracted to Zoe. When creditors cause the plantation to be put up for sale, the family anxiously awaits a letter containing money that will save the estate, but M'Closky intercepts the letter and kills the Negro messenger, unknowingly having his picture taken in the act. At the auction, amid great drama, M'Closky buys Zoe. Later, through the exposed photographic plate, M'Closky is revealed as a murderer; the letter is found, and M'Closky is pursued to his death. Unaware of the change in events and having heard George say that he would rather have her dead than owned by M'Closky, Zoe takes poison and dies.

(Discussion) A tremendously prolific playwright, adapting or writing more than one hundred plays, Boucicault was always an Irishman wherever he lived -- England, America, Australia -- and he dominated the stage during his time in America (1853-1860, 1872-1890). His plays are mainly melodramas, and *The Octoroon* has the sentiment and the exciting action which are typical of Boucicault's best work. Based on Mayne Reid's novel *The Quadroon* (1856) and using the photographic device from the English novel, *The Filibuster* (1859) by Albany Fonblanque, the play also contains much of Boucicault's original thought. Appealing to all popular trends, it includes an Indian, a Yankee, an Irishman and various Negroes. Although the theme of a white man falling in love with an octoroon in Louisiana might have aroused some sectional passions in 1859, the play was discreetly noncommital.

C. The Indian Character

The first Indian play written by an American, *Ponteach; or, the Savages of America* (1776) was not acted, and it was not until 1808, when James N. Barker's *Indian Princess* was performed, that an American play on an Indian theme saw the stage. From that time until mid-century, more than fifty plays on Indian themes were performed. Of these plays, *Pocahontas* (1830) by George Washington Parke Custis best uses the Pocahontas theme, and *Metamora* (1829) by John Augustus Stone was the most successful on stage. Romanticized and idealized, the Indian reached the height of popularity during the 1830s and 1840s. Then, quite suddenly, undermined by the clever burlesques of John Brougham, the Indian play lost its appeal. One result was the growth of the American backwoodsman plays -- James Kirke Paulding's *The Lion of the West* (1831) and the dramatization of novels by Cooper and Simms -- which became extremely popular after the Civil War. Such were the changing romantic tastes of the American public.

1.   *THE INDIAN PRINCESS; OR, LA BELLE SAUVAGE* (1808) BY JAMES NELSON BARKER (1784-1858)

(Plot) As preparations are being made for the marriage of Pocahontas, daughter of Chief Powhatan, and Miami, Captain Smith interrupts the Indians and is captured and threatened with death until Pocahontas saves him. Time passes, and Pocahontas' friendship with Rolfe, one of Smith's men, so angers Miami that he makes war on Powhatan's tribe, which is victorious through the help of the English. The guileful Miami then arranges to kill Smith and Rolfe at a banquet, but Pocahontas thwarts his plans and leads the English to Smith's rescue. At the climax, Rolfe and Pocahontas are engaged, and Powhatan becomes an ally of the English.

(Discussion) The subject matter of the play comes from John Smith's *General History of Virginia* (1624), but the play is not documentary. With its main interest in romantic love, it becomes not so much a plea for the noble Indians as praise for the hardy explorers. This strong patriotic note is typical of Barker's writing. Neither in structure nor language, however, is this play as well written as Barker's *Superstition,* and with the exception of Pocahontas the characters are conventional and poorly developed. Yet it was widely performed, and one critic for the New York *Evening Post* (June 13, 1809) called it "one of the favorite modern productions."

2.   *POCAHONTAS; OR, THE SETTLERS OF VIRGINIA* (1830)
BY GEORGE WASHINGTON PARKE CUSTIS (1781-1857)

Raised at Mount Vernon under the care of President Washington (his father's step-father) and Mrs. Washington, Custis was more than a dabbler in literature, writing prose (largely recollections), verse and nine dramas, four on Indian themes. His first play, *The Indian Prophecy* (1827-1828), is based on an event in George Washington's life. In *Pocahontas; or, the Settlers of Virginia,* a popular play of this time, Custis was more effective as a playwright, but his work is still weak, with stiff and excessively long speeches and generally undeveloped characters. Both Pocahontas and Matacoran, the villain, are hobbled by impossible rhetoric, but Matacoran manages to be the most interesting individual in the play, with his hatred, bravery and treachery.

(Plot) Returning to Virginia with John Smith, Rolfe falls in love with Pocahontas, daughter of Powhatan and promised in marriage to Matacoran. In the name of the Queen, Smith crowns Powhatan, who fears Smith's guns but is still influenced by a vengeful Matacoran. Discovering the watchword of the English guard -- "Pocahontas, the friend of the English" -- Matacoran prepares for battle but is foiled by Pocahontas who naturally says the watchword as she comes to warn Smith of the Indians' treachery. In the battle, both Smith and Matacoran are captured, and Smith is finally saved from the executioner's axe by Pocahontas. As a noble Smith allows Matacoran to escape, Powhatan pledges his friendship to the English and his daughter to Rolfe.

3. *METAMORA; OR, THE LAST OF THE WAMPANOAGS* (1829) BY JOHN AUGUSTUS STONE (1800-1834)

(Plot) The two plot lines of the play are held together by a feather, an eagle's plume -- one that Metamora gives Oceana as a symbol of his protection. As the play begins, Mordaunt explains to Oceana, his daughter, that rather than marry Walter, her intended, she must accept Lord Fitzarnold because he can identify Mordaunt as one of the regicides. At an English council meeting, Metamora, accused of a murder, recognizes his Indian betrayer, kills him and escapes to lead an attack on the English. The attack interrupts Oceana's wedding to Fitzarnold, but the feather protects the house of Mordaunt. Walter, however, is captured by the Indians, while Metamora's wife, Nahmeokee, is taken by the English, until threats and negotiations by Metamora bring her release. In the subplot, Fitzarnold is killed by Metamora, and Walter is discovered to be the son of Sir Arthur Vaughan and therefore a suitable mate for Oceana. Defiant to the last, Metamora is beaten but not defeated -- "Yet we are forever!" His Indians scattered, his child killed, he stabs Nahmeokee and curses the white man before he is shot down by the Indians.

(Discussion) When he wrote *Metamora,* Stone had only a slight reputation as an actor and playwright in the New York-Philadelphia area. With the spectacular success of *Metamora* everyone appeared to gain -- audiences, managers and especially Edwin Forrest -- everyone except the playwright. Although he wrote at least five more plays (and perhaps eleven during his brief life), one -- *The Knight of the Golden West* (1834) -- a popular Yankee vehicle for "Yankee"

Hill, Stone was typical of neglected American playwrights. Despondent and in ill health, he jumped from the Spruce Street Wharf in Philadelphia into the Schuylkill River on May 29, 1834.

On November 22, 1828, *The Critic* printed a proposal by Edwin Forrest, the actor: "To the author of the best tragedy, in five acts, of which the hero or principal character shall be an aboriginal of this country, the sum of five hundred dollars, and half of the proceeds of the third representation, with my own gratuitous services on that occasion." Of the fourteen plays which the advertisement elicited, *Metamora* was considered the best. Produced by Forrest the following year, it earned him more money during the next thirty-five years than any other play. The language, the action, the spectacle, the suspense -- every part of the play gave Forrest the kind of role that best fitted his bombastic style.

Termed an Indian tragedy, the play might be more accurately described as romantic melodrama, with all of the violence, the action, the love and the sentiment that melodrama of this period required. The character Metamora is modeled on the famous New England Chief, King Philip, whose attacks upon the English in 1675-76 became known as "King Philip's War." Metamora's valiant but unsuccessful attempts to keep the white man from overrunning his lands provide the main thesis of the play. Metamora is also cleverly involved in the secondary theme, a conventional love episode among the English.

4.   A VARIETY OF INDIAN PLAYS

The Indian appears in numerous plays as both a major and a minor character. Mordecai Noah's *She Would Be a Soldier* has a minor Indian character; so does Boucicault's *The Octoroon*. A majority of the plays, however, are about particular Indians: *Logan, the Last of the Race of Shikellemus, Chief of the Cayuga Nation* (1823), a dull but historically accurate play by Joseph Doddridge (1796-1826); *Carabasset* (1831), based on the life of the Jesuit missionary Sebastian Rasles and his friendship with the Norridgewock Indians, by Nathaniel Deering (1791-1881); *Tecumseh; or, The Battle of the Thames* (1834), concerning the Indian chief who fought for the British

in 1812, by Richard Emmons; and many others. The single
character which appealed to the most playwrights, however,
was Pocahontas. Robert Dale Owen (1801-1877) attempted a
more complete picture than usual in *Pocahontas* (1837).

5.   THE INDIAN RIDICULED:
BURLESQUES BY JOHN BROUGHAM (1810-1880)

The exaggerated characterization and interpretation of the
"Noble Redskin" by dramatists and actors finally brought
about his fall from popularity. The man most responsible for
helping change public tastes was John Brougham, a superb actor
and productive playwright who was dubbed the "American
Aristophanes" by Laurence Hutton (*Curiosities of the American
Stage*, New York, 1891, p. 164).   In no plays was he more
deserving of this title than in his burlesques of the Indians.

Brougham's *Met-a-mora; or, the Last of the Pollywogs* (1847) is
an obvious satire on the Stone-Forrest success. The plot follows
Stone's play, but names are changed, speeches are parodied and
the "eagle's plume" becomes a "tail, plucked from a mongrel
rooster." Forrest's stage mannerisms and his declamatory
delivery of lines are ridiculed, and the evening of broad
farcical entertainment is enlivened with one-liners of minstrel
show humor.

Burlesques of plays and people were popular with the
pre-Civil War generation, particularly at William Mitchell's
Olympic Theatre in New York during the 1840s. Brougham
further perfected his art with *Po-Ca-Hon-Tas; or, the Gentle
Savage* (1855), an "Original, Aboriginal, Erratic, Operatic,
Semi-Civilized, and Demi-Savage Extravaganza."   Captain
Smith's description of the court of "Pow-Ha-Tan I, King of the
Tuscaroras -- a Crotchety Monarch, in fact a semi-brave"
suggests the humor of the play:

> I visited his Majesty's abode,
> A portly savage, plump and pigeon-toed;
> Like Metamora, both in feet and feature,
> I never met-a-more-a-musing creature.

6.   THE INDIAN REPLACED:
APPEARANCE OF THE BACKWOODSMAN

About the time the Indian became popular on the American stage, the backwoodsman, another native American character, appeared as Nimrod Wildfire in James Kirke Paulding's *The Lion of the West* (1831). The Indian, however, held the stage through the mid-1840s, while the backwoodsman appeared only occasionally. Not until after the Civil War did the backwoodsman achieve sustained popularity on the stage -- long after the Indians had ceased to be "noble savages" and had become "varmint Redskins."

In the years between 1830 and 1870, there were a scattering of plays about frontier men or backwoodsmen. In *The Lion of the West*, Nimrod Wildfire -- "half horse, half alligator, and a touch of the airthquake" -- was the attraction. Another popular backwoodsman play was *Nick of the Woods* (1838), a novel by Robert M. Bird dramatized by Louisa Medina (1813?-1838). One of the most successful creators of spectacles on the American stage during the 1830s, Medina was the author of eleven plays, including *Wacousta; or, the Curse* (1833); *Guy Rivers; or, the Gold Hunters* (1834), evidently a dramatization of William Gilmore Simms' novel; *The Last Days of Pompeii* (1835) and *Ernest Maltravers* (1838), both stage adaptations of novels by Edward Bulwer-Lytton. Other backwoodsman plays include several dramatizations of some of Cooper's novels, Modecai Noah's *The Frontier Maid* (1840) and W. R. Derr's *Kit Carson, the Hero of the Prairie* (1850).

During the 1830s Kentucky was The West. Twenty years later, the frontier had changed; the frontiersmen considered the Indian more of a menace than a "noble savage"; the Homestead Act of 1862 opened more land for settlement; wars were fought; and legends grew -- legends of the backwoodsman's powers. Soon plays appeared with a new hero! And lo, the poor Indian vanished -- at least, the stage Indian, who fits well Mark Twain's description of the Indian of fiction: a member of "an extinct race which never existed."

IV. DRAMA: A MIRROR OF THE TIMES

The years from Jefferson's Presidency to Lincoln's -- mirrored by the drama -- saw growth and change, war and confusion, opportunity and idealism. A new nation was trying to establish itself; a new social culture was beginning to develop as numerous social problems appeared: war and border disputes, economic panics, political arguments, religious differences, population increases, transportation difficulties and unbridled expansion both across the continent and in the minds of the new Americans. By mid-century, America was becoming a vast and rapidly developing country, whose changes were reflected among its people and in its social affectations. It was gaining a reputation as a nation of hustlers, "dollar grabbers" -- optimistic and boastful, rough-and-tumble individuals who practiced Ralph Waldo Emerson's doctrine of self reliance and worked for their future, "Root hog, or die." The East became distinct from the West.   People everywhere asserted an individuality that was expressed through the American Temperance Society, founded in 1826, the Mormon trek to Utah in 1846-47, the gold rush to California, agitation for women's rights, anti-foreign attitudes and the political and social difficulties that anticipated the Civil War.

Strictly speaking, there was no established genteel society during the first half of the nineteenth century, although the families of Tidewater Virginia and Back Bay Boston and the Patroons of New York were the main pretenders. Consequently, dramatists may have lacked the material for comedy of manners, but they had much material for melodrama; and it was mainly in farce and melodrama that they provided the many caricatures of American society and brought to the stage diverse attitudes toward the problems of this period.

One accepted criterion for the success of a work of art was its reception by literary critics in America and by the audiences and critics in England. The major literary figures in America had little to say about the drama, but that it had an appeal for them there is no question. Irving, Cooper, Paulding, Bird, Poe, Longfellow, Willis, Sargent, Boker -- all wrote plays. Perhaps they hoped to improve the drama by improving the literary quality of American theatre fare, but they were as unsuccessful in their efforts as were Shelley, Browning, Tennyson and Byron in England. As for the contributions of American playwrights, the English attitude ranged from abuse to amused tolerance to enthusiasm. Generally, the effect of American drama was theatrical rather than literary, and perhaps that distinction suggests a major characteristic of the times. It was a time of idealism, individualism and romance when the open, frank movement of life was apt to be sensational and spectacular. Reflecting the Spirit of the Times, the drama, with all of its theatrical distortions, became a mirror-image of society.

A.   The Comedy of America

In a strict sense, the comedy of this period in America was farce, or to be quite liberal, farce-comedy. The witty portrayal of some aspect of a fashionable society with well-drawn characters who are logically motivated in both speech and action and whose thoughts and struggles direct the plot of the play -- these characteristics of good comedy are largely lacking. Plays with a foreign setting come nearest to being comedy; American people and society are caricatured, with fashionable life, such as it existed, a favorite target. As America's economy flourished, self-reliance sometimes became self-indulgence. The natural social ego of an enterprising and successful nation more than once found itself in a ridiculous situation, ready-made for the satirical writer of farce-comedy, who doubled in nationalistic sentiment while emphasizing a romantic realism which was becoming popular in fiction. Comedy in America during the first half of the nineteenth century, then, variously emphasized three important aspects of American drama at that time: a dependence upon foreign settings; a nationalistic attitude toward the American people, their society and morals; and a concern for realistic touches.

1.   THE COMIC IDEA WITH A FOREIGN SETTING

For the most part, America's playwrights seemed content either to express opinions about social or political issues or to exploit a currently popular fad or fashion. They wrote to moralize, to satirize, to inform and to entertain. They were not interested in presenting objective views or detached attitudes.

Consequently, the writer of pure comedy was rare, as was the American play which deserved to be called a comedy. Only a few plays could boast some of the characteristics of the genre: detachment, wit, clever dialogue and well-developed characters. Invariably, the writer of anything approaching such comedy either adapted a foreign play and kept the foreign scene, because it was too difficult to change it to American circumstance, or wrote of a foreign scene because it somehow facilitated a certain detachment. The following are among the best that American dramatists had to offer.

(a) *How to Try a Lover* (1817) by James Nelson Barker
(Plot) The scene is Catalonia in medieval Spain. Into the castle grounds of Count Almeyda, father of Eugenia, Carlos and his servant Pacomo, both accomplished lovers, come in search of the fair Eugenia. The fathers of Carlos and Eugenia, however, are intriguers. Believing that true love must conquer something, they plot to "try the lover," to put obstacles in his path. When, after much confusion, Carlos reaches Eugenia and declares his love, he is arrested. At the Court of Love, prepared by the fathers, Eugenia presides and, having secretly discovered the fathers' intrigue, amazes and horrifies them by seeming to condemn Carlos. But she finally relents. His punishment is, of course, that he must marry Eugenia, and everyone is happy.

(Discussion) Indebted in both plot and characterization to Pigault-Lebrun's picaresque novel *La Folie Espagnole*, Barker's *How to Try a Lover* is a well-wrought and sprightly farce-comedy, complete with interesting dialogue and fast-moving intrigues. Theatre audiences demanded certain dramatic conventions of the time. There appear, therefore, secret letters, disguises and stock characters, such as the pure and innocent ingenue, the heroic young nobleman and servants who imitate their masters. But it is all done very well.

(b) *Charles the Second; or, the Merry Monarch* (1824)
   by John Howard Payne and Washington Irving
(Plot) As the play opens, Lady Clara proposes a bargain with her lover, Rochester, "the King's prime companion in all his excesses": she will consent to marry him if he will disgust the

King with his "nocturnal rambles and bring him to reason." Mulling over his task, Rochester learns that Edward, his page and protegé, is wooing Mary the barmaid and immediately decides to see Mary himself and, at the same time, teach the King his "first lesson in morals." Disguised as common seamen, Rochester and the King visit the tavern of Captain Copp, Mary's uncle, who, it turns out, hates Rochester intensely. When Rochester leaves the penniless King to pay the tavern bill, the King is locked in a room until he bribes his way to freedom with a diamond-studded watch. At the palace the next morning, Copp and Mary return the watch to its owner and recognize the King and Rochester. But they can keep a secret, and all ends happily: Rochester will become a "rational and submissive husband"; Mary will marry Edward; and Charles swears that he will henceforth abjure nightly frolics.

(Discussion) Although the play contains more than a fair amount of farce, *Charles the Second* is the best comedy of this period and, doubtless because of Washington Irving's contribution to its composition, one of the most readable. A quite free adaptation of Alexandre Duval's *La Jeunesse de Henri V*, the play owes its great success in part to Payne's creation of Captain Copp and to Irving's humorous touch in the dialogue, although Irving's part in its creation was kept secret for many years. A fine comic character, Captain Copp has a suggestion of humanity about him -- a sentimental heart, an honest mind, the language and temper of a sailor and a sense of humor. Equally significant are the comic dialogue and the language of this play, which set it apart from contemporary comedies and made it popular on both American and English stages.

2.   FASHIONABLE LIFE

Various aspects of social life in America are caricatured in a number of farce-comedies, but few plays attempted realistic portrayals of fashionable life. As the century progressed, however, social structures became recognizable in major cities from Boston to Charleston, and both a genuine and an imitated sophistication became evident. When the break with England and Europe widened, it appeared more slowly in fashion than in politics and literature. At the same time that one part of American society was reacting positively to nationalistic pressures, another part (the *nouveau riche*) was attempting to gain social standing through obvious adulation and imitation of foreign manners and customs. It was an awkward period for a developing society, but for a playwright with a nationalistic bias or an inclination toward satire, America provided incomparable opportunity.

Plays about anything resembling fashionable life are part satire, part farce, with a strain of melodrama, a pretention toward social comedy and a liberal amount of frank nationalism. All of these ingredients had appeared on the American stage for a number of years, but the more dominant interest in social commentary that appeared by mid-century, plus the greater wit and sophistication of the playwrights, provided some distinction for these plays. From their earliest ventures American playwrights showed an interest in satiric comedy and caricature -- of people, events and institutions. Nineteenth-century playwrights carried on this tradition. James N. Barker's *Tears and Smiles* (1807) contrasts the falseness of French fashion with America's more sterling national traits; *Fashionable Follies* (1809) by Joseph Hutton (1787-1828) stresses the silliness and stupidity of fashion-minded people; an anonymously written play, *The Moderns; or, A Trip to the Springs* (1831) ridicules the absurdities and idiosyncracies of life in a summer colony. James K. Paulding's *The Bucktails; or, Americans in England* (1815, 1847) contrasts, quite favorably of course, the American heroine with the Englishman who wants to marry her. *'Tis Ill Playing with Edged Tools* (1854) was written, according to the anonymous author, to illustrate fashionable life in New York -- and some of its vices. In *Fashion and Follies of Washington Life* (1857) Henry Clay Preuss proposed "to exhibit a panoramic view of characters and events" with a view to their reform.

(a) Anna Cora Mowatt Ritchie (1819-1870)
In her *Autobiography of an Actress* (1854) Mrs. Ritchie tells of her early prejudices against the theatre, which "melted" away as she grew older. After writing her first "positive attempt as a dramatist," *The Gypsy Wanderer; or, the Stolen Child*, at

seventeen, she was forced by circumstances as well as by her own desires to pursue a career in the theatre. When her husband lost his fortune, she reluctantly accepted a suggestion that she give public readings, which brought her an offer to appear in the legitimate theatre -- an offer she indignantly refused because people of her social station did not appear on the stage. Then she wrote *Fashion*, and its success on the New York stage changed her views: she now "determined to fulfill the destiny which seemed visibly pointed out by the unerring finger of Providence . . . . I would become an actress." And in this career she was also successful. By the time ill health forced her to retire from the stage in 1854, she had raised the reputation of theatre in America and through her written plays had added to the stature of American drama.

Fashion; or, Life in New York (1845)
(Plot)   Once a milliner, now the fashion-minded, social-climbing wife of a rich man, Mrs. Tiffany explains to her daughter, Seraphina, how she must "catch" Count Jolimaitre, a fashionable fraud who finds "but one redeeming charm in America -- the superlative loveliness of the feminine portion of creation -- and the wealth of their obliging papas." In contrast to Mrs. Tiffany, who worships all that is foreign, Adam Trueman personifies American independence. He is shocked to find that his old friend, Tiffany, has committed a forgery and is being blackmailed by Snobson, his clerk, who will exchange his silence for the hand of Serafina in marriage. When Millinette, the French maid, recognizes the Count as an imposter, Gertrude, the wholesome governess, overhears their talk and tries to trick the Count into confessing his true identity, only to place herself in a compromising position. So great is her shame that she is turned out of Tiffany's house but not before she writes an explanatory letter, which Trueman reads and learns that Gertrude is really his granddaughter and heir. Trueman, the Yankee, then goes into action. He explains to Tiffany that Snobson is as much at fault as he and then exposes the Count as a fraud. All ends happily: Millinette will marry the fake Count, really a nice fellow; Gertrude and Colonel Howard, a stuffy but true American, will also marry; and Trueman will rescue the Tiffanys from their financial difficulties if they learn "to prize at its just value -- Fashion."

(Discussion) *Fashion* is Mrs. Ritchie's major contribution to the drama and has since become a landmark in the progress of American social comedy, providing as it does a half-way point between Royall Tyler's *The Contrast* and the transitional social comedies of Bronson Howard, W. D. Howells and Clyde Fitch. Mrs. Ritchie's Preface to the London edition of her play, 1850, reveals her objectives:

> The Comedy of *Fashion* was intended as a good-natured satire upon some of the follies incident to a new country, where foreign dross sometimes passes for gold, while native gold is cast aside as dross; where vanities rather than the virtues of other lands are too often imitated, and where the stamp of *fashion* gives currency even to the coinage of vice.

In spite of obvious inadequacies, *Fashion* illustrates better than any American play of its time the characteristics of social comedy. Its theme is the relationship of the individual to society, and its characters, though mainly caricatures, suggest a variety of social levels. The manner in which society is satirized, the wit and the epigrammatic quality of the lines also add to the comedy: "A woman of fashion *never* grows old! Age is always out of fashion"; fashion is "an agreement between certain persons to live without using their souls! to substitute etiquette for virtue -- decorum for purity -- manners for morals!" Mixed with this comic caricature, and frequently dominating it, are aspects of farce and melodrama. The gestures, the exaggerated actions of Mrs. Tiffany, the cudgel waving by Trueman -- all are farce actions. Disguises, letters, forgery, a dastardly villain -- these are the hallmarks of melodrama. There is still, however, a great deal of charm and brilliance in *Fashion;* Mrs. Ritchie understood her society well, and she was a clever writer.

(b)   *Self* (1856) by Mrs. Sidney F. Bateman (1823-1881)
(Plot) Extravagant and irreponible, Mrs. Apex has ruined her husband with her excesses. When her stepdaughter, Mary, refuses to lend her legacy of fifteen thousand dollars, Mrs. Apex persuades her equally extravant son, Charles, to forge a check for that amount. But Mary has written a check for fifteen

thousand dollars to help save her father's business, and when this check is returned "without funds," Mr. Apex turns Mary out of the house. It is now up to John Unit, a Yankee who has been disgusted with the excesses of the Apex family, to put things in order. Thanks to Mary's persuasion, he will supply the needed money if the flagrant buying stops. Everyone forgives anyone who needs forgiveness, and all are finally happy.

(Discussion) Sidney Cole Bateman, daughter of actor Joe Cowell, and mother of the sensation child actresses Kate and Ellen Bateman, wrote several plays and was herself a fair actress and the manager of the Lyceum Theatre in London. One of the more memorable plays on city life in America during the 1850s, *Self* is laced with local allusions. Its characters, objects of satire and theme of forgery, however, appear to be modelled on Mrs. Ritchie's *Fashion*. Although distinguished by its thesis -- that "our labors are prompted by that great motive power of human nature -- Self!" -- Mrs. Bateman's play suffers from her limited talents and methods.

(c)   *Young New York* (1856)
       by Edward G. P. Wilkins (1829-1861)
(Plot) Mr. Ten-pen-cent, a wealthy retired merchant, pleased with his accomplishments, is persuaded to run for Congress. Self-satisfied and society-conscious, all the Ten-per-cents except Rose are disagreeable people. When Rose, a sweet but independent girl who reads Emerson, marries her music teacher, Skibberini, she is ostracized by the family. Later, Mr. Ten-per-cent, defeated in his political campaign and having somehow lost his fortune, discovers that Rose is giving a concert. He attends and is so overwhelmed by the beauty of her singing that he forgives Rose and her husband. All are happy at the final curtain, and, as Rose says, "every man and woman is to be tried by the standard of their acts alone, and upon them is to stand or fall. How do you like Young New York?"

(Discussion) Hardly a social comedy, *Young New York* is typical of a rather large number of farces which satirize various social conditions and conventions. Edward G. P. Wilkins, drama critic for the New York *Herald,* was praised for his "complete success" in a play filled with biting comments on congressional elections, journalistic practices, "money campaigns," current prices and popular health cures -- "if the good people of Gotham would only profit from this lesson" (*Spirit of the Times*, November 29, 1856, p. 504). One character in the play tells of a train wreck in which twenty-eight immigrants were killed. There would be no fuss -- they were second-class passengers. This comment anticipates by several years Mark Twain's observation about a steamboat blowing up -- "nobody hurt, killed a nigger."

(d) Attitudes Toward Fashion
The Very Age (1850) by Edward Sherman Gould (1805-1885) was described in *The Knickerbocker* (August 1850, p. 186) as a "satire upon the fashionable apes of foreign follies and vices" with "biting and incessant" insights into "upper tendom." Another playwright, Thomas Blaydon De Walden (1811-1873), examined that society rather well in *The Upper Ten and the Lower Twenty* (1854), which a writer for the *Spirit of the Times* (November 25, 1854, p. 492) called an "excellent exposé of New York Life." Sentimental and sensational views of New York City, however, captured the attention of many of the journeyman dramatists of the period. Thaddeus Mehan's *Modern Insanity; or, Fashion and Forgery* (1857) shows the dark side of city life, as do J. Burdette Howe's *The Mysteries and Crimes of New York and Brooklyn* (1858), De Walden's *Wall Street* (1857) and an anonymously written play of localized horrors entitled *Life in Brooklyn, Its Lights and Shades -- Virtues and Vices* (1857).

**3.   THE MOSE PLAYS: *A GLANCE AT NEW YORK* (1848)
       BY BENJAMIN A. BAKER (1818-1890)**

Of the variety of plays which dramatize life in the city or attempt to capitalize on the peculiarities of New York City, none achieved a more popular success than those built around the character of Mose, the New York fire b'hoy. Sketchy, episodic, with no finesse and little plot, these plays probably have dramatic ancestors in *The Fireman's Frolic* (1831), written by a fireman from Philadelphia, and *Beulah Spa; or, Two of the B'hoys* (1834). Whatever his background, Mose made his first full-length appearance in *A Glance at New York* (1848) by Benjamin A. Baker, a prompter at Mitchell's Olympic Theatre, where the play opened. Francis S. Chanfrau (1824-1884) was the fortunate New York actor who dressed in the red shirt, plug hat and turned-up trousers of the New York fireman and claimed the role of Mose. A roughneck who enjoys physical action and practical jokes and who will fight a fire, sing a song or love a girl with equal zest, Mose became a spectacular success. Baker featured him again in 1848 in *New York As It Is.* Then the imitations began: *Mose in California, A Glance at Philadelphia, Philadelphia As It Is, Mose in China, Mose in France.* Baker deserves the credit with *A Glance at New York,* which, flimsy, stilted in language, verbose and farcical, is nevertheless interesting as characteristic of a brief trend in American drama.

(Plot) Called a "Local Drama," this fast-moving play has numerous and episodic short scenes. It opens with a song on the steamship pier, as George, the country greenhorn, arrives in New York City to visit Harry. Immediately, Jake and Mike, two con men, sell George an old watch for ten dollars. After Mose arrives on the scene, the men dress as women and invade a woman's bowling alley. Next they go to Loafer's Paradise, where Mose hankers for a fight and finally manages to create one in which, of course, poor George gets the worst of it. In Act II there are six scenes, more incidents, more greenhorn jokes and more characters. Only though careful manipulation can the play reach a final curtain. About to run off to help a friend in a fight, Mose explains to the audience: "And if you don't say no, why I'll scare up this crowd again tomorrow night, and then you can take another Glance At New York."

4.   COMEDY AND ROMANTIC REALISM: *RIP VAN WINKLE*

For purposes of classification, *Rip Van Winkle* remains an anomaly, its history as a play covering nearly three-quarters of the nineteenth century. While it is romantic in theme, its interpretation, particularly by Joseph Jefferson, III, shows realistic detail as well as valid psychological insights into character. Considerably more melodramatic in the stage version than in Washington Irving's story, *Rip Van Winkle* more than any other play of the period, earns the title of domestic comedy.

(a) The History of *Rip Van Winkle* as a Play

It all started with the publication of "Rip Van Winkle" in *The Sketchbook* (1819) of Washington Irving. From that date until *Rip Van Winkle* by Jefferson and Dion Boucicault opened at the Adelphi Theatre in London on September 5, 1865, and played for one hundred and seventy nights, at least four versions of the story had appeared in theatres. First, an anonymous adaptation was staged in Albany, New York, in 1828. John Kerr's *Rip Van Winkle; or, The Demons of the Catskill Mountains!!! A National Drama*, produced in Philadelphia in 1829, became the model for all subsequent dramatizations. By inventing a love subplot between Rip's daughter, Alice, and Knickerbocker, an ex-school teacher, Kerr created a romantic story. This, he turned into a melodrama by introducing a contract through which a greedy slob named Derrick Van Slous hopes to get the better of Rip. An 1850 version by Charles Burke, Jefferson's half-brother, softens the patriotic touches in Kerr's play, adds local color in the form of Dutch dialect and includes several songs. Called *Rip Van Winkle, a Legend of the Catskills, a Romantic Drama in Two Acts*, this play begins with a song and makes Rip a jolly, fun-loving person adored by all except his wife, who berates his friends and beats Rip when she finds him drinking. A later British adaptation by Thomas H. Lacy draws from both the Kerr and Burke plays. Unlike the Kerr version it contains dialect but different from the Burke dialect. A major distinction is that Dame Van Winkle is alive in the second act and married to Nicholas Vedder; Lacy produced an ironic twist by having Vedder abuse her as she once abused Rip.

(b) *Rip Van Winkle* (1865)
    as Acted by Joseph Jefferson, III (1829-1905)

(Plot) In the village of Falling Waters, Gretchen Van Winkle complains of Rip's foolishness and of the villainy of Derrick, her former suitor, who takes mortgages on Rip's land and gives him money for drink. To protect the houses he has built on Rip's land, however, Derrick must own the property, and to this end he gives Rip a contract, actually a bill of sale, which he explains as an acknowledgement for a loan. Rip, a bit drunk and a bit suspicious, puts the paper in his pocket unsigned. Time passes, and one stormy evening Rip comes home drunk, with an empty game bag, having shot nothing but the family bull. Furious, Gretchen orders him out of the house, and Rip wanders off, falls asleep and dreams of cavorting with Henrick Hudson's "little men." His sojourn lasts for twenty years. When Rip awakens and returns to his village, he is saved from abusive treatment from strangers by Hendrich, who as a young boy had playfully promised to marry Rip's favorite daughter, Meenie. Then Gretchen appears. Married to Derrick, browbeaten and changed, she invites Rip to sit by her fire. In a dramatic scene, Gretchen stands up to Derrick and refuses to have Meenie marry his nephew. Meenie then recognizes Rip, who produces the paper showing that Derrick does not own the house and land. As Derrick leaves, Gretchen gives a cup to Rip, who ends the play with a toast: "Unt ladies and gents, here is your goot health and your fortune and your future families; and may you all live long and prosper!"

(Discussion) In America Joseph Jefferson, III means Rip Van Winkle. In 1881, he wrote to a friend: "I think I have played 'Rip Van Winkle' about twenty-five hundred times." And he continued playing the role until his death twenty-four years later. Reviews were generally excellent, and in Odell's *Annals of the New York Stage* (viii, p. 279) Jefferson is called a "one-part actor *par excellence.*" Although Rip already had a long stage history, Jefferson first became interested in him during the summer of 1859, when he fashioned a three-act play from the three printed versions and Irving's story. Dissatisfied with the result, however, six years later he persuaded Dion Boucicault to rewrite his work. The resulting three-act play, which Jefferson performed throughout his life (and which, according to A. H. Quinn, he later made into four acts by dividing Act One), bears some resemblance to Burke's play and, as in Lacy's version, keeps Dame Van Winkle alive until the final curtain.

B.   An Active and Growing Society

Changes in American society were clearly reflected in its drama. Significant social movements, events and social problems provided subject matter for those playwrights and theatre managers who were ever eager to woo a fickle public.

From 1830 to about 1865 the developing nation responded immediately and aggressively to any change.

The most obvious social changes stemmed from population increases and shifts. From 1830 to 1860 the population grew by 150 per cent, and a major reason for this growth was the immigration of Europeans, particularly Irish and Germans. Along with their native cultures, however, the immigrants brought problems which were immediately recognized by outbursts of anti-foreignism. Because of their individuality in language and their striking personal idiosyncrasies, the Irish provided ready-made characters for the theatre and, just as Jonathan and Mose had been, they were exploited on the stage. Plays about the Germans -- or "Dutchmen," as they were usually called -- were less popular, possibly because the Germans seemed less flamboyant than the Irish.

Social problems frequently became theatre fare. At mid-century the demands for women's suffrage came to a head. Temperance movements grew in response to the drinking habits of the Irish and Germans -- and the number of temperance plays multiplied. Americans also perceived a threat in the Roman Catholicism of the Irish. Although the Mormon trek westward was mainly motivated by a desire for religious freedom, it was also part of the geographical expansion in which immigrants became involved even before the discovery of gold in California sent the wagons rolling westward.

Between 1830 and 1860 seeds of war were planted: the abolitionists' arguments, the underground railroad, the Compromise of 1850, "Bleeding Kansas," the Dred Scott Decision and the activities of John Brown. If the dramatic growth of the country brought new characters and examples of romantic individuality to the American stage, the spreading social, political and religious upheavals provided play-wrights with an abundance of dramatic conflict.

1.   ETHNIC GROUP: THE IRISH

If Paddy the Irishman cannot be placed with Jonathan the Yankee, Sambo the Negro and Metamora the Indian as an original American character, he can most certainly be called the most popular adopted son of nineteenth-century American drama. Although the Irishman had appeared by about 1800 in such plays as John Murdock's *The Triumph of Love* (1795) and John Minshull's *Rural Felicity* (1801), the character reached his greatest popularity about mid-nineteenth century, when his heroic actions and comic traits made him a popular hero. Introduced to America during the 1830's by the English actor Tyrone Power (1795-1841), Paddy soon became a vehicle for such actors as John Collins, John Brougham, Barney Williams and William J. Florence. The best writers of Irish-American plays were Brougham, James Pilgrim and Dion Boucicault. Like the Yankee, the Irishman went many places and tried his hand at a number of things, as play titles suggest: *The Irish Attorney, The Irish Outlaw, The Irish Porter, The Irish Schoolmaster, The Irishman in Cuba, The Irishman in Greece*. Of the Irish vehicle actors, Barney Williams (1823-1876) achieved the greatest success both in America and in Great Britain.

(a) John Brougham (1810-1880)

An actor-manager-playwright, born in Dublin and with some success in the London theatre before coming to America in 1842, Brougham contributed to American drama mainly with his popular burlesques. He also achieved considerable success as a comedian, particularly in Irish roles, and displayed both wit and talent as a writer of farces. Among his best Irish plays were *The Irish Fortune Hunter* (1850) and *Temptation; or, the Irish Immigrant* (1856). During his fifty years upon the stage, Brougham provided substance to many facets of American drama -- the light, ridiculous and ephemeral popular entertainments as well as more thoughtful plays such as *The Game of Life* (1853), *Columbus El Filibustero* (1857) and *The Ruling Passion* (1859). Like Aristophanes, to whom he was compared, he created amusing diversions for the theatre public while flagging social conditions demanding serious attention.

(b) James Pilgrim (1825-1879)

Along with Samuel D. Johnson (1813-1863), whose *Brian O'Linn* (1851) well exemplifies his contribution to Irish plays, and Charles H. Saunders (1818-1856) with his popular play, *Bumpology*, James Pilgrim wrote a large percentage of the numerous Irish-American farces. Although he wrote a serious tragedy laid in Ireland, *Robert Emmett* (1853), he was much more successful with plays like *Paddy the Piper* (1850) and *Shandy Maguire; or, The Bould Boy of the Mountains* (1851). Shandy is the typical Irishman of the farces -- quick with his wits, his fists and a joke, but in reality a soft-hearted hero who protects widows, saves the heroine from the villain and beats up the ruffians. Pilgrim also brought the Irishman and the Yankee together on stage with *Irish Assurance and Yankee Modesty* (185?) and *Ireland and American* (1852), plays fitting the acting skills of Mr. and Mrs. Barney Williams and Mr. and Mrs. William Florence.

(c) Dion Boucicault (1820-1890)
Boucicault claimed to have "invented the Irish drama," but his plays are concerned with Ireland rather than with the Irish in America and do not reflect the American scene. As "sensational drama," his own phrase, his plays -- *The Colleen Bawn* (1860), *Arrah-na-Pogue* (1864), *The O'Dowd* (1873) and *The Shaughraun* (1874) -- were excellent and very successful melo-dramas. Before *The Colleen Bawn*, Boucicault had used the "faith-an-begorra" Irishman in such plays as *West End* (1842) and *Andy Blake* (1854). With *The Colleen Bawn*, however, Boucicault changed his methods, and his Irish plays began to emphasize qualities of character rather than to rely solely on amusing speech and antics.

(d) Popular Irish Vehicle Play: *Handy Andy*
Handy Andy, adapted in 1844 by Thomas D. English from a novel (1842) by Samuel Lover, became a vehicle for William Florence and other Irish actors. Subsequent versions were claimed by H. Montgomery in 1860 and W. A. Floyd in 1862.

(Plot) As the play opens, Squire Egan tells young Edward O'Connor that marriage to Fanny Dawson is impossible until O'Connor gets a deed for some property "given by Scatterbrain to your father." Enlivening this situation is Andy, "filius nullius" (son of nobody), an orphan whose blunders and witty comments are the major attraction of the play. For mystery there is Mad Nance, who raves about a son who is heir to "his father's title" and about Squire O'Grady, a "man of fraud and wrong." Following a drunk scene, a pistol and knife scene, a switched bundle scene and numerous other incidents, Mad Nance visits O'Grady and gets the deed along with her marriage certificate, identifying her as Ann Fitzgerald, and the record of her son's birth. With the deed, Edward and Fanny can be happily married, while Andy, obviously, is Mad Nance's son, the Earl of Scatterbrain.

2.   ETHNIC GROUP: THE GERMANS

No other ethnic group offered the dramatic possibilities of the Irish. Although German immigrants rivaled them in number, they ranked a poor second in theatrical appeal. Misunderstood and disliked, the "Dutchmen" most frequently reached the stage as objects of ridicule. Two plays featuring "John Schmidt" type Germans were written by Summerfield Barry, an actor from Baltimore who, as a youth, performed with Edwin Booth and Stuart Robson, both stars of the American theatre. *The Persecuted Dutchman* (1854) and *The Dutchman's Ghost* (1857) are, perhaps, typical of more abundant theatre fare.

The Persecuted Dutchman; or, The Original John Schmidt (1854) starred Samuel W. Glenn, a recognized "Dutch comedian" of the 1850s who also acted in an anonymous play, *The Dutch Guardian,* that same season in New York. As *The Persecuted Dutchman* opens, the honorable Augustus Clearstarch arrives at Mrs. Plentiful's hotel with Miss Arabella Blowhard, whom he wishes to marry so that he may get her father's fortune. Discovering that she has no money, he decides to send her back to school. Then the hero enters, John Schmidt, a tightfisted and tired businessman who wants only a bed and sleep. He is immediately disturbed, however, by Arabella's father, who arrives, whip in hand, and mistakes Schmidt for the villain who took his daughter. "Oh, I am a persecuted Dutchman. Mine Cot in Hemmel!" moans Schmidt. Soon Arabella straightens everything out; apologies are made and Schmidt will visit the Blowhards in New York if he can bring his friends -- the audience.

3.   PLAYS ABOUT MORMONS

Led by Brigham Young, the Mormons made their famous trek to Utah in 1846-48. During the 1850s, numerous Mormons and immigrants from Europe made the arduous trip, until several thousand had homes in the valley of the Great Salt Lake. Soon the Mormon adventure appeared in the theatre: *Deseret Deserted; or, the Last Days of Brigham Young* (1858) and *Life of the Mormons at Salt Lake* (1858), both anonymously written, and *The Mormons; or, Life at Salt Lake City* by Thomas Dunn English (1819-1902), doctor, lawyer, poet, and crusty New York journalist who wrote at least twenty plays, all lost to history.

The Mormons; or, Life at Salt Lake City (1858)
Obviously anti-Mormon propaganda, this play dramatizes the activities of a new group of arrivals at Salt Lake City. There is Noggs, a crooked New York civil official turned Mormon to escape the law. There are the Woodvilles, new converts. There is Mary, wooed by Pratt, an unscrupulous Mormon elder. And there is the mysterious fellow Eagle Eye, really Walter Markham, who is trying to track down the murderer of his sister. When Mary decides to marry Pratt, Eagle Eye decides to save her. Pursued by the Danites, the Mormon military division of Brigham Young's ambitious venture, Eagle Eye and Mary escape to the mountains. After several incidents, Mary is threatened by another Mormon named Blair, whom Eagle Eye recognizes as the murderer. Overcome by his own guilt, however, Blair kills himself before a U.S. Army scouting party rescues Mary, Eagle Eye and the now disenchanted Woodvilles.

4.   PLAYS ABOUT THE WEST

A number of plays describe the movement westward to California and the brand of society found there. Early in January of 1849, Charles Burke acted in an anonymous play entitled *A Trip to the California Gold Mines*. Other plays are *A Live Woman in the Mines* (1857) by Alonzo Delano, showing some of the admirable and fearless characteristics of Western people, and *Fast Folks; or, Early Days in California,* by Joseph A. Nunes, presumably acted during the 1858-59 theatre season in Philadelphia. These plays present a miscellany of social history, local color and folk drama.

Texas is featured prominently in Augustus W. Fenno's *The Campaign of the Rio-Grande* (1846), a melodramatic also claimed by Walter M. Leman, and in such anonymously written plays as *Crockett in Texas* (1839), *The Lone Star* (1849) and *The Texas Struggle* (1850). Thomas Barry, a Boston theatre manager, wrote about *The Battle of Mexico* (1850), and William Gilmore Simms (1806-1870), a Southern novelist and critic, followed his hero through the battle of the Alamo in *Michael Bonham; or, the Fall of Bexar* (1855).

5. TEMPERANCE DRAMA

Within a few years after the American Temperance Society was formed at Boston in 1826, a thousand-odd local groups had sprung up. Temperance crusades used pictures and pamphlets and featured as lecturers such reformed drunkards as John B. Gough, whose popularity was phenomenal. Alcohol was a natural enough ingredient in nineteenth-century American melodrama, and the fervor of temperance supporters merely served to increase, and not only figuratively speaking, the dependence of playwrights upon it. The best temperance plays were written near the middle of the century: Charles W. Taylor, *The Drunkard's Warning* (1856); Harry Seymour, *Temperance Doctor* (n.d.); and two minor classics, William H. Smith's *The Drunkard; or, the Fallen Saved* (1844) and William W. Pratt's dramatization of the novel by Timothy S. Arthur, *Ten Nights in a Bar Room and What I Saw There,* which was presented on the New York stage in 1858. Both of the latter had long original runs and are still occasionally produced.

The Drunkard; or, the Fallen Saved **(1844)**
Ten Nights in a Bar Room **(1858)**
This play opened at the Boston Museum and ran for 140 performances. It tells of the weak but well-meaning Edward Middleton, who is tempted to drink by the villain Cribbs and goes from bad to worse until, urged by Mr. Rencelow, he takes the pledge. He is then reformed and becomes successful while the villain is punished. Although not as theatrically effective as *The Drunkard, Ten Nights in a Bar Room* was second in popularity only to *Uncle Tom's Cabin* in the theatre of the late nineteenth century. In Pratt's dramatization, John Morgan, the hero, is made the slave of drink sold to him by Simon Slade, who in turn, victimized by his own greed, is finally killed by

his own son in a drunken quarrel. Other men are slain, good men; mothers and daughters die or go insane. Finally, when Morgan's little daughter ("Father, dear Father, come home with me now. The clock in the belfry strikes one.") is accidentally killed, Morgan reforms and leads a movement to close the tavern.

6.   SLAVERY AND THE CIVIL WAR

There had been slaves in all thirteen colonies before the Revolution, but with Congressional action in 1808, the importation of slaves to America became illegal. This action, however, did not solve the social or moral problem, the question of the "fortunate" slave versus black bondage. Plays reflects the turbulent events that immediately preceded the war -- such as the Fugitive Slave Law of 1850, the publication of the novel *Uncle Tom's Cabin* in 1852, the Kansas-Nebraska Act of 1854, John Brown's Pottawatomie Massacre of 1856, the Dred Scott Decision of 1857, the incident at Harper's Ferry in 1859 and the subsequent hanging of Brown.

Most famous among plays, of course, were the many adaptations of *Uncle Tom's Cabin,* billed as "The World's Greatest Hit." Another very popular melodrama about Southern slave life was Dion Boucicault's *The Octoroon* (1859). Mrs. Stowe's second novel about slavery, *Dred: A Tale of the Great Dismal Swamp* (1856) was dramatized several times but never successfully in America. J. T. Trowbridge's stage adaptation of his own novel, *Neighbor Jackwood* (1857), dramatizes the bitter Northern attitude toward the Fugitive Slave Law by showing the chase, capture and rescue of an octoroon slave. "Bleeding Kansas" and John Brown's fanatical activity appear in several plays. In O*ssawattomie Brown; or, the Insurrection at Harper's Ferry* (1859), for example, J. C. Swayze tried to foreshadow Brown's martyrdom through scenes of his final confrontation.

Both Union and Confederate points of view were presented on the American stage. *The Traitor's Doom; or, the Fate of Secession* and *Anderson, the Patriot Heart of Sumter,* portrayed the fall of Fort Sumter in New York theatres during 1861, the same year that Benjamin E. Woolf (1836-1901) wrote *Off to War.* One of the best-known war plays was *The Guerillas; or, the War in Virginia* (1862) by James D. McCabe (1842-1883). Particular battles are represented by *The Scouts; or, the Plains of Manassas* (1861) by John H. Hewitt (1801-1890) and *Bull Run; or, the Sacking of Fairfax Courthouse* (1861) by Charles Gayler (1820-1892), which was performed in New York less than a month after the actual event.

7.   WOMEN'S RIGHTS

The Women's Rights Movement had a spectacular beginning at Seneca Falls, New York, with a convention in 1848 at which Elizabeth Cady Stanton read her "Declaration of Sentiments." Press and pulpit reacted immediately, while the stage generally belittled the seriousness of the movement in comedies and "amusements" that were popular in parlor theatricals. Typical are such plays as *The Rights and Wrongs of Women* (1856), anonymously written, and *Women's Rights* (1856) by William B. Foule (1795-1865). A more commercially acceptable play on the issue of women's suffrage is *The Rights of Man* (1857) by Oliver S. Leland (1834-1870).

C.   The Appeal of Melodrama

That melodrama fascinated the majority of those who attended the theatre is perhaps the only undebatable statement that could be made about American drama before the Civil War. Since the theatre of the time was controlled by a manager who wanted to make money and an actor who desired popularity, it is not surprising that a high percentage of the plays that were written or adapted during that period were melodramas. From Dunlap, who made a career of Kotzebue, to Boucicault, a master of melodrama, whether the play was written in poetry or prose or was concerned with political issues, native characters or social problems, the techniques of melodrama were prominent. (Farce, of course, was also relished by the people who came at eight and should be linked with melodrama as popular theatre entertainment.) Nor was this interest in melodrama a passing fad. As the century progressed, plays became more violently, more spectacularly and more purposefully melodramatic. The following plays illustrate the kinds of melodrama most enjoyed by audiences.

1. *MAZEPPA; OR, THE WILD HORSE OR TARTARY* (1825)

(Plot) Grandson of a Tartar chiefton, Mazeppa loves Olinska, who is being forced to marry Count Premislas. In anger, Mazeppa tries to fight the Count, is caught and sentenced to be tied to a wild horse and let loose in the desert. Later, at the entrance to a cavern where Korella, the prophetess of the Tartars, speaks of the return of a leader, Mazeppa rides in on the back of the horse. Fulfilling Korella's prophecy, Mazeppa persuades the Tartars to get Olinska for him. As the Tartars attack, Olinska, fearing for her life and virtue, tries to stab herself, but is prevented by Korella, who also enlightens her. All ends happily, as the marriage of Mazeppa and Olinska brings peace to the Poles and the Tartars.

(Discussion) *Mazeppa* is a spectacular melodrama which, either in a version by John Howard Payne or -- more likely -- an anonymous revision of it, achieved considerable success on the American stage. (There is some doubt that Payne's play was ever produced.) Whatever the version, the daring historical ride of Mazeppa, Cossack leader and ally of Peter the Great, provided all of the excitement and pageantry necessary to melodrama. During the early 1860s, in an amazing novelty performance, the exuberant actress, Adah Isaacs Menken, created a sensation as she acted the male role of Mazeppa strapped "naked" (in flesh-colored tights) to the back of a "wild" horse.

2. *PUTNAM, THE IRON SON OF '76* (1844)
   BY NATHANIEL H. BANNISTER (1800-1834)

(Plot) As a chorus sings "we shall be free," and a lion and an eagle descend from the flies, Goddesses of War and Liberty in Roman chariots point to Benjamin Franklin and others signing the Declaration of Independence and a group of American generals: Washington, Putnam, Cadwallander and Greene. As William prepares to leave his village and his beloved Clara to fight for his country, Indians attack. General Putnam on horseback dashes on stage to save Clara, but William is captured by the Indians. Putnam befriends Oneactah, an Indian who has been duped by a Renegade to fight for the British. With the help of Clara and Oneactah's daughter, the Indians (sympathetically treated by Bannister) are persuaded to fight for General Washington. Meanwhile, Putnam is captured by the British from whom he manages a clever and exciting escape in Act III, Scene 5, on his miraculous horse, Black Vulture. There is comic relief in the forced induction of Cabbageall into army life by a Yankee officer and their subsequent capture by the British. The play ends with the Battle of Yorktown -- "Red fire for the whole scene, and drums and trumpets" -- and a recreation of the famous painting showing Cornwallis surrendering to Washington.

(Discussion) A masterful blend of patriotic themes and horses on stage, this military melodrama in three acts fascinated audiences nightly, as Black Vulture raced down the rough trail of Horse Neck, 150 feet from the heights of the theatre down to the stage. Other plays capitalized on Bannister's idea, and by 1874 actress Kate Foster and her horse Wonder were performing in *Mazeppa, Eagle Eye, Three Fast Men, Putnam* and *The Cataract of the Ganges.*

3.   THE SENSATIONALISM
OF DION BOUCICAULT (1820-1890)

The name of Dion Boucicault must appear frequently in any review of American drama. His reputation rests on (1) a few comedies; (2) his successful efforts to help secure in America a copyright law giving the author of a play "the sole right to print and publish the said composition, the sole right also to act, perform or represent the same" (August 18, 1856); (3) his revision of *Rip Van Winkle;* (4) his Southern play, *The Octoroon;* (5) his Irish plays; (6) his numerous "sensational dramas" or melodramas; and (7) his major contributions to American dramatic criticism. Although a man of the theatre, he tended to emphasize the play and the characterizations within the play rather than the personalities of the actors. He initiated the traveling company which performed a single play; he devised new advertising methods, and he invented a solution which made scenery fireproof. His ideas concerning acting brought him distinction, while his essay on "The Art of Dramatic Composition" showed his concern for Aristotle and the classical Greek and French dramatists. His thirteen essays in the *North American Review* (1877-89) form his defense of a drama which he saw as "the necessary product of the age in which it lives." For the theatre as well as the drama, he was a significant figure in America.

Although he bowed to the demands of his audience and resorted excessively to the burning of ships and houses, Boucicault tried to make the sensationalism of his melodramas realistic and to bring social significance to his plays. *The Octoroon* was concerned with the evils of slavery; his Irish plays brought sympathy for Ireland's struggle for freedom. *The Poor of New York*, adapted from *Les Pauvres de Paris* by Edouard Brisebarre and Eugène Nus, shows Boucicault at his melodramatic best -- spectacular realism, sensationalism and social interest. George C. D. Odell (*Annals*, vii, 22) noted that it was "among the first of those local melodramas of crime, poverty, and riches."

The Poor of New York (1857)
(Plot) Frightened by the financial Panic of 1837, Paul Fairweather deposits one hundred thousand dollars in Gideon Bloodgood's bank. Discovering that the bank is about to fail, Fairweather attempts to withdraw his money. When his request is refused, he becomes hysterical and dies of apoplexy, dropping his deposit receipt on the floor. Next morning his body is found in the street; Bloodgood keeps the money, and the only witness to the event, a clerk named Tom Badger, keeps the receipt. Twenty years pass, and people are in the depths of the Panic of 1857. Fairweather's widow and children, Lucy and Paul, are poverty-stricken. Bloodgood is well off but is still trying to get the receipt from Badger, whom he has had arrested, hoping to find the receipt on his person. In a final desperate attempt to destroy the receipt, Bloodgood sets fire to the house where Badger lives. The scene is spectacular; police arrive and the villain is arrested, while the lives of Badger and the Fairweathers will be filled with the serenity that only melodrama can provide.

4. *EAST LYNNE* (1863)

(Plot) Archibald Carlyle has just brought his bride, Isabel, to the Old Homestead in East Lynne, but their serenity is soon disturbed by Barbara Hare, who begs Archibald to help her brother, a suspected murderer. Without confiding in his new wife, Archibald accepts this humanitarian task which necessarily brings him closer to Barbara. As time passes, Isabel grows suspicious and jealous and is easily deceived by Francis Levison, a scoundrel, and runs away with him. Years later, abandoned and repentant, Isabel, disguised as Madame Vine, returns to East Lynne, where, working as a governess for Archibald and Barbara, who have married, she finally reveals herself when one of her own children dies in her arms. In the final act, it is necessary only to punish the villain, who has been identified as the murderer in question, and to forgive Isabel, who conveniently dies, relieving Archibald of any possible charge of inadvertently committing bigamy.

(Discussion) To many modern Americans, *East Lynne* means melodrama. Based on a novel by Mrs. Henry Wood, an English-woman, and adapted by Clifton W. Tayleure (1830-1891), it opened at the Winter Garden in New York in 1863. William Winter, dramatic critic (*Albion,* March 28, 1863), declared that a "flimsy and stupid novel has been resuscitated into a flimsy, unnatural, incongruous and feverishly sentimental play." Yet the play is still in print, still read as an example of weepy, sentimental melodrama and still occasionally produced.

D. Shortcuts to Popularity: Adaptations, Translations, Burlesques and Novelties

Managers and actors had always been rather suspicious of American authors, believing that Europeans were more accomplished in the arts. Generally, the theatre manager, who was most frequently an Englishman trying to make a living in America, thought it more expeditious to produce a successful French play altered to suit an American audience or to adapt a popular novel for the stage than to speculate on an untried homegrown play. His or her reasons were threefold: lack of American participation in international copyright protection made pirating European plays a profitable and safe undertaking; in America there was still a strong dependence on the "Mother Country" for art and entertainment; and, because the better American writers had no financial incentive to write for the theatre, few good American plays existed. Translations and adaptations, then, were faster and easier for the journeyman playwrights, safer for the theatre managers and usually popular with the audience.

From the beginning, American dramatists looked to Europe -- especially England -- for characters, settings, themes and plots. In spite of his enthusiasm for purely American drama, William Dunlap was a prodigious borrower, adaptor and translator -- from the English, French and German drama. John Howard Payne, Nathaniel Parker Willis, James Nelson Barker, Richard Penn Smith -- many of the better American dramatists at one time or another borrowed material from Europe, either (1) a complete play adapted to American circumstances or translated for an American audience, (2) particular characters or story lines from successful plays or (3) the diction and rhetoric of foreign dramatists. As the century progressed, John Brougham and Dion Boucicault became the major adaptors of foreign literature.

The three most successful adaptations for the theatre in mid-nineteenth century were *Ten Nights in a Bar Room* from the novel by T. S. Arthur, *Uncle Tom's Cabin* from H. B. Stowe's novel and *Rip Van Winkle* from Washington Irving's story. A great number of the historical adventure novels, however, were put into play form, almost always by a person other than the novelist. Quite popular were the dramatized novels of James Fenimore Cooper, Robert Montgomery Bird, William Gilmore Simms and John Pendleton Kennedy. Poe's *The Gold Bug* was dramatized in 1843; Hawthorne's *The Scarlet Letter* was adapted for the stage at least twice, in 1857 and 1858. Most successful of all were the adaptations of the popular sentimental and sensational novels of the immediate pre-Civil War years: *The Hidden Hand* (1859), for example, by E. D. E. N. Southworth, whose sixty novels captivated readers during the 1850s; *Hot Corn: Life Scenes in New York Illustrated* (1854) by Solon Robinson; and the abundant outpourings of writers such as Sylvanus Cobb and Ned Buntline.

Burlesques of plays -- ridiculous mockings of original works -- were not as frequent as adaptations or translations, but the reasons for writing them were somewhat the same. If a play had been a hit, it was assumed that a burlesque of that play would also be a hit. John Brougham was one of the most able and successful writers of burlesques with his attacks on *Metamora* in 1847 and *Pocahontas* in 1855. Charles M. Walcot, Sr. (1815-1868), close friend of Brougham, was also a superior writer of burlesques, with *Fried Shots* (1843), a burlesque of *Der Freischutz*, and his ridiculing of Longfellow's poem in *Hiawatha; or, Ardent Spirits and Laughing Water* (1856). Many more burlesques appeared, such as *The Lady of Irons* (1842), a reworking of Bulwer-Lytton's *The Lady of Lyons,* and *Clam-eel* (185?), a ridiculing of *Camille.*   Apparently, the genre was well appreciated by audiences.

Even the most pretentious legitimate theatres resorted to novelties and spectacles during hard times, while popular theatres, such as the Bowery Theatre in New York, depended upon such entertainments: minstrel shows, dog shows, child actors, individual performances by actresses such as Lola Montez and by Jenny Lind, concerts and lectures. An 1858 play by Harry Seymour (c. 1819-1883), *Jessie Brown; or, Havelock's Last Victory,* features Hindoo dancing girls, a feast of Vishnu, wild Brahma dances and an attack on Fort Caunpore showing the massacre of American missionaries. Actress and theatre manager Laura Keene occasionally saved her theatre season with such novelties as *The Sea of Ice; or, a Mother's Prayer* (1857), *Young Bacchus; or, Spirits and Water* (1857) and *Love and Lightning; or, the Telephonic Cable* (1858), which celebrated the laying of the Atlantic cable.

E.   Poets and Novelists as Playwrights

The drama seems always to have had an almost irresistible appeal for writers. Something about the immediacy of the audience's response and the fascination of seeing one's characters brought to life on the stage impels both those with and those without the dramatic touch to put their thoughts into dialogue and action. The results, however, have not always been happy. In no instance, for example, did a first-rate American novelist or poet of the early nineteenth century become a successful dramatist. Of America's major writers, Washington Irving collaborated -- anonymously -- with John Howard Payne in the successful play *Charles the Second* (1824); Poe wrote a fragment of a poetic drama which he called *Politian* (1835); and Longfellow wrote some poetic dramas -- *The Spanish Student* (1842), *The Golden Legend* (1851) -- which did not suit the needs of the theatre.

Several lesser figures achieved moderate success, both in literature and in the drama. Robert Montgomery Bird became a successful novelist after he stopped writing plays. Nathaniel Parker Willis wrote extremely popular essays and poems, and George Henry Boker was a poet of some reputation. Poet Julia Ward Howe wrote plays, including *Leonora; or, the World's Own* (1857). George H. Miles, another minor poet, achieved some success with such plays as *De Soto* (1852). The author of the novel, *The Dutchman's Fireside*, James Kirke Paulding, wrote the equally popular play, *The Lion of the West* (1831) and *The Bucktails; or, Americans in England* (1847). John Neal, the gothic novelist of *Logan* (1822) and a critic, wrote *Otho* (1819), a tragedy based on the Byronic hero, Otho the Bastard. Another novelist, William Gilmore Simms, wrote *Michael Bonham; or, the Fall of Bexar* (1852) and a tragedy in blank verse, *Norman Maurice; or, the Man of the People* (1851).

Among the numerous playwrights of this period, several wrote fiction, poetry or essays. Samuel Woodworth, the author of *The Forest Rose* (1825), is best known to the American public as the author of "The Old Oaken Bucket." T. D. English, author of *The Mormons* (1858), a doctor by profession, as well as a critic and journalist, gained some reputation as the writer of "Ben Bolt." Many were editors or journalists: Isaac Harby (*The Gordian Knot*, 1807), Epes Sargent (*Velasco,* 1849), Cornelius Mathews (*Witchcraft; or, the Martyrs of Salem,* 1846) and Oliver Bell Bunce (*Marco Bozzaris,* 1850).

F.   Transatlantic Evaluation:
American Drama in England Before the Civil War

Ever since certain Colonists decided to distance themselves from English domination, others have been equally determined to judge excellence in the arts and literature by the products of

English and European minds. This has been particularly true -- and remains true today -- of theatrical activity. Long before the Civil War, however, American plays were produced in London theatres with a certain regularity and some success. Although a few American plays had been produced in London early in the century, the production of J. H. Payne's first play at Covent Garden in 1815 established a foothold for American drama in the London theatre which it has never relinquished. Most enthusiastically received were those plays which exhibited the peculiar traits of Americans. Yankee plays, Negro minstrels and skits and pioneer adventure plays enjoyed long runs. American social caricatures were also applauded, as were *Uncle Tom's Cabin* and *Rip Van Winkle*. For this liberal attitude which many English people had toward American plays before the Civil War, much credit is due such actors as Edwin Forrest, Charlotte Cushman, James Hackett, Negro impersonator Thomas Dartmouth Rice and Yankee actors George Handel Hill, Dan Marble, Josh Silsbee and John Owens.

1.   JOHN HOWARD PAYNE (1791-1852)

Payne's success in the English theatre can be traced through the records of the Enthoven Collection of the Victoria and Albert Museum in South Kensington, London. After the production at Covent Garden in 1815 of his first translation, *Trial Without Jury*, Payne was a well-known playwright in London for the next fifteen years. Mainly, the critics approved. During the 1822 season, Payne had seven plays produced in London theatres -- a considerable achievement for an American dramatist. His most successful plays were *Clari; or, the Maid of Milan* (1823), *Charles the Second; or, the Merry Monarch* (1824) and *The French Libertine* (1826), later entitled *Richelieu*, which inspired exciting critical debates from political as well as dramaturgical points of view.

There can be little doubt that Payne's work paved the way for a more appreciative view of American drama. After William Dunlap's *Tell Truth and Shame the Devil* was performed at Covent Garden on May 18, 1799, American plays only occasionally found their way across the Atlantic. As the new century progressed, the number of American plays produced in

England gradually increased. When M. M. Noah's *Wandering Boys; or, the Castle of Olival* was presented at Covent Garden on February 24, 1814, it was anticipated by this comment: "It will no doubt resemble melodrama in general, in being full of sound and show, and good for nothing -- too dull . . . and too absurd to entertain the maturer frequenters of a theatre." Then Payne came to London and ten years passed. On September 13, 1824, at Sadler's Wells, Samuel Judah's *The Mountain Torrent* was reviewed in the *Theatrical Observer*: "In our opinion, it is decidedly the best piece of the kind ever witnessed here: the plot is completely original, the incidents peculiar and pleasing . . . the characters . . . finely delineated." Both Noah and Judah have been reduced by time to very minor roles in the history of American drama, but the individual receptions accorded their plays in England suggest a turning point in the attitude of English reviewers toward American plays.

2.   POETIC DRAMA ON THE ENGLISH STAGE

American poetic tragedy had a mixed reception in England. Edwin Forrest, the actor, took J. A. Stone's *Metamora* and R. M. Bird's *The Gladiator* to London in 1836. While *Metamora* was condemned as "utter rubbish" by the English critics, *The Gladiator* met with a varied response. Representative is the critic who saw "great crudity in this work, taken altogether" but went on to call Bird's play "an ornament to the literature of any country."   When Charlotte Barnes Conner's tragedy, *Octavia Bragaldi*, played at the Surrey Theatre in 1844, advertising capitalized on the American authorship of a play that had been very successful in the United States. On May 10, 1849, G. H. Boker's tragedy, *Calaynos*, was produced with "merited success." Generally, however, poetic dramas were not among America's successful dramatic exports.

3.   YANKEE PLAYS

The most popular plays of this period exported to England were the Yankee plays; next in popularity were Irish plays, backwoodsman plays and minstrel sketches. The American Yankee actor took the character to England in such plays as *Yankee Land, The Yankee Pedler, The Forest Rose* and *The People's Lawyer*. And the Yankee's popularity grew. In 1852, for example, at the Adelphi theatre, Josh Silsbee played Hiram Dodge in *The Yankee Pedler* for 125 nights, having just completed ninety-nine performances as Jonathan Ploughboy in *The Forest Rose*.   In general, English audiences found the Yankee great fun and kept him on their stages for nearly thirty years, even enticing English playwrights to try their hands at writing Yankee plays.

4.   IRISH PLAYS

The Irish character acting of Barney Williams helped promote the success of American Irish plays in London. *Irish Assurance and Yankee Modesty* was standard in Mr. and Mrs. Williams' repertory.   Another couple long associated with Irish farces, Mr. and Mrs. W. T. Florence, were also successful in London, particularly in T. D. English's Irish play, *Handy Andy*.   In a later production of *Handy Andy* at the Haymarket, December 1, 1860, the American actor John Drew was extremely popular.

5.   BACKWOODSMAN PLAYS
AND THE WESTWARD MOVEMENT

Among the backwoodsman plays, *The Kentuckian; or, a Trip to New York,* adapted by William Bayle Bernard from Paulding's *The Lion of the West,* was one of the most popular.   Bernard (1807-1875), born in Boston, the son of actor-manager John Bernard, moved to England in 1820 and made his reputation as a writer of plays about America and as an adaptor of American plays and fiction to English circumstance.   After the Covent Garden production of *The Kentuckian,* beginning March 9, 1833, one critic wrote: "At Covent Garden the novelty has been a farce called *The Kentuckian,* in which a good satire is conveyed against old Mother Trollope, the lady who obtained so much reputation by exhibiting a due disgust for American vulgarity." Adaptations of James Fenimore Cooper's novels were more successful in England than in America. One version of *The Pilot* by Edward Fitzball, an English playwright, played for two hundred nights at the Adelphi Theatre in 1825-26.

6.   *UNCLE TOM'S CABIN* AND THE SOUTH

Almost immediately after Harriet Beecher Stowe published her novel in March 1852, it became a theatrical hit in England.

Before the year was out, there were at least eight versions at different London theatres, including an equestrian version at the Adelphi and a pantomime at Drury Lane. Opening at the Olympic Theatre on September 20, 1852 (only a month after C. W. Taylor's version had been presented in New York, and before the successful Aiken version was produced), Tom Taylor and Mark Lemon's version was entitled *Slave Life* and subtitled "Negro Life in America," rather than "Life Among the Lowly." It also provided a happy ending for the play with the freeing of Tom and Harry. One reviewer hoped that these changes would "make America ashamed of herself." Other Englsh dramatists quickly created new interpretations.

Other American plays treating Southern problems include *Ida May; or, the Secrets of the Slave Trade*, opening at the Victoria Theatre in May 1855; *Dred, a Tale of the Great Dismal Swamp*, adpated by a Mr. H. Young, which was a tremendous success at the Victoria Theatre during the fall of 1856; and Dion Boucicault's *The Octoroon*, enthusiastically received by the audiences at the Adelphi Theatre in 1861. The English, however, could not tolerate the ending of a play in which a beautiful and charming slave girl commits suicide. In letters to the London *Times*, Boucicault argued his case but eventually succumbed to rising indignation and reluctantly provided a happy ending and an entirely different tone to his play.

7.   OTHER PLAYS AND CRITICAL REACTION

A number of other American plays were produced in England before the Civil War, among them Mrs. A. C. M. Ritchie's *Fashion*; many of Boucicault's plays; *Nick of the Woods*, a version of Bird's adventure novel; and *Pocahontas*. In both scope and quality, the English got a reasonable idea of American drama. Although on occasion critical reaction was stuffy, the critics themselves seemed interested and not a little amazed. Moreover, it remains historically significant that English audiences at this early date found entertainment in American plays and that criticism was sufficiently favorable for theatre managers to find it to their advantage to produce American plays.

G. The English-American Playwright

Echoing Emerson's plea for an American literature in "The American Scholar," 1837, were fervent demands for an American drama. Yet, well past mid-century, critics persisted in accepting American writing only as a "condition of English literature." Such an authority as Duyckinck's *Cyclopedia of American Literature*, 1855, declared it still "thoroughly and essentially English." In a manner more pronounced than in other genres, the theatre remained essentially English: English actors and actresses flocked to America; at mid-century a majority of theatres were managed by Englishmen, who naturally produced English plays. Authors themselves caused a confusion of identity. John Howard Payne wrote most of his plays in England; Dion Boucicault is claimed by Americans, English and Irish; John Brougham lived thirty-eight of his seventy years in America.   The nationality of other playwrights is also difficult to define, but all contributed those ephemeral pieces that kept American theatres open during the mid-century years: J. Burdette Howe (1828-1908) wrote for both English and American theatre; James Pilgrim (1825-1879) came to America in 1849 and over the next thirty years wrote more than 200 plays; Henry W. Grattan Plunkett (1808-1889), born in Dublin, spent twenty-three years in America as playwright, actor and manager; Thomas DeWalden (1811-1873) came to America in 1844 and returned to England only once. John F. Poole (1835-1893) came to America as a young man and succeeded as playwright and theatre manager. By the 1880s Americans had gained control of their theatres, and the confusion as to identity began to disappear.

V. YANKEE ORIGINALITY: AMERICA'S CONTRIBUTION TO WORLD THEATRE
THE MINSTREL SHOW, THE SHOWBOAT, THE TOM SHOW

It is generally agreed that the minstrel show is America's contribution to world theatre; certainly, nowhere else could it have had its beginnings. Although the Tom show and the showboat were not original theatre in the same artistic way that the minstrels were, each was a distinctive theatrical innovation. And in a sense, all three -- the minstrel, the showboat and the Tom show -- were bound together by a common philosophy and technique. They created excitement; they reached out to the ordinary American and made him or her laugh and cry. As soon as possible after the minstrel railway car pulled onto its siding, or the showboat docked, or the wagons of the Tommers appeared in town, the person on the street was made aware of the arrival by a parade as colorful as the company's resources could provide. "Come one! Come all! Here is the kind of entertainment and excitement that you want, born in America!"

A. Introducing Sambo and Bones!

One night in 1828, an itinerant actor named Thomas Dartmouth Rice (1806-1860) was walking behind a hotel in Louisville, Kentucky (or was it Cincinnati, Ohio?) and happened to see a Negro currying a horse. He was an unhappy-looking Negro with a deformed right shoulder and rheumatism in his left leg and his knees, but he sang as he worked and, at the end of each verse of his song, he gave a little jump and set his "heel a ricken'" as he landed. Rice was fascinated. Watching closely, he soon learned the song and mastered the little jump:

Turn about and wheel about,
    An do jis so;
And ebery time I wheel about,
    I jump Jim Crow.

With clothes borrowed from the old Negro, Rice began performing the song and dance between the acts of the play in which he had a part. Surprisingly enough, his success was astounding both in America and in England, and his Jim Crow routine earned him the title Father of American Minstrelsy.

The first public presentation of a minstrel show was that of the Virginia Minstrels -- Daniel Emmett, Billy Whitlock, Dick Pelham and Francis Brower -- at the Bowery Amphitheatre in New York, February 6, 1843. Actors had impersonated Negroes on stage since the late eighteenth century, and Rice had performed a single blackface act. The quartet of Virginia

Minstrels added instrumental music -- fiddle, tambourine, banjo and bones -- and jokes. By the last quarter of the nineteenth century, minstrel companies sometimes included a hundred people, and the minstrel show with its established pattern was an evening's entertainment. There were six or eight blackfaced end men, having either bones or tambourines, who were introduced in pairs by the whitefaced interlocutor before being seated in a shallow half circle on either side of him. Behind them was the chorus. E. P. Christy is usually credited with inventing the role of the interlocutor and dividing the night's entertainment into two parts. After the introduction of the end men, Part I consisted of songs and jokes; Part II was an "olio" of variety acts and a sketch or afterpiece.

After the success of Christy's Minstrels in New York in 1846, scores of minstrel companies were started. Some flourished. Bryant's Minstrels had a run of eighteen years in New York (1857-1875). Other companies left their names and memories and usually great debts -- Spencer's Minstrels, Gorman Brothers Minstrels, Beach and Bowers Minstrels. In 1878 J. H. Haverly combined four troupes into the United Mastadon Minstrels. By 1908, when one of the most elaborate minstrel companies, the Cohan and Harris Minstrels, toured the country starring "Honey Boy" George Evans with "One Hundred Honey Boys," the character of the minstrel had changed to become a spectacle show. Songs were still important, but little of the original imitation of Negro life remained. The afterpiece, also, could not compete with the better-quality farces written by such dramatists as Charles Hoyt, and the variety acts were rivaled by vaudeville entertainment. By the second quarter of the twentieth century, America's only "original contribution to world theatre" had been left to the movies and the amateur stage for whatever means of survival it could manage.

B. Here Comes the Showboat!

Perhaps all theatre should answer a felt need, but there are few better examples of a theatrical institution designed for a particular purpose than America's showboat theatre. Although Noah M. Ludlow had probably used a Mississippi flatboat as a theatre in 1817, it was not until July 1831, when

William Chapman's "drama barge" floated down the Ohio and Mississippi Rivers giving one-night shows that the era of the showboat started.

With the success of Chapman's "floating theatre," imitations of all kinds appeared by the dozens. Chapman had produced legitimate plays. Soon the entire gamut of theatre fare (Shakespeare, minstrels, melodramas, circuses, the latest New York plays) could be seen on showboats run by some of the most colorful theatre people. Captain Augustus Byron French -- banjo player, magician and general showman, married to a wire walker -- started on the rivers in the late 1870s with a small barge called the *Sensation*, seating only eighty-nine people. Soon he added the luxury of a pusher boat; and by 1887, his newest *Sensation* boasted a steam calliope that could be heard for several miles on the river, a ten-piece band for parades and an advance man who plastered his advertising on available fences and trees. In 1909 W. R. Markle's *Goldenrod* was an extravagant boat: two hundred feet long and forty-five feet wide, with lots of gilt, 2500 lights, draperies, carpets, full-length mirrors and a seating capacity of 1400.

The problems of the showboat actor were many and varied, but they are not the reason the showboats nearly stopped running. By the late nineteenth century, the need which stimulated the showboat theatre business was being filled by stock and touring theatre companies. Revived as a curiosity in the early twentieth century, the showboat was sinking fast by the Great Depression of the Thirties. By 1938 only five showboats were in operation. Now, used mainly for tourism and municipal festivals, showboat entertainment can still be enjoyed. The *Goldenrod*, for example, is tied up at St. Charles, Missouri, and the *Majestic* at the Cincinnati landing presents plays nightly from May through September.

C. "The World's Greatest Hit"

"Poor old Uncle Tom," mourns George Shelby, "he's gone!" And perhaps this is true. After more than a hundred years on the stage, *Uncle Tom's Cabin* has joined the minstrel show and the showboat as a curiosity in the history of American drama and

theatre. Based on Harriet Beecher Stowe's novel, this play --
which the New York *Herald* in 1852 warned would "poison the
minds of our youth with the pestilent principles of
abolitionism" -- owed its early success to its attack on slavery
and then continued to be produced as a melodrama and spectacle
play. It truly deserves the title "The World's Greatest Hit."
Rather than a play, however, it is a powerful theatrical
tradition because its innumerable stage interpretations make it
impossible to discuss as a single work.

Although Mrs. Stowe never gave permission for the
dramatization of her novel because, as she wrote to one actor,
"the world is not good enough yet for it to succeed," in August
following the March 1852 publication of the novel, C. W.
Taylor's dramatization appeared on the New York stage and
ran for two weeks. The real tradition of *Uncle Tom's Cabin* as a
play, however, began with an adaptation by George L. Aiken
(1830-1876) at The Museum in Troy, New York, on September 27,
1852. To this three-act play ending with the "Death of Eva"
Aiken added a four-act sequel which in combination ran for one
hundred performances in Troy before being transferred to the
National Theatre in New York, where it broke a record with
325 consecutive performances. It starred Cordelia Howard, who
became famous as Little Eva. Four other versions of the play
appeared in New York that fall, and the novel also spread its
message: more than one million copies in twenty-three editions
of the novel were sold by May 1853.

One distinctive characteristic of *Uncle Tom's Cabin* is the
variety in the stage versions. The play simply grew. By 1879,
Great Danes masquerading as bloodhounds were pursuing Eliza
across the river. Simon Legree got meaner and meaner and more
adept with his whip. But it must have been an extravagant
enthusiasm for novelty that caused one company to double the
number of its parts: two Simon Legrees and two Uncle Toms.

As time went on, members of the theatre companies that played
Uncle Tom's Cabin became known as Tommers, and their shows
were called "Tom Shows." Interested in only one play, these
players were quite like a family of troubadours, living the
various characters in the melodrama. A girl who started as

Little Eva might eventually become Eliza. The boys and the men needed several talents -- tending Mark's mule, playing in the band and perhaps acting two or three minor characters in a single performance. But the Tommers were a dauntless clan, and however varied the scenes, the aim of the play was always the same: virtue must be rewarded and sin punished!

The complexity of Mrs. Stowe's novel is mainly responsible for the great number and diversity of play versions. Some scripts, almost sketches, follow a simple theme, while others lasted as long as five hours and include some fifty scenes. One of the better-known dramatizations is by A. E. Thomas, who, modeling his version on the earlier one by Aiken, wrote a play of three acts and twenty-three scenes.

Uncle Tom's Cabin (1852)
(Plot) George Harris, a mulatto slave owned by Haley, a villainous slave trader, appears at the Shelby Plantation to tell his wife and son, Eliza and Harry, who are Shelby's slaves, that he is running away to Canada. Eliza, learning that Shelby is in debt and must sell Harry and Uncle Tom, warns Tom, who will not leave, and flees with little Harry, only to be stopped by the ice-filled Ohio River. Faced with capture by Haley and Lawyer Marks, she jumps through a window of the tavern where she has been hiding and is next seen floating down the river on a piece of ice.

At the St. Clair household, Mr. St. Clair has just bought two new slaves: Topsy for Ophelia, the would-be social reformer from Vermont, and old Uncle Tom for his daughter Little Eva, a sickly but overwhelmingly sweet and virtuous child. Meanwhile, George, Eliza and Harry are united with the help of Phineas Fletcher, although they are continually hunted by Haley and Marks. Back at St. Clair's, Little Eva dies with a final wish that Uncle Tom be given his freedom, but before the papers can be signed, St. Clair is killed in a fight. With the St. Clair plantation in debt, the slaves are sold -- Topsy to Ophelia; Uncle Tom and Emmeline, a good woman, to Simon Legree, the most heartless slave owner in the entire country. At Legree's plantation, Uncle Tom is ordered to flog Emmeline, who has refused to go with Legree into his house, and is whipped when he disobeys and left to suffer with another slave, Cassie. In the meantime, Shelby, who has come to buy back Uncle Tom, and Marks have found a man who swears that Legree stabbed St. Clair. At Legree's house, they accuse him of murder and are dramatically saved from his anger by Cassie, who fatally stabs Legree. Then the end comes rapidly as Uncle Tom dies in Shelby's arms: "Poor old Uncle Tom -- he's gone!"

VI. THEATRE BEFORE THE CIVIL WAR

From 1800 until the Civil War, the American theatre developed from a largely imitative form of entertainment to a point where it could contribute to world theatre. It had produced some very capable actors and actresses and some startling innovations in production methods; and it now reached -- although with some gaps -- from coast to coast. No serious critic of the drama or theatre had yet appeared, but this only meant that anyone who wished had an opportunity to fling bats or bouquets. Meanwhile, the actors -- deserving or undeserving, tyros or artists -- carried on their tradition.

A. Criticism of the Theatre

In a column entitled "The Stage" appearing in *The Philadelphia Repository and Weekly Register* (April 11, 1801, p. 171), the comment was made that "such a thing as a well conducted theatre has never existed nor can it, because a sufficient number of good plays cannot be collected to support a public theatre." Other critics saw the problem in the institution itself: "The stage is the direct School of Vice." Still others could find fault with the physical theatre, with its poor lighting and the odor and smoke of the oil-pots and stoves. There was frequently violence in the gallery, assorted improper activities in the boxes and rats and vermin in the pit.

Theatregoers could sympathize with the recommendations of Jonathan Oldstyle (Washington Irving):

> To the actors -- less etiquette, less fustian, less buckram.
> To the orchestra -- new music, and more of it.
> To the pit -- patience, clean benches, and umbrellas.

To the boxes -- less affectation, less noise, less coxcombs.
To the gallery -- less grog and better constables; and
To the whole house, inside and out -- a total reformation,
    And so much for the theatre.

For many people the theatre remained a rowdy place. It is perhaps little wonder that Mrs. Frances Trollope, in her report on American manners during the 1830s, was shocked by what she saw in the theatre: men spitting and drinking, "a lady performing the most maternal office possible," and "a general air of contempt for the decencies of life." Nor did such activities in the theatre cease before the Civil War. As the "Wild West" was opened, the theatre, perhaps an index of civilization, was only slightly aware of the "decencies of life."

To help the reformation which Washington Irving suggested, there were the critics; at least, there were people throughout the first half of the nineteenth century who undertook to comment on plays, point out flaws and suggest opportunities for improvement. Newspapers and weekly magazines had theatre columns; some magazines, such as *The Theatrical Censor* and *The Thespian Monitor,* were devoted entirely to theatre criticism. Irving's witty and intelligent observations on the theatre in the *Salmagundi* papers (1807-08) are outstanding.

In defining the objectives of theatre criticism, a writer in *The Theatrical Censor* (December 9, 1805) noted that the critic was not the enemy of the drama nor of the public, but the "voice of an enlightened audience." Unfortunately, few who wrote about the drama and the theatre seemed to meet these qualifications. Of the numerous critics, John Neal commented bitingly on the drama but with some insight; Poe was erratic in his observations but was one of the most astute observers of the period. On occasion, theatre criticism became little more than theatre advertising, which Walt Whitman, writing for the Brooklyn *Eagle* in 1847, condemned when he said that he found no independent drama critics, only "slaves of the paid puff system."

A healthy criticism of drama and theatre, however, was being created. In 1831 *The Spirit of the Times* was established as a reliable source of theatre criticism with its "Theatre Column" and essays on a variety of theatre subjects by writers, mainly in New York, but also from cities across America. James Oakes from Boston, writing under the name of "Acorn," was one of the best theatre correspondents for *The Spirit of the Times* around the middle of the century. During the 1850s readers of the *Spirit* found essays, anonymously written, on such subjects as "The Drama in New York," "Originality in Dramatic Writing," "Foreign and American Critics," "The Theatre and Its Enemies" and "The Decline of the Drama." Theatre columns from the *Spirit* usually commented on the actors but covered a broad spectrum of theatre problems. A good many literary figures and journalists also commented on the theatre, including Robert Walsh, Edmund Morris, James Rees, James Kirke Paulding, Margaret Fuller and Cornelius Mathews, who founded the Copyright Club in 1843 and urged passage of a bill covering "Dramatic Pieces" in 1844. Although Dion Boucicault receives much of the credit for the copyright law of 1856, which supported the dramatist's control of his or her work, many literary figures wrote in support of international copyright protection from 1820 to 1891, when America finally signed an international agreement.

B.   Westward Ho! and Southward, Too!

Well before the Revolution, the American theatre had its beginnings in Southern cities such as Charleston and Williamsburg. Philadelphia and New York had also been responsive to theatrical entertainment. Although Boston had no theatre until the 1790s, by the early nineteenth century, most of the cities on the East Coast had theatres. Gradually, however, a center for theatrical activities became a necessity, and by 1825 New York was the place. Meanwhile, the theatre was spreading westward, and by 1860 there were American theatre companies in California and many cities in between.

The push westward and southward started soon after the new century began. From 1815 through 1830, an intrepid actor named Samuel Drake brought plays to Kentucky and the Ohio River Valley. In 1817 a member of Drake's company, Noah Ludlow, started his own theatrical company and was soon producing plays in Tennessee (1817), New Orleans (1818) and St. Louis (1819). A little later, an ambitious actor, James H. Caldwell, began a chain of theatres along the lower Mississippi River. Theatre along the upper Mississippi was not long in coming.

Theatre in California existed before the Gold Rush days, but the 49ers provided a tremendous stimulus for theatrical activities. Professional theatre came to Sacramento in 1849; within a year, San Francisco had a theatre and by 1851 enjoyed three theatres and a circus.

C. To Build a Theatre

To build a theatre was no easy task in a new nation where society was only slowly being established and independence of character was considered a prime virtue. Some audiences enjoyed English drama; other strongly nationalistic people rejected it. Some liked poetic drama; others would attend only farcical entertainment. Theatre managers, struggling to please as many people as possible, adopted a number of devices to stimulate success. Of these, the so-called Star System was most significant before the Civil War. Supplementing it were such novelties as child actors and actresses, "breeches roles," animals on stage and the sensationalism produced by the stage carpenters. On the other hand, struggling to combat the overwhelming power of the Star System, there were resident companies formed in the large cities.

1.   ENGLISH ACTORS AND ACTRESSES

One of the earliest attempts to infuse some excitement into the theatre was the importation of English actors, a finesse still employed. Two English actors who made reputations in America early in the nineteenth century were the talented Thomas Abthorpe Cooper and the erratic and alcoholic George Frederick Cooke. Charles Mathews' visit to America in 1822-23 provided him with a character idea -- the Yankee -- which made his fortune. As the century progressed, nearly every celebrated English thespian visited America: Edmund Kean, romantic and successful but so arrogant as to antagonize Boston audiences forever; Charles Kemble and his lovely daughter, Fanny; and William Charles Macready, whose professional and personal feud with Edwin Forrest helped stimulate the greatest theatre disaster of the nineteenth century -- the Astor Place Riot of 1849. Most theatres in America before the Civil War, however, were managed by Englishmen, a fact resented by struggling American actors.

2.   AMERICAN ACTORS AND ACTRESSES

English performers added a touch of Old World culture to New World society, but the American theatre also produced notable performers. John Howard Payne had been a successful young actor before he went to England. Junius Brutus Booth emigrated to America in 1821 and provided competition for Edmund Kean. His sons -- Edwin Booth, John Wilkes Booth and Junius Brutus Booth, Jr., the least talented of the three -- made theatre history in America. Charlotte Cushman received ovations as an actress on both sides of the Atlantic before mid-century and enjoyed her reputation for the next twenty years. Joseph Jefferson, III, of Rip Van Winkle fame, was just starting his outstanding career during the period before the Civil War.

Dwarfing all others in acting style, pecuniary success and violence of temperament was Edwin Forrest, a man who prided himself on his physical and personal power. The popular acting style of the day was declamatory, and Forrest has been compared to Daniel Webster, their elocutionary presentation being not significantly different. There was no question of Forrest's leadership in American theatre, and his interest in plays by American authors (those plays, that is, tailored to his specific acting requirements) adds to his position. His success in England was marred only by his "Edinburgh hiss" of William Charles Macready's Hamlet. Beginning with this incident, a personal antagonism between the two actors developed until it reached a climax in the infamous Astor Place Riot. On May 10, 1849, when Macready played MacBeth in New York's Astor Place Opera House, supporters of Forrest precipitated a riot, which ended when the militia fired into the mob, killing thirty-one people and wounding at least 150. But for Forrest, this was only the climax of one act of an exciting life: a scandalous divorce suit provided another. The success of his acting career is matched only by the sensationalism of his life.

No less important to the development of the acting tradition in America were the specialist performers: the Yankee, the Negro, the Irishman, the Dutchman and the New York fireman, Mose. There were also a number of lesser actors and actresses, popular with contemporary audiences, who had substantial reputations in the theatre: McKean Buchanan, J. A. Neafie, Edward L. Davenport, Anna C. M. Ritchie, Josephine Clifton, William Burton, James Murdoch and such actor-managers as Thomas Hamblin of New York's popular Bowery Theatre, Olympic Theatre manager William Mitchell and Laura Keene.

3.   THE STAR SYSTEM

During this part of the nineteenth century, theatre was governed by the Star System, a technique used by theatre people to add interest to a production by "puffing" the talents of a single actor or actress to extravagant proportions. It did add interest, fortune and glamour; but it also had its bad effects, and opposition to it grew throughout this period. In his *Personal Recollections of the Stage,* 1855, William B. Wood cited some of its evils. In its excessive concern for a single star, the theatre suffered from a lack of good supporting actors -- and a surfeit of poorly prepared actors who were wrongly billed as stars. Such "puffing and lying" did not contribute to a healthy theatre. In addition, the Star System rarely allowed time for adequate rehearsals, good casting or the making of effective scenery. There was also the evil of the benefit nights for which an actor might give a superb performance, while slacking off on the nights when the management would get the receipts.

4.   THE GROWING POWER OF THE RESIDENT COMPANY

From the beginning of the century the only form of professional theatre organization was the resident acting company composed of actors and actresses who could, idealistically, perform with or without the support of a visiting star. At first these stock companies were obliged to tour to neighboring towns, but gradually, as cities grew in size, the theatre companies served their public from one location. One of the early managers to build a resident company was William Mitchell at the Olympic Theatre in New York in 1839; in 1843, W. H.

Smith started a resident company for the Boston Museum. Later, William E. Burton in 1848 and James W. Wallach in 1855 opened permanent acting companies in their New York theatres. After reaching a certain point of success before the Civil War, such companies were increasingly weakened by the touring of the complete casts of single plays and by the turn of the century had virtually disappeared.

VII. SUMMARY

From the beginning of the nineteenth century through the Civil War, American drama was clearly that of a new nation imitating what it considered the fashionable and cultural best of Europe and England, while experimenting with the various possibilities for a drama of its own. At the same time, the drama mirrored contemporary social, political and historical movements very closely. Concerned with an immediate appeal to popular tastes in a nation that was strongly nationalistic, playwrights dramatized current events and created and romanticized heroic national characteristics. That the plays of this period were not better may be partially explained by certain factors: the control of the theatre by actors and actresses, the narrow commercialism of mostly English theatre managers, the unsophisticated tastes of the theatregoing public and the lack of copyright protection and, therefore, financial reward for playwrights. It is also true that there were only a handful of playwrights with sufficient imagination and skill to create a play with both high literary quality and audience appeal. In general, this was a weak and stumbling period in the history of American drama, a time of interest in plays for their social, historical and theatrical significance and, for only a few plays, for their excellent qualities. It was also a time of great promise -- when there appeared both theatre entrepreneurs and playwrights whose ideas and productivity clearly foreshadowed better things to come.

It is perhaps ironic that a new and strongly nationalistic country should have produced its best drama in romantic tragedies and melodramas imitative of Europe in style, plot and theme. In many ways, however, these heroic plots and themes suggested to Americans their own struggle for freedom, while the romantic style reminded them of their own adventures in the New World. Barker's *Superstition* claims its distinction among these plays with its purely American theme, in contrast to two other poetic dramas, Bird's *The Gladiator* and Boker's *Francesca da Rimini*. Other plays which deserve to be included among the best are Anna C. M. Ritchie's *Fashion*, with its clever farce-comedy and caricature of American manners; Payne and Irving's *Charles the Second*, another witty farce-comedy with literary pretentions; Nathaniel Bannister's *Putnam, the Iron Son of '76*, a popular spectacle for more than a generation; the accumulative play of *Uncle Tom's Cabin*, the "World's Greatest Hit"; Boucicault's *The Octoroon* and Taylor's *East Lynne* as representative of the best melodramas written during this century; and *Witchcraft; or, the Martyrs of Salem*, the major work of the playwright identified by his generation as the "Father of American Drama," Cornelius Mathews.

This period is also noteworthy for the creation of certain character types and for original contributions to American and world theatre. The characters were Jonathan, Sambo and Metamora, with Jonathan the most popular because he was a national symbol as well as a comic figure. The theatre innovations were the minstrel show, arising from a social phenomenon in America; the showboat, a product of American geography; and the Tom shows, which resulted from the overwhelming success of a sentimental melodrama based on a serious social problem.

As part of the history of American drama, this period has significance, but compared with American literature of that time, the plays are much less important. During these years Irving produced his short stories and essays; Emerson his celebrated essays on "Nature," "Self-Reliance" and "The American Scholar"; Thoreau his *Walden*; Bryant, Longfellow, Lowell, Holmes and Whittier some of their best and most popular poems; Hawthorne and Melville their greatest novels; Poe his stories and poems; and Whitman his *Leaves of Grass*. Obviously, the drama of this period is a country cousin to such lasting literary accomplishments. Yet it was a living and developing drama. As a critic, Poe thought Mrs. Ritchie's *Fashion* worthy of serious consideration. Writing in the

Brooklyn *Eagle* in 1847, Walt Whitman pleaded for "American plays" featuring American opinions and institutions and employing American talent -- as Emerson and others had asked for an American literature. The need for an American drama to match American fiction and poetry was being recognized.

SELECTED BIBLIOGRAPHY

Barnes, Eric W. *The Lady of Fashion.* New York: Charles Scribner's Sons, 1954.

Birdoff, Harry. *The World's Greatest Hit -- Uncle Tom's Cabin.* New York: S. F. Vanni, 1947.

Clapp, W. W., Jr. *A Record of the Boston Stage.* Boston: J. Munroe & Co., 1853.

Foust, Clement. *The Life and Dramatic Works of Robert Montgomery Bird.* New York: The Knickerbocker Press, 1919.

Graham, Philip. *Showboats: The History of an American Institution.* Austin: Univ. of Texas Press, 1951.

Grinsted, David. *Melodrama Unveiled, American Theatre and Culture, 1800-1850.* Chicago: Univ. of Chicago Press, 1968.

Harrison, Gabriel. *John Howard Payne, Dramatist, Poet, Actor and Author.* Philadelphia: J. B. Lippincott & Co., 1885.

Hewitt, Barnard. *Theatre U.S.A., 1665-1957.* New York: McGraw-Hill Book Co., 1959.

Hodge Francis Richard. *Yankee Theatre: The Image of America on the Stage, 1825-1850.* Austin: Univ. of Texas Press, 1965.

Hutton, Laurence. *Curiosities of the American Stage.* New York: Harper & Brothers, 1891.

Jefferson, Joseph. *The Autobiography of Joseph Jefferson.* New York: The Century Co., 1890.

McConachie, Bruce A. *Melodramatic Foundations: American Theatre and Society, 1820-1870.* Iowa City: Univ. of Iowa Press, 1992.

Meserve, Walter J. *Heralds of Promise: The Drama of the American People During the Age of Jackson, 1829-1849.* Westport: Greenwood Press, 1986.

Moody, Richard. *America Takes the Stage.* Bloomington: Indiana Univ. Press, 1955.

_____. *Edwin Forrest, First Star of the American Stage.* New York: Knopf, 1960.

Musser, Paul H. *James Nelson Barker.* Philadelphia: Univ. of Pennsylvania Press, 1929.

Winter, William, ed. *Life, Stories and Poems of John Brougham.* Boston: James R. Osgood, 1881.

Wittke, Carl. *Tambo and Bones.* Durham: Duke Univ. Press, 1930.

Chapter Three

From Profession to Art
The Civil War to World War I

Dramatic changes in literary movements or theatre trends come slowly, with suggestions of things to come first intruding upon the scene for a number of years. Clearly, America's developing drama lost momentum during the Civil War. John Brougham and Dion Boucicault returned to England for the duration, and the seriousness of the conflict narrowed people's thoughts and attitudes. With the coming of peace, theatre in America began to flourish in ways that had once been only dreams. Whether the war had anything to do with these changes is a moot point, but a new kind of theatre person appeared -- the entrepreneur -- and the playwright gained status in the theatre. During the years from the Civil War to the formation of the Provincetown Players and the appearance of Eugene O'Neill just before World War I, the writing of plays changed from a profession in which a playwright could eke out a living by combining hack work with acting or theatre management to an art in which the dramatist achieved financial reward, and his or her play was considered a literary form subject to critical standards.

Although the kinds of plays written during the first half of the nineteenth century persisted in later decades, distinctive changes took place in form and purpose. Melodrama continued to contrast the sweet and sentimental with the vivid and violent, but during the decade and a half before World War I, it assumed obligations which caused critics to talk in terms of "Social Melodrama." Farce had always been popular, and so it remained; yet, it too undertook to comment on society. During the last half of the nineteenth century, poetic drama very nearly disappeared, only to return during the first decade of the twentieth century. Spectacles remained popular -- from vaudeville, Honky Tonk and Wild West Shows to minstrels, burlesques, circuses and musicals.

A major change during the period was a more serious emphasis on realism. Following, although at a distance, the literary realism which distinguishes such major writers as Mark Twain, William Dean Howells and Henry James, all of whom tried to write for the theatre, the drama of the last third of the nineteenth century reluctantly released its firm hold on romantic stories and occasionally shocked its audiences by emphasizing more realistically and more effectively than before the problems plaguing this period which historians have variously called The Gilded Age, The Age of Excess or The Great Barbeque. Dramatists adopted disparate attitudes toward Herbert Spencer's "survival of the fittest" concept. The success of the socially conscious play, plus the growing demands for a literary drama from a developing core of dramatic critics, stimulated an interest in social comedy. A final new trend -- called "A New Seriousness" -- appeared in the plays of those more thoughtful dramatists of the early twentieth century who not only concerned themselves with social and moral issues of a more enduring nature than their predecessors, but also brought greater artistic imagination and insight to their work.

General criticism of American drama before World War I tends to be severe, but the best plays of the late nineteenth and early twentieth centuries pointed toward America's debut into world drama. Ibsen's plays had influenced American dramatists, particularly James A. Herne, and the plays of other foreign dramatists had made an impression. At the same time, American plays were being well received in England and had been produced with some success in European countries. By World War I, America needed the stimulus of dedicated theatre artists and an outstanding dramatist, whom it discovered in Eugene O'Neill.

I. THE RISE OF REALISM IN AMERICAN DRAMA

The Rise of Realism in American literature was a major trend during the last half of the nineteenth century. Starting with local color writers, including Harriet Beecher Stowe, and articulate humorists such as Artemus Ward and Bill Nye, realism followed a European trend which was stimulated by Balzac's *Père Goriot* (1834-35). According to William Dean Howells, who is frequently referred to as the "Father of

American Realism," realism is nothing more than a truthful representation of life. As a reaction against the sentimental writers of the past, however, realism was also a focusing of the universe according to the writer's concept of truth, although his or her ideas of good taste were also involved.

An understanding of realism also requires a knowledge of the consequences of the twin forces of Science and Democracy which affected all aspects of life in late nineteenth-century America: Darwin's *Origin of Species* (1859), Sir Charles Lyell's discoveries concerning the Glacial Age, Friedrich Ingels and Karl Marx's *Communist Manifesto* (1848), Auguste Comte's writings in sociology and Herbert Spencer's attempt to apply Comte's theories to biology, the Civil War, the Homestead Act of 1862, Reconstruction in the South and politics in Washington, the so-called Robber Barons, Thorstein Veblen's age of "conspicuous waste," Samuel Gompers and the American Federation of Labor in 1866. Realism in literature came about because people were forced to look at life less romantically, and a more thoughtful and socially conscious literature mirrored this view. This was the trend that the drama followed.

Certain extremes in the Rise of Realism in the drama can be clearly described, but realism also exists in a variety of forms which may be noted in the work of particular playwrights. Touches of realism appeared before the Civil War in plays that depict certain sections of America through their particular characteristics.   Later, this local color drama became mainly pictorial of New England and the West.   An underlying sense of realism next appeared in the plays of Howells, Steele MacKaye and William Gillette. Realism in the production of a play was another thing altogether, and even the wildest melodramas of David Belasco and Augustin Daly could boast some quite realistic stage scenery. The climax of realistic drama in the nineteenth century, however, was James A. Herne's *Margaret Fleming* (1890).

A.   Local Color Drama: Things American

In literature, the term "local color" describes those stories and poems which clearly suggest some particular locale distinct

from other places.   The distinction is usually made through
characters, dialect (using cacography), customs and scene. The
most frequently mentioned writers of local color could be found
in New England (Sarah Orne Jewett), the South (George
Washington Cable), the Midwest (Edward Eggleston) and the
Far West (Bret Harte).

As do works of fiction and poetry, numerous plays have as an
objective the presentation of life in a particular section of
America. These plays focus on the same areas as the stories and
poems -- New England, the Midwest and the Far West -- while
showing some interest in the South and, continuing a fascination
discovered before the Civil War -- life in New York City.
Frequently, neither characters nor ideas in these plays were
new, but there was a concern for realism in custom, character or
dialect. In a sense, earlier character creations now assumed
legendary characteristics, and the local color plays written
after the Civil War suggest that the population was becoming
increasingly aware of the unique qualities of America.

1.   THE YANKEE BACK HOME:
      NEW ENGLAND LOCAL COLOR

During the 1860s, the Yankee continued to be popular on New
York and London stages, but this Yankee remained a caricature,
a symbol of America. Following the traditions of Seba Smith's
Major Jack Downing and James Russell Lowell's Josea Biglow,
the local color dramatists tried to make the Yankee a
believable New Englander, poised against the customs and
scenes of his native land. Of all New England local color
dramas, none was more popular than *The Old Homestead*.

(a)   Denman Thompson (1833-1911)

After fifteen years as a wandering actor, Thompson finally
found success in 1875 as a Yankee farmer in a thirty-minute skit
called *Joshua Whitcomb,* which he toured for three years in
variety houses. Its phenemal popularity on the road -- 124
nights in Chicago in 1878 -- prompted Thompson, with the help
of George W. Ryer, his business manager, to create a full-length
play called *The Old Homestead,* which opened at the Boston
Museum to "instantaneous success" on April 5, 1886. Happily for
Thompson, who performed the role of Uncle Josh Whitcomb

until his death in 1911, the success of the play was as long lasting as it was instantaneous, supposedly earning him three million dollars.   W. D. Howells ["Editor's Study," *Harper's Monthly*, LXXIX (July 1889), 317] considered Thompson the originator of a typically American drama and *The Old Homestead* one of the "sweetest and simplest" of plays: "On a wider plane than anyone else has yet attempted, Mr. Thompson gives us in this piece a representation of American life."

The Old Homestead did not die with Denman Thompson. Numerous revivals were staged; film versions were made in 1914, 1922 and 1935. In 1927 the play was first published, and performances of *The Old Homestead* may yet be seen each summer at the Potash Bowl near Keene, New Hampshire, and West Swanzey, where Thompson died and is still remembered as a "famous theatrical trouper."

The Old Homestead (1886)
(Plot) At the Whitcomb farmhouse in New England, Josh and his sister, Matilda, entertain Frank and Ann Hopkins, the city-bred son and daughter of Josh's old school chum, Henry. Josh, worried about his son Reuben, who ran away after being falsely accused of stealing, agrees to visit the Hopkins family in New York and there look for Reuben. Then, as a quartet approaches from behind the barn to sing a few sentimental songs, Happy Jack appears, a victim of drink but a clever talker. Soon Josh gives him ten dollars if he will promise to stop drinking.

At the Hopkins mansion in New York, Josh, as "the very embodiment of honesty and rural simplicity," both shocks and charms his host. The next day he hunts for Reuben and becomes involved in the usual greenhorn problems. Meanwhile, Happy Jack, now apparently prosperous, enters, sees a young man in the hands of the law, bribes the policeman and gives the young man a dollar to get something to eat. Then he sees Josh and repays him the ten dollars, as the young man staggers into view again and into the arms of Josh, who sobs, "My boy, Reub!"

Later, back at the Old Homestead on New Year's Eve, fiddle music announces a dance and Reuben's homecoming. After some homespun New England advice for the young'uns, Joshua says a word to the audience -- "Now, you fathers that have got wild boys, I want you to be kind o' easy with them. . . . And, mothers, . . . your hearts are always biling over with love and kindness for the wayward child!" The music starts and all take their places for the Virginia Reel.

(Discussion) Essentially a sentimental melodrama with a strong moral and lots of farce humor, the play includes traditional themes of temperance and the conflict between city and country life. Realistic touches are exploited: New England customs (country dances, a sleigh ride and milking problems), country scenes, references to the Panic of '73 and the actions and speech of the main character, Josh, who is sentimentalized in somewhat the same way as are the characters in local color stories and poems.

(b)   More Local Color from New England
Throughout the nineteenth century, plays set in New England were regularly produced. A good example of the Down East play is *The County Fair* (1889) by Charles Barnard and Neil Burgess. The main character is Miss Abby Prue, a New England old maid who combines a liberal amount of shrewdness with an equal amount of sentiment. The plot tells of a farm, a mortgage, a villainous mortgage holder and a horse that wins enough money at the county fair to pay off the mortgage. Another equally popular play about mortgages, horses and New England is *David Harum* (1900), a dramatization of E. N. Westcott's very popular novel. *Way Down East* (1898), by Lottie Blair Parker, exploits the peculiar dialect of New Englanders in a romantic melodrama that was performed for more than two decades.   D. W. Griffith turned the play into a movie masterpiece starring Lillian Gish in 1920. Several plays by James A. Herne fairly bristle with New England local color: *Drifting Apart* (1888) and *Shore Acres* (1892).

2.   THE WILD WEST IN THE EASTERN THEATRE

The appetite for western drama, started by James Kirke Paulding's *The Lion of the West* (1831), when Kentucky was the West, continued with such plays as Joseph A. Nunes' *Fast Folks; or, Early Days in California* (1859?). Then, in 1868, the sensational appearance of Bret Harte's "The Luck of Roaring Camp" in *The Overland Monthly* suggested characters and actions ready-made for the theatre. The romantic adventures touched Eastern audiences, and playwrights followed the lead of such writers as Harte and Joaquin Miller. The dramatists' major objective, however, was sensational melodrama: violent actions, exciting escapades and exaggerated characters. A good example is Joseph Arthur's *Blue Jeans* (1891), set in rural Indiana and distinguished by a buzz-saw device employed to intimidate the heroine. Local color is secondary, but it is part of the appeal of these plays.

(a)   *Horizon* (1871) by Augustin Daly (1838-1899)

(Plot) Going west to occupy lands from a Congressional grant, Sundown Rowse is accompanied by Captain Van Dorp, an adopted son whose foster father left his haughty wife and, with his daughter, ran away to the West years before. At the land grant, Rogue's Rest, young Van Dorp is attracted to Med, the daughter of Whiskey Wolf (actually the elder Van Dorp). The rest of the play shows how the sentimental gambler, Loder, protects Med against the Indian, Wannemucka, and prepares the way for their marriage.

(Discussion) Augustin Daly, one of the major figures in late nineteenth-century American theatre and drama, contributed to the development of American theatre in the two major trends of the late nineteenth century -- the Rise of Realism and the development of social comedy. Alert to the potential audience appeal of popular fiction, Daly dramatized a Bret Harte story in *Horizon*, copyrighting it as "a play of contemporaneous events upon the borders of civilization." Suggestive of his interest in realism and social events is this comment [A. Daly, "The American Dramatist," *North American Review*, CXLII (May 1886), 485-92]: "Possibly our national drama, from a literary point of view, will reach its best period when native writers vie with each other in illustrating native character and contemporaneous fashion and follies."

Although the main figure in *Horizon* is Sundown Rowse, a caricature of a crooked politician and Washington lobbyist, other characters suggest the West and Bret Harte's creations:

the gambler, the drunkard who wants to take care of his daughter before he dies, the bad Indian and the various citizens of Rogue's Rest. Most of the play is laid in the West, but the atmosphere is very moral and romantic. The scene and the characters present local color; the plot involves the melodrama of murders, Vigilante Committees, Indian raids, mysterious letters and rescue by American soldiers.

(b) Adaptations of Frontier Life:
Joaquin Miller (1839-1913) and Bret Harte (1836-1902)
Many stories by Harte and Miller were adapted to the stage. These writers also adapted their own works of fiction or wrote original plays. Miller, known popularly as the "poet of the Sierras," wrote four plays -- *The Danites of the Sierras* (1877), based on two of his short stories; *Forty-Nine* (1881); and *Tally Ho* and *An Oregon Idyll*, both published with his poems in 1910 but presumably never performed. *The Danites*, about a rough but goodhearted group of miners whose lives are changed by the arrival of a widow, was quite successful on the stage.

A more ambitious playwright, Bret Harte wrote several weak plays, five of which never saw the stage. *The Two Men of Sandy Bar* (1876) was a failure in the theatre; and *Ah, Sin* (1877), in which Mark Twain collaborated, fared scarcely better. The best dramatizations of Harte's stories were written by other people, and of these playwrights Bartley Campbell (1843-1888) was the most successful with *My Partner* (1879). Generally, literary figures who were part of the local color movement could not please theatre audiences.

(c) Other Plays Across the Continent
T. W. Henshaw's *The Forty-Niners* (187?), advertised as a "great national drama of pioneer life, faithful to the civilization and incidents it portrays," is typical of plays set in the West but shows little knowledge of it. Laid in the Sierras, it has an extremely artificial and melodramatic plot which is not related to the Sierras. *Nevada; or, the Lost Mine* (1882) by George M. Baker is another of the frontier plays in which Bret Harte's characters find themselves in amazingly melodramatic situations. Other plays include *How Women Love* (1876) by Bartley Campbell, revised as *The Vigilantes; or, the Heart of*

the Sierras (1878), and *A Gold Mine* (1887) by Brander Matthews (1852-1829) and George Jessop (d. 1915).

James J. McCloskey (1825-1913)

McCloskey is best known for *Across the Continent* (1870), a sensational melodrama, sensationally acted by Oliver Doud Byron. Building upon a temperance theme and the violence of big city life until Act III, which is set in a Far West station of the Pacific Railroad, the play is replete with Indians, a gallant hero, a despicable villain, a trainload of soldiers and complete reliance upon certain telegraph messages. *The Far West; or, the Bounding Fawn of the Prairie* (1871), also based upon McCloskey's knowledge of the West, is one of the "hundred or so" plays he presumably wrote.

Augustus Thomas (1857-1934)

Remembered as the author of well-made melodramas of a more subtle nature than the frontier drama could boast, Thomas also contributed to the local color drama of the West and Midwest. *In Mizzoura* (1893), a play of rural setting in which realism of customs and character is emphasized, has a melodramatic plot in which a girl, returning from college to a home of poverty, finds excitement and love. *Colorado* (1901) was a failure. An earlier western play, *Arizona* (1899), with the usual melodramatic plot but better than average characters, is set in a part of Arizona that Thomas had observed closely in 1897 and which he recalled successfully to provide scene and atmosphere. Thomas' work is distinguished by his serious concern for portraying aspects of life realistically.

David Belasco (1853-1931)

A strong advocate of realism in the American theatre, Belasco was a writer of successful melodramas, mainly in collaboration with others. During one period of his complicated career, he wrote plays which show not only his great skill in writing melodrama but also his knowlege of the West, where he lived as a young man. *The Girl of the Golden West* played for three years after it opened in 1905 and was later made into a grand opera by Puccini. As an example of local color, it became popular through its language, characterization, background scenery and western traditions. Briefly, the play dramatizes the story of Minnie Falconer, known as The Girl, and her first love, Johnson (or Rammerez) the highwayman. She gives him her first kiss, hides him when he is wounded, gambles with the sheriff for his life and cheats to assure victory, wins over the jury of miners with her pleas for Johnson's life and finally leaves with her hero for a bright future.

Davy Crockett (1872) by Frank Murdock (1843-1872)
(Plot) Raised in the backwoods with Davy Crockett but now part of city society, Eleanor passes through Davy's settlement with her fiancé, Neil, and a group going west. Worried about a mysterious plot in which Neil is involved, she appeals to Davy. Later, separated from their group by a blizzard, Eleanor and Neil arrive at Davy's hunting cabin. While Neil sleeps, Eleanor inspires Davy to declare his love by reading the story of young Lochinvar. Having burned all the cabin furniture, even the bar to the door, to keep warm, they find only one way to keep the door closed against marauding wolves: "The strong arm of a backwoodsman." The next day, swollen arm and all, Davy hikes ten miles to save Neil, who is dangerously ill. When Eleanor later learns that Neil's uncle has power over her guardian and demands the marriage so that he may control her fortune, she tells Davy that she is his if he rescues her. This he does, quoting young Lochinvar as they ride away. At last she is happy in the "heart and home of Davy Crockett."

(Discussion) With Frank Mayo in the title role, *Davy Crockett* was a box office success in England and America until Mayo's death in 1896. Owing some debts to the life of Davy Crockett and others to Scottish history and Sir Walter Scott's *Marmion,* this play uses the background of the Tennessee trapper against the contrasting falseness of city and foreign society to build an idealized picture of the American backwoodsman. Davy is a "naturel gentleman" who follows his father's motto: "Be sure you're right, then go ahead." In local color terms, the play emphasizes something of the language of the backwoodsman and the peculiarities of his life.

3. LOCAL COLOR IN THE SOUTH

Plays set in the South vary from the popular war plays to numerous melodramas of the romantic South. Civil War plays appeared with such titles as *The Union Spy* (1871) by L. W. Osgood, *The Virginia Veteran* (1874) by Thomas Power and *Hal Haggard; or, the Federal Spy* (1883) by Fred Andrews. These plays, however, show only incidental interest in anything but romance and excitement. Both David Belasco and William Gillette exploited the theatricality of the war with a modicum of realism, but *Shenandoah* is the epitome of the romantic Civil War melodrama and, with its extravagant use of horses, achieved tremendous popularity.

(a) *Shenandoah* **(1888) by Bronson Howard (1842-1908)**
(Plot) After a ball in a Charleston home, some of the guests wait to see if Fort Sumter will be shelled. Among those waiting are Kerchival West and Robert Ellingham, lieutenants in the U.S. Army, who discover that they are in love with each other's sisters, Madeline West and Gertrude Ellingham. But Kerchival and Madeline are from the North, and the Ellinghams are from the South. As the shells burst over the Fort, the friends must part to fight on opposing sides. After many complications, lovers are reunited and all ends well.

(Discussion) Whatever Howard's reason for writing this play -- perception of the tastes of the time or in imitation of William Gillette's successful *Held by the Enemy* -- it is a thoroughly romantic tale in which the author attempts some realism in his characters and in his picture of Southern society.

(b) Southern Local Color Melodrama
Among the Southern melodramas, one was much like another, as the following review of Charles Calahan's *Coon Hollow* (1894) makes clear (New York *Herald*, August 28, 1894):

> You know the recipe for making a play of this sort. The scene can be laid in Tennessee, because you can thus get a background of the Mississippi by moonlight. The principal ingredients are invariably an extremely chivalrous 'Southern gentleman,' a mountaineer, 'rough on the outside, but true at the core' -- at fitful moments; a callow youth, who generally wears riding boots and acts foolishly, and a maiden of preternaturally smart naivete. You season it with a villain of inordinate wickedness and

of perfectly incredible shortsightedness. Add a dash of steamboat races, Negro quartets and cotton compresses. Garnish with wild mountainous scenery.

4.   **LOCAL COLOR IN NEW YORK:
     EDWARD HARRIGAN (1844-1911)**

In the "Editor's Study" of *Harper's Monthly* (July 1886), William Dean Howells praised Harrigan's various immigrant characters, whose touches of realism suggested to him "the spring of a true American Comedy." He called him "the American Goldoni," after the Venetian dramatist who presented the working people of Venice in such a lifelike manner. Others, for comparable reasons, called Harrigan "the American Dickens." Harrigan, a native of New York, did not fulfill the prophecy, but he did contribute good farces to American drama and paid shrewd attention to realistic detail in his creation of the street life of lower Manhattan. Each of his little plays, he wrote in *Harper's Weekly* [XXXII (February 2, 1889) 97-99], was intended as a "series of photographs of life today in the Empire City." To provide these he used authentic places and character types, made realistic by close attention to speech, dress, gestures and lifestyle. Although he felt that human nature was "most virile and aggressive among those who know only poverty and ignorance," Harrigan believed in portraying "the fact that right-doing, kindness, and good nature are in the majority."

Joining an acting company about 1867, Harrigan formed a very popular acting team for his farces, playing the male roles himself, while Tony Hart (Anthony J. Cannon, 1855-1891) impersonated the women. As "Harriganandhart" they sang, danced and performed in more than sixty of Harrigan's high-spirited farces, first at the Theatre Comique and then at Harrigan's Theatre Comique, until this theatre burned and they separated in 1884. Many of the sketches deal with the Mulligans of Mulligans' Alley in New York's Sixth Ward, which Harrigan, born in New York, knew well. Here, with elaborate stage business, meticulous attention to realistic detail and a comedian's enthusiasm for the "general melee" which characterize many of his plays, Harrigan assembled his interracial community. There are the Wee Drop Saloon, run by

Walfingham McSweeny, an Italian junk shop, a Chinese laundry-lodging combination and a Negro social club called the Full Moon Union. The Boston *Herald* once aptly referred to Harrigan's plays as the scene of the "war of the races in cosmopolitan New York."

As riotous fun, Harrigan's farces are both the reflection of the serious activities and social movements of his generation and an antidote to the grimness which they frequently unveil. *Reilly and the Four Hundred* (1890) contrasts social levels; *The Mulligan Guard Nominee* (1880) is a broad satire on politics; *The Mulligan Guard* (1873) is a burlesque of the target-shooting expeditions of military organizations. His plots provide excitement; the temperaments of the characters add the necessary violence; and Harrigan, confessing to being provincial and optimistic, tried always to be "truthful to the laws which govern society."

The Mulligan Guard Ball (1879)

(Plot) With more chaos than logic, the play revolves around the planned elopement of Dan Mulligan's son, Tommy, and Katy, the daughter of Lochmuller, the butcher. Although both sets of parents are violently opposed to the marriage, the couple elopes during the intermission of the Grand Ball, which explodes into a great fight when the ceiling collapses and the ball of the Skidmore Guards, a Negro group, being held in the Red Man's Hall above the Harp and Shamrock Ballroom, joins the Mulligans in a "Grand Crash." Finally, the Lochmullers and the Mulligans are reconciled when Gus Lochmuller and six of his butchers, armed with meat cleavers, help Dan Mulligan get rid of the bill collectors for the Ball.

B.   Realism and Melodrama

The beginnings of realism in the drama can be described only in general terms. Howells' definition of realism as the "truthful representation of life" may be interpreted to include the truthfulness that appears in many aspects of a pre-Civil War play -- the characters, the scene, the incidents, the background customs or the ideas. A new approach to a "truthful representation of life," however, did come after the war, bringing with it certain problems for the dramatist, whose success depended upon an immediate appeal to a large, unsophisticated audience. Realism as a genre became suspect as people felt that, in their effort to be truthful about life, playwrights were forsaking the bounds of good taste and were sometimes even immoral. James A. Herne suffered particularly from this criticism. As late as a few years before World War I, one playwright lamented that "the conflict between romanticism and realism leaves the American playwright in a quandry almost cruel." ["Cruel Dilemma of the American Playwright," *Current Literature*, LI (September 1911)] Consequently, few dramatists writing during the fifty years between the Civil War and World War I concentrated on presenting realistically truthful incidents and views of life or avoided idealizing and exaggerating their characters. Suggestions of an interest in the literary movement of Realism, however, can be found in many plays.

1.   "AUTOCRAT OF THE STAGE":
      AUGUSTIN DALY (1838-1899)

Augustin Daly made his reputation in both playwriting and in the theatre. His tremendous energies brought him acclaim as a drama critic, theatre manager, original playwright, adaptor of foreign plays, producer and adaptor of Shakespeare and manager of a company of actors that successfully carried Shakespeare and other dramas to Europe in 1884. His career reached its pinacle in 1893, when he opened his own theatre in London. As a drama critic and theatre manager, he encouraged American playwrights to a limited extent, but he was not an innovator. He did little to promote realism, and he did not try to improve the audience's taste or to encourage a literary drama. Rather, his constant advice to dramatists was that they write according to the requirements of theatre managers. It was as a theatre manager that Daly is best known, as the "Autocrat of the Stage" who controlled his actors more tyrannically than other entrepreneurs of the period. Not having the promotion of American drama as a primary interest, he became, in both theory and practice, a negative influence on its development. With the secret collaboration of his brother Joseph, however, he wrote or adapted more than ninety plays

-- sensational melodramas, farces and a few social comedies. As a creator of exciting melodramas, in fact, he had few peers among his contemporaries.

Under the Gaslight (1867)

(Plot) This is the story of Laura Courtland, the extremely virtuous heroine, whose engagement to the wealthy Ray Traffort is broken when the dastardly villian, Byke, claims her as his daughter. Snubbed by society, she leaves New York, protected by Snorkey, a Civil War veteran, and Peachblossom, a girl of the streets, but is constantly pursued by Byke and old Judas. For a while Laura lives with her cousin, Pearl, who now plans to marry Ray; but the villains appear once more, and Laura, planning to leave on the morning train so as not to mar the happiness of Pearl and Ray, has herself locked in the baggage shed of the railroad station for the night. Faithful Snorkey follows to protect her, but is overcome by Byke and tied to the railroad tracks before the eyes of Laura, who grabs an axe from a handy bundle in the shed, breaks down the door, and rescues him just in the nick of time. For melodrama, this scene is hard to beat. In the last act, all ends happily for the good and the virtuous: Ray and Laura are to be married; Snorkey and Peachblossom have matrimony in mind; and the goodness of Laura makes it possible for Byke to "emigrate."

(Discussion) Although the plot of Under the Gaslight is as fantastic as any of the nineteenth-century melodramas, there are suggestions of realism in the railroad scene; in the one-armed Civil War victim, Snorkey, whose condition is a social comment; in the satirical picture of the snobbish high society; and in the general authenticity of the scenes: Delmonico's in New York, the Tombs and the Pier on the Hudson River.

2.   ERRATIC GENIUS: STEELE MACKAYE (1842-1894)

Among the late nineteenth-century theatre entrepreneurs, Steele MacKaye was an actor, a teacher of actors, a theatre manager, an architect, a playwright and an inventor. Best known for his improvements in stage design and equipment, such as the elevator stage, his ultimate theatrical dream was the Spectatorium (480 feet long, 380 feet wide and 275 feet high), conceived as part of the Chicago World's Fair of 1893 for the production of MacKaye's chronicle of Columbus, *The World Finder.* The building process, however, was disrupted by the Panic of '93, and the structure itself was destroyed by a storm, reducing his dream to a much less ambitious theatre called the Scenitorium. MacKaye was a dreamer and a genius, to whom theatre was a temple of art and culture, and his determination to provide the most favorable aesthetic conditions for both actors and audiences was enhanced by his crusade for realism in acting and "true-to-life" dialogue.

Although playwriting was a secondary part of MacKaye's career, his plays have significance in the development of American realism. Three of them boast a distinctive realism in characterization. *Won at Last* (1877) is a tender and romantic farce-comedy with a believable hero and a well-drawn heroine who discovers on her wedding day that her husband is cynical and has married her simply because, as he states, she is "well bred, cultivated, and good; she will make me at least a tolerable companion and save me the ridicule and disgrace of a fashionable wife's flirtations." Although the play becomes melodramatic in the last act, it took a firm step toward both realism of character and social comedy. In *Paul Kauver* (first performed as *Anarchy* in 1887), MacKaye revealed his indignation over what he considered the unfair trial of the anarchists in connection with the Chicago Haymarket Riot of 1886. The immediacy of the theme and the sincerity of the author produced a realistic tone in both character and dialogue.

Hazel Kirke (1880)
(Plot) The setting is England. When, many years back, Aaron Rodney loaned him money that saved his mill, Dunston Kirke promised him his daughter, Hazel, for his wife. Now, when Dunston discoveres that Hazel has fallen in love with Arthur Carringford (Lord Travers), he turns her out of his home with a curse: "May my eyes never more behold thee." Believing themselves married, but tricked by Arthur's valet with a Scottish ceremony on the English side of the border, Arthur and Hazel face difficulty when Arthur's mother insists that he marry another girl. Shocked and contrite, Hazel returns home and promises to be Rodney's wife if he will ask Dunston to accept and forgive her. But Dunston, now blind, refuses.

Seconds later, he hears that Hazel is drowning in the mill race. She is, of course, saved by Arthur, who promises her marriage, and is forgiven by Dunston: "Hazel, coom to my heart!"

(Discussion) The success of MacKaye's best-known play, *Hazel Kirke*, at the Madison Square Theatre in New York was so great that during the 1882-83 season there were fourteen companies touring the play. Basically, it is a sentimental melodrama, although without a real villain; speeches are sometimes exaggerated, and emotions are frequently made melodramatically vivid. Casting a refreshing light over all this are a quality of humor and a tendency toward naturalness in both characters and incidents. Dunston is a stubborn man, willfully wrong in his actions, but his honor and his passion are, in Hazel's character, the very qualities which determine her ways and precipitate the conflict.

3.   REALISTIC ACTOR: WILLIAM GILLETTE (1855-1937)

Whereas MacKaye was a playwright whose main concern was for stage settings, William Gillette was a playwright whose chief interest was in realistic acting: "the artistic representation of reality." As an actor, William Gillette's most effective role was that of the calm, clear-headed person who works quietly, quickly and efficiently in very trying circumstances. Almost all of the plays that he wrote, whether farce or melodrama, contain such a character. Of his twenty full-length plays, Gillette acted in nine and was particularly successful as Thomas Beene in *Held by the Enemy* (1886), Captain Thorne in *Secret Service* (1895) and Sherlock Holmes in Gillette's popular dramatization of that fictional character's exploits: *Sherlock Holmes* (1899), whose title role he recreated on stage more than 1300 times during the remainder of his life. In a 1913 lecture entitled "The Illusion of the First Time in Acting," Gillette explained his approach to realistic acting in his plays, which are now remembered more for his performance than for literary merit.

Secret Service **(1895)**
(Plot) Edith Varney, daughter of General Varney of the Confederate Army, loves Captain Thorne and tries to keep him in Richmond by persuading President Jefferson Davis to appoint

him to duty in the telegraph office. Meanwhile, Captain Arrelsford of the Confederate Secret Service, suspecting Thorne of being a Union spy, one of two brothers operating in Richmond, brings the brother they have in prison to the Varney house. When the brothers meet, the prisoner whispers a message, grabs Thorne's gun and shoots himself, allowing Thorne to turn him over to Arrelsford. Later, Thorne appears at the telegraph office and starts to send the whispered message. Amidst a great deal of action and frustration, Edith shows Thorne's commission from President Davis, which she says is only to save Thorne's life -- not for "anything else." Sentimental love wins when Thorne revokes his message and allows himself to be arrested. Because he did not send the message, Thorne's death warrant is set aside, and, aware of Edith's undying love, he is marched away to prison.

(Discussion) Encouraged by the success of *Held by the Enemy,* a Civil War play plotted around the love of two men for the same woman and the heroism of a Confederate spy, Gillette wrote *Secret Service.* It is noteworthy that the play was not a popular success until Gillette started acting the role of Captain Thorne in 1896. There is realism in the economy of language in the play, and, as usual with Gillette's work, in its action. Suggesting a realistic unity of action, the four acts take place at 8, 9, 10 and 11 o'clock on a single evening.

C.   William Dean Howells (1837-1920): The Reticent Rebel

Called the "Father of American Realism," W. D. Howells is usually considered a critic and a writer of fiction illustrative of the "commonplace" realism which he championed. He was also a serious dramatist who wrote thirty-six plays, proposed a theory of realistic drama and contributed significantly to both the Rise of Realism in the drama and the development of a social comedy. Opposed to sentimentality in both fiction and drama, he was a definite rebel among his literary and theatrical contemporaries. His reticence was suggested by his strong concern for taste and morals in his own writing. Although he could approve of the more realistic plays of Ibsen and Herne, he could not write as these dramatists did. He was, however, a realist, reticent or not, whose novels such as *A Modern Instance* (1882) shocked many of his readers; and his plays are an excellent illustration of the Rise of Realism.

1.   THEORY OF REALISTIC DRAMA

Howells' theory of drama was simply a logical extension of his theory of fiction (*Criticism and Fiction,* 1891) with the added qualifications made necessary by the limitations of the stage. He saw the drama as "distinctly a literary form" the purpose of which was to illustrate life in terms of morality and truthfulness.   The dramatist should avoid verse drama, soliloquies, asides and the *deus ex machina,* which were not a part of life. By the turn of the century, Howells' comments on truthfulness in drama matured from truthfulness of characters and action to a fundamental truthfulness of idea.   Employing these criteria, he assessed America drama.

2.   REALISM IN SCENES, CHARACTERS AND INCIDENTS

Realistic detail was fundamental to Howells' writing, and his plays are filled with references to contemporary events and real persons -- the invention of the phonograph, the cholera epidemic in New York in 1893, the humor of Bill Nye and Josh Billings.   Actors' speeches were loaded with commonplace phrases and the overused expressions of everyday conversation. Plays were based upon his own experiences and those of his friends. (Twelve of Howells' plays employ the same major characters: Mr. and Mrs. Willis Campbell are modeled on Mr. and Mrs. Samuel L. Clemens; Mr. and Mrs. Edward Roberts are Mr. and Mrs. Howells.) Equally realistic and more significant are the social events or situations around which Howells' plays are built. There are formal dinners or afternoon teas -- events in which the social background has an important effect on the action and meaning of the play. The activity is of real and orginary life; people stay in hotels, by flowers, write letters of introduction and lament the Christmas rush.

3.   REALISM IN IDEA

Accompanying Howells' concern for the more or less superficial characteristics of realism was his insistence on truthfulness and moral value. In his own plays he tried to present problems of real life in which truthfulness was a central issue. *A True Hero: Melodrama* (1909), for example, suggests a way in which man may equate truth and reality in life. *The Unexpected Guests* (1893) describes the failure of the socially convenient lie and the triumph of truth. Writing mainly farces, Howells faced difficulties in achieving his objectives, but he was able to involve his characters in his one-act plays in the more meaningful of life's situations by using the same characters in a dozen plays and thereby allowing them to develop over time. In a few of his longer plays, he maintained his realism of ideas by dramatizing his own novels -- *A Foregone Conclusion* (1886) and *The Rise of Silas Lapham* (1898).

4.   A REALISTIC FARCE: *THE GARROTERS* (1885)

(Plot) The scene is the Roberts' living room a few moments before a dinner party on a cold, stormy night. Having been sent out on an errand, Mr. Edward Roberts enters, exhausted, disheveled and frightened. Believing that a thief snatched his watch as he crossed Boston Common, he was obliged to wrestle the man to the ground and recover his property. Mrs. Roberts is at first astounded, but as the guests arrive, she begins to brag about her husband's exploits. Then in the doorway appears poor old Mr. Bemis, Sr. -- exhausted, disheveled, a woeful creature and not a little angry. He, too, has been garroted on Boston Common, and his watch has been stolen. The situation is now clear to Roberts -- who has gone to his room and found his own watch on the dresser -- and to Willis Campbell, who tries to get him to make a joke of the experience. As Roberts faces Bemis, however, his humor deserts him, and he flounders helplessly until Dr. Lawton, another guest, exposes Campbell's trick, having already disclosed to the other guests that Roberts is the garroter, a badly mistaken and frightened one at that. And even old Bemis agrees to forgive. Given an intelligent and sophisticated society, the situation is not complicated. Roberts quickly promises to mend the watch chain that he broke and -- dinner is served!

(Discussion) When Howells started writing plays, theatre managers wanted full-length plays with exciting, violent and passionate action. Howells, on the other hand, was interested in dramatizing the common, everyday actions of the average person. Although Howells was not completely successful in satisfying commercial theatre audiences, his attempts are significant; his plays, filled with the realism of everyday life, combine some quiet drama with a literary quality that could not be matched by his contemporaries.

The Garroters was one of Howells' more successful one-act plays, even praised by G. B. Shaw, who saw a production in London under the title *The Dangerous Ruffian*. As a farce, it has the clever intriguer, the good man who is fooled, the victim, the hysterical and not-so hysterical observers. One of his Roberts-Campbell plays, it has the characters familiar to his audiences; and, typical of Howells' farces, the plot is based on an actual event of which Howells had become aware.

D. James A. Herne (1839-1901): An Epoch Marking Realism

In the history of American drama, the career of James A. Herne is an obvious milepost of distinction. Like other theatre entrepreneurs of the latter part of the nineteenth century, he was an actor-manager-playwright. Unlike his peers, Herne felt the forces of science and democracy that challenged all sensitive Americans. Breaking out of the confining network of theatre people, he became friends with William Dean Howells, Hamlin Garland and Stephen Crane and was influenced by the writings of Henrik Ibsen, Thomas Hardy and Emile Zola. Interested in the trend toward realism in literature, he attempted to combine and focus a sensitivity for good literary drama and a sound knowledge of the theatre. Although his success was only relative, his significance lies mainly in (1) his development of realistic themes and character in his plays, particularly in *Margaret Fleming*, (2) his interest in a literary drama and (3) his creation of a realistic creed in "Art for Truth's Sake in the Drama."

1. A THEORY OF REALISTIC DRAMA

Unlike theatre realists who emphasized authenticity in scene construction and acting, Herne attempted to create a drama of ideas in the same realistic vein that had altered the development of fiction in America. No American dramatist came nearer to Ibsen's playwriting style than Herne. When, in February 1897, the magazine *Arena* published "Art for Truth's Sake in the Drama" (XVII, 361-70), Herne was merely trying to do for the drama what had already been done for fiction.

"Art for Truth's Sake," wrote Herne, "emphasizes humanity." As a serious mode of expression, according to Herne, "Art for Truth's Sake" perpetuates everyday life, develops the commonplace aspects of life, dignifies labor and abhors injustice. The drama, Herne declared, must "express some *large* truth" which "is not always beautiful but in art for truth's sake it is indispensable." Like Howells, Herne believed that the drama had a "higher purpose" than to amuse: "Its mission is to interest and to instruct." Although these ideas seem harmless enough and Herne seems a weak imitation of Ibsen, his most realistic play, *Margaret Fleming,* was as unacceptable to American audiences as Ibsen's *Ghosts.* With this play and his essay on "truth," Herne suggested the real beginnings of modern American drama, but he did not have an immediate following. "Epoch marking" rather than "epoch making," his influence was lost until a later generation of dramatists who -- although most of them had never heard of James A. Herne -- were impressed by the same voices that had inspired him and by the upheavals in modern European drama.

2.   EARLY PLAYS

Herne started his acting career in 1854, toured with Helen Western's company and became a stage manager in San Francisco, where he met David Belasco. Writing plays with Belasco or in the Belasco manner for the next twenty years, Herne gave little evidence of his later accomplishments. *Within an Inch of His Life* (1879), which he and Belasco adapted from a story by Gaboriau, and *Hearts of Oak* (1879), also written with Belasco, were melodramas with typical sensations and spectacles. With *The Minute Men of 1774-75* (1886), his first original play, he employed New England local color and Yankee dialect. Not until *Drifting Apart* (1888), with his realistic portrayal of a New England fishing village, did he attract the attention of Howells and Garland. Four years later, with Uncle Nat Berry in *Shore Acres* (1892), Herne created the true "Downeaster" and later became a millionaire.

3.   *MARGARET FLEMING* (1890)

(Plot) The play opens in the private office of Philip Fleming, an easygoing fellow whose motto is "Live and Let Live." Then Dr. Larkin enters, angrily stating that he has just delivered a child to Lena Schmidt and that Philip is the father.   He demands that Philip visit Lena.   Reluctantly, Philip agrees and calls home, lying easily as he creates a story to explain his absence to his wife, Margaret, who is concerned for their baby's nursemaid.   Maria, the nursemaid, is upset because her unmarried sister has just had a baby and is now near death. The next day, after Dr. Larkin has explained that Margaret has glaucoma and must not become excited, Margaret complies with Maria's plea to visit her sister.   When she arrives, however, the sister -- Lena -- is dead, and Maria bitterly tells Margaret that Philip is the father of the child.   In a strong scene, Margaret sends a note to Philip: "I am waiting for you here.   That *girl* is dead."   Then she takes the baby, and "scarcely conscious of what she is doing, suddenly with an impatient, swift movement, she unbuttons her dress to give nourishment to the child." A week later at the Fleming home, Margaret, now blind and with Lena's baby as well as her own, awaits news of Philip, who has run away.   When he appears, ashamed and contrite, Margaret forgives him, although "the wife-heart has gone out of me."   Pleased, Philip tells of his hope to win her back again; and Margaret replies: "I don't know. That would be a wonderful thing . . . . And we must get to work." Inspired, Philip goes to see the children, and a "serene joy illuminates her [Margaret's] face" as the curtain falls.

(a)   The Reception of *Margaret Fleming*

After a brief tryout in Lynn, Massachusetts, in 1890, and the subsequent refusal of theatre managers to produce his play, Herne was forced to rent Chickering Hall in Boston, where, before Howells, Hamlin Garland and other realists, the play was presented on May 4, 1891, and ran for three weeks. In December, it was taken to New York, where it failed.   After that it was seldom produced. Its reception clearly suggests the romantic inclinations of the average theatre audiences of that time and supports a consensus that the American theatre simply was not ready for a play of that kind, just as it had refused to accept Ibsen's *Ghosts* two years previously.

Some people, however, those interested in more realistic drama, were enthusiastic in their approval. Hamlin Garland's review of the Boston performance ["Mr. and Mrs. Herne," *Arena* (IV, October, 1891), 543-60] applauded the "utter simplicity and absolute truth to life" that made this play superior to others on the American stage "in purpose, in execution, in power." New York critics were less sympathetic. The reviewer for the *Dramatic Mirror* (December 12, 1891) found no pleasure in *Margaret Fleming*, only "the details of unpleasant and unhealthy forms of unruly life." Edward A. Dithmar, in the *New York Times* (December 10, 1891), noted the realism in the play, which he compared to the news in the morning paper, but did not see the artistic creation. Although his view had some validity, his general approach relegated the play to the obscurity which other critics suggested.

(b)   Realism in *Margaret Fleming*
Reminiscent of Howells' work, Herne's play calls attention to the small details which show realism in character and incident: the general conversation, the instructions to the cook and -- though shocking to the audience -- Margaret's gesture of nursing the baby. From the beginning, Philip is an easygoing fellow, insensitive and materialistic. Herne cleverly compares him to Joe Fletcher, a secondary character who turns out to be Maria's husband and provides some comic relief. Joe is the bad example of what liquor and immorality can bring to a man; they are very much alike, but Philip has been luckier. Margaret is a sensitive and emotional, yet protected, person; but when she does face the ugly world, she has all of the strength and power that her faith in the goodness of mankind has made possible. Conscious of rights and wrongs, her moral fiber and her forceful will give her a control over her destiny that Philip lacks. At the end of the play, she feels contentment in the knowledge that she has done what was right, and this feeling can sustain her.

The theme of the play shows Herne's interest in social philosophy, particularly social determinism. Philip's status in society saves him from suffering the consequences of being the kind of man he is. It is different for Lena, as Dr. Larkin explains: "The *girl's* not to blame. . . . Under present social conditions, she'd probably have gone wrong anyhow." Herne's use of a rose as a symbol of social growth is well integrated into this theme. Margaret's lullaby tells of blossoms that must go out into the world and weep. She had hoped a particular rose would bloom on her baby's birthday, but it did not, and Philip later plucked it. She loves flowers and in Act IV appears with an armful of roses. The doctor, however, confesses that his roses are full of bugs, and she advises him to spray them: "Don't you know that the time to prevent trouble is to look ahead? From potatoes to roses, spray before anything happens -- *then* nothing *will* happen." But who can do the spraying? Only those who rise above their fates!

4.   *THE REVEREND GRIFFITH DAVENPORT* (1899)

Based on a novel by Helen H. Gardener entitled *An Unofficial Patriot,* Herne's play tells the story of a southern man who is morally opposed to slavery, although he has slaves of his own. When the Civil War begins, one of his sons fights for the North, the other for the South. He himself is misunderstood by the slaves he has freed, and his anti-slavery theories arouse bitterness among his neighbors. Forced to leave his home, he goes to Washington and, at Lincoln's request, prepares a map of Virginia and leads Union troops to his home, where he is captured by his own son. In his review of the play, John Corbin ["Drama," *Harper's Weekly*, XLIII (February 11, 1899), 139] calls it an essay in stage realism -- "quiet, humorous, sincere, deeply intelligent, and artistic."

II. THE BEGINNINGS OF SOCIAL DRAMA: COMMENT, COMEDY AND MELODRAMA

Hand in hand with the Rise of Realism in drama was the development of a drama built around various aspects of society. Although plays had mirrored society -- albeit with some distortion -- since Revolutionary times, by the beginnings of the twentieth century there were melodramas dealing with serious subjects, as well as strong beginnings for a social comedy. The American drama critic, John Corbin, noting these beginnings in "The Dawn of American Drama" [*Atlantic Monthly*, XCIX (May 1907), 632-44], as well as the difficulties involved, pointed out the refusal of theatre managers to produce a play by G. B. Shaw as an illustration of their lack of artistic judgment.

It is questionable whether any of the playwrights during this period were capable of writing true social comedies. Howells could write witty dialogue and accurately describe society, but he lacked the sophisticated detachment of the comic writer and the dramatic instinct that contemporary audiences required. Daly was mainly interested in supplying a commodity; Gillette wrote to satisfy his own acting demands; Steele MacKaye was concerned mainly with the development of the theatre proper; Belasco and Boucicault emphasized spectacles; Bronson Howard understood good plotting but lacked literary skills and could not seem to avoid melodrama; Henry C. DeMille, David D. Lloyd and Archibald C. Gunter showed potential, but Clyde Fitch came closest. Social comedy, in its best sense, required an interested theatre management, a sophisticated audience and the talents of an imaginative playwright. Hence, America enjoyed mainly comedy and melodrama that commented on society.

In an essay entitled "The Development of American Drama" [*Harper's*, XLII (December 1920), 75-86], William Archer, the English critic, wrote: "A favorite generalization with regard to the American stage is that it excels in 'shirt-sleeve drama' and is weak in the drama of society." It is a combination of the "shirt-sleeve" or realistic drama with an awareness of society and its problems which distinguishes the drama of this period. Mainly in melodrama, and more or less seriously, the playwright began to treat the social, economic, political and religious issues of the day. It was an active period for American playwrights -- from the Civil War until World War I -- and a time of growing social problems that frequently appeared, in one form or another, on the American stage.

A. Toward a Social Comedy

Social comedy is usually defined as a witty portrayal of fashionable life in which the complex manners or moral actions of the characters become a major concern of the dramatist, who must create motivated actions and believable characters with a facile pen and a detached attitude. The attempts at social comedy written during those years, unfortunately, do not fulfill completely these requirements, but the faults and foibles of high society were beginning to attract dramatists. John Geoffrey Hartman, in *The Development of American Social Comedy from 1787-1936* (1939), called the years between the Civil War and 1900 the Transition Period, placing it between the Period of Caricature, 1787-1860, and the later Establishment of Social Comedy by Clyde Fitch. With due consideration for Fitch's dramatic skills, his plays, and those of Langdon Mitchell, can only be accepted as prominent among plays most nearly approaching social comedy in America. A handful of other dramatists of this period also showed interest in the themes and techniques of social comedy.

1. AUGUSTIN DALY AND SOCIAL COMEDY

Two plays by Daly which indicate his concern for social comedy are *Divorce* and *Pique*. Both were popular successes, and both were adapted, at least in part, from English novels. The basic situations in both plays suggest social comedy -- marriage problems, divorce -- but in each instance, Daly failed to achieve comic detachment and manipulated his characters and action into melodrama. In *Divorce* his satire on the hypocrisy of divorce lawyers provides an interesting side issue.

(a) *Divorce* (1871)

Encouraged by her ambitious mother, Louise Ten Eyck marries the old but wealthy Dewitt, while her sister Fanny accepts Alfred Adrianse, a childhood beau who has just inherited his father's fortune. Grace, a cousin of the Ten Eyck sisters, is in love with Harry, a young minister; but, being poor, they must postpone marriage. Three years later, Louise and Dewitt are about to separate, and Alfred is jealous of Fanny's attentions to a Captain Lynde. The plot then becomes farcical, as the lawyers try to create good cases for divorce and fail when the two couples forget and forgive. Grace and Harry become part of that sentimental group of poor but happily married people.

(b) *Pique* (1875)
Lovely Mabel Renfrew, part of a very fashionable society and much sought after by men, is refused by Raymond, the man she loves, because she has no money. To make the insult more stinging, Raymond then addresses his attention to Mabel's rather young and widowed stepmother. But Daly does not take advantage of this situation to create effective social comedy. Instead, Mabel reacts impulsively and with pique: she hastily accepts the marriage offer of Arthur Standish, an honorable and likeable fellow whom she had once refused. Unable to adjust to life with Arthur, she angrily tells him that she married him only from hurt pride and that she still loves Raymond. Then the play becomes melodramatic. Arthur leaves; their child is kidnapped; with the help of her father-in-law, Mabel foils the villain; she and Arthur are reunited; and Raymond marries her stepmother.

2.   "THE DEAN OF AMERICAN DRAMA":
BRONSON HOWARD (1842-1908)

A serious dramatist who evolved his own principles of dramaturgy ("The Laws of Dramatic Construction") and was one of the most successful of late nineteenth-century American playwrights, Bronson Howard earned the title of "Dean of American Drama" by making a professional career out of playwriting. Although he was not interested in drama as literature, he was concerned with the playwriting profession. He founded the American Dramatists Club in 1891 (later the Society of American Dramatists and Composers, the forerunner of the Dramatists Guild) and worked to extend legal protection to the dramatist's art. His established success in both England and America was along the lines frequently suggested by Augustin Daly: he was a fine craftsman who collaborated with the theatre people and used well his expert knowledge of the stage and the actor's art.

Although Howard was a member of the "Syndicate School" -- dramatists for the Theatre Syndicate that controlled many theatres at the turn of the century -- he had greater vision than his commercial-minded contemporaries. He saw, for example, that the direction of the drama was toward social comedy and that in America the businessman was becoming increasingly important. He also emphasized the international aspect of social life and by so doing attempted to dramatize themes which W. D. Howells and Henry James had exploited in popular novels. Original in much of his work and interested in a theory of drama, Howard was limited by the many conventions and requirements of the theatre, but he did point the way for others who, with greater talent and more interest in literary drama, were to follow him.

Both Brander Matthews, American writer, teacher and critic, and A. H. Quinn emphasized the point that Howard wrote during a transitional period. Before him, a staple of the American stage had been foreign plays; yet, during his lifetime Howard was able to give the American dramatist greater importance in the theatre. Although a few of his plays were adaptations and he retained in his work many of the conventions and devices that had made foreign drama popular in America, he forced managers to see the value of American playwrights and paved a more secure way for the younger dramatists who would follow him.   Much of this he accomplished through personal force and written precept. His creative work may be divided into three general categories: the plays that deal with some aspect of society, those that emphasize American business and his single war play, *Shenandoah* (1888).

(a)   A Theory of Drama
Bronson Howard's "Laws of Dramatic Construction," as he described them in *The Autobiography of a Play,* present his more important ideas on the drama. Mainly, he demanded a well-constructed or "satisfactory" play -- which meant that the play must be satisfactory to the audience. For example, audiences in England and America would not accept, Howard believed, the death of a good person in a tragedy; death must be deserved. He also declared that those who err (for example, a wife who has soiled her moral character) must always die before the final curtain falls. Similarly, a love triangle must always bring disaster.   Obeying his laws of dramatic

construction, Howard stated, was "merely the art of using your common sense in the study of your own and other people's emotions." The playwright, he noted, should deal "so far as possible, with subjects of universal interest." Playwrights should put upon the stage only their best work, acknowledging the advice and assistance of others; and they should always keep in mind the sympathies of their audience, as well as the motives and actions of their characters.

(b)   The Social Plays

Howard's early farces were distinctive only for their better-than-average dialogue and some ingenuity in plot; but they only suggest his interest in contemporary society. *Saratoga* (1870) is a good example. Using a favorite American resort as its scene, it presents the farcical involvement of Bob Sackett with four women, while fashionable society provides a background for the comic situations. The fact that *Saratoga* was adapted by Frank Marshall for the English stage under the title *Brighton* (1874) suggests a current popularity more than a universal appeal. *Diamonds* (1872), called a "comedy of contemporaneous manners" by Brander Matthews, follows society downstate to New York City and Staten Island. *Hurricanes* (1878) is a similar type of play.

As American fortunes began to increase, an awareness of European culture became fashionable among the *nouveau riche*. Consequently, the international comedy of manners intrigued writers, and Howard plumbed its possibilities in several plays. *Met By Chance* (1887) uses an international contrast as a basis for its plot. Howard's last play, *Kate* (1906), dramatizes the story of a rich American girl who becomes engaged to an English earl. *One of Our Girls* (1885) contrasts Julie -- living in France and engaged to a French count to satisfy her desire for a title and his interest in her dowry -- with her rich cousin from America, Kate. The plot is melodamatic, but the freedom in choosing a mate which Kate enjoys is effectively justaposed to the restrictive traditions which bind Julie.

(c)   The Business Plays

Howard's understanding of the importance of American business during the late nineteenth century and his ability to portray this characteristic of society effectively in his plays are both evidence of his insight and an achievement which distinguishes his work. His conscious use of a socio-economic movement and his employment of fashionable society as a background are significant contributions to American drama.

Young Mrs. Winthrop (1882)
This play was praised by Odell (quoting "some critics," *Annals of the New York Stage*, XII, 19) as "the great American drama so long and so ardently awaited." "This beautiful piece," Odell wrote (p. 18), was in accomplishment and solid effect one of the finest things yet written for the American stage. In this play, Howard dramatized that increasing complexity of the business and social worlds which can prevent a man and a woman from finding happiness together in their home. Left alone by a husband immersed in business, Mrs. Winthrop finds some relief in the social whirl. After a brief separation, husband and wife are reunited through Howard's preachments.

The Henrietta (1887)
An extremely successful play satirizing life on the Stock Exchange, *The Henrietta* is concerned with the financial rivalry of Nicholas Vanalstyne, Sr., known as "the Napoleon of Wall Street," and his son, Nicholas, Jr.   Both are unscrupulous men to whom business is "health, religion, friendship, love -- everything." Taking its title from the Henrietta Railroad, control of which is an issue, the play was erroneously hailed by critic John Corbin as the earliest of a new kind of play -- the business play.

Aristocracy (1892)
This play presents the American businessman in the international situation. Jefferson Stockton is a California capitalist, a millionaire who knows that new millionaires -- like him -- are not of good society. When his daughter, Virginia, is refused by Stuyvesant Laurence, the son of an old and proud New York family, Stockton realizes immediately that the quickest way to enter New York society is via London society. The rest of the play caricatures society in London before the Stocktons return to New York and, presumably, happiness.

3.   WILLIAM DEAN HOWELLS (1837-1920)
AND THE COMEDY OF PROPER SOCIETY

Howells identified most of his one-act plays as farces, but this judgment cannot always be accepted without reservations. Several of these plays show the characteristics of social comedy. In addition to his one-act plays, Howells wrote two long comedies early in his career: *Out of the Question* (1877), concerned with a problem of propriety -- What constitutes a gentleman? -- and *A Counterfeit Presentment* (1877), one of his more successful stage plays, with Laurence Barrett in the leading role.   With its charming and witty comments on society, the latter play tells of a delicate heroine, who is brought to a New England resort hotel by her parents to recover from an abortive romance, only to meet a man whose appearance is identical to the man who she thinks jilted her.

It was mainly in his one-act plays, however, that Howells presented the society that he knew best -- Boston's Back Bay aristocracy. As a group, these plays clearly reveal his acute powers of observation, as well as the high degree of critical insight required by the writer of the social comedy. His favorite scene was the formal dinner, and his favorite people the Robertses and Campbells, whom he featured in a dozen plays which explore various social emergencies.

(a)   The Roberts-Campbell Plays
The first of the Roberts-Campbell plays appeared in 1883, and during the next ten years, Howells wrote ten more plays with these characters, returning to them only once after that period. Although there is a disparity in the dramatic value of these plays, a good number of the characters are believable and human. Amy Cambell is a shrewd woman, while Mrs. Roberts is as scatterbrained as she is kind. Dr. Lawton is a delightful talker, and Willis Campbell a charmer as well as a schemer. Enacted within an atmosphere of propriety, the Roberts-Campbell plays show a mature, sophisticated, convention-bound society, in which tradition has replaced thought, and action and words have become nearly equal in importance.

What may be called a twelve-act play starts when Mrs. Roberts returns to her home in Boston in *The Sleeping Car* (1883) with her baby and her Aunt Mary, whom she has just visited in Albany. Christmas is doubly meaningful this year because Mrs. Roberts' brother, Willis Campbell, is returning to Boston from California, where he has lived for a number of years. Two Christmases later, in spite of an elevator mishap (*The Elevator*, 1884), the Robertses give a formal dinner, and the audience meets their friends -- the Millers, the Curwins, old Mr. Bemis, his son Alfred, Dr. Lawton and his daughter, Lou. Alfred and Lou will be married before the next Christmas dinner, at which poor old Mr. Bemis will be mistakenly garroted by Mr. Roberts in *The Garroters* (1885).

The next three plays follow the activities of Willis Campbell: first, he flirts with Amy Somers, a young widow, in *The Mousetrap* (1886); then he becomes engaged to Amy, who, in *Five O'Clock Tea* (1887), has waited the proper period of time since the death of her husband; finally he becomes involved in the problems of being a husband in *A Likely Story* (1888). Other plays show Willis as a farce intriguer: in *The Albany Depot* (1889) he taunts Mr. Roberts, who is meeting a new cook whom Mrs. Roberts has just hired; in *Evening Dress* (1892) he helps Roberts find his dress suit. Much closer to social comedy are *A Letter of Introduction* (1892), in which Roberts' absent-mindedness is exploited, and *The Unexpected Guests* (1893), in which Amy Campbell faces that social emergency. *A Masterpiece of Diplomacy* (1894), in which the Robertses face the problem of having called two doctors of different medical persuasions to treat a very simple illness, shows much of the Howells wit and charm. *The Smoking Car* (1900), the last play in the series, however, turned out to be a weak and disappointing farce.

(b)   Social Comedy and Satire

One comic theme which seems to have fascinated Howells was the ever-present struggle between man and woman -- a frequent theme in his Roberts-Cambell plays. Numerous times, Howells treated this conflict in a plot involving an engagement, which is either being made for the first time or being patched up after some confusion. No fewer than seven plays have similar plots on this theme: *The Parlor Car* (1876), *The Register* (1883), *A Previous Engagement* (1895), *An Indian Giver* (1897), *Her*

Opinion of His Story (1907), *Parting Friends* (1910) and *Self-Sacrifice* (1911).

One of Howells' major strengths in the drama was his ability to write brilliant conversation -- far more witty and clever than anything else being written in America at this time. (James A. Herne believed that Howells wrote the "most charming comedies" he had ever read and once proposed that Howells write a "comedy in connection with a play like *Margaret Fleming*.") Enhancing his wit was his gift for satire. With a certain mischievousness, Howells pointed out the ridiculous attitudes and foibles of society and the socially acceptable person. A good illustration of his skill is *A Letter of Introduction* (1892), in which he ridicules Englishmen, New Yorkers, critics, Boston snobbery, the cultivated family of Boston, American artists, American language and American culture. In his later plays -- *The Night Before Christmas* (1910) and *The Impossible* (1911) -- Howells was more serious, less flippant and more pessimistic in his satire.

4.   OTHER WRITERS OF SOCIAL COMEDY

It is tempting -- and quite necessary in "outline histories" -- to illustrate a popular fad or even a serious movement with reference to only the major practitioners. But, of course, many other dramatists (for various reasons less successful) contributed substantially to the trend toward social comedy. In addition to major newspapers and such journals as *Harper's* and *The Dramatic Mirror* during the last quarter of the nineteenth century, magazines such as the New York *Clipper, Puck, The Critic* and *Century* provided supporting evidence of their work.

(a)   Henry C. DeMille (1850-1893)

DeMille's first play, *John Delmer's Daughter* (1883), dealing with family problems and social climbing, did not succeed on stage, but a later play, *The Main Line* (1886), a frontier melodrama written with Charles Barnard, toured the country. But it was in collaboration with David Belasco that DeMille made his reputation, and four of their plays were among the most popular of the period. *The Wife* (1887) dramatizes a husband's resolve to win the love of his wife, who has married him out of pique. E. H. Sothern, acting the title role in *Lord*

Chumley (1888), made a memorable theatre experience out of a manipulated story involving the adventures of an English nobleman. *The Charity Ball* (1889) contrasts a strong clergyman with his weak brother. *Men and Women* (1890) builds upon the banking and business worlds.

(b)   David D. Lloyd (1851-1889)

Lloyd, a journalist for the New York *Tribune,* advocated realism in the drama and might have contributed more substantially to American drama had he not succumbed to an early heart attack.   *For Congress* (1883) and *The Senator* (1889) show the backroom politicking and the society of Washington, D.C., which supported such activities. In *The Woman Hater* (1885) he created a minor vehicle for John T. Raymond, a comic actor who was best known for his role as Colonel Mulberry Sellers in an adaptation of Mark Twain's *The Gilded Age.*

(c)   Archibald C. Gunter (1847-1907)

Born in England, Gunter worked as a mining engineer in San Francisco before moving to New York, where he wrote novels and plays. Not a serious critic of society's faults and foibles, Gunter nevertheless enjoyed poking fun, as he did in *Ada* (1879), which deals with social-climbing people in New York and their marriage problems, and in *The Deacon's Daughter* (1887). In his best-known play he adapted his own successful novel, *Mr. Barnes of New York* (1888), concerned with the adventures of a rich and impudent American.

5.   CLYDE FITCH (1865-1909) AND THE SOCIAL WORLD

The traditional criticism of Clyde Fitch describes him as a skillful man of the theatre and a master of stage effects who brought with him the practiced eye of the observer of society and a singular talent for writing realistic dialogue. Although he lacked genius, he was immensely clever at capturing the idiosyncrasies of individuals and society -- particularly those of New York. To satisfy the actors and theatre managers for whom he wrote, Fitch used some of the devices of melodrama that had proved successful, but he otherwise became absorbed in detailed observations of particular social or personal foibles which, in his most successful plays, he exploited to create social comedy. When he carried his enthusiasm for truthful detail to excess, however, the result was either a caricature or an over-abundance of what his detractors termed "Fitchian detail."

(a)   Popular, Prolific and Prosperous

A colorful figure who sported a twirlable black mustache, Fitch was a conscientious and hard-working playwright. Asked to write a play for Richard Mansfield, the actor, he produced *Beau Brummell* (1890). During the next nineteen years he wrote thirty-three original plays and adapted twenty-two novels or foreign works. Writing easily and without haste, he was able to work on as many as five plays at the same time. His popularity is illustrated by the 1901 theatre season in which four of his plays were running in New York theatres at the same time. Clearly helped by America's signing of an international copyright law in 1891 and his membership in the "Syndicate School," Fitch became the first millionaire dramatist in America. In England, several of Fitch's plays met with considerable success, particularly *The Truth* (1906), which -- acted in several European countries -- gave him an international reputation.

(b)   Theory of the Drama

In *The Clyde Fitch I Knew* (1909), Archie Bell quotes the information which Fitch usually gave to aspiring playwrights:

> Write the play as it seems to you. Brevity is important. Things must move fast. Study the works of others, but don't imitate. Don't follow rules, but there are guiding principles. Revise your work thoroughly. Study doubtful situations. Prune out superflous words. Try to be truthful.

According to Bell, Fitch wanted to reflect "absolutely and truthfully the life and environment about us; every class, every land, every emotion, every motive, every occupation, every business, every idleness!" But his concern for truth was without the larger prospective of life. His plays, combining aspects of comedy and melodrama, were written with a sensitivity which inspired critics to describe Fitch as a man of whom better work might be expected.

(c)   Social Plays: On Married Life

Of Fitch's fifty-five plays, only six or seven warrant serious consideration as social comedy.   Fitch's first full-length play on society, *A Modern Match* (1892), tells the story of a flippant and selfish wife, who refuses to assume the responsibilities of marriage and therefore must suffer the consequences of the unfaithful wife.   There is, however, little of Fitch's later talent here among his exaggerated characters, artificial stage directions and melodramatic plot.

Her Great Match (1905), which shows Fitch's understanding of European as well as American manners, involves an international contrast between an American girl and the Crown Prince Adolph of Eastphalia. The dinner scene at the beginning of *A Happy Marriage* (1909) is excellent Fitch, but the play later dissolves into an uninspired discussion of marriage.

(d)   Social Plays: Social Climbers

In *The Social Swing* (1893), an adaptation of Sardou's *La Maison Neuve,* Fitch described two people who embark on an extravagant social life and become frivolous, immoral and bankrupt. Beneath a melodramatic plot, *The Climbers* (1901) satirizes aspects of the New York social life and, in particular, the "climber."   Although considered shocking by some New York managers, the opening scene of the play is one of its best from the point of view of social comedy as it ridicules the hypocrisy and unfeeling materialism of the members of the Hunter family after the funeral of Mr. Hunter: "Oh, my dear, that's just it! The watchword of our age is self! We are all for ourselves; the twentieth century is to be a glorification of selfishness, the Era of Egotism."

(e)   Social Vices: Individual and Collective

Fitch never became a social dramatist of the first order because he wrote for the "Syndicate" and remained "a man of the commercial theatre." In his most successful plays, however --- *The Girl with the Green Eyes, The Truth* and *The City* --- he emphasized social vices and concerned himself with character development, the realistic details of conventional society and a more socially significant conflict and struggle.

The Girl with the Green Eyes (1902)

(Plot) Jinny Tillman is a jealous, nervous person who shows her weakness on the day she marries Jack Austin. When Jack tries to help Jinny's brother Geoffrey, who made an unfortunate marriage during his college days and now loves Ruth Chester, Jinny is inflamed with jealousy at Jack's apparent attentiveness to Ruth. Circumstancial evidence further clouds the situation, as a thoughtless Jack causes Jinny to attempt suicide. As in all good melodrama, however, she is saved by the dramatist's manipulation of time and Jack's inconsistent character. All ends happily.

(Discussion)   The exposition for this play employs the traditional servant scene, and the jealousy is clearly fore-shadowed. Minor characters provide humor in a Dickensian fashion. Only Jinny is a well-developed and clearly motivated character. There is some good wit, as well as irony and excellent satire, not only on New York society but also on American tourists and European guides. The happy ending was a requirement of the "Syndicate School."

The Truth (1906)

The heroine of *The Truth* is Becky Warden, who, like Jinny Austin, has inherited a particular vice: she is a pathological lier, whose husband is an honest as Jack Austin is blindly unsuspecting. Called "the greatest play ever written by an American author" when it was tried out in Boston, *The Truth,* nevertheless, failed on the stage in New York in 1907. Soon afterwards, however, it was produced in several European countries and played in London for over a year. Barrett Clark, theatre historian, called it "one of the few genuine American comedies of manners."

The City (1909)

(Plot) In Middlebury, New York, the Rand family is preparing to move to New York City, until George Rand, Sr., tells his son, George, that he is being blackmailed by his illegitimate son, Hancock. He then dies from the shock of his confession. Years pass; the family has moved to New York; and George is about to become a candidate for governor. As he prepares to show that his record is clean, Cecily, his sister, arrives to tell him that she and Hancock were married that morning. When he tells the newlyweds that they share the same father, a mentally deranged Hancock kills Cecily and tries to commit suicide. George is forced to explain everything to the police, and the scandal ruins his political career. He and his wife, now facing the truth, turn their backs on "the city" and try to find hope for the future.

(Discussion)   In this play, Fitch changed his theme from individual vices to the evils that characterized society: for people bred in a small town the city has an evil influence. This thesis, however, is not well managed in the play.   The unhappiness of Fitch's people comes, at least in part, as a consequence of the plotting of a degenerate offspring born of moral hypocrisy in that very same small town. The evil is in the person, not the city. The language, like some of the ideas in the play, is stronger than Fitch's usual fare and suggests a more naturalistic tendency in his work, but the tone is still that of social melodrama.

(f)   Achievements in Social Drama
Fitch contributed to the reputation of American drama abroad by being the first American playwright to gain a significant international reputation.   In the development of American drama he has a place of importance, but he was less a literary figure than a product of the commerical theatre.   Walter Pritchard Eaton, in the "Dramatist as Man of Letters" [*Scribner's Magazine*, XLVIII (August 1910), 490-97], considered him a theatre craftsman who combined acute powers of observation with skill in characterization and a concern for careful productions.   Rather than establish a social comedy in America, Fitch defined more clearly than his predecessors a base from which social comedy could be written.   Just as Howells presented his truthful observations of society in farce, Fitch developed some believable characters and painted his social observations on the backdrop of melodrama.

6.   LANGDON MITCHELL (1862-1935): ONE "STERLING COMEDY"

Langdon Mitchell was a dramatist and poet whose reputation rests on one play, *The New York Idea* (1906), which A. H.

Quinn called a "sterling comedy." Since its first production with the celebrated American actress Mrs. Fiske in the leading role, *The New York Idea* has been successfully revived and translated into several foreign languages. Other plays by Mitchell include a poetic tragedy, *Sylvian* (1885), and a successful adaptation of William Thackeray's *Vanity Fair* entitled *Becky Sharp* (1899).

The New York Idea **(1907)**
(Plot) In the Phillimore living room, the mother, sister and aunt of Philip Phillimore, a pompous Supreme Court Judge just divorced from Vida Phillimore, cooly greet Philip's fiancée, Cynthia, the ex-Mrs. John Karslake. When Vida Phillimore and John Karslake drop by, a farcical chaos results. Disturbed by the Phillimore family, Cynthia, a race horse enthusiast, delays the wedding in order to make a trip to Belmont Park. She is also tormented by indecision and is jealous of Vida's attentions to John. Finally, when the wedding starts and the bored choirboys burst into song, Cynthia realizes her mistake and runs off to prevent John from marrying Vida. She is successful, of course, and after she and John talk things over, the play turns into a melodrama and love finds its way.

(Discussion) The play is filled with quotable lines about marriage, divorce, society and family. "Marriage is three parts love and seven parts forgiveness of sin." The wit and literary quality of some of the dialogue contrast with the farce action and elevate the theme.

B. Issues and Attitudes

Writing of "the tendencies of the American stage" [*Cosmopolitan*, XXXCIII (November 1904), 15-22], Daniel Frohman, the American theatre impressario, noted that the theatre had made inroads into many aspects of everyday life. He was optimistic that there was "much that should furnish good, sound, convincing and interesting material for a successful American play." And he was right. Beginning in the late nineteenth century and becoming stronger in the early twentieth century, there was a rising interest among playwrights in various issues and attitudes. Using farce, comedy or melodrama, playwrights now joined other writers who were trying to say something meaningful about the many forces and institutions that were America.

1.   SOCIAL ISSUES AND ATTITUDES

Just as American dramatists early in the nineteenth century had grasped at nearly every social aberration or problem, as well as any event that took the public's attention for any length of time, dramatists eagerly found material for their plays in the increasingly complex society of late nineteenth-century America. In some instances they showed a commitment to Horace's dictum which turned melodrama and comedy into progaganda, bending that advice to the advantage they sought. In so doing, they foreshadowed the more determined behavior of their followers in the 1930s.

(a)   The Temperance Issue

Temperance has always been a thesis dear to the hearts of reformers and sensation hunters. Major dramatists, such as James Herne, showed the evils of drink in a number of plays. Another popular playwright, Charles H. Hoyt, attacked intemperance in *A Temperance Town* (1893) by pointing out that forced prohibition may not be a good thing, but temperance certainly is.   Alice Brown's *Children of Earth* (1915) dramatizes the serious problem of the drinking wife. There are also numerous plays by journeyman playwrights like George M. Baker and the professional reformers who used the drama to promote their objectives: Mrs. L. D. Shears, *The Wife's Appeal* (1878); T. S. Denison, *The Sparkling Cup* (1879); George H. Booth, *The Drunkard's Dream* (1882); and Charles Alkisson, *Ruined by Drink* (1889).

(b)   Race Differences

Illustrating one of those inconsistencies in a land where "all men are created equal," Americans were fascinated by racial and national differences.   In the early American plays, dramatists had exploited the distinctive characteristics of Negroes and Indians, as well as Yankees, who were almost a race in themselves. Soon these characters were joined by the Irishman and the German.   After the Civil War, Edward Harrigan emphasized the international flavor of New York, and the Yankee became a New Englander. Meanwhile, the Indian character nearly disappeared from the stage; the Negro continued to be portrayed as a minstrel and as a sentimental retainer, occasionally becoming the subject of serious drama. Then the Jew made an appearance.

The Jew as a Stage Character

The Jew was seen on stage primarily as a businessman. George H. Jessop (d. 1915) was born in Ireland and died in London but contributed abundantly to the theatre in New York with farces, most written in collaboration. In *Sam'l of Posen* (1881) he showed Sam as a Jewish immigrant store clerk who vows to own the business in a year. Odell (*Annals of the New York Stage*, XI, 257) wrote that "*Sam'l of Posen* was the Jewish commercial traveler, with most of the brass required by his profession." *Caught in a Corner* (1886), by W. J. Shaw, portrays Isaac Greenwald, the Chicago Board of Trade and an attempt to corner the wheat market by a woman speculator. In a more serious but still melodramatic picture of the Jew, Augustus Thomas created Dr. Seelig, who acts as the *raisonneur* in *As a Man Thinks* (1911). Edward Harrigan also pictured the Jew in his numerous New York farces. One of the most successful plays featuring Jews (outside the developing Yiddish theatre in New York City) was *Potash and Perlmutter* (1913), adapted from stories of Montague Glass (1877-1934) by Charles Klein with the help of Glass. In this play, two Jewish businessmen are transformed into Hebrew comedians, arguing incessantly and wittily, yet sharing joys and sorrows.

The Indian Character

The Indian lost his popularity as a highly romanticized hero when John Brougham burlesqued *Metamora* and *Pocahontas* in mid-nineteenth century. After the Civil War the Indian continued his stage career as a friend or foe of the "white man," either singularly or in groups. Throughout most of the nineteenth century there seemed to be theatre audiences eager for Indian plays. Ned Buntline's *The Scouts of the Prairie* (1873) starred Buntline, Buffalo Bill Cody (who made his fortune with the Wild West Shows), Texas Jack Omohundro and twenty Indian warriors. There were *The Red Mazeppa* (1872), featuring Jinnie Arnott Silver Spear; *Oroloso; or, the*

Dead Shot of the Sierra Nevadas (1873), with Frank Fayne, Clara Butler and Little Frank Fayne; and Harry Seymour's *Sitting Bull; or, Custer's Last Charge* (1876).

Slowly a change came, and the Indian finally became part of the social climate. *Squaw Man* (1905) by Edwin Milton Royle (1862-1942) dramatizes the romantic struggle of an English soldier who must choose between the Indian woman whom he loves and has married and the girl and the earldom waiting for him in England. That same year, 1905, William C. DeMille (1878-1955) wrote *Strong Heart*, which presents the love story of an American Indian boy and a white girl. The heroine is determined to marry the boy until she discovers that he must return to his tribe as chief. Realizing that she could not tolerate the primitive living, she changes her mind. By far the best portrayal of the Indian is found in *The Arrow Maker* (1911), the story of medicine woman's love for a young Indian, by Mary Austin (1868-1934).

The Negro Character

A familiar sight in minstrel shows and as the sentimental or humorous servant in plays, the Negro was occasionally dramatized as an object of racial discrimination, as shown in Herne's *The Reverend Griffith Davenport* (1899). One of the few plays to show a Southern view of the Negro was *The New South* (1893) by Clay Greene (1850-1933) and Joseph Grismer (1849-1922), which emphasizes that the Negro should be "kept in his place because he was an undesirable character." A different treatment of the race problem is illustrated in *The Nigger* (1909) by Edward Sheldon (1886-1946), the story of a Negro-hating governor who discovers that he has a Negro ancestor. As a melodrama, it is artificial and improbable, but it shows a forceful character in Governor Morrow, who, at the end of the play, leaves the southern girl to whom he is engaged and prepares to tell the people about his heritage. Clayton Hamilton ["New Theatre and Contemporary Plays," *Bookman*, XXX (January 1910)] found it impossible to consider the play seriously, but its serious theme would be dramatized many times. George J. Nathan, writing near the middle of the twentieth century, cited *The Nigger* as one of the ten dramatic shocks of the century.

(c)   The Marriage Scene and the Woman's World

The play for which Bronson Howard is best known, *The Banker's Daughter* (1878) tells the story of a woman who quarrels with the man she loves and marries an older and wealthy man to save her father from financial ruin. Circumstances cause her to reveal her perfidy to her husband, thus creating a triangle which Howard resolves through the death of the first love and the strengthening of the husband-wife relationship. When World War I broke out, Howard's play was still being produced, and his subject matter had become stock-in-trade on the American stage. In the *New York Times* of April 8, 1900, Edward A. Dithmar writes of *A Man and His Wife* by "George Fleming," pseudonym of Julia C. Fletcher, that it has the "old, old subject of marital infidelity, the subject of so large a portion of all the comedies."

The marriage scene -- struggle, separation and reunion -- was a more than frequent theme. A woman's world seemed to absorb the thoughts of many of the more successful dramatists: Clyde Fitch, Langdon Mitchell, Henry C. DeMille, David Belasco and Rachel Crothers (1878-1958). *The Woman Hater* (1885) by David D. Lloyd (1851-1889) gave John T. Raymond a fine role. In 1890 Augustus Thomas' wrote *A Woman of the World* as a sequel to *A Man of the World* (1889).   Ann Crawford Flexner examined *The Marriage Game* (1913), and two plays by A. E. Thomas (1872-1947) stress husband-wife relationships: Thinking that she is dying, a woman decides to choose *Her Husband's Wife* (1910) but is too successful and decides to live in order to compete with her "choice" when her husband mentions divorce to shock her into contentment; *The Rainbow* (1912) shows how the daughter of separated parents brings about their happy reunion.

(d)   A Woman's Place

Henry Adams, historian and author of America's most distinguished autobiography, *The Education of Henry Adams*, once wrote that "the proper study of mankind is woman." Playwrights have evidently always agreed. From such a play as Dion Boucicault's *Formosa: The Most Beautiful; or, the Railroad to Ruin* (1869), which dramatizes the fate of the "fallen woman," to Rachel Crothers' plays featuring the

self-sufficient woman, however, was a tremendous step. A new
force of women was beginning to be apparent as the century came
to a close; more realistic struggles of women were dramatized.
W. D. Howells' plays -- *The Mousetrap,* for example --
frequently emphasize the moral superiority of women. James
A. Herne's *Margaret Fleming* shows a woman of great moral
strength and courage. By the time Percy MacKaye wrote
Tomorrow (1913) it was clear that great things were expected of
women. Explaining his play in a preface, MacKaye wrote:
"the concept of women as the creative arbiter, through selection
of our race and its future, must constitute a living theme for
national thought and action." Florence Keper discussed "Some
American Plays" in *Forum,* 51 (June 1914), 921: "Any play
produced on the American stage, with perhaps a few negligible
exeptions, has its say on the feminist question."

Women's rights plays had existed for half a century, although
most were inconsequential -- Alfred Ford's *Jael and Sisera*
(1872); anon., *The Late Convention of Strong-Minded Women*
(1873); Eleanor Freeman's *When the Women Vote* (1885).
During the decade immediately preceding World War I,
however, the consequences of women's suffrage activities in the
real and theatrical worlds became more interesting. While
Margaret Fleming suggests a double standard for men and
women, Rachel Crothers attacked this idea in *A Man's World*
(1909): When an independent and self-supporting woman
writer named "Frank" Weir, living with an adopted child,
discovers that the man she loves is the father of that child and
the destroyer of the child's mother, she expects him to assume
responsibility. But he demurs: "What do you expect? We don't
live under the same laws. It was never meant to be. Nature
made men different." Other plays by Crothers emphasize
similar themes: *He and She* (1911) and *Ourselves* (1913).
Augustus Thomas' *As a Man Thinks* (1911) presents another
view. Dr. Seelig, the voice of truth, declares: "There is a
double standard of morality because upon the golden basis of
woman's virtue rests the welfare of the world."

Differing views appeared and disappeared, but the feminist
question remained popular in the theatre. Edward Sheldon's
The High Road (1912) traces the spiritual growth of a modern

woman who is self-supporting and therefore responsible for her own decisions. George Middleton's *Nowadays* (1914) treats the equality of woman; his heroine proposes to a man and also assumes that she has the right to have a career. As plays dramatized the woman's growing strength in the world at large, however, the inevitable burlesques appeared. One was William C. DeMille's one-act farce, *In Nineteen Ninety-Nine, a Problem Play of the Future* (1914); in which the man cares for the child while the woman has become the breadwinner and the family protector. A double standard still prevails in the play, however, and while she "flits around from sin to sin, " he fears the false step which will damn him forever. Boucicault's *Formosa* had returned!

(e)   Problems of Immorality
Another social issue that some dramatists treated was that of immorality, which they, of course, opposed in proper fashion. Adultery is often suggested but always indirectly, and the woman involved is never allowed to escape condemnation. Bronson Howard had made such a denouncement mandatory in his discussion of *The Banker's Daughter:* "The wife who has once taken the step from purity to impurity can never reinstate herself in the world of art on this side of the grave." Seduction is treated in such plays as *The Charity Ball* (1888) by Henry C. DeMille and David Belasco, in which the seducer is made to marry the girl; or in the western plays, in which a villain makes an "honest woman" of the girl before he is hanged. Howells had stated that every dramatist was also a moralist, and dramatists in the late nineteenth century generally took it upon themselves to be judges, too.

When a house of prostitution was portrayed on stage by Bayard Veiller in a play called *The Fight* (1913), the critics voiced bitter indignation at "all its tawdry horrors." Veiller, however, defended his play in the *New York Times* (September 21, 1913), stating that it "was taken incident for incident from a warning sent out last year by the Traveler's Aid Society to girls in all parts of the country." That same year, 1913, Charles Rann Kennedy completed his one-act play on prostitution, *The Necessary Evil*. Witter Bynner's short play, *Tiger* (1913), shows how a girl is lured into a house of prostitution, thinking that she will marry the man who takes her there.   In a sensational climax, she is saved by her first customer, who turns out to be her own father.   As the theatre was becoming increasingly realistic in presenting the more sordid aspects of life, critics became more vocal.

The Easiest Way (1908) by Eugene Walter (1874-1941)

Eugene Walter was a newspaper man who became a writer of well developed and skillfully constructed melodramas. *Paid in Full* (1908) contrasts the strong woman and the weak man in a realistic manner, but *The Easiest Way,* as a study of a weak woman, is one of the most effective melodramas of the period, showing definite changes in theatre tastes and a concern for disagreeable truths. Laura Murdock is the money-loving, easy-going heroine. When she falls in love with John Madison, she has already lived with many men, most recently with Willard Brockton. An agreement is made: if she will stop living with Brockton, John will marry her when he has made enough money. Later, in New York, Laura pawns everything as things go from bad to worse; finally, she goes back to Brockton but tries to deceive and marry John when he arrives in New York, his fortune made. But Brockton forces her to tell the truth. John then rejects her, and Laura, after a weak attempt at suicide, heads for the theatre and "to hell with the rest." Brockton is a worldly person; he knew what Laura would do. The study of Laura, however, as a woman defeated by her basic desires, provides a strong drama with some psychological insight.

2.   ECONOMIC ISSUES AND ATTITUDES

American drama made spectacular and melodramatic use of economic and industrial advances and problems.   When Augustin Daly created his sensational railroad scene in *Under the Gaslight,* he introduced a bit of economic progress which appealed to his audience. Soon Daly's success prompted other playwrights to look closely at industrial America -- with noticeable results. The heroine of Joseph Arthur's *Blue Jeans* (1891) nearly has her head sawed in half by a buzz saw, while the heroine of William Haworth's *A Nutmeg Match* (1892) prevents the villain from releasing a steam pile driver which will crush her husband's skull.   In the South -- Charles

Calahan's *Coon Hollow* (1894) -- the cotton press replaced the buzz saw and the railroad tracks as a means of intimidation.

Many plays did, however, either comment on economic issues or use an issue to some purpose. In this way, the struggles of capital and labor, the problems of speculators and financiers and the troubles wrought by money (still the root of all evil) became a part of American drama. Reform is occasionally an issue, and plays such as William Hurlbut's *The Writing on the Wall* (1909) suggest varied places where reform was needed. In this melodrama, for example, the objective is reform in city building laws and fire safety in tenement dwellings.

(a) The Struggles of Capital and Labor
In "The Future of American Drama" [*Arena*, II (November 1890), 625] Dion Boucicault proposed a drama concerned with social problems, such as "the great struggle between labor and capital." He was, of course, asking for serious drama in contrast to the sentimental melodrama which for the previous twenty years had used poor working girls as heroines and dramatized the consequences of criminal labor conditions. Charles Foster's *Bertha, the Sewing Machine Girl* (1871) chronicles Bertha's life from her fourteen-hour work day for $6-$8 a week, to prison for a theft she has not committed and almost to "a fate worse than death" before she is rescued. *The Waifs of New York* (1871) by Thaddeus W. Meighan recounts the trials of an orphaned pair, a bootblack and a sewing girl, among the villains of New York. The heroine of Leonard Grover's *Lost in New York* (1887) says: "I work sometimes eighteen hours a day for a bare living. They say slavery is abolished, but there is more slavery among women who sew in New York than was ever known among the Negroes."

Few plays presented a definite protest against labor and economic conditions until well after the turn of the century. The workingman is treated very slightly in Bronson Howard's *Baron Rudolph* (1881), and James A. Herne provided only a brief picture of the common workers in *Margaret Fleming*. Hamlin Garland's *Under the Wheel* (1890) is much more realistic in its presentation of labor conditions. Playwrights saw the sensational aspect of the Molly Maguires: Albert W.

Aiken's *The Molly Maguires* (1876) and an anonymous play, *The Molly Maguires; or, the Black Diamond of Hazelton* (1881). There were occasional plays about strikes -- *The Strike* (1877), *The Workingmen's Strike* (1881), R. G. Whittey's *The Pullman Strike* (1895) and James E. Coggin's *The Strike Breaker* (1906) -- and in 1891 Henry C. DeMille used a social philosopher to win both a factory strike and the factory owner's daughter in *The Lost Paradise,* an adaptation of a foreign work. Another play, Augustus Thomas' *New Blood* (1894), is sympathetic to labor as it dramatizes conditions in a manufacturing company.

During the early years of the twentieth century, the outstanding labor play was Edward Sheldon's *The Boss* (1911), which uses labor-management struggles as a background to portray the breakdown and humanizing of a political and economic boss. Other plays which stress labor's problems include Charles Klein's *Daughters of Men* (1906), which deals with a labor strike, and Charles Kenyon's *Kindling* (1911), which dramatizes the poverty and desperation that a strike can precipitate. Between 1870 and World War I, records show the existence of about sixty plays dealing with working conditions in America.

(b) Speculators and Financiers
In the public's mind the successful businessman merged with the financier and the speculator. *The Gilded Age,* a novel by Mark Twain and Charles D. Warner, gave its name to a period of speculation and created a character who will always be remembered as a speculator: Colonel Muberry Sellers. G. S. Densmore's 1874 dramatization of the novel provided John T. Raymond with a successful vehicle as Colonel Sellers. Bartley Campbell's *Bulls and Bears,* in which a professor pits his intellect against the skill of a Wall Street broker, is an 1875 adaptation of the same foreign play that Augustin Daly dramatized that year as *The Big Bonanza.* William Winter, writing for the New York *Tribune,* found "four acts of hopeless commonplace in which there is not one spark of wit, not one bright thought, not even a gleam of smartness," but *Bulls and Bears* ran from February through the end of the season. That same year, 1875, Benjamin E. Woolf's *The Mighty Dollar* dealt

with a political speculator who, like Colonel Sellers, is involved in a railroad land grant.

In the 1880s Henry C. DeMille's *John Delmer's Daughter* (1883), Bronson Howard's *The Henrietta* (1887) and Brander Matthews and George H. Jessop's *A Gold Mine* (1887) reflected the financier's popularity in the theatre. When a critic for the New York *Dramatic Mirror* (May 9, 1891) mentioned "the average Wall Street play, of which we have had so many," it can be assumed that George Broadhurst's 1896 failure, *The Speculators*, was just another play on the financial situation. But the trend continued. Charles Klein with *The Money Makers* (1914), concerned with "the moral end of the money question," was only one of many to build on a popular topic.

(c)   Men and Money
By the beginning of the twentieth century, playwrights were beginning to find out just what money could do. Winchell Smith and Byron Ongley's *Brewster's Millions* (1906), which introduces the theatre's favorite fictional performer, George Spelvin, was one of the more successful plays of this new type. How does one get rid of a million dollars? Charles Klein's *The Lion and the Mouse* (1905) depicts financial interests that circumvent the law. In *Get Rich Quick Wallingford* (1910) George M. Cohan provides a hero who does just that. *Fine Feathers* (1913), by Eugene Walter, shows the power of money to corrupt a man and create a greed that will drag him to ruin. *It Pays to Advertise* (1914) is an amusing farce by R. C. Megrue and Walter Hackett built around a rich man's bet that his son can make more money than another man's son. In all of these plays and many more, it is money that makes the plot go.

3.   POLITICAL ISSUES AND ATTITUDES

Political themes are as old as American drama -- *Androboros*, 1714, for example -- and occasionally from the Revolution throughout the nineteenth century politics and politicians became the central issues of full-length plays. There are also many references in nineteenth-century melodrama to political maneuvers, campaigns, elections and graft: the dramatization of Mark Twain's *The Gilded Age* (1874) satirizes politicians; Edward Harrigan's *The Mulligan Guard Nominee* (1880) ridicules all politics; David Lloyd's *For Congress* (1884) satirizes Congressional practices. One of the best plays to have a plot woven around the maneuverings of a politician was *The Senator* (1889) by Lloyd and Sydney Rosenfeld. A mixture of romance and politics with humorous but loosely plotted incidents, the play burlesques Washington society through the love life and political activity of Senator Hannibal Rivers, an honest gentleman who stirs the sensitive heart.

(a) The Eighteen Nineties
Numerous plays on political issues and politicians came to the theatre during the 1890s. In 1895, Henry G. Carleton's *Ambition* pictured the self-made man of integrity, Senator Obadiah Wreck, and Augustus Thomas' *The Capitol* suggests the financial and religious influences exerted in Washington. That same year, Charles Klein's *The District Attorney* attacked political corruption and Tammany graft. Washington had always been a target for satire, and a major political issue on the stage during this decade was the imperialism in Cuba, with such titles as *Cuba's Vow*, *The Maine Avenged* and *Devil's Island*.

(b) Influence and Corruption
With the new century, playwrights began to probe the world of the politician, and soon the wide political scene came to the stage -- from the importance of the First Lady to the trickery of the county chairman. Casper Nannes (*Politics in the American Drama*, 1960) called George Ade's *The County Chairman* the "finest play on the subject yet to come out of American drama." The 1903 play shows the small-town politican to perfection -- a shrewd but cynical trickster whose interest is winning. That same year George M. Cohan wove a love story into a mayoralty campaign in *Running for Office*. In Charles Klein's very successful political melodrama, *The Lion and the Mouse* (1905), the influence of big business in Washington politics becomes an almost overwhelming force. Two other political plays -- George Broadhurst's *The Man of the Hour* (1906) and *The Undertow* (1907) by Eugene Walter -- successfully reveal the political machinery in a large city, New York.

4.   RELIGIOUS ISSUES AND ATTITUDES

Although American dramatists were generally concerned with strong moral quality, they stayed away from strictly religious topics.   By the late nineteenth century, however, there was clearly a growing interest in religious figures and ideas -- an interest which was to develop as World War I approached.

(a) Stereotypical Religious Figures

During the two or three decades before the new century, religion was sometimes mentioned in plays but never discussed, and the representative of a religion was presented as a safe figure working for the public good. If a Biblical thesis were put into a play, it was customary to make it a poetic drama: G. H. Hollister's tragedy, *Thomas á Becket* (1866). In other plays of this period, ministers or priests appear seldom and briefly. Charles Hoyt in *A Temperance Town* (1893) created the Reverend Ernest Hardman, a limited but good man who works doggedly for what he believes to be right.   A more sophisticated presentation of religion appears in Augustus Thomas' *The Capitol* (1895), which discusses the lobbying practices of the Catholic Church in Washington.   It was a difficult thesis, and Thomas took care that it would offend no one. James A. Herne's *The Reverend Griffith Davenport* (1899) focusses on a humanitarian minister, but his basic religion is not dramatized -- only his interpretation of human rights.

(b) Religious Historical Drama

Historical melodramas of the spectacular type occasionally portrayed the Christian theme.   In 1901 there were two dramatizations of Henryk Sienkiewiczs' *Quo Vadis* -- the Whitney version and an adaptation by Jeanette Gilder. Thomas Ewing, Jr.'s poetic tragedy, *Jonathan*, appeared in 1902. Most memorable of this period, however, is William Young's ambitious and spectacular melodrama, *Ben Hur* (1899), a dramatization of Lew Wallace's famous novel. Much of the excitement in this play was due to the art of the stage manager and his carpenters -- in particular, the tremendously effective chariot race with eight horses on treadmills prancing before the audience.

Ben Hur **(1899)**

At the palace of the Hurs, who are Jewish, Ben Hur is insulted by Messala, a Roman and a former friend. When Ben accidentally causes the death of a Roman leader, he is arrested by Messala and is sentenced to row in a Roman galley. During the battle in which the galley is destroyed, Ben saves the life of a Roman officer and then lives with him as an adopted son until the man dies, whereupon Ben returns to his home and searches unsuccessfully for his mother and sister. But he learns of the coming King, and with the Arabian horses of Ilderim, he wins a desperate chariot race with Messala. Later, having discovered that his mother and sister have leprosy and hide in a cave, Ben finds them healed by Jesus and is happily reunited with Esther, his very faithful sweetheart of earlier days.

(c)   A More Serious Concern

Consistent with nineteenth-century practice, dramatists used poetry more frequently than prose when writing on religious themes. Outstanding examples appear among the plays of William Vaughn Moody (1969-1910): *The Masque of Judgment* (1900), *The Fire Bringer* (1904) and *The Death of Eve* (unfinished). A superior poetic drama, presenting the Christ figure as "the Lonely Man," *The Piper* (1910) by Josephine P. Peabody Marks tells the story of the Pied Piper of Hamelin.

Moody, the Anglo-American Charles Rann Kennedy and Edward Sheldon used clergymen and religion to help dramatize the ideas in their plays. Sheldon's Archbishop in *The Boss* (1911) is a strong and powerful figure who thoroughly cows the belligerent Regan.   Kennedy, an advocate of Christian principles and one of the few dramatists of the period who combined a searching mind with good dramatic technique, created an effective Christ figure in *The Servant in the House* (1907) and presented a crucifiction theme in *The Terrible Meek* (1912). Moody's *The Faith Healer* (1909) is a penetrating study of a practitioner of the occult who finds love and the fulfillment of his mission at the same time. Undertaking a very difficult problem in *Rebellion* (1911), Joseph M. Patterson dramatized the inner struggle of a Catholic woman who has to decide whether to divorce her drunken husband and marry again or remain true to her beliefs in a Catholic marriage.

5.   ATTITUDES TOWARD SCIENCE

Science and democracy -- truth and equality -- are considered the twin forces most responsible for the movement toward realism in late nineteenth-century American literature. Few playwrights were concerned with the effect of science on society, but Dion Boucicault used the camera in *The Octoroon* and Howells frequently employed new inventions such as the telephone and the elevator. It was a long time, however, before playwrights would use anybody other than the family doctor to suggest an attitude toward science.

(a)   Scientist as Doctor

In spite of the inadequate training of the medical doctor of the late nineteenth century as compared with modern medical school requirements, most playwrights saw the doctor with his interest in chemistry, anatomy, biology and psychology as a representative of science and used him to suggest truth. In James A. Herne's *Margaret Fleming* the doctor is the voice of truth. Dr. Littlefield in *The Faith Healer* represents the dogmatic skepticism that science has toward the occult.   In Steele MacKaye's early comedy, *Won at Last* (1877), there are both Professor Tracy, "a man of science," and Dr. Sterling, "a man of fact." The distinction is interesting, although the different points of view of these two characters are not dramatized. As World War I approached, the scientist would be identified more specifically and made more human. In *Fine Feathers* (1912) Eugene Walter had Bob Reynolds, a chemist-scientist, take a bribe and suffer the consequences of the damned.

(b)   Science in the Drama

Among the significant American dramatists of the period, James A. Herne and W. D. Howells seem to have had the most inquiring minds about science. Most of Howells' concern was combined with an interest in psychical research and was developed in novels rather than in plays, although *The Mother and the Father* (1909) and *The Impossible* (1910) show this interest. Relating science and realism, Herne believed in evolution, made references to the beliefs of Darwin and Herbert Spencer in his plays -- scientific agnosticism in *Shore Acres;* social determinism in *Margaret Fleming* -- and wrote that he had an "unbounded respect for scientists and the scientific method." Curiosity and imagination produced more distinctive views of the scientist, as seen in *Tomorrow* (1913), a study of positive eugenics concerned with "the improvement of the human breed through selection," by Percy MacKaye, the son of Steele MacKaye.

III. THE AGE OF MELODRAMA

Taking his title from the best-remembered line of Owen Davis' popular melodrama, *Nellie, the Beautiful Cloak Model*, "'Why do you fear me, Nellie?' The Melodrama of Forty Years Ago" [*Harper's*, CLXXXIII (July 1941), 164-70], Walter Prichard Eaton mourned the passing of the old-fashioned melodrama of intense excitement and unsophisticated emotion. Before the movies usurped this type of entertainment for their stock-in-trade, theatres did a rushing business in sensational melodrama. Vivid and violent, sweet and sentimental, these melodramas combine simple emotions, complicated plots and uncomplicated characters and intricate stage machinery. The object of the play was to thrill, and the playgoer had only to weep, scream, hiss or shout for joy as emotion dictated.

Modern melodrama is more complicated than Eaton suggested, but the type that he described dominated the American stage from the Civil War until shortly after World War I. It is also quite different from Jean Jacques Rousseau's *Pygmalion* (1766), the play for which Rousseau created the term "melodrama." In Paris, toward the close of the eighteenth century, the Boulevard du Temple became a laboratory for this type of play which exhibits physical and emotional thrills with a villain-hero conflict, a musical accompaniment and a happy ending. Pixerécourt originated the stock characters -- the pure heroine, the dark villain, the intrepid hero and the comic. America's master of the melodrama was David Belasco, but he shared popularity with many others during the twenty years before 1900 and the dozen years that followed.

Best defined through what it is supposed to do, melodrama must thrill rather than comment on life. Limited by one-dimensional development, characters must provide excitement or comedy. "For every smile a tear, for every tear a smile," announced the posters. Because the objective is vivid sensation and violent emotion, there is little logic and even less plot, but an abundance of situations -- usually well-tried situations made novel by the skill of the actor or the stage carpenter. One of the key words in any melodrama is "Saved!" Any rescue -- though sure to come -- is always delayed until the last second, and manipulation of "time" is the playwright's greatest asset.

Because the periods of the Rise of Realism in the drama and the beginnings of social drama were also the Age of Melodrama, most of the plays are melodramas. In America there were many masters of the genre: Dion Boucicault, Augustin Daly, David Belasco, Bartley Campbell, Clay M. Greene, James M. McClosky and Owen Davis. The structure of their plays remained consistent. Still, they might vary their subject matter from historical and romantic material to the more theatrical problems of society or the scandals of crime and detection. In all such plays, however, the major characteristics of melodrama remained: the objective was to stimulate feeling rather than thought, and the scenes were put together with a view toward sensational entertainment.

A.   Melodrama:
Vivid and Violent, Sweet and Sentimental

Melodrama evokes visions of stock situations that have excited so many for so long. H. J. Smith described the standard reaction clearly in a March 1907 essay on "Melodrama" in the *Atlantic Monthly*. There is the heroine, he wrote, looking demure and helpless as she tremulously cries, "I swear to you that I am in-no-cent," while the audience breaks into cheers; later, bound and gagged and left on a railroad track, she is rescued at the last minute by her two Landseer dogs, "possessed of an intelligence almost human." Meanwhile, the not-too-bright hero nearly succumbs to the wiles of the scheming "Zidella of the purple gown and reptilian eyes." Across the stage slithers the arch-villain with a horrible leer upon his mustachioed face, and -- well, the story goes on until all are saved. It was that simple, but it was awfully exciting. This is one kind of melodrama, and nineteenth-century American dramatists have no peers in its creation.

1.   DION BOUCICAULT (1820-1890)

When William Winter wrote down his thoughts about Dion Boucicault for his book, *Other Days, Being Chronicles and Memories of the Stage* (1908), he listed Boucicault's "supreme achievements" in drama as "the ticking of the telegraph, in 'The Long Strike'; the midnight farewell of the schoolmaster in 'The Parrish Clerk'; the incident of Jessie's concealment of the broken floor, in 'Jessie Brown'; the heroic self-sacrifice of Shawn, in 'Arrah-na-Pogue'; the sentinels in the opening scene of 'Belle Lamar'; and the pathetic situation wherein the poor old father learns that his son's honor has been vindicated, in 'Daddy O'Dowd.'" Few modern students of the drama would find themselves in agreement with many of Winter's ideas, but he obviously showed good sense in choosing the creation of melodramatic incidents as Boucicault's forte.

Boucicault's type of drama, however, declined soon after his death, and within a few years critics were beginning to apologize for his work and wonder how they ever enjoyed his plays. Once considered "the apostle of realism on the stage," with his fire-and-water spectaculars, Boucicault lost his reputation and his style became a casualty to changing techniques in acting and writing melodrama.

Boucicault's first play to be produced after the Civil War was *The O'Dowd* (1873), an adaptation of a French play, whose scene and circumstances he transported to Ireland. Emphasizing the prodigal son theme, the play dramatizes both the sacrifice that the father must make to save his son from ruin and the heroic actions of the son to redeem his name and fortune. More traditional as melodrama, and very successful on the stage, was *Led Astray*.   Also adapted from a French melodrama and produced the same year as *The O'Dowd*, *Led Astray* manages to change a French love triangle into an Irish triangle and even heighten the effect. *Belle Lamar* (1874) is a melodrama of the Civil War. Boucicault's last popular melodrama was another in the Irish vein, *The Shaughraun* (1874), loosely translated as "The Wanderer."   Based on an incident in the Fenian insurrection of 1876, it tells of the adventures and escapes of an Irish gentleman under sentence of death as a Fenian.

After these successes, Boucicault wrote and adapted several plays, but his fortunes slowly melted away. Finally, he was reduced to teaching in a school for actors, a melancholy end for one whose contributions assure him a niche in the history of American drama and theatre.

2.   AUGUSTIN DALY (1838-1899)

In *The Theater of Augustin Daly*, Marvin Felheim entitled his chapter on Daly's major melodramas "Blood and Thunder Dramatist." These plays include *Under the Gaslight* (1867), *A Flash of Lightning* (1868), *The Red Scarf* (1868), *Horizon* (1871) and *Undercurrent* (1888). Of these plays, *Under the Gaslight* is the most famous and was the most successful, its railroad scene becoming a hallmark of melodrama.

A Flash of Lightning (1868)
(Plot)   Having two daughters, Garry Fallon shows his partiality for Rose by giving her a necklace, and his dislike for Bessie by accusing her of theft when the necklace is missing and turning her over to the villainous policeman Skiffley. By accepting her fate, Bessie tries to shield the man she loves, Jack. The rest of the play shows Skiffley trying to gain control of Bessie, while Jack tries to save her and prove that he, too, is innocent of the theft. Somehow they get aboard a Hudson River steamer, which blows up and burns -- providing equally heroic opportunities for Jack and for the stage carpenter. Both are successful; and in the final act, Jack proves that lightning destroyed the necklace, but not before Bessie almost does away with herself in anticipation of a jail sentence.

(Discussion)   The water and fire spectacles in *A Flash of Lightning* provided nothing new for New York audiences, who had seen burning buildings in *The Poor of New York*, a burning ship in *The Octoroon* and a water spectacle in *The Colleen Bawn* -- all by Boucicault. The play was successful, however, and Daly soon wrote *The Red Scarf; or, Scenes in Aroostook*. In this play, he tied his hero to a log which was about to be sawed in two in a sawmill before he burned down the mill.

Such action was typical of the Daly melodrama, but Daly's heroines were inevitably brave and quick on their feet, and all actors were able to appear for their bows at the final curtain.

3.   DAVID BELASCO (1853-1931)

In his bitter and cynically clever work, *The Devil's Dictionary,* Ambrose Bierce defined a dramatist as "one who adapts from the French." The phrase is an apt description of a number of American dramatists during the nineteenth century, especially David Belasco, master of sentimental and romantic melodrama. As actor-manager-playwright and innovator in the theatre, Belasco paid attention to every detail in his productions. His interest in the use of electricity caused Montrose Moses (*The American Dramatist,* 1918) to relate his discussions of Belasco to the "Switchboard Theater." Mainly Belasco collaborated with other playwrights: James A. Herne (*Hearts of Oak*), Henry C. DeMille (*The Charity Ball*), Franklin Fyles (*The Girl I Left Behind Me*), John Luther Long (*Madame Butterfly*). Belasco had that skill of being able to add the particular touch which made a play successful on the stage. With DeMille, he wrote social melodrama; with Long, romantic melodrama; but his forte was the robust melodrama of violence and sentiment. Of the sixty plays he wrote after 1872, twenty-three are adaptations or dramatizations of material not his own; in nineteen plays, he collaborated with a total of twelve people.

(a)   *The Girl I Left Behind Me* (1893)
In an intense and violent melodrama of life on an army post in Sioux country, the General's daughter, who is engaged to a scoundrel, discovers that she loves another. Outside the fort, the Indians attack, led by Scarbrow, the Sioux chieftan. Complications arise when it is clear that Scarbrow's daughter and the General's daughter love the same man. The Indian girl's death solves the love triangle, although for a while it seems that the General may have to kill his daughter, to prevent her from being captured by the Indians, and leave the melodrama without a heroine. But "Saved!" is the byword, and the rescue comes as the Indians retreat before the U.S. Cavalry.

(b)   Belasco and His Stars: Mrs. Leslie Carter

As a theatre manager, Belasco was interested in creating stars. Mrs. Leslie Carter, one of his greatest stars after her sensational divorce from a socialite family, tells in her memoirs how intense his training was -- in gesture, in voice projection and in physical feats. Her physical actions and her stamina never failed to bring comments from the critics. Belasco wrote several plays for Mrs. Carter before they parted ways, the first one being *The Heart of Maryland* (1895), in which Mrs. Carter played the part of Maryland Calvert, who risks life and limb for her lover. For three years she brought joy to the hearts of audiences by refusing to let the curfew sound which would bring doom to her lover. Her method was simple but startling -- she clung to the clapper of the bell, swinging with it. Three years later, in 1898, Belasco adapted *Zaza* from the French especially for Mrs. Carter. As Zaza, "the wicked and of course irresistible music-hall singer," Mrs. Carter had ample opportunity to exploit her beauty, the violent ebb and flow of her emotions and her limitless energy. Because the scene was a theatre, Belasco exercised his tremendous talent in stage management with exhibitions of theatre machinery. *Zaza* well exemplifies his melodramatic art: a play adapted from the French, a plot filled with sensationalism, a single star with an emotional appeal, an exhibit of the stage manager's skill -- in essence, a spectacle in character, action and scene.

4.   OWEN DAVIS (1874-1956)

Al Woods and Owen Davis as theatre manager and playwright, respectively, may have produced more "thrillers" than any other team in the American theatre. Starting in 1899 with *Through the Breakers,* Davis found the market pressing and the results so lucrative that for nearly fifteen years he wrote a melodrama every month or six weeks -- one hundred and twenty-nine melodramas -- before he wrote *The Family Cupboard* in 1913. The titles of some of his better-known melodramas are *Convict 999; Confessions of a Wife; Nellie, the Beautiful Cloak Model;* and *Gambler of the West,* which he considered the best of these works. Eventually, he tired of writing sensational melodrama, began to write more realistic plays and finally won a Pulitzer Prize for *Icebound* in 1923.

The most successful American writer of melodrama at the turn of the twentieth century, Davis explained his change in writing style in an essay entitled "Why I Quit Writing Melodrama," *American Magazine* (September 1914). For the potential writer of melodrama, he also listed the rules for his former success: the play's title is seventy-five per cent of its success; the third act belongs to the stage carpenter; the play should be divided into no fewer than fifteen scenes, each ending with "a moment of perilous suspense or terrifying danger." Cheap to produce and seventy per cent successful in theatres, the Davis melodrama was a product of his knowledge of the theatre and the audiences who wanted not serious and political speeches but "amusement or some excitement or something that will bring about a mood of hope, faith, or exaltation."

5.   BARTLEY CAMPBELL (1843-1888)

Starting his playwriting career in 1871, Campbell wrote thirty-five plays and became America's most popular writer of melodrama before his mental breakdown in 1885. A man of great ego as well as talent, he advertised busts of himself and Shakespeare on his stationery and finally leased the Fourteenth Street Theatre in New York for the 1885-86 season to produce his own plays. As many as five of his plays were on tour at one time.

Not only was Campbell the most popular dramatist of that day, but many critics considered him one of the best. *The White Slave* (1882) was one of his most successful plays, as was *My Partner* (1879), a dramatization of Bret Harte's story. *The Galley Slave* (1879) has a foreign setting, and *Paquita* (1885) dramatizes a surgeon's struggle as he performs a life-saving operation on his wife's lover. Most of his plays were performed in England with considerable success. After its initial run in New York, *The White Slave* toured coast to coast.

The White Slave (1882)
Lisa, the illegitimate white child of the Judge's daughter, is loved by Clay, the Judge's adopted son; but they are kept apart by the assumption that Lisa has Negro blood. When the old Judge dies, his debts force the sale of his plantation and the slaves, including Lisa. Lacy, the villain, buys Lisa, who goes to

work in the fields rather than meet Lacy's demands. "Rags are royal rainment when worn for virtue's sake!" she explains in one of those memorable lines from popular melodramas; "Rather a hoe in my hands than self-contempt in my heart." Finally, Clay rescues Lisa, who is shown by a baptismal record to be the Judge's white granddaughter; Lacy is accused of murdering a Negro; and Lisa, Clay and their slaves return to the Judge's plantation and a wedding.

6.   CLAY M. GREENE (1850-1933) AND MELODRAMA OF THE WEST

The author of seventy-eight plays and librettos, Greene combined his love of music with his skills as a writer of melodrama. Some of his better plays were written with David Belasco, such as *Pawn Ticket 210* (1887), the story of Mag, pawned ten years before the action starts by her mother. When love and hope of marriage, along with all the frills of sentimental melodrama, come to Mag, "Pawn Ticket 210" hopes that she will be able to redeem herself.

Like a number of his contemporaries, Greene, born in San Francisco, wrote many plays about the West. *M'liss* (1878) is based on a Bret Harte story; other titles include *Sharps and Flats* (1880), with hero Slauson Thompson involved with the financial activity in San Francisco, and *The Golden Giant Mine* (1887), set in Golden Run, Idaho. Other comparable western melodramas by Greene's peers include *A Gentleman from Nevada* (1880) by George Jessop and J. B. Polk, *The Angel of the Trail* (1884) by Howard Hill, *Poverty Flats* (1885) by James J. McCloskey, *Queen of the Plains* (1888) by Ned Buntline and *Chick* (1889) by Joseph Clifton.

7.   HISTORICAL MELODRAMA

Historical events and personalities did not appeal as strongly to playwrights of the late nineteenth and early twentieth centuries as they had to dramatists writing during the early 1800s. Bronson Howard and Brander Matthews wrote *Peter Stuyvesant* (1889), embellishing the life of the early New York governor. Clyde Fitch wrote *Beau Brummell* (1890), *Nathan Hale* (1898) and *Major André* (1903). The most popular historical melodramas, however, were either of a religious nature or had a foreign setting.

8.   ROMANTIC MELODRAMA

Most melodramas have at heart a touch of the romantic, but seldom do they have the romance of fantasy and of distance places with strange-sounding names. Only a few dramatists seem to have been interested in writing such plays. David Belasco's collaborations with John Luther Long are outstanding: *Madame Butterfly* (1900), *The Darling of the Gods* (1902) and *Adrea* (1904). Richard Tully's *Bird of Paradise* (1912), George C. Hazelton and J. H. Benrimo's *The Yellow Jacket* (1912) and Edward Sheldon's *The Garden of Paradise* (1914) based upon Hans Christian Anderson's "The Little Mermaid" -- all suggest a kind of romantic fantasy. Most of the plays of Edward Knoblock are romantic melodramas, such as *The Cottage in the Air* (1909) and *Kismet* (1911), his greatest success.

Collaborations by David Belasco and John Luther Long
Madame Butterfly **(1900)**
This play is based on a story by John Luther Long. Highlighted with tender and romantic songs, the play tells of Cho-Cho-San, Madame Butterfly, who waits with her child, Trouble, for the return of Lieutenant B. F. Pinkerton, an American naval officer to whom she feels herself married. All night long she waits -- a night created by lights, lasting fourteen minutes during which no words are spoken -- only to discover that Pinkerton has brought an American wife with him. Going behind a screen, Cho-Cho-San wounds herself with her father's sword -- "To die with honor, when one can no longer live with honor" -- binds her throat with a scarf and dies embracing her child.

The Darling of the Gods **(1902)**
Another play with a Japanese background, this drama has the exotic quality of the oriental fantasy. Yo-San, the daughter of the Prince of Tosan, who wants "only to be perfectly happy all my life," falls in love with Kara, the outlaw leader of the two-sword men, and protects him when he is wounded. But she is later tricked into betraying the hideout of Kara and his men. For her betrayal, Yo-San must wander one thousand years before entering heaven, but as Kara promises to wait, they kill

themselves saying, "Sayonara." In the last scene, the thousand years have elapsed; Yo-San and Kara meet in the first Celestial Heaven and ascend to the next together.

9. MELODRAMA OF CRIME AND DETECTION

With Indians to fight, the wilds of nature to contend with and the most horrible of black-mustachioed villains to foil, writers of melodrama during the nineteenth century did not bother much with criminals. Generally, the heroes or the heroines solve their own mysteries and hand the villains over to some nebulous person called "The Law," whom the good people respect while the bad show their disdain in many ways. The cops-and-robbers evidently had to wait in line behind cowboys who killed Indians and heroes who subdued tall-hatted malefactors.

For some reason Edgar Allan Poe's great detective, Monsieur Dupin of "The Purloined Letter" and "Murders in the Rue Morgue," did not attract playwrights, although William Gillette's *Sherlock Holmes* (1898) owes something to Poe's creation as well as to Conan Doyle's. One of the few popular American detectives of the period, Dick Brummage of *The Great Diamond Robbery* (1895), knew many disguises and tricks and was as incorruptible as he was persistent; but though he shared their self-confidence, he clearly lacked the wit, finesse and intelligence of the two detectives of short-story fame. This play by Edward M. Alfriend (b. 1843) and A. C. Wheeler (1835-1903) illustrates the type of melodrama popular in the Ten-Twenty-Thirty (10¢-20¢-30¢) Theatre -- simple, clean-cut characters, complicated situations and fast-paced action, all requiring an emotional rather than a thoughtful reaction.

With the new century scarcely a decade old, crime melodrama reached new heights of popularity. In the spring of 1912, Bayard Veiller wrote *Within the Law*. Combining action and sentiment, this play tells of a girl, unjustly convicted of stealing from a shop where she worked, who seeks revenge by marrying her former employer's son and leading a gang that works just within the law. Extremely successful, it presaged a fad in crime-and-detection plays -- a "flood of melodrama featuring criminals hunted by detectives and police." [*Bookman*, XXXVI

(February 1913), 638-49] *The Conspiracy* (1912) by John Emerson and Robert Baker tells of a girl who helps round up criminals by working for an amateur criminologist. *Under Cover* (1914) by Roi Cooper Megrue is concerned with some jewel smugglers and a girl whose misplaced love tempts her to help them. *On Trial* (1914) by Elmer L. Reizenstein (later Elmer Rice) is the dramatization of the prosecution and defense of a man charged with murder.

(a)   *Seven Keys to Bald Pate* (1913)
       by George M. Cohan (1878-1942)
A mixture of melodrama and farce, *Seven Keys to Bald Pate* is one of the best examples of the early crime melodrama. Having bet the owner of the Bald Pate Inn that he can write a novel there within twenty-four hours, Mr. Magee discovers in the inn some crooks and a newspaper girl who is trying to expose their crime. One by one, the crooks are caught by Magee and the girl. Then the farce begins: the crooks seize control, kill the girl, blame Magee and fool the police, until the owner of the Inn appears and calmly kills the two policemen before he explains that the people are all actors in his employ. Presumably Magee has lost his bet, but in the epilogue he is typing: everything portrayed has been his story!

(b)   *On Trial* (1914) by Elmer L. Reizenstein (Rice, 1892-1967)
On Trial is a social melodrama of the criminal courts. Its numerous stage devices, particularly flashbacks, added to its effect on the stage. According to the *New York Times* reviewer, August 20, 1914, it was a "new thing to have an entire play written out of the record of a murder trial." Deceived by a man before her marriage, a young woman is forced by circumstances to visit this man. Finally, he is killed by her husband, who complicates his trial by trying to shield his wife.

B.   Social Melodrama

In an article on the "Characteristics of American Drama," Alfred Hennequin [*Arena*, I (May 1890), 700-09] maintained that the French melodrama had combined with English melodrama to produce a very prevalent type of American play -- social melodrama. Perhaps a compromise on the part of the playwrights, managers and audiences, social melodrama kept safely within the bounds that managers and playwrights knew were successful at the box office, while suggesting a tendency toward the modern drama of Ibsen and Shaw.   Clayton Hamilton, a popular writer-critic of the period, saw the change from early melodrama as a degeneration. ["Melodrama, Old and New," *Bookman*, XXXIII (May 1911), 309-14] He found "a new species of melodrama that is ashamed of itself" taking the guise of "a serious study of contemporary social problems." Social melodramas, however, retain the characteristics of melodrama and use or comment on social problems and conditions rather than treat them intelligently and imaginatively.

Among the melodramas which comment on social problems and conditions, Clyde Fitch's work provides a good starting point with two social melodramas, both written in 1901: *The Way of the World*, concerned with life in New York City, and *The Girl and the Judge*, which shows the reactions of the daughter and the husband of a kleptomaniac.   Charles Klein's plays are mainly melodramas involving social, political and economic issues.   George Broadhurst's *Bought and Paid For* (1911) exploits the problems of a wealthy, self-made man who feels that he "owns" his wife among his other assets.   Life in a newspaper office is exaggerated dramatically in *The Fourth Estate* (1909) by Joseph M. Patterson and Harriet Ford.   In general, the writer of social melodrama was restricted in choice of material only by what he or she considered unprofitable for the box office.

1.   EUGENE WALTER (1874-1941)

The most significant writer of social melodrama was Eugene Walter, whose best play, *The Easiest Way*, was written in 1908. *Paid in Full*, written that same year, is a study of human weakness in a husband, contrasted with the strength of the wife. It capitalizes on a melodramatic situation in which the husband, accused of embezzlement, begs his wife to visit his employer and bargain for his freedom with her physical charms. *Fine Feathers* (1913) dramatizes the evils of greed and temptation, as a young chemist is bribed to use poor quality materials in a dam which breaks with appalling loss of life. Faced with running or staying, the chemist stays, calls the police and then ends his life with a bullet.

2.   AUGUSTUS THOMAS (1857-1934)

A master of the well-made play who achieved success by exploiting the interests of a changing society, Thomas wrote for the commercial theatre, generally with a particular star in mind. In his best-known play, *The Witching Hour* (1907), a conventional melodrama of sentiment and morality, he dramatized the story of a young man who, under the influence of hypnotism, has killed a man.

IV. THE POPULAR FARCE

There will always be farces in the theatre, and it is likely that they will always be popular. Before the Civil War, the farce in America was mainly an afterpiece or a means to exploit a character such as the Yankee. By the turn of the century, it had become an evening's entertainment. Amidst the social and industrial difficulties of late nineteenth-century America, people wanted mainly the vicarious excitement of melodrama and the laughter of farce. At that time farce reached its highest point of popularity in the history of American drama.

A. Farce and Its Varieties

If farce is successful, the audience laughs. Dramatizing either novelty or the common life, the farceur presents no major conflicts but a series of minor incidents in which external, physical and trivial situations are exploited. Following an improbable thesis, the playwright creates confusion and embarrassment purely for their own sake. Characterization is avoided. Generally, yet with the single exception of the intriguers who may start the confusion, stock characters and unalert people become the *dramatis personae* in farce. If the characters used intelligence, in fact, there would frequently be no play. Specifically, characters do not determine or influence events, and the play progresses, not by what the characters do, but by what happens to them. Farces, then, are compounds of absurdity, improbability and contrivance. There must be, however, sufficiently recognizable human traits in the characters or verisimilitude in the situation that the audience will want to see how it all ends.

1.   SITUATION FARCE

The situation farce was the most successful of the period, and one of the popular figures of this time was also a prolific writer and adaptor of farces -- Augustin Daly. One of his most frequently performed farces was *A Night Off* (1885), which tells of an absent-minded professor who loves the theatre and, while his wife is away, has numerous adventures when a romantic tragedy he wrote in college is produced. Another effective writer of farces was William Gillette, author of *The Private Secretary* (1884) and *Too Much Johnson* (1894). Typical of the farces of George Broadhurst is *Why Smith Left Home* (1889), which describes the problems of Smith and his bride, who are visited by so many relatives that they can never be alone. Two of the better-known farces of this period are *Brewster's Millions* (1906), by Winchell Smith and Byron Ongley, and Margaret Mayo's *Baby Mine* (1910).

2.   SECONDARY PURPOSE: RIDICULE

Objects of ridicule in farce are unlimited, and almost all playwrights who attempted satire did so with farce techniques. Politics seems always an object of ridicule. *The Nominee* (1890), adapted from the French by Leander Richardson and William Yardley, describes an election in which a man runs for Congress as a Jacksonian Democrat and is elected as a Republican Protectionist. *For Revenue Only* (1892), attributed to Milton Nobles, exaggerates aspects of politics and tells of a candidate for Congress whose unscrupulous campaign manager turns out to be his long-lost son. *It Pays to Advertise* (1914) by Roi Megrue and Walter Hackett is an early play ridiculing the advertising business. George M. Cohan's *Broadway Jones* (1912) makes fun of the business and advertising worlds. Numerous plays, mainly of doubtful merit, exploit the absurdities of the stock character, the speculator -- Benjamin E. Woolf's *The Mighty Dollar* (1875) and Daly's *The Big Bonanza* (1875). From Bronson Howard's *Saratoga* (1870) to the plays of Charles Hoyt, farce was the popular means for ridiculing society.

B.   Everyone Writes Farce

Most playwrights of this period wrote farce -- some intentionally, some because they lacked the skills to avoid it. Farce as a genre, however, has its admirable qualities. Of the many who specialized in farce for the commercial theatre, two of the most talented and successful were Charles Hoyt and George Ade. Both relied heavily upon satire and situation, but whereas Hoyt wrote straight farce that followed in the footsteps of Edward Harrigan, Ade emphasized effective dialogue and more recognizably human characters. Their contemporary writers of farce included Clyde Fitch, Augustus Thomas and William Dean Howells.

1.   CLYDE FITCH (1865-1909)

Some critics may contend that Fitch wrote mainly farce; certainly, he resorted to contrivance in creating both plot and characterization. In several plays, however, he clearly illustrated his talent for creating the unpretentious but entertaining farce. *The Blue Mouse* (1908), adapted from the German, is a good example. A young man, ambitious to advance in his business and knowing that his boss is susceptible to pretty women, hires a chorus girl to act as his wife. As both boss and young man are already married, the misunderstanding between "hired" wife and real wives produces ludicrous entertainment.

2.   AUGUSTUS THOMAS (1857-1934)

Many of Thomas' plays are farces. *On the Quiet* (1901) tells of the complications which result when a college student, rebelling against an earlier promise, secretly marries an heiress. Wishing to be anonymous while visiting America, an English earl (*The Earl of Pawtucket,* 1903) borrows an American's name and, of course, his problems.

3.   WILLIAM DEAN HOWELLS (1837-1920)

Over the course of his career, Howells wrote twenty-five one-act plays, most of which he called farces. A few of them came closer to being comedies through his development of a basic situation, characterization and dialogue. Many, however, are simple farce -- *Evening Dress* (1893), in which

Campbell exploits Roberts' wardrobe while trying to find his dress suit; *Room Forty-Five* (1900), in which a woman cannot sleep because the man in the hotel room beneath hers snores; *Parting Friends* (1911), in which two young people are so beleaguered by visitors that they cannot kiss goodbye before she leaves on a steamer for Europe. Few of Howells' farces were actually produced on the professional stage, but they were tremendously popular in amateur theatricals.

4.   CHARLES H. HOYT (1859-1900)

Called the forerunner of George S. Kaufman and Moss Hart, Hoyt exploited farce and satire to become the most popular writer of "hilarious confusion" in the late nineteenth century. Drawing his material from his own experiences -- small-town life in *A Rag Baby* (1884), superstition in *The Brass Monkey* (1888), politics in *A Texas Steer* (1890), temperance and suffrage meetings in *A Temperance Town* (1893) -- he developed his plays from an early emphasis on slapstick comedy to an awareness of social problems.

In a Puritan but careless fashion, he poked genial fun at American society. *A Milk White Flag* (1893) burlesques the hypocrisy of home guard companies; *A Runaway Colt* (1895) tells of a gambler's attempt to bribe a baseball player. Hoyt's objective was to entertain, and his box office success suggests his place in American farce-comedy. *A Trip to Chinatown* (1891), with such popular songs as "Reuben, Reuben, I've Been Thinking" and "After the Ball," had the longest run of any play in America at that date, with 657 performances. Playwriting was Hoyt's business, and he took it seriously, revising his work with extreme care with the result that he would earn nearly half a million dollars in a good year. But with success came severe strain, and he died at the Retreat for the Insane in Hartford, Connecticut, at a young age.

A Texas Steer; or, Money Makes the Mare Go (1890)
A satire on Washington politicians and their methods, the play opens in Texas.   Maverick Brander's daughter, Bossy, and Captain Bright are arranging to have Brander elected to Congress because Bright is being transferred to the Capitol and they would like to be together.   The election is chaotic but not

too expensive at five dollars a vote. With the Branders in Washington, there are the usual greenhorn problems, from elevators to blackmail, but the Texans are fearless with their guns every-ready. Brander, of course, does nothing as a Congressman and is investigated by three gun-toting Texans who shoot up the place and cause Brander to lose friends in Washington while assuring his reelection in Texas.

5.   GEORGE ADE (1866-1944)

Undoubtedly using Hoyt as a model, Ade wrote numerous farces and farce-melodramas. He employed satire yet was not a penetrating satirist, nor was he seriously critical in his plays. Enjoying people and situations more than plot construction, he became a popular playwright during the first decade of the twentieth century. In *The College Widow* (1904) he created a typical farce situation: In order to persuade a certain boy to come to Atwater College to play football, the coach asks his girlfriend to show interest in the boy. She is successful, and the football team wins its big game. The crisis comes when the coach's plot is revealed, as is his girlfriend's love for the football player. *The Sultan of Sulu* (1902) is a musical farce which uses an army base in the Philippines to poke fun at government procedures. *Just Out of College* (1905) satirizes the value of a college education in the business world. *Artie* (1907) describes a clever and flippant young man who jollies his way to success. Ade continued to write plays but was eventually lost in a theatre scene dominated by Eugene O'Neill.

V. POETIC DRAMA
THE CIVIL WAR TO WORLD WAR I

From the beginnings of American drama to the Civil War period, the most significant plays were written in poetry. The best actors emphasized poetic drama in repertories slanted toward an artistic as well as a commercial success. After the Civil War and until the turn of the century, poetic drama became less popular because it did not fit the requirements of the Rise of Realism. Then, during the decade before World War I, there was a revival of interest in poetic drama.

A.   Poetic Drama and the Rise of Realism

With the exception of the work of George Henry Boker, the poetic drama of the period from the Civil War to the turn of the century was less inspired than what had come before. Times had changed, as had the demands of the theatre. People were being forced to look at life more realistically, and the drama mirrored that change. Therefore, when W. D. Howells, the spokesman for realism, declared that any play which proposed to be a faithful representation of lives of men and women should not be written in verse form, few dared disagree. The Rise of Realism in literature not only did not promote poetic drama but laid down a dictum under which poetic drama would be considered false. Poetry, in fact, was not a significant part of the Rise of Realism.

1.   POETIC PLAYS (1865-1900)

Between 1865 and 1900, few poetic dramas reached the stage. A number of poets of the period, however, attempted to write dramas, such as *Prince Deukalion* (1878) by Bayard Taylor. In 1881 William Young dramatized part of the Arthurian legend in *Pendragon,* and two years later Ernest Lacy wrote *Chatterton,* a study of that poet's life, for the actress Julia Marlowe. Other writers of poetic drama included G. H. Hollister, who sold *Thomas á Becket* (1866) to Edwin Booth; Henry Guy Carleton with *Memnon* (1881); Thomas B. Aldrich, whose *Mercedes* (1884) won high praise from A. H. Quinn; and Elwyn A. Barron with *The Viking* (1888). In general, these plays are neither good theatre nor good poetry.

2.   THE POETIC DRAMA OF W. D. HOWELLS

During the 1870s and early 1880s, there was a slight revival of interest in poetic drama, occasioned mainly by the temperament and acting abilities of Lawrence Barrett. One poetic drama in which Barrett acted for more than twenty years was written by none other than W. D. Howells, the Father of Realism, who occasionally condescended to write alongside the romantics. For his first poetic play, Howells chose Ippolito D'Aste's *Samsone,* which he translated and adapted as *Samson* (1874) for the actor Charles Pope. In 1878 he translated and adapted Tamayo y Baus' *Un Drama Nuevo* as *Yorick's Love*, in which Barrett acted until his death in 1891. Employing a play within a play, it tells the story of an actor, Yorick, who discovers that his young wife loves another when she acts the part of an unfaithful wife with him in a play.

Howells also wrote three other poetic dramas: *Priscilla: A Comedy* (1879-82), a dramatization of Longfellow's "The Courtship of Miles Standish"; *A Sea Change; or, Love's Stowaway* (1888), an operetta with music by Georg Henschel; and *The Mother and the Father* (1909), a series of three plays showing the reactions of a mother and father to the birth of a daughter, her later marriage and her untimely death. But Howells was not an exceptional poet, and these plays were never produced by professionals.

B.   A Revival of Interest in Poetic Drama

From about 1900 until World War I, there was renewed interest in poetic drama in America and Europe. In England, William Poel was reviving Elizabethan plays with popular success in productions of *Everyman* and Shakespeare's plays. William Butler Yeats was writing exceptional poetic drama; and on the Continent, Rostand, Maeterlinck and Hauptmann contributed poetic plays. America, however, was still not ready for poetic drama, although Percy MacKaye had declared that "the drama of democracy will be a poetic drama." It was a period ruled by pragmatism, described by the Muckrakers and interpreted by naturalistic moralists like Theodore Dreiser. Poetic drama presented a great contrast to reality because it did not seem to mirror life, and people did not look to poetry for truth. The poetic dramatists, however, wanted to portray both beauty and truth. Hence, they copied from the past, choosing for themes historical events, romantic legends or Greek myths. Several of them attracted favorable attention from both audiences and critics.

1.   RELIGIOUS AND UNIVERSAL THEMES: WILLIAM VAUGHN MOODY (1869-1910):

Among American poet-dramatists writing before World War I, the one with the best reputation as a poet was William

Vaughn Moody, the stern teacher of English at the University of Chicago, best known for his "Ode in Time of Hesitation." As a poet, Moody was a transitional figure. Ever aware of his new ideas and a moving, progressive culture and society, he employed the style and form of the older poets. In the history of American drama, Moody is most noteworthy for two prose plays -- *The Faith Healer* and *The Great Divide* -- which indicate his concern for serious, realistic and progressive drama. His poetic plays suggest similar themes and contain some effective poetry, but they did not reach the stage.

"A Poetic Trilogy" (1900-1912)
Based on the Bible and dramatizing the conflict between God and the creatures He had created, Moody's trilogy begins with the Incarnation and continues through the Day of Judgment, with the Angel Raphael as the protagonist. The first play, *The Masque of Judgment* (1900), shows that man's desires, for which God is responsible, make him susceptible to evil. When man rebels and is conquered by the serpent, it is God's mistake. Another story of rebellion -- Prometheus' struggle with the gods and his subsequent punishment -- *The Fire Bringer* (1904), the second in the trilogy, presents an unreconciled god at the end of his tyrannical attempt to destroy man. The third play is a fragment, *The Death of Eve* (1912), concerned with the reconciliation of God to man through woman, who had first separated them. To Moody, who saw disunity as oblivion, man and God must be united.

**2.   ROMANTIC EXPERIMENTER:
PERCY MACKAYE (1875-1956)**

Percy MacKaye is known in drama circles through the work of his father, Steele MacKaye, and through his own work in poetic, pageant and experimental drama.   His contributions, particularly in spectacular pageants, are undeniable, although his works were never popular in the theatre. His first poetic drama, *The Canterbury Pilgrims* (1903), is a blank-verse comedy in four acts which emphasizes the character of the poet Chaucer and his sentimental attitude toward the Prioress, as the Wife of Bath tries to make him her next husband. *Sappho and Phaon* (1907) tells the sad story of the Lesbian poetess in love with the slave Phaon. One of his best poetic plays was

Jeanne d'Arc (1906), a five-act play in blank verse which presents a romantic and sentimentalized Jeanne who is driven toward her destiny by the guardianship of St. Michael and by her love for her people.

3.   HUMANITARIAN POET-DRAMATIST:
     JOSEPHINE PRESTON PEABODY MARKS (1874-1922)

Josephine Peabody Marks is the most significant of the early twentieth-century poet-dramatists. A poet with a dominating interest in historical and literary material, Marks owed some of her skill in dramatic writing to William Vaughn Moody, one of her college teachers. After a one-act verse play, she wrote *Marlowe* (1901), an idealized if unsuccessful play which views the poet through his "passionate shepherd" poem. *The Wolf of Gubbio* (1913), shows the struggle of selfishness versus love in men's lives against the background of Christmas and the influence of Francis of Assisi, whose love controls even aminals.

The Piper (1910)
(Plot) After ridding the town of Hamelin of rats, the Piper is refused his fee by the greedy townspeople. Only Veronica, who is not Hamelin-born, and her crippled little boy, Jan, have sympathy for the Piper. Barbara, the Burgomaster's daughter, falls in love with Michael, the sword swallower, a member of the Piper's group of strolling players. Into the hills, the Piper takes the children, and there he struggles -- his prideful wish to punish the villagers conflicting with his love for the children and his human sympathy. When he discovers that Barbara will be placed in a nunnery as penance for the village and hears of Veronica's faith that he will return the children, he brings them back to the village. People are still greedy, but there is love in the world, and this knowledge seems to have changed the Piper.

(Discussion) This play won the Stratford Prize Competition in 1910. For Marks, the Piper became not a fairy but a human being, a "fanatical idealist," and the play, in which the poetry provides a decidedly emotional appeal, is a character study.   The forces of greed among the villagers, love represented by Jan and Barbara, Christianity and the supernatural (the pipes of the Piper) act upon the complex struggle within the Piper, who is torn between pride and human sensitivity, cynical bitterness and self-denying love. Pitting himself even against God, he is finally overcome by the Christian force.

4.   MORE POETIC DRAMA (1900-1914)

Other poetic dramas written during these years include T. B. Aldrich's *Judith of Bethulia* (1904), the story of a woman who resists love and assassinates the ruler of the army which surrounds her town, with the consequence that the town is saved and she is honored; George Cabot Lodge's *Cain* (1904); novelist Mary Johnson's *The Goddess of Reason* (1907), a blank-verse play in four acts concerned with the love of a lord for a peasant girl during the French Revolution; Cale Young Rice's *A Knight in Avignon* (1907), a one-act play; and plays by Ridgely Torrence and Edwin Arlington Robinson.

VI. A NEW SERIOUSNESS

In early America, tradition suggested to playwrights that poetry -- rather than prose -- was the language of serious drama. With the change of attitudes which permeated American society after the Civil War, the medium for seriousness in drama changed. Thoughtful themes attempted by romantics who wrote in poetry were generally lost upon audiences who expected good dramatists to use prose. Thus the drama of the last part of the nineteenth century became realistic in the style of Howells and Henry James. By the turn of the century, others joined the ranks of those who not only sought commercial success on the stage but had something of importance to say, but the means of presenting a serious theme had changed yet again. Convention now dictated that drama be at once comedy, problem play and criticism of society. Even David Belasco changed his approach with *The Return of Peter Grimm* (1911), asking whether the dead may return to life as we know it.

Few of the plays of this particular period are outstanding, but those few have significance for that misunderstood and underestimated decade and a half before World War I. It was a time of change and movement, but it was also a time of

innocence.   Most of the dramatists, therefore, dealt with
questions of simple propriety and never penetrated into the
deeper concerns of morality and truth.   A few tried, with
varying success and failure: William Vaughn Moody, Rachel
Crothers, Edward Sheldon and Charles Rann Kennedy.

A.   William Vaughn Moody (1869-1910):
Believer in Humanity

A poet rather than a commercial playwright, Moody wrote
only on themes which he felt significant in modern life, themes
involving intense emotional conflicts, both within individuals
and between ideological and social groups.   In *The Great
Divide*, sometimes called the first modern American drama, he
contrasted the independent freedom of the West with the
inhibiting traditions of Puritan New England, but the major
conflict of the play is the internal struggle of a New England
girl whose basic desires war against her heritage. It is a "great
divide" of opposing values presented by the East and the West.
Melodramatic touches mar the hero and the plot development,
but sensational subject matter and the serious intent of the
playwright in idea and language was impressive in the
theatre. *The Faith Healer* dramatizes the conflict between
earthly love and a sense of divine mission, between science and
faith, between love and duty. In all of Moody's plays, there is
the strong thesis of the necessary unity of humankind and a
Spiritual Being. A somber realist, Moody was both practical
and profound -- bringing meaning to a commercial theatre.

1.   *THE GREAT DIVIDE* (1906)

An Easterner visiting the West with her brother and fiancé,
Ruth Jordan falls into the clutches of three brutish men. Unable
to protect herself, she offers herself to the strongest, Stephen
Ghent, who buys her with a string of gold nuggets. Later,
married to Ghent, Ruth buys back the nuggets and returns alone
to the East, where Ghent's child is born. But life is meaningless
for Ruth until Ghent appears, explains his love and promises to
begin life again in order to bring her happiness and to remove
the guilt of the past.

2.   *THE FAITH HEALER* (1909)

Mary, the wife of a midwestern farmer who believes in the ideas of Darwin and Spencer, is able to walk for the first time in five years when treated by Michaelis, a faith healer. But Michaelis begins to doubt his divine mission when he feels the strength of his love for Rhoda, Mary's niece. When his subjection to the scorn of a medical doctor and an orthodox clergyman causes him to lose his powers, Mary finds that she can no longer walk. Only through his own inner searching and his love for Rhoda, is he able to regain his power.

B.   Rachel Crothers (1878-1958): Historian of Manners

Although her name has only recently been retrieved from the roll of forgotten dramatists, for a period of more than twenty-five years, Rachel Crothers contributed a play of some significance to American drama almost every season. It has been suggested that her plays form a study of the manners of women during the first quarter of the twentieth century, and to a degree this is true. The heroine of *The Three of Us* (1906) defends her right to freedom and demands the respect of others; *He and She* (1911) challenges male and female stereotypes; *Ourselves* (1913) deals with a woman's moral responsibilities; *Young Wisdom* (1914) discusses trial marriages. But many of her strong observations of that early period later became standard fare: a woman's place is in the home (*He and She*, 1911); parents can disillusion their children (*Mary the Third*, 1923); self-expression doesn't mean freedom (*Expressing Willie*, 1924); saying you believe doesn't make you believe (*Susan and God*, 1937).   Dressed in the craftsmanship which marks Crothers' plays, these ideas become more impressive than a mere list can reveal. If she did not chronicle the life of Modern Woman, she emphasized her problems. If she was not a profound commentator, she had thoughtful opinions. If she did not provide radical solutions, she did raise searching questions.

The plays which Crothers wrote before World War I mark a decided step in the development of serious social comedy. Neither as person nor as playwright was she a dedicated feminist. "Drama is drama," she said in a speech in 1912 before the Drama League, "and what difference does it make whether women or men are working on it?" Offering a wide range of commentary on the condition of twentieth-century women, Crothers wrote at least thirty-eight plays with an appeal that made her the most commercially successful American woman playwright prior to World War II.

He and She (1911)
Tom and Ann Herford, both sculptors, decide to enter separate designs for a commission. So as not to bother them while they work, their teenage daughter remains away at school. Keith, Tom's assistant, at the indirect urging of a family friend, the dramatist's raisonneur, decides that he really doesn't love Ruth, a prim career girl, but sees great possibilities in Daisy, Tom's home-loving sister. Tom is shattered when Ann gets the commission, but the tables turn quickly as the daughter comes home from school, having decided to marry her school's handyman. Ann immediately gives Tom her designs and decides to spend her time winning back the faith of their daughter, and a traditional family balance is restored.

C.   Edward Sheldon (1886-1946): Romantic Realist

The variety of plays by Edward Sheldon makes him difficult to classify, but his early plays brought him a reputation as a precursor of the realists of the 1920s. Although he wrote mainly melodrama, he represents an interesting combination of the realist and the romanticist, and his significance comes from his imaginative experimentation and his courage in tackling social themes. When poor health apparently incapacitated Sheldon after World War I, he collaborated with such dramatists as Sidney Howard (*Bewitched,* 1924) and Charles MacArthur (*Lulu Belle,* 1926). Although none of this later work is outstanding, he remained a source of inspiration and help on dramaturgical problems for a number of prominent dramatists, including Robert E. Sherwood.

Sheldon's first professionally produced play, *Salvation Nell* (1908), suggests realism in the barroom scene, although it is clearly a melodrama of a girl who works for, waits for and wins to the right cause the man she loves. *The Nigger* (1910) courageously dramatizes the story of a Southern governor who discovers that one of his grandparents was a Negro slave. After *The Boss* (1911), Sheldon's concern for romanticism became dominant. The search for beauty in *The High Road* (1912), for example, was treated not as realistic tragedy but as romance. *Romance* (1913), one of his most successful plays, uses the story of a young American clergyman's grand passion for an Italian opera singer to prepare for the marriage of the clergyman's grandson to an actress. Sheldon's romantic and poetic imagination is seen at its height in *The Garden of Paradise* (1914), a dramatization of Anderson's "The Little Mermaid." Essentially, Sheldon always tried to present a truthful theme, but his early concern for realism disappeared from his later plays.

The Boss (1911)
(Plot) When Griswold and Company, Contractors, are forced to near-bankruptcy by Regan, a rival contractor, and the bank which Griswold directs is in danger of losing money, Regan offers to join forces, with the stipulation that he be allowed to marry Griswold's daughter, Emily, and thereby gain social position. Over family objections, Emily, a very serious-minded social worker, agrees to the match -- but in name only. Complementing this conflict is young Griswold's union activity in organizing Regan's workers, their subsequent strike and the riot during which Griswold is hit by a brick. The aggressive Regan is accused of instigating the incident and put in jail, where his belligerent spirit is broken. With Emily's help, however, Regan's moral spirit is strengthened and, freed after the real culprit confesses to throwing the brick, he goes home, a good man, with his wife.

(Discussion) As do *Salvation Nell* and *The Nigger*, *The Boss* shows Sheldon's interest in the realistic portrayal of life. Against a background of business, political and labor conditions, the dramatist created a romantic incident -- the forced marriage -- and a stageworthy, if melodramatic, hero. The play is frequently realistic in character, scene and action, but it is not a realistic study of labor problems or a labor boss.

D. Charles Rann Kennedy (1871-1950): Christian Idealist

A scholarly Englishman who married an actress, Edith Wynne Matthison, and became an American citizen in 1917, Kennedy was an advocate of Christian principles, which he dramatized with more ardor than theatrical effectiveness. His concern for social problems and the religious and sociological implications in his plays reflect the Social Gospel Movement. Although after World War I Kennedy continued to write plays and work with students at Bennett College, he had already reached the height of his playwriting career.

Kennedy's Christian idealism is the dominant aspect of his work. Believing that "God does things as a dramatist would," he set out to dramatize Christianity. In *The Servant in the House* (1907) he presented a Christ-figure (Manson), who reveals the hypocrisy of organized religion and the idealism of love and truth. Another play, *The Winter Feast* (1908), portrays, as he said, "the hate and lies in life that destroy." These were the first two of a proposed but unfinished five-cycle play; the third, *The Idol Breaker* (1914), dramatizes the thesis of freedom. A later trilogy consists of *The Chastening* (1922), on Jesus of Nazareth; *The Admiral* (1923), on Columbus as discoverer, which G. B. Shaw called a "magnificent play"; and *The Salutation* (1925), on the love of Paolo and Francesca.

1. THE TERRIBLE MEEK (1912)

A daring play, *The Terrible Meek* "portrays a soldier's awakening consciousness." In the darkness, a woman whose son has been killed talks with the Captain and the soldier who executed him. Finally, the scene is faintly revealed, with the crucified Christ in the background. Exploring a thesis that "the real meek are beginning to inherit the earth," Kennedy sent his published play to all kings, emperors, presidents, war ministers, munition-makers and every other leader he knew of.

2. THE IDOL BREAKER (1914)

Concerned with individual freedom and humankind's relationship to God and society, this play tells of Adam, a bastard blacksmith bound to the village of Little Boswell, and of Naomi, the gypsy girl who represents that quality which "unites all men beyond time and space." Adam has made a clock -- "God's clock!" -- with a living heart and a tongue which tells the truth as well as the time, thus revealing humanity's hypocrisy and awakening the antagonism of the people, who misunderstand and condemn Adam as an atheist, an egotist and an anarchist. Into this situation comes Jake, Naomi's husband, who represents the freedom of hate in contrast to Naomi's freedom of beauty and understanding. Jake is killed in a fight. In the last act Adam and Naomi return to Boswell, where Adam will become "Blacksmith of the World."

VII. BEGINNINGS IN DRAMATIC CRITICISM

Many years had passed since Washington Irving called critics the "pests of society," but the label stuck in people's minds. During the first hundred years of American drama, theatre developed and plays improved, but dramatic criticism remained essentially an unenlightened passtime. With few exceptions, dramatists before the Civil War had not bothered to evolve theories of drama, and criticism of plays generally meant paid "puffing" or biased comment on the way the play had been produced. Toward the end of the nineteenth century, however, attitudes toward dramatic criticism began to change.

A.   Whither American Drama?

By the last quarter of the nineteenth century, many people were beginning to ask this question, and the answers suggested a new period in dramatic criticism.   Although Augustin Daly accepted "The American Dramatist" [*North American Review*, CXLII (May 1886)] only in terms of the dramatist's willingness to collaborate with a theatre manager, Brander Matthews viewed more openmindedly "The Dramatic Outlook in America" [*Harper's*, LXXVII (May 1889)]. Alfred Hennequin described the "Characteristics of American Drama" [*Arena*, I (May 1890)] and Dion Boucicault was optimistic about "The Future of American Drama" [*Arena*, I (November 1890)].

Although it is difficult for some post-World War II critics to sympathize with the achievements of pre-World War I dramatists, there is much to be said for dating the beginnings of modern American drama in 1890. During this year James A. Herne, America's most serious imitator of Ibsen (whose plays generally designate the beginnings of modern drama), produced his best play, *Margaret Fleming*. And by this time, critics and dramatists were writing in terms of an American drama and were concerned with what it was and where it was going.

B. American Dramatic Theory

"American Playwrights on the American Drama" [*Harper's Weekly*, XXXIII (February 2, 1889)], an important document in theatre history, consists of essays by Edward Harrigan, William Gillette, John Grosvenor Wilson, Steele MacKaye, William Winter, Bronson Howard and Augustin Daly. In contrast to earlier times, later in the century it became normal for a dramatist to proclaim his theories of the drama in a published essay. Bronson Howard wrote "The Laws of Dramatic Construction," in which he described a "satisfactory" play. In numerous essays, W. D. Howells propounded his dramatic theory, which inspired James A. Herne to write "Art for Truth's Sake in the Drama," (*Arena*, February 1897). Dion Boucicault's theories are clearly recorded in his *North American Review* essays, and David Belasco explained his theories of the drama in magazine articles and in his book entitled *The Theatre Seen Through the Stage Door* (1919). By the turn of the century, some dramatists, such as Langdon Mitchell, were lecturing on their theories of drama. Others were being interviewed adroitly by newspaper and magazine writers, with the consequence that a playwright had increasing opportunities to discuss his or her theories.

C. Dramatic Criticism

Historically, criticism of the American drama came from three different views -- moralistic, technical, literary. In practice, there were (1) critics who were paid to "puff" a certain play, (2) newspaper and magazine critics who might lack completely the necessary intellectual or imaginative equipment to criticize a play and (3) a few literary critics concerned with the drama as literature rather than theatrical performances.

1.   PUBLICATIONS FEATURING DRAMATIC CRITICISM

Throughout the first half of the nineteenth century, numerous writers had commented on drama and theatre in America, and even a few periodicals -- such as *The Thespian Monitor, The Thespian Mirror* and *The Theatrical Censor* -- had existed for brief periods of time. Not until after the Civil War, however, did the first significant theatrical papers appear: The New York *Dramatic News and Society Journal,* 1874; The New York *Dramatic Mirror,* 1879; The New York *Dramatic News,* 1881. About this time, *Leslie's Monthly Magazine,* along with such publications as *The Critic, Puck, Century* and *The Brooklyn Magazine,* gave special attention to the theatre. During the late 1880s, W. D. Howells used his "Editor's Study" column in *Harper's* to comment as he wished on the drama and theatre. Among the better-known drama critics of the late nineteenth century were Edward G. P. Wilkins, William Winter, Stephen R. Fiske and Andrew C. Wheeler (Nym Crinkle). A significant step was the appearance in 1900 of *Theater Magazine,* edited by Arthur Hornblow. As newspapers and magazines more consistently reported theatre activities, dramatic criticism increased in quantity and improved in quality.

2.   THE NEW CRITICS

Dramatic criticism retreated from its earlier emphasis on morality, although the subject still appeared in such essays as "Filth on the Stage" and "Indelicacy of Modern Plays." Criticism from a technical point of view was still a major interest of the reviewers -- William Ellsworth's observations on *Ben Hur* in *The Critic* (XXVI, March 1900) and many comments by prominent theatre figures such as Steele MacKaye, William Gillette and Dion Boucicault. The innovation of this period was an interest in drama as literature. W. D. Howells evaluated the plays of every major contemporary dramatist during the two decades that surround the turn of the century. He was particularly effective in his criticisms of Edward Harrigan and James A. Herne, as well as Ibsen and Shaw. Henry James spent considerably less time writing about

American drama, but he published several interesting essays on contemporary drama. Among the most active of the other serious critics were Brander Matthews, Laurence Hutton (*Curiosities of the American Stage*, 1891) and Walter Prichard Eaton (*The American Stage of Today*, 1908).

3.   JOURNALISTIC CRITICS

It is possible here only to note the increased number and great variety of journalistic critics. Howells complained that the same reporter who described a fire in the morning reviewed a theatre performance that evening. That was one problem; another was paid "puffing." The Theatre Syndicate, for example, controlled not only theatres and playwrights but also newspaper critics. The reviews of certain critics, then, are completely unreliable. A few critics, however, were independent and astute in their observations. William Winter wrote many criticisms of plays and dramatists (some collected in *The Wallet of Time*, 1913), but his close association with dramatists such as Daly limits the value of his work. Alan Dale and James G. Huneker were among the best reviewers. John Corbin deserves attention for his observations, particularly those in "The Dawn of American Drama" [*Atlantic Monthly*, XCIX (May 1907)]. Clayton Hamilton was a prolific critic of all drama, although he was inclined to be more conservative than inspired.

VIII. A DEVELOPING THEATRE

During the fifty years that separated the Civil War from World War I, the American theatre changed drastically. Following a past inclination toward spectacular melodrama and stimulated by the realistic movement in literature and the products of a developing industrialism, theatre performances became more realistic. The style of acting, as well as the entire procedure for producing a play, underwent changes in the hands of the new director-producers. With the social and economic development of the spreading country, the need for entertainment grew, and new forms became popular. Growth meant money, and one consequence of potential wealth was the establishment of the monopoly known as the Theatre

Syndicate. If a phrase were needed to describe the theatre of the early twentieth century, it would be "Big Business!"

A.   Realism in the Theatre

Realistic theatre did not necessarily mean a truthful theatre in terms of ideas presented in plays. Essentially, it meant that the audience need not "suspend its disbelief" quite so willingly. The acting, the action, the scenery and the stage properties became more realistic. Dramas which suggested realism of idea, such as Ibsen's *Ghosts*, did not become acceptable in the American theatre until after the turn of the century.

1.   REALISM IN SCENE

Before the Civil War, Boucicault produced realistic spectacles, such as a building burning in New York City or a boat exploding. Later melodramas employed the buzz saw, the pile driver or the cotton press in an effort to capitalize on the popular appeal of realism. The log cabin and the wolves in *Davy Crockett,* as well as the storm, suggest the realism made possible by the stage carpenter. Such plays as *Ben Hur*, with palaces, horse races and galley fights on water, are outstanding examples of stage realism. On the other hand, Edward Harrigan and W. D. Howells were interested in more detailed stage realism of a less spectacular nature.

2.   "THE BELASCO METHOD"

As director and producer, David Belasco insisted on a realism limited only by the abilities of his stage carpenters and property masters. Details interested him, and critics referred to "The Belasco Method." If soldiers were supposed to be tramping through North Carolina, Belasco demanded North Carolina mud. For one play that required a certain kind of room, he visited a poverty-stricken neighborhood in New York and bought the contents of a room -- wallpaper and all. Many props for *DuBarry* came directly from Paris.   He was meticulous, even to the indentation in a pillow which would suggest that a character had just arisen from bed, or the right kind of bisquit in the cupboard of a down-on-her-luck actress. This was the realism of which Belasco was a master.

3.   CHARACTER ACTORS

A number of actors achieved reputations for realism through their development of details in their character portrayals. Joseph Jefferson III was such an actor in *Rip Van Winkle;* so were Frank Mayo in *Davy Crockett* and James O'Neill in *The Count of Monte Cristo.* William Gillette's acting of Sherlock Holmes and Denman Thompson's in *The Old Homestead* also showed a concern for particular realism.

B.   Innovations in Theatre Management

The theatre manager was usually the person who owned the theatre, chose the plays, hired the actors and collected the money. Actors learned their "lines of business" and as "walking gentlemen" or "leading ladies," for example, performed in plays. This arrangement changed when the producer-director-entrepreneur -- such as Augustin Daly -- appeared on the scene. This new breed of manager, opposed to the star system as it had been, now created the stars and promoted the tyranny of the actor, to which was added the autocracy or tyranny of the so-called "director." A helpful innovation in management was the establishment of the booking office, and with this service came the means of controlling both performers and plays, a development exploited by the Theatre Syndicate.

1.   THE AUTOCRAT OF THE STAGE

No one could have become more absorbed in the theatre than Augustin Daly, and few were as powerful. He "lived" in his theatre; he chose, wrote or adapted his plays; he selected his cast, not for "lines of business" but as he understood the roles; and he controlled and rehearsed his actors in a dictatorial and effective manner. His standards in art and personal morality were high, and his achievements in encouraging a certain kind of play, and in taking his productions of Shakespeare to England and the Continent, are significant.

2.   A MAN OF CREATIVE IMAGINATION

A theatre manager, Steele MacKaye was fascinated with the technical aspects of theatre. His innovations include the elevator stage, improved ventilating systems, fireproofing for scenery and a curtain of light. MacKaye is also remembered for the theatre he planned for the 1893 Chicago World's Fair -- the Spectatorium. With a stage opening of 150 feet by seventy feet, a seating capacity of ten thousand and numerous devices for a variety of stage spectacles, it was the product of an extravagant imagination. Unfortunately, when the economic Panic of 1893 curtailed expenses for the Fair, the plans for the Spectatorium were cancelled.

3.   THE THEATRE SYNDICATE

The key to theatre success in the late nineteenth century was the booking agency. Theatre entrepreneurs agreed: Control bookings and you also control theatres, actors and playwrights. With the growth of a nationwide network of theatres, it was little wonder that a theatre monolopy would appear on the American scene. It happened on August 31, 1896, with the combining of already existing partnerships which controlled theatre in different parts of the country: Sam Nixon and Fred Zimmerman (Philadelphia to Chicago), Charles Frohman (New York, New England and the Continent), Al Hayman (the important towns west of the Mississippi and the Far West), Marc Klaw and Abe Erlanger (south from New York to New Orleans and north to Chicago).

The objective of these individuals was power -- control. A Syndicate theatre, for example, could not hire independent actors; Syndicate acting companies could not play in free theatres. The Syndicate took five per cent of the box office gross, and there were obvious economic abuses including unfair competition and restraint of trade. Technically, it was within the law, and an investigation by the U.S. Attorney General in 1908 found no grounds for prosecution. It was a tough system, however, and only a few tried to buck it -- Belasco, Minnie Maddern Fiske, James A. Herne. For ten years, the control was strict, but it finally weakened -- from internal discord, excessive greed, questionable contracts and competition from such ambitious empressarios as Keith and Albee and the Shubert brothers. The last Syndicate agreement expired in 1916. Although it was a significant force, the Syndicate probably never controlled more than seven hundred theatres.

C. Theatre Activity: Expansive and Experimental

During the last quarter of the nineteenth century and the first decade of the twentieth, American theatre was a varied and frequently extravagant business. The minstrel shows, the Tom shows and the showboats were major innovations. Burlesques and variety acts probably started when the first dance-hall girl climbed onto the bar and began to sing or dance. But greater publicity came with Lydia Thompson and her British Blondes in 1869. Musical comedy goes back to the eighteenth century, but *The Black Crook* by Charles M. Barras is usually considered the first of the modern musical comedies. This four-act extravaganza built upon the Faustian legend opened on September 12, 1866, and ran for 474 performances by combining scenic splendor, huge ballets, popular music and scantily clothed dancers. Critics saw the "utter rubbish" beneath the spectacles, but this "monster hit" grossed over one million dollars in its first engagement, toured frequently and was revived throughout the remainder of the century.

Other kinds of entertainment included the Wild West Show, the Can Can, the Circus and the Honky Tonk. Actors continued in vehicle roles and added protean or multiple parts to their repertoires. In 1871, for example, Johnny Thompson played nine parts in James McCloskey's *On Hand; or, True to the Last*, emphasizing ethnic roles, and performed on twelve musical instruments from bass viol to cow's horn. Tony Pastor created a variety entertainment for family audiences, and amateur theatricals flourished during the late nineteenth and early twentieth centuries. The work of George M. Cohan enhanced American musicals after the turn of the century; and in 1907 the Ziefeld Follies began their unique kind of revues. American vaudeville was born in the variety houses toward the end of the nineteenth century, with such memorable acts as Weber and Fields and McIntyre and Heath, and reached top popularity during the First World War.

1. ACTORS, IMPORTS AND EXCITEMENT

Beyond variety, this was the age of big names in American theatre. Lawrence Barrett and Edwin Booth were matinee idols; Nat Goodwin, a foremost comedian. Richard Mansfield and Minnie Maddern Fiske were leaders of the theatre when Ethel Barrymore made her stage debut in 1894. It was also the age of the "international star," as European stars, particularly from Italy, Germany and France, visited the United States. Soon after the turn of the century, America was importing popular melodrama and, with some daring and some dissension, the plays of Ibsen, Shaw, Synge, Barrie and Rostand. Both the plays and the players caused excitement, but the single greatest spectacle was also a catastrophe: on December 30, 1903, the Iroquois Theatre fire in Chicago claimed more than 500 lives.

2. TWO NOTABLE EXPERIMENTERS

Among various theatre experiments, two plays by dramatists of particular imagination and theatrical skill are outstanding. Percy MacKaye's *The Scarecrow* (1908) takes its theme from Hawthorne's story, "Feathertop," and tells how a scarecrow, created before the audience's eyes, comes to life as Lord Ravensbane and achieves a considerable sense of humanity before it succumbs to its own artificial construction. The fantasy of the play, its challenge to actor and director and its literary quality make it distinctive. Belasco's play of the supernatural, *The Return of Peter Grimm* (1911), is another experimental fantasy. Peter returns from the dead to be an unseen influence on the lives of the living and finally to carry away with him the little boy who dies. Although its thesis is love encumbered with ample sentiment, the play was effective theatre fare at the time and rose above maudlin experimentation.

IX. SUMMARY

From the Civil War to World War I, drama developed from a profession demanding certain acquired skills to an art showing seriousness and imagination -- from the commercial plays of Boucicault and Daly to the artistry of Herne, Moody and Crothers. Plots became more sophisticated; characterization revealed the dramatists' more probing attitudes. Early stereotypes -- the Indian, the Negro, the Yankee, the Irishman and the Jew -- developed into the individuals which distinguish the plots of many modern American plays. Before the turn of the century most plays were melodramas or farces, but the

significant trends were toward realism -- as seen in the plays of
Steele MacKaye, Howells and Herne -- and the development of
a social comedy by Howard, Howells and Fitch.

European influences helped the twentieth-century American
dramatist become successful.   A new interest in language
promoted an interlude of popularity for poetic drama.   Social,
economic and political theses were treated seriously; and social
melodrama replaced the vivid spectacle that had owned the
stage during the last third of the nineteenth century.   Drama, in
general, although not yet great nor even very memorable as a
body of literature, had become a more meaningful genre.
Breaking away from the traditions of the past -- in both theme
and technique -- the theatre and the audience were now ready
for what was to come: an independent and courageous theatre
company and an outstanding dramatist.

SELECTED BIBLIOGRAPHY

"American Playwrights on the American Drama," *Harper's Weekly*,
 XXXIII (February 2, 1889), 97-100.
Dickinson, Thomas H. *Playwrights of the New American Theater.* New
 York: The Macmillan Co., 1925.
Felheim, Marvin. *The Theatre of Augustin Daly.* Cambridge: Harvard
 Univ. Press, 1956.
Hartman, John Geoffrey. *The Development of American Social Comedy
 1787-1936.* Philadelphia: Univ. of Pennsylvania Press, 1939.
Herne, James A. "Art for Truth's Sake in the Drama," *Arena*, XVII
 (February 1897), 361-70.
Herron, Irma Honaker. *The Small Town in American Drama.* Dallas:
 Southern Methodist Univ. Press, 1969.
Hughes, Glenn. *A History of the American Theatre, 1700-1950.* New
 York: Samuel French, 1951.
Hutton, Laurence. *Curiosities of the American Stage.* New York: Harper
 & Brothers, 1891.
McArthur, Benjamin. *Actors and American Culture, 1880-1920.*
 Philadelphia: Temple Univ. Press, 1984.
Meserve, Walter J., ed. *The Complete Plays of W. D. Howells.* New York:
 New York Univ. Press, 1960.
_____. *American Drama to 1900: A Guide to Information Sources.*
 Detroit: Gale Research, 1980.
Moses, Montrose J. *The American Dramatist.* Boston: Little, Brown &
 Co., 1925.
Quinn, Arthur H. *A History of the American Drama from the Civil War to
 the Present Day.* New York: Appleton-Century-Crofts, Inc., 1943.
Wilson, Garff B. *Three Hundred Years of American Drama and Theatre.*
 Englewood Cliffs: Prentice-Hall, 1973.

Chapter Four

American Drama Between the World Wars
From the Provincetown to World Renown

With the appearance of the Provincetown Players and Eugene O'Neill, American theatre and drama achieved a significance which by the time of World War II had changed American drama into a recognized force in world drama. The substantial advances made during the twenty-five years preceding 1915, however, should not be forgotten. The Provincetown Players, for example, were only one group of several in a Little Theater Movement rebelling against commercial practices in America. Foreign influences, which were highly significant in the development of modern American drama -- from the Moscow Art Theatre to the works of Ibsen and Strindberg -- were seen long before World War I in the plays of a few serious dramatists. Essentially, the direction had been clearly pointed out by 1915, although implementation was urgently needed. This was supplied through the creative work of the Provincetown Players and the imaginative genius of Eugene O'Neill -- a necessary combination. Within a few years, American drama was transformed into something more vital than it had been, but the result obtained was the product of forces at work in America since the beginning of the century.

The dramatic impetus having been established and the moment in social and intellectual history being appropriate, several dramatists of the 1920s began writing plays which were distinguished by imaginative thought and characterization. Dramatists, as Thomas H. Dickinson (*Playwrights of the New American Theater*, 1925) pointed out, were no longer concerned only with amusement; they began to feel the more dynamic responsibility of the literary and theatre artists toward society and truth -- Maxwell Anderson, Paul Green, S. N. Behrman, Sidney Howard, Philp Barry, Robert Sherwood. Also, the greater freedom which the dramatist now enjoyed was mirrored in the kind of plays he or she wrote -- a new realism, a more poignant social drama, folk drama, pageant drama, poetic drama.

It is always difficult and a bit presumptious to attempt to impose order on creative work, but the attempt is sometimes necessary and the results, in the historical sense, valuable. Underlying a good part of the drama of the 1930s is a social consciousness which may be oriented through the dramatist's intellectual persuasion -- left to right, from the most liberal of propaganda plays to the traditional high comedy. Along the spectrum between these two points are plays of social commentary, problem plays, satirical plays and plays of domestic and light comedy. In addition to these expressions of social attitudes, there were, as in the nineteenth century, always light farces and entertaining melodrama. Outstanding in this period were those few dramatists who revealed psychological insight. Among those searching for a meaningful interpretation of life, not limited by commercial interests or intimidated by audience demands, were Eugene O'Neill, Philip Barry, Maxwell Anderson, Thornton Wilder and William Saroyan.

One particular achievement in American drama of this time was the development of a substantial dramatic criticism. Before World War I, there were important sojourns into this field, chiefly by those oriented in literature, but no tradition was established. With this necessary adjunct to a more meaningful drama, American plays at the outbreak of World War II assumed a new importance. A perennial but increasingly persistent intruder on the international theatre scene before World War II, American drama during the years following 1945 became accepted as a major force in world drama.

I.   AN APPROACHING TRANSFORMATION

American drama and theatre at the time of World War I enjoyed a potential, largely unrecognized, that it could not have claimed ten years previously. Activity throughout the theatre suggested a spirit and vitality which were unknown during the Augustin Daly and Charles Frohman periods of influence. The work of university teachers such as George Pierce Baker, for example, was creating a healthy influence on playwrights, and art rather than commercialism was becoming a more common objective. Of particular significance in theatre history is the Little Theater Movement, which took its impulse from foreign theatres, although for the moment, foreign influence was less impressive on the work of the dramatist. Consisting mainly of melodrama, with increasing emphasis on social and psychological interests and some concern for experimentation and form, American drama offered little for Eugene O'Neill to imitate. He could, however, follow the direction that the more daring of his immediate predecessors suggested -- imitate foreign drama -- and he could revolt. The seeds of change in American drama and theatre had already been planted. The conditions in the theatre, the poverty of good plays and the world situation helped bring about a transformation toward which numerous playwrights, theatre people and critics had been working for a number of years.

A.   The Condition of the Theatre

Simply stated, the theatre during the second decade of the twentieth century was marked by steady change.   The monopoly of the Theatrical Syndicate had been broken. Of the older director-producers, Belasco was the only remaining major figure, and, although he was still active, his particular style was losing its appeal. More impressive was the influence of André Antoine's Théâtre Libre, the Abbey Theatre and the Moscow Art Theatre. In America, as universities began to train playwrights, the nature of commercial theatre production was changing. Statistics also indicate a change in the theatre. In 1900, for example, there were sixteen first-class theatres in New York; in 1910, there were thirty; in 1925, sixty-one. These theatres produced seventy-two new plays in an average year at the turn of the century; ten years later, they were producing 130 plays; at the quarter-century mark, they produced 208. Plays on tour during these years, on the other hand, dropped in number from 308 to 198 to 68. The magazine *Drama* started publication in 1911 and *Theatre Arts* in 1916. The Drama League of America was founded in 1910. As New York asserted its power, there was also a tremendous growth of community theatres across the country.

1.   UNIVERSITY THEATRES AND GEORGE PIERCE BAKER

During the late eighteenth century, American universities made a contribution to the drama which they were unable to continue during the nineteenth century. In the early twentieth century, however, they became important only in the development of American drama. Some of the more effective contributions came from Frederick Koch at the University of North Dakota and later at the University of North Carolina, A. M. Drummund at Cornell, Thomas H. Dickinson at the University of Wisconsin, Thomas Wood Stevens at Carnegie Tech and E. C. Mabie at the University of Iowa.

No teacher was more influential than George Pierce Baker (1866-1935) at Harvard University and later at Yale University. Actor, playwright, director, critic and teacher, Baker created a graduate course in English Composition (English 47), "The Technique of the Drama," known as the "47 Workshop," which has become a familiar landmark in theatre history. First taught in 1905, the course eventually enrolled, among others, Edward Sheldon, Philip Barry, Eugene O'Neill and Sidney Howard. Baker's essay on "Practical American Drama" in 1911 suggests his approach, which was not, unfortunately, looked upon with complete satisfaction by Harvard administrators. After pleading without success for a Harvard School of Drama, Baker left for New Haven in 1924 to help establish the Yale School of Drama.

2.   LITTLE THEATER MOVEMENT
AND THE PROVINCETOWN PLAYERS

Eva LeGallienne, an American actress and director, once wrote that "the true theatre of America must be created by the people themselves." Her statement effectively describes theatre activity during the early twentieth century. Stimulated by the revolt of little theatres abroad and the work of Adolphe Appia and Gordon Craig, it was a protest against the commercial theatre. When the Abbey Players from Dublin toured America in 1911 and Max Reinhardt's spectacular *Sumurûm* was produced in 1912, the necessary impetus had been provided, and several little theatre groups sprang up: the Chicago Little Theatre, the Toy Theatre in Boston, Stuart Walker's Portmanteau Theatre and the Washington Square Players. The *Little Theatre Monthly* appeared, edited by Harold A. Ehrensberger, and soon listed more than one thousand community and university theatres. Pageantry, which used amateur actors, was spurred on at this time by Percy MackKaye. Essentially, the changes in theatre had been brought about by inspired amateurs, many of whom later became professionals. From among the Washington Square Players, for example, the Theatre Guild was formed in 1918.

The Provincetown Players
The best known of all little theatre groups was the Provincetown Players, started by some theatre enthusiasts on a wharf in Provincetown, Massachusetts, during the summer of 1915. The next year they gave themselves a name, selected George Cram (Jig) Cook as president of the twenty-nine members and settled at 139 Macdougal Street in Greenwich Village as a subscription theatre -- "to give American playwrights a chance to work out their ideas in freedom." Eugene O'Neill joined them during the summer of 1916, and with him and Susan Glaspell as their major playwrights, the group's success mounted. Soon they moved to different quarters; and during the 1920-21 season, they took O'Neill's *The Emperor Jones* uptown.

With success, however, came difficulties. The informality was gone; the spirit that held the group together vanished and members parted company -- some interested in experimental theatre, others seeking commercial success. After Jig Cook sorrowfully left, a triumvirate took over: O'Neill as playwright, Robert Edmund Jones as designer and Kenneth Macgowan as director. Again the Players attained success, and again they disagreed on their objectives. In 1925, a third Provincetown group reaffirmed the old ideas but almost immediately met financial difficulties. Helped by Otto Kahn, they forged ahead into the fall season of 1929, hoping to recoup losses with a production of Thomas H. Dickinson's *Winter Bound*. Too late! The Crash ended an era in the theatre, too, but not before the Provincetown Players had changed the course of American drama and theatre.

B.   Suggestions Without Excitement: 1915-1919

During these five years, there were suggestions of potential among dramatists but little of the excitement of artistic achievement. War conditions prevailed; older playwrights were losing their effectiveness; new playwrights had not yet gained control of their art. The transformation was slow in coming, as social melodramas and comedies commented on society's follies -- one of them receiving the first Pulitzer Prize in Drama. Worthy of comment, however, were the beginning works -- one-act plays -- of playwrights who would soon do better things. Not until 1919 did the drama seem to suggest in over-all productions the creativity which would characterize the plays of the 1920s.

1. SOCIAL MELODRAMA AND COMEDY: THE OLD AND THE NEW

Among the established dramatists writing during these years -- Eugene Walter, Charles Rann Kennedy, Rachel Crothers, Percy MacKaye and George Middleton -- were several new names. Louis Anspacher wrote *The Unchastened Woman* (1915), which enjoyed a measure of popularity, portraying, as it does, a wealthy but unconscionable society woman's fight for power. Clare Kummer (1873?-1958) started her prolific and popular career with *Good Gracious, Annabelle* (1916), a lively situation comedy distinguished by witty dialogue as a girl gets her millionaire. Jessie Lynch Williams (1871-1929) is remembered primarily as the winner of the first Pulitzer Prize for the Best American Play: *Why Marry?* (1917). Satirizing and defending the institution of marriage, Williams presented a couple who feel that love is enough, that they do not need marriage. Finally, they are tricked into marriage because it is "the best we [society] have to offer you." Williams' next play, *Why Not?* (1922) dramatized two mismatched couples whom he brought properly back to an acceptance of social standards by providing each with a child. The new realism in social comedy had not yet arrived.

As the 1920s approached, the pace and character of the drama suggested the explosion of good plays to come. *Clarence* (1919), a cute but silly farce by Booth Tarkington (1869-1946, the author of some twenty-one plays who was rightly more recognized for his novels), provided good roles for Helen Hayes and Alfred Lunt and shows how a young soldier-scientist-Ph.D. solves the problems of the Wheeler family. *Déclassée* (1919) by Zöe Akins (1886-1958) describes a love triangle, the resulting divorce and the woman's suffering from being déclassée, or lowered in social position. *The Famous Mrs. Fair* (1919), by James Forbes (1871-1938), tells of a woman whose war career overshadows her return to civilian life until she sees what her place must be. Essentially, Forbes emphasized the small-town living which had brought him minor success in *The Traveling Salesman* (1908) and *The Commuters* (1910), but this time with more serious insight. Other plays produced in 1919 include Susan Glaspell's first full-length play, *Bernice;* O'Neill's *The Dreamy Kid* and Elmer Rice's *For the Defense.*

2. MODERN DRAMA IN ONE-ACT

The university and the Little Theater Movement changed the nature of one-act drama in America from the frequently farcical curtain raisers of the past to something of dramatic significance. Generally, these plays were the initial efforts of dramatists who were to do better things. Lewis Beach's *The Clod* (1914) takes place during the Civil War in a frontier house and shows how little things reveal the basic person -- even the clod. In Susan Glaspell's *Trifles* (1916) a farm woman has strangled her earthy and unimaginative husband with a rope while he slept. As women at the farmhouse wait for their husbands to investigate the crime, they deduce the motive when they discover the woman's canary, her sole company and comfort, with its neck wrung. *Aria Da Capo* (1919), by Edna St. Vincent Millay, is a poetic satire on war, using the traditional Harlequin characters. Particularly outstanding are the one-act plays of Eugene O'Neill -- *Bound East for Cardiff, Thirst, In the Zone, Ile, The Rope,* among others -- which suggest the character and themes of his later plays.

II. EUGENE O'NEILL: CREATIVE SEARCHER

Whatever the final criticism of O'Neill's work may be, he arrived on the American dramatic scene at a time when he was most urgently needed. Moreover, through his sense of good theatre and his obsessive determination to explain human existence by the exploitation of his own life and family, he made a significant contribution to American drama and theatre. Writing mainly plays (his poetry is extremely slight and of interest only to the historian), he refused to be lionized when his work achieved popular acclaim, and he persisted with a single exception -- *Ah, Wilderness!* (1933), a comedy -- in writing a mixture of melodrama and tragedy which reveals his own somber outlook on life within the confines of American circumstance. His connection with nineteenth-century American theatre though his father, James O'Neill, the actor, warred with his own dramatic instincts, which were stimulated by European innovations in experimental theatre.

Throughout his career, conflicting agonies arising from personal and family difficulties led O'Neill to contemplate psychology and philosophy, which he was unable to master but which added strength and insight to the human conflicts in his plays. Through a tangled path of dramatized experiments, he searched -- haunted and cursed! -- finding different answers, none completely satisfying either in form or idea. His lack of detachment presents a problem; his stylistic demands upon audiences may be an even more serious limitation. All considered, however, his achievements have earned him more critical attention than any other American playwright and an international reputation which ranks him among America's greatest dramatists. Regardless of changing critical opinions, O'Neill will always be remembered as a vital, moving force in the establishment of modern American drama.

A. Life and Influences

Because an individual is the sum of all experiences and influences, a review of certain events and ideas will increase an understanding of the emotional and intellectual complexity that was Eugene O'Neill. The story of his life, fascinating and not a little horrible, is suggested by the titles of books about him: *The Haunted Heroes of Eugene O'Neill, Eugene O'Neill and the Tragic Tension, The Curse of the Misbegotten.*

1. "TRIAL BY EXISTENCE," EUGENE O'NEILL (1888-1953)

Within ten years, the shy young man whom Terry Carline introduced to the Provincetown Players in the summer of 1916 became a major figure in American drama. In another ten years, he had won the Nobel Prize for his contribution to dramatic literature. To accomplish this he had traveled a long way from his birth in a family hotel on the northeast corner of Forty-Third Street and Broadway in New York City, the son of James O'Neill and Ellen Quinlan O'Neill, to life as a sailor on assorted tramp steamers, to six months in a tuberculosis sanitarium, to George Pierce Baker's "47 Workshop" at Harvard and on to the Provincetown Players and his first theatre success. The way had not been easy.

O'Neill's father considered himself a tragic person, doomed to act in a single play, *The Count of Monte Cristo*. With self-pity, alcohol and a miserly attitude toward money (of which he had plenty), the elder O'Neill created a family life of misery and horror, which his son revealed in one of his last plays, *Long Day's Journey into Night*. That his mother innocently became addicted to drugs, that his brother Jamie was an alcoholic and that his Catholic faith brought him no solace haunted Eugene O'Neill throughout his life. Married in 1909 to the first of three wives, he immediately left his bride and started on aimless adventures -- Honduras, Argentina, the open sea -- until his confinement in a sanitarium for tuberculosis gave him an opportunity to read and to think. After his recovery in 1913, his admission the following year to Professor Baker's "47 Workshop" and his association with the Provincetown Players, he began his climb to success with the first of three Pulitzer Prize plays, *Beyond the Horizon* (1920). Ever restless and plagued by doubts, he divorced his second wife, Agnes Bolton, in 1929 and married actress Carlotta Monterey. Meanwhile, his plays kept appearing until *Days Without End* in 1934.

During the 1930s O'Neill worked on a dramatic cycle entitled "A Tale of Possessors Self-Dispossessed," which at one time was to "include eleven individual plays." Ill health and despair prevented him from completing his projected work, and although he destroyed most of his manuscripts in the early 1940s, two of his masterpieces -- *The Iceman Cometh* (1939) and *Long Day's Journey into Night* (1939-41) -- among others, have survived. Haunted by alcholism, disease, love and hate and the frustration of his own personal and artistic ambitions, he isolated himself in later years from all but his understanding wife. His son by his first wife, Eugene O'Neill, Jr., a brilliant classical scholar, committed suicide in 1950. He had two children by Agnes Bolton: Shane, who lived haphazardly in the O'Neill shadow, another victim; and Oona, who married Charlie Chaplin.

2.   INFLUENCES ON O'NEILL

In his book entitled *Twentieth Century Drama*, Bamber Gascoigne questioned the "academic parlour game" of discovering sources and influences. For the immediate enjoyment of a particular work of art, the point is well taken. For the literary historian, however, the placing of an artist's work within a developing social and intellectual frame has its value.

In American drama, O'Neill found almost nothing to imitate. He was, however, influenced by it to the extent that melodrama reminiscent of the late nineteenth century is a recognizable quality in his plays. In *Desire Under the Elms* he even burlesqued some of the traditional aspects of American melodrama. Admitting the influence of no dramatist except Strindberg, he was clearly interested in other European dramatists, particularly Ibsen and the European Expressionists. Beyond the theatrical experimentation, O'Neill borrowed ideas from Freud, Jung and Adler (*Strange Interlude* and *Mourning Becomes Electra*). References to the Bible, orthodox religions and classical myths appear often in his plays. Philosophy fascinated him, particularly that of Nietzsche; and he frequently retreated into a kind of mysticism. The Greeks -- their practices and doctrines in drama -- became central in his experimentation. A restless, searching person who flirted with ideas for their own sake, O'Neill was stimulated, although momentarily, by various philosophies, types of literature and modes of contemporary thought.

B.   Experimentation in Form

By inclination and circumstance, O'Neill experimented with technique. Concerned with the predicament of individuals, their struggles and inner conflicts, while searching for meaning and order, he became aware of -- and fearful of -- indescribable forces and confusing human attitudes. In America, however, with only a few exceptions -- Percy MacKaye, for example -- O'Neill had inherited a theatre in which realism was the major objective, brought about mainly by devices and artifices of the stage manager. In dealing with an individual's inner strengths and the subconscious, O'Neill discovered that mere realism failed to probe deeply enough. For him Expressionism became a major technique, complementing the earlier Naturalism against which this style of presentation was a distinct revolt. He further experimented with monologues, trilogies, symbols, divided characters and masques.

1.   *THE EMPEROR JONES* (1920)

Primarily a monologue, *The Emperor Jones* shows the destruction of a man's sense of dignity and pride as he retrogresses through a Darwinian chronology to a primitive state.   Elaborate stage sets, strong lighting effects ("the formless fears") and the divisions within this play suggest its experimental nature.   Concerning the use of sound, O'Neill wrote (quoted in *The Curse of the Misbegotten*, p. 131):

> One day I was reading of the religious feasts in the Congo and the uses to which the drum is put there -- how it starts at a normal pulse and is slowly accelerated until the heartbeat of everyone present corresponds to the frenzied beat of the drum. Here was an idea for an experiment. How could this sort of thing work on an audience in a theater?

2.   *MOURNING BECOMES ELECTRA* (1929-1931)

Rewriting the Greek myth concerning the House of Atreus, O'Neill took the Mannon family, placed them in a Civil War setting and motivated them in terms of Freud and Jung. The play became for O'Neill "a modern tragic interpretation of classic fate," "a modern psychological play -- fate springing out of the family." *Mourning Becomes Electra,* a trilogy composed of three plays -- "The Homecoming," "The Hunted," and "The Haunted" -- follows Aeschylus' *Oresteia* in character and action, although O'Neill, with greater severity, provides no escape for any of his characters. The Greek influence is also seen in the use of the villagers as a choral response and in the mask-like quality of certain characters, as well as the Mannon house itself.   The emphases on sex, the psychological motivations and the Oedipus and Electra complexes point clearly to Freud and Jung.   *Strange Interlude* (1926-27) is another trilogy with Freudian implications.

3.   SYMBOLS AND SPLIT CHARACTERS

Used variously in O'Neill's plays, the symbol is most obvious in *Dynamo* (1929).   Meant to be the first play of a trilogy (which was not continued) investigating the failure of science to fill the void left by a dead Christianity, the dynamo, a symbol of science, becomes in this play a god -- a mother-god, because O'Neill had seen the failure of the father-god in Christianity.   Even in physical appearance, the huge dynamo with its dual commutators suggests the female god.

In *Days Without End* (1934), O'Neill used two characters to suggest two conflicting qualities within a single person.   John Loving is the whole person: Loving is vicious and bitter, "a death mask of a John who has died with a sneer of scornful mockery on his lips."   The struggle in the play is between John and Loving, but the other characters see and hear only John.

4.   MASKS

O'Neill made several notes on the use of masks, contending that all characters in plays should wear them, and suggesting masks -- or a mask-like quality -- for several of his plays.   One of his most complicated plays using masks is *Lazarus Laughed* (1928). All members of the Chorus wear masks representing the Seven Ages of Man and seven kinds of people.   With such masks as the Simple, Ignorant, Young Manhood Type or the Sorrowful, Resigned, Old Age Type, there is the possibility of forty-nine masks.   His most interesting play of masks, however, is *The Great God Brown* (1926) with Dion Anthony wearing the mask of Pan, which changes into a cynical Mephistopheles.   When Dion dies, Billy Brown steals his mask, thinking that he is stealing his creativity.   Soon Brown is forced to wear a second mask, William A. Brown, successful businessman.   It is a difficult play to understand, and even O'Neill felt obligated to attempt an explanation in an essay.

C. Search for Self

To "justify the ways of God to man" is perhaps the greatest challenge for the creative imagination. In nineteenth-century America, the attempt to know God became an attempt to see one's own relationship to society and to other people. One's concept of nature gained, accordingly, greater import. In this questioning of life, creative artists searched for meaning, for values, for truth. With the appearance of Darwin, Comte and Spencer, this search became an analysis of the various forces that worked upon the individual in society. Modern writers, however, influenced by the principles of modern psychology, particularly the introversion-extroversion concepts of Jung and Kierkegaard's idea of self, understood that any search would be concentrated in "self." Consequently, through self-analysis many modern artists attempted to "justify the ways of God to man," and Eugene O'Neill was such an artist. He took as his task the expression of the torment and tension within the human mind and attempted to understand the predicament of humanity and therefore recognize values in life by dramatizing an individual's search for the secrets of self. Mainly, O'Neill discovered, human beings are destroyed by such a search; only once did he see victory. Finally, even a life of illusion in which one no longer needs to make searches proved unsatisfactory.

1.   THE PREDICAMENT OF THE HUMAN BEING

In an attempt to understand his fellow beings and to discover basic truths, O'Neill made many observations which he once described as "the sickness of today." This sickness, thought to result from various forces at work, becomes the predicament of the sensitive individual who, in a search for his soul, finds cultural elements which destroy humanity. It may be the force of materialism, which hardens and dehumanizes Marco Polo in *Marco Millions* (1928). Or an individual may be destroyed by an inability to be true to self and at the same time be successful in life, as Dion is doomed in *The Great God Brown* (1929). If this "sickness of today" permeates the forces of society which make sensitive people miserable and eventually destroy them, the desire to "belong" is a possible if frustrating response -- frustrating because humanity is destined never to "belong."

Yank in *The Hairy Ape* (1922) is symbolic of the predicament O'Neill created for those who try to understand life; these men are the "haunted heroes."   Obsessed, driven, and suffering, "everyman" is pictured by O'Neill as searching for truth, trying to discover both himself and his place in the universe.

2.   THE SEARCH DEFEATED

With the exception of *Ah, Wilderness!* (1933) and *Desire Under the Elms* (1924), O'Neill's major plays written before he stopped publishing in the mid-1930s show humanity defeated in any search for meaning.

(a) *Beyond the Horizon* (1920)

Robert Mayo, poet and mystic, is planning to leave his family farm to go on a voyage with his uncle and see "beyond the horizon." But Ruth Atkins, one of O'Neill's early dominating women, persuades Robert to stay and marry her, while Robert's brother, Andrew, who really loves the farm, goes on the planned trip. All three search for meaning in life, though not consciously, and all fail. Ruth loses even her will to seek; Andrew sees nothing in the wonders of the world he visits; Robert, having been unhappy with Ruth and having failed to satisfy his dream, dies without seeing "beyond the horizon."

(b) *The Hairy Ape* (1922)

Using the social problems created by the Industrial Revolution as a background for a psychological search for meaning, *The Hairy Ape* is, O'Neill wrote, a "symbol of man, who has lost his old harmony with nature, the harmony which he used to have as an animal and has not yet acquired in a spiritual way . . . . The struggle used to be with the gods, but is now with himself, his own past, his attempt to belong." Yank, a stoker on a steamship, attempts to show the world who he is after being called a "hairy ape" by a member of so-called polite society. Physically strong and continually assuming the position of Rodin's "The Thinker," Yank is completely ineffective in his attempt. Nobody understands him -- the policemen who arrest him for disturbing the peace, the Industrial Workers of the World who consider him a spy. All he wants is "to belong." Finally, he sees a gorilla in a cage as a possible companion, but, once freed, the gorilla crushes him: "Even him didn't tink I belonged. Christ, where do I get off at? Where do I fit in?" The answer, of course, is "nowhere!"

(c) *The Great God Brown* (1926)

As a boy, Dion Anthony (Dionysus, "the creative pagan acceptance of life" combined with St. Anthony, "the life-denying spirit of Christianity") wore the mask of Pan to conceal his sensitive spirit from those around him. Later, after he is grown and married, his mask becomes Satan even to Margaret, his wife, and he can remove his mask only in the company of Cybel, the prostitute and mother of all men. Professionally, he is a fine architect in spite of his alcoholic addiction, his outward response to his inner frustration. Finally, destroyed by his inability to be creative in modern society, he dies, and his mask is stolen by William Brown, his childhood friend, his boss in the contracting firm and a successful businessman. Brown thinks that he is stealing Dion's creativity, but he is actually taking only Dion's cynical paganism. Wearing the mask, he assumes his place as Margaret's husband, but soon he must wear another mask -- William Brown Businessman -- and patronize Cybel. He can be himself to no one. Frustrated by his fate, he finally abandons the mask of Brown (thus killing him and being accused of his murder) and dies with Dion's mask beside him. Ironically, it is to this mask of Dion that Margaret promises to be true forever, while the body of Brown is identified by Cybel as "Man!" "Howd'yuh spell it?" asks the police captain.

(d) *Lararus Laughed* (1928)

This play shows the search in conjunction with faith. When Lazarus was brought back from the dead, he laughed. This was his answer to those who asked what lay beyond the grave: "There is only laughter!" For those who follow Lazarus in life, there is laughter, the symbol of knowledge. At the end of the play, Lazarus is burned at the stake by Caligula and answers questions as to what is beyond life with laughter: "Fear not, Caligula! There is no death!" At first Caligula laughs, too; then he changes and boasts that he has killed Lazarus, proving that there is death. Finally, however, he becomes humble: "Fool! Madman! Forgive me, Lazarus! Men forget!" Men will search for meaning, O'Neill seems to say, and be defeated because they cannot learn from the past. "Men forget!" Each must make his own discovery. Only partial success in the search is attained, but the play anticipates *Days Without End*.

(e) *Dynamo* (1929)

The theme of this play is, in O'Neill's words, "the death of an old God and the failure of science and materialism to give a satisfactory new one for the surviving primitive religious instinct to find a meaning for life in and to comfort its fears of death with." As Reuben Light searches for a god and meaning in life, he is influenced his father, a devout but cowardly minister, and by the atheist next door who taunts Reuben, and whose daughter Reuben loves. Losing his faith, Reuben leaves home and becomes a hardened cynic and worshipper of science. The conflict still exists, as Reuben, O'Neill's symbol of modern man, requires both a cold, intellectual father-god and a warm, emotional mother-god. The dynamo suggests both science and, with its dual commutators, woman; but in his attempt to worship it, Reuben is destroyed by its electrical force.

3.   THE SEARCH ENDING IN FAITH

In *Days Without End* (1934), O'Neill dramatizes a search for meaning which clearly leads to Christianity. The play is, according to O'Neill, "primarily a psychological study . . . revealing a man's search for truth amid the conflicting doctrines of the modern world and his return to his old religious faith." The struggle between John and Loving, two aspects of John Loving, is dramatized through a novel that John is writing. The theme of the novel -- Can a man who has sinned against his wife be forgiven? -- is also John's personal problem. Loving, whom nobody sees or hears, answers the question with "No!" Aided by Father Baird, who tries to make John repent, John finally becomes conscious of his soul and starts for the church; his wife forgives him; and Loving dies at the foot of the cross, as John shouts, "Life laughs with God's love again." With love, one's search for truth ends in a meaningful faith.

4.   THE SEARCH AND MAN'S ILLUSION

After a single burst of optimism following a period in which damnation seemed a part of life, O'Neill stopped publishing his plays until *The Iceman Cometh* appeared in 1946 (copyright, 1940). In his later plays his attitude toward the search for meaning focussed on illusions in life. Humankind may seem to find value in self-deception rather than in self-analysis, O'Neill admitted, but in a life of illusion there is neither truth nor happiness -- only sickness and stagnation.

(a) *The Iceman Cometh* (1940)

A motley group of has-beens waits in Harry Hope's saloon for the annual visit of Hickey, a happy salesman who jokes about his wife being home with the iceman. The men are all failures: Harry hasn't been out of the bar for twenty years; a Harvard-trained lawyer took to drink and now only dreams of his potential; Jimmy Tomorrow is always waiting for tomorrow to act; an anarchist talks of the worthlessness of life as he tries to forget his past; and so on. But when Hickey arrives, he is changed. He now insists upon facing the truth, and he tries to make each bum accept himself for what he is, see life truthfully and be happy. Reluctantly, all do as he says. But they are not happy, and Hickey cannot understand this development. Unnerved by his failure, he confesses to having killed his wife; she lived in a dream, he says, and he killed her to prove the dream. The men are stunned and can reach only one conclusion -- Hickey is crazy! If this is so, of course, all of his talk has been insane, they can return to their old lives, their old illusions and safety. Only the anarchist has learned. Having preached suicide but now a convert to Hickey's truth, he realizes his own failure because he is too weak to take his own life. Years before, O'Neill had abandoned Hickey's philosophy; here he shows the inadequacy of the life illusion.

(b) *A Touch of the Poet* (1935-42; first produced, 1957)

Part of the cycle entitled *A Tale of Possessors Self-Dispossessed*, *A Touch of the Poet* suggests the spiritually desolate life of those who would live by illusions. Major Con Melody, his wife and his daughter, Sara, run an inn near Boston. A prideful, would-be aristocrat, Melody lives in his past glories as a soldier and rides a thoroughbred mare in spite of approaching poverty. The crisis occurs when Sara falls in love with a wealthy young Bostonian, Simon Harford, who is taken sick at the inn. When the Harfords try to interfere with

the young lovers and even attempt to bribe Melody, he is
infuriated. Dressed in his officer's uniform, he goes to Boston to
challenge Mr. Harford to a duel and is beaten by the Harford
servants. His pride destroyed, Melody returns home, shoots his
mare and relapses into a thick Irish brogue. Sara, meanwhile,
has seduced Simon so that he will marry her. She, too, has lost
pride but become more understanding of her mother's love for
her father. The illusion of aristocracy lost, Melody resorts to
another life, equally inadequate. Although Sara may face life
happily, sustained by love alone, she has not escaped reality
nor found peace and understanding, as *More Stately Mansions*
(1936, unfinished), another play from the abandoned cycle,
effectively dramatizes.

D.   O'Neill's Contribution to American Drama

O'Neill's Promethean characteristics are accentuated by the
lack of substantive competition during the early years of his
career, but in many ways O'Neill is Promethean.   To the
American drama, he brought a knowledge of the theatre and a
creative desire to examine its potential at a time when
America most urgently needed a fresh approach.   His
familiarity with dramatic literature and his interest in
philosophy and psychology make him a popular subject of
criticism and scholarship.   Essentially, he was the first
American dramatist who gained the respect of both theatre
people and literary scholars.

It is also true that his skills and insight have been
exaggerated. His language has been severely criticized for its
weakness. His plots have been shown to be melodramatic. He
has been called an "emotional hemophiliac" who could never
recover from "family-inflicted wounds." There is no doubt that
he built his plays on his own tensions, attacking cherished
values and beliefs in American society and wallowing in his
pessimistic view of life. But he had, as John Gassner pointed
out in *Theatre at the Crossroads,* "the courage of his
discontent." When he did portray, as in *Long Day' Journey into
Night,* "a stranger who never feels at home, who does not
really want and is not really wanted, who can never belong," he
was expressing a basic conflict, a struggle which places him

with Herman Melville, Thomas Mann and Albert Camus. In spite of his many weaknesses, his contribution to American drama may be found in his meaningful ideas, expressed frequently with great emotional, if uneven, power and in a manner which can be exceptionally effective on the stage. Sean O'Casey noted, "Of course, he's left an impact on the Theater of today as Shaw has: neither the English nor the American Theaters can ever be quite the same since these giants leaped onto the stage." This is high praise and indicative of the international reputation which O'Neill brought America.

Among O'Neill's plays, the following are a distinguished part of his contribution to American drama: *Desire Under the Elms* (1924), a naturalistic New England tragedy of adultery, murder and pride, which employs classical comparisons, attacks on religion and a theme of loneliness with conflicting greed and sense of freedom; *Mourning Becomes Electra* (1931), a modern psychological version of Aeschylus' *Oresteia; Ah, Wilderness!* (1933), a major contribution to American comedy, in which O'Neill shows an uncharacteristic sense of balance and humor, as well as a number of major character types that appear in his other plays, and a sentimental story of love and innocence and the nostalgic conflicts of youth; and *Long Day's Journey into Night* (1939-41; first staged in 1956), a dramatization of the torments, horrors and struggles within the O'Neill family.

III. LET FREEDOM REIGN: REALISM TO POETRY

The sense of freedom that O'Neill stimulated was immediately seen in other plays of the 1920s. In both idea and technique, this new decade in American drama was distinctive. Critics were enthusiastic about the new realism, and Alexander Woollcott joyfully announced the "waning tyranny of the happy ending," that "fine, bosom to bosom, lip to lip finale." In their fervor for portraying life truthfully, playwrights like Maxwell Anderson and Sidney Howard proved to be shocking (but enjoyable), while those who experimented in form -- Elmer Rice, John Howard Lawson -- brought gasps from their audiences with their borrowings from German Expressionism. Throughout the decade, numerous dramatists commented on society's shortcomings, employing mainly the ideas of social melodrama adopted by Eugene Walter earlier in the century. One of these writers, Sidney Howard, provided a key for the decade with his thesis: "They knew what they wanted."   It was a decade in which the independence of the individual was a byword, and this sense of freedom allowed dramatists greater scope in the kind of plays they wrote.   Although these plays were part of a slowly developing transformation, writers of folk drama, pageant drama and poetic drama also found new energy during the 1920s.

A. Insurgent Realism

No plays suggest the change in realism more than *What Price Glory?* and *They Knew What They Wanted*.   Produced the same year, 1924, they suggest the robust and liberal characteristics of the time.   The previous year Owen Davis had shown his talent for realism in the Pulitzer Prize winning *Icebound*. Susan Glaspell, a seriously undervalued playwright, provided not a violent or controversial realism, but a truthful portrayal of life that indicates the insight of the emotionally and intellectually mature.   Numerous other dramatists contributed to this new realism.

1.   TWO STARTLING PLAYS

What Price Glory? and *They Knew What They Wanted* are essentially comic-melodramas, but both are vivid theatre -- one through its realistic action and language, the other through its "new" morality.

(a) *What Price Glory?* (1924)
by Laurence Stallings (1894-1968)
and Maxwell Anderson (1888-1959)

This war play takes place in a French village during World War I and tells of the rivalry between Sgt. Quirt and Capt. Flagg for Charmaine de la Cognac.   After many adventures together, they hate but respect each other, and when Quirt steals Charmaine's affection during Flagg's absence and gets into trouble with her father, Pete Cognac, Flagg is tempted to make Quirt marry the girl.   Then orders for an advance come, and Flagg backs down rather than leave Quirt in jail for refusing to obey his order.   In the military action, both Quirt and Flagg show their courage, but Quirt is hit in the leg and hospitalized until he escapes to Pete's place to see Charmaine. There, he meets Flagg. As the two argue and get drunk, they begin to fight. When orders come for a return to the front, Flagg rushes out followed by Quirt -- "Hey, Flagg, wait for baby!"

(b) *They Knew What They Wanted* (1924)
by Sidney Howard (1891-1939)

Tony, a wealthy but lonely old Italian wine grower in California, has wooed and won a girl, Amy, through letters alone. He has, however, deceived her by sending her the picture of a young radical friend of his, Joe. On the day Amy arrives at Tony's home, Tony breaks both his legs in a car wreck, and Amy, a footsore waitress who wants security, is shocked to discover that it is the old but good-hearted Tony whom she is to marry, rather than the more physically attractive Joe. A colorful wedding has been planned, and Tony is very generous with his gifts. Physically and emotionally exhausted, Amy is drawn to Joe that first night. Though tempted to leave, she reconsiders the situation and decides to go through with the marriage. Three months later, Amy and Tony are getting along well, but she knows that she is pregnant with Joe's child. Realizing her unworthiness and now loving Tony, she prepares to leave, after telling Tony the truth. At first he is furious; then he, too, reconsiders. Amy has not been with Joe since that first night, and Joe is interested only in wandering through life. Amy wants security and love; Tony, too old he thinks to father a child, wants a baby. They know what they want, and they accept the happiness they have.

2.   OWEN DAVIS (1874-1956): MELOLDRAMATIC REALIST

The author of more than one hundred successful romantic and violent melodramas, Davis stopped writing that kind of play with *The Family Cupboard* (1913) and earned a Pulitzer Prize ten years later with *Icebound*. An earlier experiment in realism, *Detour* (1921), is set in New England, where Helen Hardy has finally accumulated $1000 to take her daughter, Kate, to New York to study art. At this time, however, a neighbor, Tom Lane, is about to be dispossessed because his gas station failed when a detour rerouted traffic. Land greedy and land poor, Steve Hardy, Helen's husband, wants to buy Tom's property and orders Helen and Kate out of the house when they refuse to give him their money. Later, when a visiting art critic tells Kate that she has no talent, Kate decides to give the money to her father and marry Tom. Helen must now save her money and her illusions for her grandchildren.

Icebound (1923)

The story of this play is of lost illusions and barren life in New England. The Jordans are a greedy family who wait for their mother to die and leave them her money. Of all her children, the mother loves best her youngest but dissipated son, Ben; a young cousin, Jane, who tends the sick mother, also loves Ben. When Jane inherits the Jordan money, she signs it over to Ben who then realizes his love for his mother and for Jane. Jane, however, has no illusions about the sincerity of his attitude; she has only her love, the knowledge that she is doing what she thinks is right and the bitterness of the rest of the Jordans.

3.   SUSAN GLASPELL (1876-1948): REALIST AND EXPERIMENTER

With her husband, George Cram (Jig) Cook, Susan Glaspell was a distinct force within the Provincetown Players and wrote several theatrically effective and intellectually stimulating plays. She was clearly much closer to O'Neill in her concern for intense, meaningful drama than were any of her peers. Having a more stable and mature approach to life, she brought a greater sense of universality to her interest in individuals at odds with society, a theme she treated throughout her career. Eventually, the problems of the Provincetown Players proved a source of disappointment to both Glaspell and Cook. In 1922 they left for Greece, where Cook died two years later. Thereafter, Glaspell spent part of her time in Europe. In 1930, she wrote *Alison's House,* in which she created a thought-provoking and beautifully expressed, if sentimental and sometimes awkward, play based on an interpretation of Emily Dickinson's life.

Slight but effective, *Supressed Desires* (1915), written with Cook, is a witty satire on the theory of complete freedom in self-expression. Building upon the meaningfulness of seemingly unimportant trifles and the intuitive response of women to realities that escape their husbands, *Trifles* (1916) remains Glaspell's most popular play. *The Outside* (1916) provides "an allegory of the battle between the life force and the death force," according to historian C. W. E. Bigsby. In this play and in later work, Glaspell was an inveterate experimenter whose use of symbolism further invites comparison with O'Neill. *Bernice* (1919), an insightful work although perhaps too conversational and contrived, shows how a dead woman brings a change for the better in her philandering husband by having him told (falsely) that she killed herself. *The Inheritors* (1921) dramatizes the different views which succeeding generations have toward the administration of a college founded by a liberal ancestor. As any analysis of the decline of American idealism, the play impressed such critics of dramatic literature as James Agate and Ludwig Lewisohn.

The Verge (1921)
In her most controversial play, Glaspell fused comedy with melodrama, while experimenting with modes of symbolism and expressionism to create a challenging and metaphysically oriented commentary on feminism and related social issues. More than her other plays, *The Verge* reveals her closeness to the emotional struggles that haunted and confounded Eugene O'Neill and that link her with the serious writers of her generation. A woman on the verge of insanity is searching for the answer to life in her attempt to create new forms of life and to understand her own soul. But she can only reach the "verge." Something eludes her. Rich in language and idea, this play unfortunately lacks theatricality.

4.   OTHER EXPRESSIONS OF REALISM

The urge to find realism everywhere struck many critics at this time. Even a play like *Broadway* (1926) by Philip Dunning and George Abbot (1887-) -- a melodrama about a chorus girl who learns which guy is right for her, but only after a murder, much rowdiness and some risqué language -- was called realistic. A better play, and more deserving of being termed realistic, *Miss Lulu Bett* (1920) is the Pulitzer Prize winning dramatization of her own novel by Zona Gale (1874-1938). It tells the story of a strong woman who leaves a taunting brother-in-law and her sister, on whom she is economically dependent, to marry a man who has not yet divorced his wife. Lewis Beach's melodrama, *The Goose Hangs High* (1924), describes in realistic detail the economic problems of parents whose grown children finally discover that they should be more thoughtful. *The Front Page* (1928), by Charles MacArthur and Ben Hecht, is a satiric farce on newspaper life; realistic only in language, descriptions and general vulgarity, it makes for very effective theatre. A more seriously realistic play on an old theme is Samuel Raphaelson's *Young Love* (1928), which tells of two young people who stay together for a night, show no faith in the institution of marriage and become increasingly cynical as they become involved in mate-swapping with a young married couple. Realism appeared in many guises.

B.   Expressionism During the Twenties

One reaction to realism in the theatre was a new approach to production consistent with the experimental attitude of the Twenties. Coming to America from Europe, expressionism in art was defined by Sheldon Cheney in *The Primer of Modern Art* as "that movement in art which transfers the emphasis from technical display and imitated surface aspects of nature to creative form; from descriptive and representative truth to intensified emotional expressionism; from objective to subjective and abstract formal qualities." Expressionism in the theatre came mainly from Germany, but the closeness of art and theatre is clear. According to Ludwig Lewisohn, reviewing *The Adding Machine* (*Nation*, April 4, 1923), "Expressionism has two chief aims: to fling the inner life of the dramatic figures immediately upon the stage; to synthesize, instead of describing, their world and their universe into symbolic visions that shall sum up whole histories, moralities, cosmogonies in a brief minute and a fleeting scene." O'Neill's use of expressionism is well known, but there were others who employed expressionism to even greater effect.

1.   ELMER RICE (1892-1967): *THE ADDING MACHINE* (1923)

Giving people numbers instead of names, Rice satirized a mechanical world and the ineptitude of all who succumb to this loss of humanity. The story is told quite simply in seven scenes. In a long soliloquy, Mrs. Zero explains her dissatisfaction with life, condemning Mr. Zero, a bookkeeper, for his ineffectiveness. Upon hearing that he will be replaced by an adding machine, Zero, in anger and frustration, kills his boss, is arrested, tried and executed. After being sent to Heaven, where he operates a heavenly adding machine, he willingly allows himself to be sent back to earth -- as the heavenly gods laugh at his decision -- where he will relive his insignificant life, the eternal clod and victim in a depersonalized world.

Expressionism in *The Adding Machine* is shown in the devices which reveal Mr. Zero's emotions. For example, the Boss fires Zero: "His voice is drowned by the music [of a merry-go-round]. The platform is revolving rapidly now. Zero and the Boss face each other. They are entirely motionless save for the Boss's jaws, which open and close incessantly. But the words are inaudible. The music swells and swells."

2. **GEORGE S. KAUFMAN (1889-1961)**
   AND MARC CONNELLY (1890-1980):
   BEGGAR ON HORSEBACK (1924)

Showing an artist's revolt against middle-class family ties, this play effectively uses dream expressionism. Generally, expressionism is not the choice of writers of comedy, but these dramatists were extremely successful by supplementing comedy with music, ballet and hilarious exaggerations which underline the satire of the piece. Mr. Cady, the businessman, has a telephone attached to his chest; Mrs. Cady, constantly knitting, is fitted with a rocking chair; a man's necktie grows larger and more gaudy; characters multiply in fanciful scenes as the hero's dream becomes a nightmare.

3. **JOHN HOWARD LAWSON (1895-1977):**
   PROCESSIONAL (1925)

Best known for plays which show his commitment to Marxism, Lawson also wrote one of the earliest American expressionistic plays, *Roger Bloomer* (1923). With its various anti-realistic devices and Freudian psychology, this play exposes the hero's mind as he searches for knowledge of self. Lawson explained his second expressionistic play, *Processional,* as a "jazz symphony of American life." With its thesis of class warfare, the play dramatizes a strike in which the proletarian hero, Dynamite Jim, is abused by anti-Marxist forces in America, until the workers finally revolt and win the day. Although Lawson called his technique neither realism nor expressionism but "essentially vaudevillesque in character," his episodic approach employed many expressionistic devices to create a panoramic view of America.

C. The Social Drama of the Twenties

The tendency of dramatists to present "a serious study of contemporary social problems" -- a tendency which Clayton Hamilton resented in 1911 -- took on added meaning in the 1920s. Whereas social comment had once skipped from slight to serious, dramatists of the Twenties became alert to current psychological approaches. Into this stream of American drama, Sidney Howard launched his plays, adding an imagination and a talent which, guided by a new sense of realism, gave social drama a new dignity in the eyes of audiences and critics, both in America and abroad. He was not alone, but he stood preeminent in employing a form of drama which was to be used by writers of various intellectual persuasions during the years before World War II. And in his particular approach, he caught the spirit of the social drama of the Twenties.

1. A VARIETY OF SOCIAL PLAYS

Having commented on the difficulties of divorce in *Déclassée* (1919), Zöe Akins displayed in *Daddy's Gone A-Hunting* (1921) a bitter view of the world -- "a very unsafe place," full of "shifting sands and changing minds" -- where a conventional woman is married to a morally irresponsible artist whose ego and sense of personal freedom make a normal life impossible. *Ambush* (1921), by Arthur Richman, describes a family which has become morally and spiritually bankrupt. Learning that his daughter is deceitful and sexually promiscuous and that his wife is contemptuous of him, the father degrades himself futher by accepting these aspects of life which wait in ambush for man. George Abbott and James Gleason's *The Fall Guy* (1924) is a melodrama which shows that economic problems might force a man into crime, but for the alert conniving of the dramatists. Other plays treating the problems of married life include Frank Craven's *The First Year* (1920), Gilbert Emery's *The Hero* (1921), which dramatizes the effect of the war hero on the wife whose husband stayed home, and Maxwell Anderson's *Saturday's Children* (1927).

2.   SIDNEY HOWARD (1891-1939):
FIRST MAJOR WRITER OF SOCIAL DRAMA

Neither a profound nor original playwright by his own admission, Sidney Howard knew how to mix comedy, realism and melodrama in expertly contrived scenes of fast-moving action and rapid emotional change. His own background, as a radical reporter and writer for Hearst newspapers, perhaps made his concern for social problems inevitable. He was not, however, an experimenter in the drama but followed the tradition of the "satisfactory" play. His major interest was in character portrayal, as reflected in the titles of his plays. Literary critics have also pointed out his mastery of dramatic irony of situation and his concern for ideas. A major theme in his plays is the idea of self in society -- distinguishing those who accept freedom with responsibility from those who are merely selfish and therefore damned. During a decade in which O'Neill's achievements have unfortunately eclipsed the work of other playwrights in the minds of many critics and historians, Sidney Howard escaped notice as the first major writer of social drama in modern America.

(a)   Strong Characters: They Know What They Want
After several plays -- including a poetic drama, *Swords* (1921), about the Guelphs and Ghibellines, and a pageant, *Lexington* (1924) -- Howard wrote *They Knew What They Wanted* (1924). From that point on, his best plays were built around strong characters. Sam in *Lucky Sam McCarver* (1925) uses people to get ahead and becomes a hardened, cynical man who can never love, lucky in only an ironic sense. Carrie, *Ned McCobb's Daughter* (1926), shows her determination and the superiority of her character as she overcomes a weak husband, a conniving brother-in-law and even bandits to get what she wants. Doc Haggett in *The Late Christopher Bean* (1932) thinks he knows what he wants when he tries to take advantage of a servant

girl, the wife of Christoper Bean, whose paintings become collector's items, but he changes in time. The liberal heroine of *Alien Corn* (1933) chooses a romantic escape to freedom but definitely knows her mind.

(b) *The Silver Cord* (1926)
With its well-drawn characters, sharp irony, emotion-packed action and Freudian emphasis, *The Silver Cord* is one of the best social thesis plays in American drama. Mrs. Phelps has raised her two sons alone -- David and Robert. When the play opens, David has just returned from abroad with his bride, Christina, and Robert has become engaged to Hester. Facing this situation, Mrs. Phelps fights to maintain possession of her sons. With diabolical cunning, she breaks Robert's engagement and would destroy David's marriage but for Christina's expected baby, which proves -- though barely -- a stronger tie for David than his mother's "unselfish love." The thesis probes the distinction between "life and self" -- between living in responsible freedom and being destroyed by self-love.

(c) A Key to the Decade
The title of Howard's first successful play provides a key to character portrayals in many of the social plays of the 1920s: *They Knew What They Wanted.* Jane in Davis' *Icebound* knows -- and gets -- exactly what she wants. Maxwell Anderson's *Saturday's Children* are less successful, as is Abe McCrannie in Paul Green's *In Abraham's Bosom* (1926), but they, too, definitely know what they want. S. N. Behrman's hero in *The Second Man* (1927) knows what he wants and keeps it. So do Mary Hutton in Philip Barry's *Paris Bound* (1927) and Lissa in his earlier play, *In a Garden* (1925).

D. Modern Folk Drama

"If you draw the locality with which you are most familiar, and interpret it faithfully, it will show you the way to the universal," wrote Fred Koch, director of the Carolina Playmakers at the University of North Carolina, a center for folk drama in America. Few would disagree with Professor Koch's premise, but folk plays (and the phrase is frequently synonymous with regional plays among modern critics), though successful on the stage, have rarely achieved universal significance. This problem of the folk dramatist -- to strive for the limited historical spirit and raise the particulars to universals -- was solved with some success by Paul Green, one of Koch's students. Through the efforts of Koch, Green and others who have dramatized the folklore and traditional myth characters of various areas of America, folk drama achieved a substantial popularity across the country during the years between the World Wars.

1.   BACKGROUNDS OF MODERN FOLK DRAMA

Folk literature in America was given form by men and women who sang of "Frankie and Johnny," "Picking Cotton" and "Pat Works on the Railroad." The beginnings of American folk drama appeared early with the nineteenth-century emphasis on regional characters, such as the Yankee, the Indian and the Negro. Interest in mythical characters, like Paul Bunyan, and in local color stories came later in the century. Further stimulation for dramatists appeared when the Abbey Players visited America. Both John M. Synge and William Butler Yeats had written plays for the Abbey Players based on Ireland's folklore. The suggestion was not missed, and the growth of the American little theatres and community theatres reemphasized an interest in the common people. Soon the peculiarities of custom, the superstitions, the naïveté and the mixture of sentiment and realism which make up America began to appear in plays. Few plays, however, were very effective. The danger was that the folk background would become -- as it frequently did -- mere flavoring for melodrama.

2.   THE REGIONS OF AMERICA

Representing the same geographic sections portrayed in local color drama, folk plays were created about the West, New England and the South. Lynn Riggs wrote of the great Southwest in *Roadside* (1930) and in *Green Grow the Lilacs* (1931), which became the musical, *Oklahoma!* John Steinbeck dramatized *Of Mice and Men* (1937), using a western background; *No More Frontier* (1929) by Talbot Jennings tells of three generations of an Idaho pioneer family. Dan Totheroh's *Wild Birds* (1925) makes effective use of the Middle West, although the story approaches both sensational and sentimental melodrama.   Owen Davis represented New England well with *Detour* (1921), *Icebound* (1923) and a dramatization with his son, Donald, of Edith Wharton's novel, *Ethan Frome* (1936).   O'Neill also illustrated the peculiarities of New England with *Desire Under the Elms* (1924).

Some of the best folk plays have portrayed the South, such as *Hell-Bent for Heaven* (1924) by Hatcher Hughes (1883-1945), which employs feuding, superstition and religious fanaticism in a moving portrayal of North Carolina mountain people. *Sun-up* (1923) by Lula Vollmer (1895-1955) tells how a mountain woman, after hearing that her son has been killed in the war, hides an army deserter, even though the boy's father killed her husband.   The language, the peculiar customs and the supernatural vision suggest characteristics of folk literature.   In 1927 Dorothy Heyward (1890-1961) and DuBose Heyward (1885-1940) wrote *Porgy*, which was later made into the opera *Porgy and Bess*. The story of Porgy's love for Crown's Bess has many folk aspects -- the saucer funeral, the ominous bird which will bring disaster wherever it lands, the bleeding corpse and the conjuring for Bess. One of the best-known folk dramas is *The Green Pastures* (1930) by Marc Connelly (1890-1980). Explaining the Bible in terms of Negro life, this play humanizes God as a country preacher who watches over and loves his people. "De Lawd" attends a fish-fry in Heaven and with a spectacular flurry creates the world and man. The first half of the play ends with the Flood: "I only hope it's goin' to work out all right," says God. The second part dramatizes the stories of Moses and Joshua and shows God's anger at his people -- "I repent of dese people I have made" -- and ends with the advent of Jesus.

3.   PAUL GREEN (1894-1981) AND THE SOUTH

In *The Drama* for October 1930, Paul Green wrote an essay, "Needed -- A Native American Theatre," contending that thus far no American dramatist had spoken for his country. He could not have known that, more than other playwrights, he himself would approach his ideal. His powers of observation and his philosophic turn of mind were enlivened by his years of living in North Carolina -- years which provided the background for his writing. Although he wrote protest plays as well as outdoor pageants, his best works are his dramas of Southern life, showing an instinctive understanding of racial problems. Emphasizing the folk elements of his characters, Green revealed an idealism and a feeling for America's past which made him a distinctively American dramatist.

(a)   One-Act Plays

Many of Green's one-act plays combine his basic interest in folk characteristics with his equally strong concern for social justice. *The Last of the Lowries* (1920) is imitative of Singe's *Riders to the Sea* as it dramatizes a mother's reaction to the killing of her last son, who with his brothers and father comprised an outlaw gang. *White Dresses* (1926) portrays in poignant and bitter sentiment the story of a mulatto girl who is forced to accept her future among Negroes. The white dress which the landlord's son gives to Mary is burned by her grandmother along with another one, presumably given to Mary's mother by her real father, a white man. *In the Valley* (1928) is concerned with the unfair treatment of blacks in society.

(b)   Longer Plays and the White South

Much of the strength of Green's plays comes from his insight into the conditions and problems of the Southern white, as well as the black. At his best he transcends the regional particulars on which his plays are built to reach universal significance. Hardy Gilchrist in *The Field God* (1927) is proud of his successful farm, while his sickly but fanatically religious wife, Etta, questions this pride. When Rhoda, young and pretty, arrives from the city to help on the farm, the love that springs up between her and Hardy is inevitable, but, when confessed, causes Etta's death. Later, married, Hardy and Rhoda have constant trouble -- the farm animals sicken, their son dies -- until, their pride gone, they appeal to God to find their salvation and a renewal of their love. *The House of Connelly* (1931) also treats the Southern white plantation class. Will Connelly realizes that his mother and sisters live in the past, but he is too weak to do anything about the problem until he must thwart their desires to marry him to a wealthy aristocrat who would save them from poverty. Instead, he marries, for love, the daughter of a tenant family.   The past must be buried and a new life begun. *Shroud My Body Down* (1935) is a fascinating play on the control which superstition and religious fanaticism exert on the uneducated Southern white.

(c)   *In Abraham's Bosom* (1926): A Pulitzer Prize
In this play, presented with courage and understanding, Green depicted the tragic struggle of the idealist, who is defeated by environmental forces and by the very people he is trying to help. The working songs of Negroes in the turpentine woods, the rhythm of their speech and the use of supernatural visions enhance the folk quality of the play. Abraham McCrannie, idealistic, stubborn and furiously ambitious, wants to learn and become a teacher of his people. His white father, old Colonel Mack, finally persuades the school board to let Abe teach, but the Negroes are reluctant pupils. Abe's son turns against him, and the school closes when old Mack dies. Taunted, frustrated and beaten by white men when he tries to reopen his school, Abe kills Lonnie, his white half-brother, and is lynched.

4.   MYTH CHARACTERS: TRUE FOLK DRAMA

The terms folk and regional drama are generally confused, although strictly speaking, folk drama should be built upon American myths. E. P. Conkle (1899-) is the best of the playwrights to make use of mythic material. He wrote of *Bill and the Widow Maker*, a story of Pecos Bill, his great purple stallion and his argument with Don Coyote, the last of the cowboys; *Paul and the Blue Ox*, which tells of Paul Bunyan's problems with logging bosses; *The Delectable Judge*, a tale of the prejudiced and intolerant Judge Roy Bean; and *Johnny Appleseed* -- all published in 1947. Other folk-myth plays include *John Henry* (1940) by Roark Bradford, *Paul Bunyan* (1932) by Richard L. Stokes and *Missouri Legend* (1938), a story of Jesse James by Guthrie McClintoc.

E.   Pageant Drama

Modern American pageantry began in 1905 with Louis Evan Shipman's *Saint Gaudens Masque*, for which Percy MacKaye, a major figure in American pageantry, wrote the prologue. Essentially, the pageant is a healthy expression of the community spirit and can be loosely defined as a festival, in episodes of thanksgiving, worship or history.   Types of pageants include the processional, which is the oldest; the historical, concerned with ideas or institutions and employing dialogue, pantomime, music and dance; and the masque, involving allegory and spectacle.   Pageantry in America progressed with greater activity than is frequently realized, culminating in the work of Paul Green and his contemporaries. In 1913 the American Pageant Association was founded.

1.   VARIED BEGINNINGS

Pageants celebrated a variety of events and institutions. The Boston Normal School produced *The Pageant of Education* in 1908; Thomas Wood Stevens wrote the *Pageant of Illinois* (1909), showing the history of the region from the coming of Christianity until the Black Hawk War of 1832; George Pierce Baker celebrated the American musician, Edward MacDowell, in *The Peterborough Pageant* (1910); a propaganda pageant called *The Suffrage Allegory* was staged in Washington, D.C., in 1913, the same year that John Reed produced the *Pageant of the Paterson Strike* in New York's Madison Square Garden, which, enacted by one thousand strikers, was also extremely effective propaganda.

2.   PERCY MACKAYE (1875-1956) AND AMERICAN PAGEANTS

The author of several books -- *Community Drama: Its Motive and Method of Neighborliness* (1917) -- on community theatre, MacKaye wrote a number of pageants: *The Roll Call* (1918), requested by the American Red Cross; *The Will of Song* (1919), an experiment with community singing; *Wakefield* (1932), an attempt to dramatize the contribution of "the Folk Spirit of America" to American freedom. Perhaps his most interesting pageant is *Caliban, By the Yellow Sands* (1916), produced on the 300th anniversary of Shakespeare's death. "The theme of the masque -- Caliban seeking to learn the art of Prospero -- is, of course," MacKaye wrote, "the slow education of mankind through the influences of cooperative art, that is, of the art of the theatre in its full social scope." Presenting his pageant on three stage levels, MacKaye interposed his attempt to humanize Caliban with various scenes from Shakespeare's plays. The symbolism is obscure, but the effect of the play -- with its cast of 2500 -- was spectacular.

3.   PAUL GREEN: THE SYMPHONIC DRAMA

Pageants continued in various forms. An interesting one for students of American drama is *The Masque of American Drama* (1917) by Albert E. Trombly. And there were numerous historical pageants: Frederick Koch's *A Pageant of the Northwest* (1914), George Pierce Baker's *The Pilgrim Spirit* (1921), and the *Yorktown Sesquicentennial Pageant* (1931) written by Thomas Wood Stevens. Then came Paul Green's *The Lost Colony* and a reawakening of popular interest in pageantry that remains active today.

(a) *The Lost Colony* (1937)
Using music, dance, a processional, dramatic action and dialogue, Green wrote this historical pageant at the request of the Roanoke Island Historical Society to honor the 350th anniversary of Raleigh's Colony. Peformed at the Waterside Theatre on Roanoke Island, *The Lost Colony* tells the story of the people who sailed from England in 1587 and, led by Governor White, came to the previously established but then razed Raleigh settlement on Roanoke Island. There, before White returns to England later that year, the settlers are befriended by the Indian, Manteo, and Eleanor Dare gives birth to Virginia, the first child born of English parents in the New World. In England, Governor White finds difficulties -- the Spanish Armada is not defeated until 1588 -- and when he returns to Roanoke Island in 1590, he finds only desolation at the Colony site and the word "CROATOAN" carved on a tree. By prearranged agreement, the settlers have said that, if forced to, they will leave Roanoke Island and carve their destination on a tree. The pageant ends as the settlers leave their fort for a new location, singing "Oh God that madest earth and sky." Despite numerous theories, no one has ever been able to determine where this "lost colony" went.

(b) Later Pageants
Green wrote *The Highland Call* (1939) to commemorate the Scots settlement in the Cape Fear River Valley of North

Carolina. *The Common Glory* (1947) dramatizes the contribution of Jefferson and the State of Virginia to America during the period from 1775 to 1782. Dealing with the 1783-1799 years, Green wrote *Faith of Our Fathers* (1950) to celebrate Washington's life and career. *The Founders* (1957) dramatizes the Jamestown Colony.

F.   Poetic Drama Between the Wars

There is a recognizable cyclical movement in American poetic drama. From Colonial times to the middle of the nineteenth century in America, any dramatist who considered himself or herself a serious writer wrote in poetry. Such drama obviously had severe limitations, but even with its imitative style and weak poetry, it presented the major themes of the period. Between the Civil War and 1900, poetry and poetic drama suffered in conflict with the Rise of Realism in literature and in the theatre. Although there were always dramatists who cast their thoughts in poetic form -- even at the height of the Realistic Movement -- not until the decade before World War I did the influences of European dramatists stimulate in American theatre audiences a discernible interest in poetic drama. As an emerging body of critics discovered weaknesses of language in American plays written between the World Wars, poetic drama gained status as a challenge to both poets and dramatists. During the 1920s and 1930s Edna St. Vincent Millay, Maxwell Anderson and Archibald MacLeish enjoyed success in this difficult form, although their efforts were seldom great triumphs on the stage.

1.   IN THE DISTANT PAST -- THEN THE PRESENT

For many writers of poetic drama a fear of the present was manifest. Even the successful poetic dramatists set their stories in the distant past, and this is clearly true of the early, lesser writers of poetic plays: Edwin Milton Royle, *Lancelot and Elaine* (1921); Alfred Kreymborg, *Rocking Chairs* (1921); Arthur Goodrich, *Caponsacchi* (1923). Not until Marc Blitzstein (1904-1964) wrote *The Cradle Will Rock* (1937) did dramatists envision a contemporary use for poetic drama -- as an emotional impact in propaganda plays. Archibald MacLeish saw the value of intense emotion in the contemporary themes of his radio plays.   Others also expressed their thoughts for the stage in poetry: Delmore Schwartz, *Shenandoah* (1939), concerned with the naming of a child, and N. R. Nusbaum (N. Richard Nash), *Parting at Imsdorf* (1940), a war play.

2.   **WALLACE STEVENS (1879-1955):**
      THREE TRAVELERS WATCH A SUNRISE (1916)

Explaining his intention (quoted in the Introduction to *Opus Posthumous*, 1957), Stevens, a major figure in modern American poetry, wrote: "The play is simply intended to demonstrate that just as objects in nature affect us, ... we affect objects in nature by projecting our moods, emotions, etc." On a hilltop in eastern Pennsylvania three very cultured Chinese talk about wisdom and art while waiting for the sunrise. They are joined by two Negroes. Soon there is revealed the body of a man hanging from a tree beneath which sits a girl. The poor Italian farmer and the girl were in love but were not allowed to marry, and in despair, he has hanged himself in front of her. The philosophic discussion by the Chinese indicates that love and wisdom appear in art only by the "invasion of humanity." The strong symbolism of the play enhances its poetry.

3.   **EDNA ST. VINCENT MILLAY (1892-1950)**
      OF THE PROVINCETOWN

Known as "the beautiful young actress of the Provincetown," Edna Millay became the popular poet of the 1920s who burned her candle at both ends. An excellent poet of strong emotions, with a good sense of the dramatic, she wrote several poetic plays -- a moral farce called *Two Slatterns and a King* (1916), the slight but bright romantic play *The Princess Marries the Page* (1918), the more conventional romantic story of *The Lamp and the Bell* (1921) and *The King's Henchman* (1926), a play built along the Tristram and Isolde pattern for which Deems Taylor supplied the music.

Her most successful play was *Aria da Capo* (1919), a blank-verse satire which Harriet Monroe, editor of *Poetry Magazine*, called "a masterpiece of irony, sharp as Toledo steel." Onto a stage set for a harlequinade, Cothurnus, the mask of tragedy, thrusts two shepherds who are to enact a tragedy. Prompted by

Cothurnus, they argue, arouse each other's sense of human greed and finally kill each other. Cothurnus then shuts his prompt book and the harlequin characters return to the set, where they are disturbed by the presence of the dead bodies. To their complaints, Cothurnus tells them to hide the bodies: "The audience will forget." They agree and start to repeat the dull routine with which they began the play. The poetry is effective as well as beautiful and enhances the satiric power of the play.

4. MAXWELL ANDERSON (1888-1959): POET-DRAMATIST

A controversial figure, Maxwell Anderson has been praised as second only to Eugene O'Neill in American drama and also condemned as a fourth-rate poet and a confused thinker. A poet-dramatist who believed that it was "encumbent on the dramatist to be a poet," Anderson was concerned with the political and social issues which sometimes served as a framework for his philosophical probing. During his lifetime he wrote and adapted more than thirty plays, but his best work and most of his original plays appeared before World War II. Not a first-rate poet, he seriously and with considerable talent attacked a difficult problem in modern drama -- that of combining meaningful language, effective theatre and significant ideas. His selection of traditional verse forms rather than the more flexible forms of modern poetry, however, make it difficult for some critics to appreciate him fully as a writer of poetic drama.

(a) A Theory of Drama

In *Off Broadway* (1947) Anderson collected a number of his essays concerned with dramatic theory, including "Poetry in the Theater," which reveals his idealism and his belief that "dramatic poetry is man's greatest achievement" and that the theatre should be "essentially a cathedral of the spirit." To Anderson, prose was "the language of information and poetry the language of emotion." Believing that human beings must feel in order to endure and live fully, and that such enduring could be created artistically only in the theatre, he felt that the serious dramatist must write in poetry. The serious dramatist must also believe in the strength and freedom of individuals, thus according them a singular dignity in an essentially tragic destiny. In arriving at this conclusion, Anderson relied heavily upon Aristotle's *Poetics*, particularly the theories of Recognition and Reversal. In an essay on "The Essence of Tragedy," he phrased his main point in this way: "A play should lead up to and away from a central crisis, and this crisis should consist in a discovery by the leading character which has an indelible effect on his thought and emotion and completely alters his course of action." The person who makes the discovery must have a tragic fault, Anderson declared, and must suffer as a consequence of an experience which brings an awareness of this fault. Whether the person dies, as in a tragedy, or lives, the essential point for Anderson lay in a spiritual awakening or personal regeneration.

(b)   Historical Poetic Drama
After the failure of his first poetic play, *White Desert* (1923), a tragedy of loneliness in North Dakota, Anderson decided that a contemporary theme could not be meaningful in poetic tragedy. During the 1930s, therefore, he concentrated on historical poetic plays -- with one notable exception. *Elizabeth the Queen* (1930) dramatizes the love between Elizabeth and Essex as it conflicts with their individual desires for power. *Night Over Taos* (1932) tells of the stubborn last stand of one of the large landholders in the Southwest in 1847 before the passing of the old Spanish feudal regime. In *Mary of Scotland* (1933), a popular success, Anderson shows Queen Elizabeth's persecution of the Catholic Mary, who is finally executed in the Tower because she will not release her right to the throne. *Valley Forge* (1934) is a weak attempt to dramatize that cold, desperate winter as it, and Congress, presented serious challenges to General Washington. In *The Wingless Victory* (1936) he described the hypocrisy and intolerance of the Puritans toward a Malayan princess who is brought to New England as the wife of a sailing master. In all, Anderson wrote fourteen poetic plays during the 1930s.

(c)   The Contemporary Scene
Anderson wrote several prose but few poetic plays in which he treated the contemporary scene. In one poetic drama, however, *Key Largo* (1939), which fits very well into his theory of

tragedy, he presented a man who, having refused to die with his comrades in the Spanish Civil War, goes to Key Largo to see the family of one of those who did die, and is spiritually awakened when he discovers something worth dying for. A much better poetic play on a more significant contemporary issue is *Winterset*.

Winterset (1935)
(Plot) In the spirit of revenge, Mio Romagna is searching for someone who can identify a murderer, the man who committed the crime for which his father was executed. In a New York tenement district, he meets and falls in love with Miriamne, whose brother, Garth, witnessed the murder. Not realizing who Garth is, Mio stays in the neighborhood, where he discovers Troc, the murderer, who, sick with tuberculosis and having only six months to live, wants Garth's continued silence. He also finds Judge Gaunt, the murder trial judge who, having questioned the possibility that justice was not served, has become mentally deranged. Eventually, after a mock trial over which Judge Gaunt presides, Mio learns the truth. But with the love of Miriamne he now realizes something greater than revenge, something for which he can die undefeated.

(Discussion) Basically, this play is an attempt to put modern tragedy into the pattern of the past with themes of revenge and truth and justice as meaningful issues. At the beginning of the play, Mio is defiant, bitter and cynical, filled with the desire for revenge; but under the pressure of love, he changes and makes a discovery which brings about his spiritual awakening. Like Job he accepts God's will with resignation. Although the dialogue sounds at times pretentious, several passages display considerable poetic power, and Anderson's ambition to create a new poetic drama that would be both modern and popular has become a subject for scholarly discussion.

5.   ARCHIBALD MACLEISH (1892-1982): POET-DRAMATIST

Although his plays during the 1930s were written mainly for the radio, Archibald MacLeish's achievements in both dramatic poetry and dramatic theory have made an important contribution to these genres. In an introductory statement to

Panic (1935) and in an essay entitled "A Stage for Poetry" (from *A Time to Speak*, 1941), he made significant statements on the theory of poetic drama. Convinced that poetic drama should be more truthful and realistic than plays in prose, MacLeish declared that verse should be an intregal part of the drama rather than an ornament. That he favored the precedence of "the word-excited imagination" over experimentation in staging was, of course, one reason for the success of his radio plays. Contrary to the theories of past writers of poetic drama in America, he considered blank verse completely ineffective in expressing modern speech. "The classical rhythm equivalent to American speech," he wrote, "would be more nearly the trochee or dactyl than the iamb of blank verse." Sensing a special connection in subject, form and language, he attempted to restore the importance of word and rhythm to poetic drama.

MacLeish's Radio Plays
Panic (1935) describes a time in America when banks are closing and businesses failing; its theme is the consuming power of fear. *The Fall of the City* (1937), suggesting that people invent their own oppressors, was described as "thirty minutes of the finest verbal music of its time." The City is thrown into confusion by a dead woman who comes from her tomb with a message: "The City of masterless men will take a master." When a messenger arrives to tell of an approaching conqueror, the words of the Priest and the General are ignored by the terrified people. Finally, the conqueror appears in armor and the people bow down before him. But the armor is empty! *Air Raid* (1938) was less effective in showing a city in the grip of terror; yet, the accents of American speech were considered successful.

IV. FROM LEFT TO RIGHT: PROPAGANDA TO HIGH COMEDY

Underlying a great portion of modern American drama is a social-realistic tradition -- a concern for society, its faults and foibles, expressed mainly in a realistic fashion. The scope of these plays runs from blatant propaganda to detached and sophisticated high comedy. In between are plays which vary in their objectives from bitter denunciation to a concerned comment on social, economic and moral problems; from an intellectual and psychological interest in social conditions to a light comic approach to the idiosyncrasies of humanity. This panoramic view includes plays by all of the major dramatists of the 1930s and stretches back into the 1920s for those plays which show the beginnings of trends which reached their heights in the Depression Decade.

Observations concerning the relationship of the drama to the poetry and fiction of major contemporary literary figures are highly relevant. Generally, the novelists were able to infuse more universal significance into their work than were the dramatists of this period, and they wrote with greater imagination about similar concerns and interests. Many of the best novelists of the decade, in fact, wrote plays, though seldom very good ones: F. Scott Fitzgerald, *The Vegetable* (1923); John Dos Passos, *The Garbage Man* (1926); Jack Kirkland and Erskine Caldwell, *Tobacco Road* (1933), almost a classic with its vigorous language and seven-and-a-half-year run in New York; Sinclair Lewis, *It Can't Happen Here* (1936); John Steinbeck, *Of Mice and Men* (1937). Among the poets, there were also those who considered the same economic, social and political problems which bothered the dramatists -- Archibald MacLeish, Robinson Jeffers, Carl Sandburg, Robert Frost, Edna St. Vincent Millay. In general, the finest drama of this period reflects the ideas and interests of the best literature being written in America at this time, and a number of the plays achieved a noteworthy literary significance.

A. Art as a Weapon

The use of art for persuasive purposes in America goes back to Governor Robert Hunter and *Androboros* (1714). By the turn of the twentieth century, America had a number of protest writers -- Thorstein Veblen, Henry George, Lincoln Steffens, Upton Sinclair -- and there had been propaganda playwrights since the Revolutionary War. Drama, however, did not become a particular genre for protest until stimulated by Marxists, who found meaning in the Russian Revolution as well as in the American Depression. With their various Five Year Plans the Russians attempted to regiment both art and the theatre -- art as a weapon -- to serve political purposes. Such Russian playwrights as Alexander Afinogenov with *Far Taiga,* a study of the psychological importance of the people in Siberia, and Nikolai Pogodin with *Tempo,* which contrasts the new and old regimes in Russia, indicates their efforts to persuade through the theatre.

In America, Leftist or Radical theatre groups comprised a recognizable part of the theatre during the 1930s. Capitalism had presumably failed in 1929, and Communism was considered by many people to be the logical response to this failure. Idealistic dramatists frequently espoused Communist philosophy, attacked social conditions and wrote about opposing ideologies and the conflicts between labor and capital. Generally, their plays are artistically weak, but playwrights compensated by resorting to violent or radical action and a particularly unsubtle political dogma. Their plots concentrate on strikes, evictions, unemployment, penal institutions and the oppressed and persecuted among the common people. Drama used as a weapon in American will probably never disappear, but during the 1930s it enjoyed an unsophisticated popularity that helped identify the theatre of the period.

1. "THEATRE IS A WEAPON"

The Communist Party in America established its own theatres very early during the Thirties and later tried with some success to use and manipulate other theatre groups, such as the Theatre Guild and the Group Theatre.

(a) Communist Theatre Groups
Working through the German-speaking Proletbuehne, the Communist Party first established the Workers' Laboratory Theatre, which became the Theatre of Action in 1934. From 1932 to 1934, the Communists' League of Workers' Theatre attempted to destroy the bourgeois theatre. Rarely producing good plays, however, it advised: "Make the plays short and concise and make a thorough study of the Communist Party platform before writing them." In 1933 the Theatre Union, supported by communists and, presumably, socialists, liberals and trade-unionists, was formed to provide a professional stage for left-wing dramatists. Beginning in 1935, and lasting until

1941, the Communists' New Theatre League proclaimed its intent to establish a Soviet America with plays of "highest artistic and social level." But communist theatre in America failed to control amateur theatres and failed, too, to get a good repertory, mainly because of the more varied fruits of capitalist theatre. Good dramatists found the scope of communist material very confining, both intellectually and imaginatively. Broadway offered greater freedom -- and money.

(b) The Labor Stage
A number of non-communist amateur theatre groups nonetheless produced left-wing plays. One of the best and most active of these groups was the recreational theatre program of the International Ladies Garment Workers' Union. Established with the purpose of creating a balance of humor and propaganda, the sketch-revue called *Pins and Needles* was started in 1936 and, more or less frequently revived, closed in 1940 after 1,100 performances in New York. In one *Pins and Needles* skit, Charles Foster's late nineteenth-century heroine in *Bertha, the Sewing Maching Girl* is rescued by a union man. In another, the D.A.R. is flayed in song as "Filled to the brim with bigotry." Always maintaining a topicality, *Pins and Needles* once burlesqued a Mussolini Handicap, featuring as Public Enemy # 1 the woman who could have only one child.

2.   AGITPROP

The agitprop (agitation propaganda) provided a direct means of teaching Marxism. In its simplest form, the agitprop would tell the audience what to do: Strike! Vote! Fight! It could be produced in any place -- a street corner or a factory gate. *Vote Communist,* for example, shows a capitalist with a top hat and a large dollar sign over his heart being heckled by actors in the audience. Each time he tries to masquerade as a Republican or a Democrat or a Socialist by placing cards with the appropriate word over his heart, the card is torn away to reveal again the dollar sign. Another popular agitprop was John Bonn's *15 Minute Red Revue* (1932), which extolls the excellencies of Soviet Russia and ends with a promise to fight "for the Soviet Union." The objective of agitprop was action for the cause, and the effect of slogans was not underestimated. Plays like *Dimitroff* (1934) by Art Smith and Elia Kazan are filled with communist slogans and songs -- hence the necessity for the playwright to keep abreast of the Communist platform. Clifford Odets' *Waiting for Lefty* (1935) is basically an agitprop, a very effective one, with considerably more than the usual artistry.

3.   THE LIVING NEWSPAPER

One of the many contributions of the Federal Theatre to American drama, the Living Newspaper drama documented, analyzed and called for specific action in America, such as reforms in housing, labor, public utilities and health. A number of the best plays were composed by Arthur Arent (1904-1972) and a staff of writers. Not always very different from agit-prop, the Living Newspaper used a variety of means to present well documented facts and liberal opinions directly to an audience. In *Triple-A Plowed Under* (1936), the Voice of the Living Newspaper announces the twenty-six scenes which trace agricultural depression from World War I through foreclosure of farm mortgages, farm auctions, droughts and the deliberate destruction of crops, to the creation of the Agricultural Adjustment Administration (AAA) and its termination when the Supreme Court declares it unconstitutional. The communists approved of this play and this type of theatre. Other Living Newspapers include *One-Third of a Nation* (1938), an expose of the housing problem in American cities, and the rather daring and imaginative *Spirochete* (1938), which traces the history of syphilis in the world.

4.   A VARIETY OF PROTEST PLAYS

The variety in subject matter among the protest plays was generally limited to liberal causes. It was, in fact, popular to protest and, according to William Koslenko in his Introduction to *The Best Short Plays of the Social Theatre* (1939), "no art can *serve* a loftier purpose." Among full-length plays, *Stevedore* (1934) by George Sklar (1908-1988) and Paul Peters is effective propaganda. Lonnie, an outspoken black dock worker falsely accused of raping a white woman, is pursued by a rioting mob and supported by stevedore members of the Communist

Union. Such plays, this one cleverly linking race prejudice and economic handicap, were described as "social realism" in imitation of Russia's politicizing of the literary terms. That same year, 1934, John Wexley dramatized the Scottsboro case in *They Shall Not Die*. Another play with a Southern scene, *Let Freedom Ring* (1935) by Albert Bein (1902-) portrays a strike in a North Carolina mill town.

Black Pit (1935), by Albert Maltz (1908-1985), was called a Marxian tragedy. An out-of-work union miner forced to work as a company spy betrays a fellow worker and is ostracized. Another Maltz play, *Private Hicks* (1936), shows the victory of one soldier in a National Guard Outfit who refuses to act as a strikebreaker.   Paul Green's *Hymn to the Rising Sun* (1936) condemns the cruelties of the Negro convict road gang. One of the most successful protest plays against war is *Bury the Dead* (1936) by Irwin Shaw (1913-1984), a satiric tale of the refusal of dead soldiers to be buried. *The Cradle Will Rock* (1938), by Marc Blitzstein (1905-1964), attacks capitalism through bitter satire on its paid adherents -- Rev. Salvation, Editor Daily, President Prexy and Doctor Specialist.   All do what Mister Mister demands; but when the wind blows, the cradle will rock.

5.   JOHN HOWARD LAWSON (1895-1977):
      DRAMATIST OF COMMITMENT

A true member of the Lost Generation, who spent time with the American Ambulance Service in France during World War I and marched in protest against the government's treatment of Sacco and Vanzetti, Lawson became the most zealous convert to communism among American dramatists. From an idealistic searching during which he showed considerable talent for dramatic expressionism, he progressed to the forthright position regarding society and government which brought him a prison term after an appearance before the Un-American Activities Committee.   In his plays there is remarkable vitality, supported by an integrity and a personal commitment that is distinctive in American drama.

(a) A Lashing Out
For ten years after his first major play, *Roger Bloomer* (1923), Lawson displayed both his idealism and his bitterness toward

certain aspects of humanity. Clearly searching for something in which he could believe, he wrote in *Loud Speaker* (1927) that he followed Coolidge's advice to "look well to the hearthstone, therein all hope for America lies," but all he discovered were persecution and injustice. In particular, he saw the political manipulation of the American people and their worship of success. Like *Processional* (1925), which uses a strike to dramatize class war, *International* (1928) is an experimental mixture of Freud and Marx in which love actually conquers. The Communist press had been pleased by both *Processional* and *Loud Speaker*. Although Lawson had stressed loyalty to a cause in *International* and had castigated capitalism and commented on prejudice and economic persecution, the Communist Party was bothered by the play's bourgeois sentiment and by an obvious indecision on Lawson's part. A later play, *Success Story* (1932), was even less pleasing to Communist reviewers. Although Lawson had attacked capitalism, his theme -- money does not bring happiness -- was not accepted by a Communist press which found Lawson more interested in individualism than in class struggle.

(b) The Regimented "Bourgeois Hamlet of Our Time"
Lawson's 1934 production of *Gentlewoman* dramatized a dying class but made the personal embodiment of that class quite admirable. Reviewing the play in *New Masses*, "A Bourgeois Hamlet of Our Time," Mike Gold, the chief literary spokesman for the Party, attacked Lawson severely as confused and without direction. Quite unexpectedly, Lawson was contrite; he underwent an "intensive re-evaluation" of his work in terms of Marxist orthodoxy and joined the Communist Party. Convinced that the dramatist must take sides, he began to write dramatic criticism and theory -- *Theory and Techniques of Playwriting* (1936) -- and, in 1937, wrote his final play, *Marching Song*, which was to be a model for revolutionary drama. Concerned with revolution in an American industrialized city, the play has a collective hero, a recognizable plot and much melodramatic -- though politically clear -- action. To protest the blacklisting of a fellow worker, the Auto Worker's Union goes on a strike. Bombs are thrown by the company; strike-breakers are hired; a Union organizer is killed; Union workers are attacked with guns and tear gas. Finally, the

Union men win by capturing the power station. Certainly the Communist critics could not complain. After writing this play, Lawson went to Hollywood, where he was less effective.

6.   ELMER RICE (1892-1967): A TOUCH OF MARXISM

Late in his life Rice recounted his theatre experiences in *The Living Theatre* (1959) and *Minority Report* (1963), showing clearly that he was always a liberal dreamer who preached individual freedom from all tyrannies. A fearless protester, he wrote plays that leaned toward "art as a weapon," but although he believed in certain Marxist ideals, he did not follow Marxist methods.

The Communist press was not pleased with *We the People* (1933) because Rice had not insisted on the Marxist solution in his bitter attack on Depression times. Protesting quite properly, he showed the disintegration of the proletarian family -- the father loses his job, his health, his house; a son is falsely accused of murder and is executed. The ending of the play is agitprop but calls for a return to democratic ideals rather than Marxist revolution. *Judgment Day* (1934) was little better from the Communist point of view. In this attack upon Nazi fascism, Rice re-emphasized his belief that art could serve a useful social function. Based on the trial of Georgi Dimitroff by the Nazis, the play shows a melodramatic manipulation of plot to bring about the destruction of the villainous Hitler character. In *Between Two Worlds* (1934), Rice contrasted the social-political system of America with that of Russia, emphasizing an awareness of social purpose and a concern for humanity. Although communists saw potential for him in the Party, Rice was sufficiently miffed by the Broadway reviews and the brief four-week run of the play that he announced his retirement from the theatre.

7.   CLIFFORD ODETS (1906-1963): AGRESSIVE MARXIST

The year Clifford Odets died he complained that critics would remember him only as a playwright of the Thirties. With some reason, his fear was real, and the year 1935 may hold all of Odets that is interesting to the drama historian -- the year he had four plays on Broadway: *Waiting for Lefty, Till the*

Day I Die, Awake and Sing and *Paradise Lost*.   Born of working-class Jewish parents, he became an actor and, in 1930, a charter member of the Group Theatre. In 1934 he joined the Communist Party, leaving it in 1935 because "I am a liberal, not a Communist." During his year of tremendous success, he was hailed as the most exciting dramatist since the emergence of O'Neill. In 1936 he left New York for Hollywood -- and money. The change was dramatic and a bit traumatic for some. The remark by Frank Nugent of the *New York Times* after viewing Odets' movie adaptation of *The General Died at Dawn* seemed an apt critical summary at the time: "Odets, where is thy sting?" Although he wrote three plays after World War II, he never again matched his earlier success in the theatre.

(a) "That Wonderful Year, 1935"
Odets was different from other Marxist writers because he believed not only that a play should be "immediately and dynamically useful," but that it should also be "psychologically profound." He had joined the Communist Party in the "honest and real belief" that it was a way out of the dilemma he saw in society, and his plays of 1935 show typically Marxist characteristics.   *Waiting for Lefty* is the best, with its agitprop ending. *Till the Day I Die* tells of a communist agent who has worked underground in Germany and is caught by the Nazis, tortured and released, only to be thereafter suspect by members of his cell. Even his brother does not trust him, and he can regain the confidence of his comrades only by killing himself. *Awake and Sing* dramatizes the agony, arguments and disintegration of the Berger family. Life is frustration: life is "printed on dollar bills"; the entire atmosphere created in this moving and personal play is one of spiritual death. Finally, a real death in the family resurrects individual spirits among family members, who decide to crusade for a better future. *Paradise Lost* presents a similar degradation of the middle-class Gordon family, until they, too, feel that one can "fight" for a better world.

(b) *Waiting for Lefty* (1935)
Praised by *New Masses* and *New Theatre* magazines, this militant agitprop represents protest drama in America. Its impact was so great in 1935 that the actors were arrested in

Boston, and a producer of the play in Hollywood was beaten by thugs. Odets once said that the theatre is at its best when the plight expressed by the stage action is at one with the plight of the audience. In this play he was successful because the problems and the collective action he dramatized were meaningful to audiences in 1935. As one character says, "The world is supposed to be for all of us!" Using a union meeting setting in which a group of taxi drivers wait for their leader, Lefty, before discussing a proposed strike, Odets wrote five scenes (six in some versions) showing (1) the poverty of a taxi driver and his wife, (2) a lab assistant who is asked to spy on his superiors, (3) a young cab driver who, for economic reasons, cannot get married, (4) a labor spy in the meeting and (5) prejudice against a Jewish doctor. Finally, the news comes that Lefty has been killed, and the union leaders are confronted with the compelling force of the workers' decision: Strike!

B.   The Playwright as Concerned Liberal

The twenty-odd years between the two World Wars was a time of concern for thoughtful people. The pace of the social life that characterized the Twenties suggested greed -- live all you can, get all you can, forget all you can. Inflationary in many aspects, the joy ride of the Twenties seemed feverishly unhealthy. When the stock market crashed in 1929 and government control with welfare-state characteristics appeared in FDR's administration, independent-minded people sensed difficulties. Another source of worry was the slight but frequently violent propaganda of the Communist Party and other left-wing groups.

In poetry, novel and drama, the creative world reacted to the problems that it saw or foresaw. Some dramatists protested vigorously -- having espoused a philosophy that preached revolution. Other dramatists, equally concerned but more liberal than radical in their politics, protested or commented seriously on various social and political problems.

1.   ELMER RICE (1892-1967): A DEHUMANIZED SOCIETY

Elmer Rice's career in the theatre started in 1914 with *On Trial,* an experimental play in which a courtroom scene serves as a basis for flashbacks into aspects of a crime. A native New York who graduated from law school before becoming a playwright, Rice used his legal knowledge in several plays, in various disputes with theatres and in causes he served, from Marxism to the American Civil Liberties Union. A sensitive man of action, he wrote on subjects both popular and unpopular. When his efforts with the Federal Theatre Project were threatened by government censorship, he was outraged and resigned from his administrative post. Responding to the high-handed methods of the Theatre Guild, he and four other playwrights founded the Playwrights' Company in 1938. He vigorously opposed Senator Joseph McCarthy's attacks on theatre artists in the early 1950s.

Uneven and varied, Rice's plays range from slight comedy -- *Cock Robin* (1928) with Philip Barry, *Dream Girl* (1945) -- to realistic social drama. It was during the Twenties that his plays became most meaningful in the development of modern American drama. Troubled by the growing victimization and dehumanization of individuals, he made determined efforts to arouse the public. During the Thirties he became somewhat disillusioned with the commerical theatre, but never so much so that he could not write more plays -- either as protest or as pure entertainment. A troubled liberal and a passionate debater, he spoke out against all manner of social injustice and in support of the democratic traditions of America.

(a) Victims of Society
Rice made his first real success in the theatre with *The Adding Machine* (1923). In this and two other plays -- *The Subway* and *Street Scene,* both written in 1929 -- he effectively dramatized his concern for those he saw as crushed and victimized by society. Mr. Zero, the representative man from *The Adding Machine,* is condemned as a "waste product" and a "slave to a contraption of steel and iron." Not only is he dehumanized while alive, but even after death his existance is that of a spiritless slave. *The Subway* shows humanity again as a victim of civilization. When scientists of the future dig in America, Rice proclaimed, they will find the symbols of its society -- bones, a glass eye, false teeth, blackened coins and a key to a safe deposit box -- things that suggest falseness and

materialism, "all that remains of Western Civilization." In *Street Scene* Rice struck the same thesis but from a different viewpoint: "Everywhere you look," complains a character, "oppression and cruelty!"

Street Scene (1929)

(Plot) As people gather on the steps of an apartment house in New York's tenement district to discuss the day and their feelings, everyone knows that Mrs. Maurrant and Mr. Sankey, the milk collector, are having an affair. When Mr. Maurrant comes home, his daughter Rose, who has some understanding of her mother's love of beauty and romance, begs him to move the family out of New York, but he refuses. The next day, when Maurrant is out of town, Sankey visits Mrs. Maurrant. But Maurrant returns, his suspicions having been earlier aroused, and before the lovers can be warned, he kills his wife. After the police capture him, he tries to explain to Rose his love and his beliefs, but his ineffectiveness is symbolic of the situation. As the slum area returns to normal, Rose prepares to leave with her younger brother.

(Discussion) Mrs. Maurrant is a sensitive person with hopes and dreams; Mr. Maurrant is hardworking and conservative and believes in law and order. But how does one attain happiness? What are the choices -- promiscuity, waiting and hoping, being a kept woman, Marxism? In this "small street, small scene," a cross section of life in a tenement -- where kids play games, the gossip has a vulgar daughter, a family is evicted, a baby is born -- should everyone have a chance? At the end of the play, however, nothing has changed. There is no better understanding; there is no solution.

(b) From Karl Marx to American Traditions

With the bitterness that Rice preached in *Street Scene*, there was good reason for him to become disillusioned with the effectiveness of Broadway as a medium for reform and to begin a flirtation with the radicals: *We, the People* (1933), *Judgment Day* (1934), *Between Two Worlds* (1934). Rather than find answers in radical theories, he began to realize that his tool for reform, the drama, was merely a "bond maiden of commerce," that theatre was in the hands of business and real estate operators. Consequently, in his next play, *Not for Children* (1935), he condemned the theatre as "unrelated to reality." This discovery still did not stop him from writing plays, but it did make him reevaluate his own desires for the theatre. In 1938 he wrote *American Landscape,* in which he emphasized, as before, basic values of American traditions -- "freedom and the common rights of humanity."

2.   MAXWELL ANDERSON (1888-1959): SOCIAL AND POLITICAL ANARCHY

Many of Anderson's forty-two plays are critical of the social or political institutions which inhibit individual freedom, although he usually avoided criticism of specific institutions. His distrust of social structures, evident in his early prose plays, turned to bitter satire in *Gods of the Lightning* and *Both Your Houses.* In the Thirties, he became concerned with government -- that inhuman institution which the struggle for power promotes -- and the corruption which he found coexistent with all governments. Finally, he reached the conclusion that some government was necessary and that democracy was best, although the sensitive individual who prizes freedom may still become a victim.

(a)   A Basic Independence

Even in *What Price Glory?* (1924), there is beneath the military order a basic independence of spirit which distinguishes Flagg and Quirt, satirizes visiting Congressmen and damns the authorities for useless killing. *First Flight* (1925), written with Laurence Stallings, dramatizes the independent attitude of the backwoodsmen who finally persuade Andy Jackson that not only are the rights of the state more meaningful than the rights of a federal government but that the individual should oppose any kind of government. Another play with Stallings, *The Buccanneer* (1925), dramatizes aspects of the life of Captain Henry Morgan, who tells government representatives that men are "all robbers and thieves," that government means dishonesty. It is only the individual who counts. An adaptation of Jim Tully's *Beggars of Life,* Anderson's *Outside Looking In* (1925) burlesques the injustices of society's trial by jury and shows the hoboes' proper contempt for authority. *Saturday's Children* (1927) tells of a girl who beguiles her sweetheart into marriage only to find that the institution of marriage lacks the romance and the sense of living that she wants. Her final solution, living alone and demanding romantic feats of her husband, is unconventional but only slightly rebellious. In all of these plays Anderson asserted a basic independence.

Starting with *Gods of the Lightning* (1928), written with Harold Hickerson, Anderson took a more violent view of government against a liberal interpretation of the Sacco and Vanzetti trial of the 1920s. Bitter toward the administration of biased justice, Anderson found the government "rotten"; even the District Attorney in the play is wary of it. In the Pulitzer Prize-winning play *Both Your Houses* (1933), Anderson satirized members of both houses of Congress for their stupidity and their dishonesty. He had one congressman admit that "the sole business of government is graft, special privilege and corruption -- with a by-product of order." Anderson's hero, a new congressman named Alan McLean, is shocked by such open corruption, but he keeps his idealism. By this action Anderson suggested an attitude toward democracy on which he would built later. For the moment, he was concerned with the growing powers of a government that preys on individual freedom.

(b) Corruption by Power (Poetic Plays)
"It rots a man's brain to be in power," says a character in *Valley Forge* (1934). This idea is basic in a number of Anderson's poetic dramas, although in *Valley Forge* he had to resort to a little double talk in order to make Washington a rebel-idealist rather than the kind of triumphant dictator whom Anderson detested. Elizabeth must value power over love in *Elizabeth the Queen* (1930), and she must assent to the cruelty that is power to protect her throne in *Mary of Scotland* (1933). In *High Tor* (1937) the individualist who wants freedom from the power of government must simply leave; that is his only escape. Rudolf in *The Masque of Kings* (1937) also dislikes authority, but when the logic of power is explained to him, he realizes that for the idealist escape comes only with suicide, that even an idealistic revolution will fail when the revolutionaries become corrupt, as they inevitably will. Anderson's theme again and again is social pessimism: justice and power are

incompatible. The theme is repeated in *The Feast of Ortolans* (1937) and *Second Overture* (1938). In a struggle for individual integrity and freedom in a world of socio-political power, the alternatives are accepting defeat as Essex does, becoming corrupt as Elizabeth does, escaping through suicide or running away or dying for an ideal as the hero does in *Key Largo*. In any event, power corrupts.

(c)   Compromise Through Democracy

In *Night Over Taos* (1932) and *Both Your Houses* (1933), Anderson suggested that some government is necessary and that democracy seems the best method. In *Knickerbocker Holiday* (1938), that rousing satire of the New Deal and FDR with music by Kurt Weill, he blasted the philosophy of benevolent despotism but finally concluded in some seriousness: "Let's keep the government small and funny, and maybe it'll give us less discipline and more entertainment." The individual was still uppermost in his mind, however, as he allowed the heroine of *Candle in the Wind* (1941) to voluntarily give her life for love and freedom. "A tyrant is a tyrant, beneficent or maleficent," he wrote in his "Thoughts about the Critics." But the soldiers in *The Eve of St. Mark* (1942) die for freedom and a democratic government, while Socrates in *Barefoot in Athens* (1951) defends democracy. When the king asks: "What do you trust?" Socrates (and seemingly Anderson) answers: "The Citizens -- the voters."

3.   S. N. BEHRMAN (1893-1973): COMEDY WITHOUT DETACHMENT

In the history of American drama Behrman will be remembered mainly for his contribution to high comedy with his portrayals of an urbane and usually genteel society frequented by fashionably tolerant matrons and cynically detached artists, more effete than talented. Most of his plays, however, although witty in dialogue and sophisticated in idea, lack the degree of detachment necessary for successful comedy of manners. The various aspects of the social and political life, which Behrman treated with polish, often touched the marrow of his emotions. His interest in power-mad fanatics and tyranny became in the Thirties a major aspect of his plays, until he seriously questioned the possibility and the value of detachment in the theatre.   Although he never completely abandoned the comic spirt, neither did he remove the sting of his commitments.

(a)   The Fascist World

Early in his career, Behrman presented some of the characters and ideas which he obviously found distasteful, and it became clear that he was not opposed to expressing his opinions.   He was, however, subtle in dramatizing the defeat of hated forces. Raphael Lord in *Meteor* (1929), for example, is a success in the business world because he is ruthless, and he is made to suffer for his inhumanity.   A number of people in an English country house provide generally divergent ideas in *Rain from Heaven* (1934).   Hobart, an Anglo-American fascist capitalist, and Hugo, a German-Jewish refugee, show Behrman's beliefs. Hugo, by far the most appealing character, will return to Germany to fight Nazism, while Hobart, made to see himself more clearly, can only sulk.   In *End of Summer* (1936) Behrman labels one character "the enemy," a fraudulent psychologist named Dr. Rice, who cynically woos the heroine in order to get her money for his fascist cause.   Behrman defeats him in high comic splendor.

(b)   "No Time for Comedy"

In 1939 Behrman wrote a play called *No Time for Comedy* in which he attempted to justify the writing of comedy in a world threatened by war.   His playwright-hero feels that he should leave his successful genre of comedy for serious drama, but he fails in his attempt and returns to his forte.   Perhaps one should laugh in the face of danger, but how can one laugh when people are not even allowed to live?   Behrman's troubled view is revealed as he questions the value of detached comedy in a world in which detachment should be impossible.   The previous year in *Wine of Choice* he had vigorously condemned a proletarian writer whose hatred has warped his sense of humanity by confronting this revolutionary fanatic with a person who upholds traditional values.   With his usual wit and gentility, Behrman had shown the radical defeated.   Then in *The Talley Method* (1941) he revealed a new position -- The Talley Method of Detachment which eliminates all sense of humanity.   This, too, however, Behrman found intolerable.

Unable to leave his writer-hero in this play as a victim in an animalistic world, he himself settled into the role of "playwright of social issues."

4.   SIDNEY KINGSLEY (1906-): DETAILED DESPAIR IN MELODRAMA

A newcomer to the theatre in the Depression Decade, Sidney Kingsley indulged in realistic studies which, though melodramatic in action and conception, presented a vivid picture of life. Not a prolific playwright, he wrote his most stirring and successful plays during the 1930s: *Men in White* (1933), a Pulitzer Prize winner replete with overwhelming hospital details, is about a young doctor, an agonizing love triangle and the maturing of the hero; and *Dead End* (1935) is memorable for its detailed accuracy. After the failure of *Ten Million Ghosts* (1936), a severe protest against war and munitions makers, Kingsley returned in a few plays to vivid and romantic melodrama and farce.

Dead End (1935)

(Plot) Into a squalid East River scene where several boys swim in the filth-covered water, comes a wanted criminal, "Baby Face" Martin, to see his mother and his first sweetheart. To his shocked surprise, his mother has only contempt for him, while his sweetheart has become an obviously diseased prostitute. Life in the slums is a struggle. A gang of boys, led by Tommy, indoctrinate a new boy, fight with the Second Avenue gang and steal the watch of a rich kid living in a nearby hotel. When the kid's father tries to catch the boys, Tommy cuts him with a knife, and the police are called. There is also love in the slums. Drina, Tommy's sister, tries in vain to take care of him. Gimpty, a crippled young architect, and Kay are in love, but she fears his poverty and chooses to become the mistress of a rich man. Finally, Martin is killed by G-men on a tip from Gimpty, and the police catch Tommy, who seems destined for a life of crime, although Gimpty will give his reward money to Drina to pay Tommy's lawyer. Life in the slum goes on.

(Discussion) Brooks Atkinson, drama critic, called the play a "public social document." Gimpty, the intellectual, says to Tommy's sister: "Yeah, Drina, the place you live is awfully

important. It can give you a chance to grow, or it can twist --
like that." Although the play is infused with melodrama, the
realistic scene, dialogue and action produce a shocking drama.
In sensation rather than lesson, it can be compared with Rice's
Street Scene, and from its characters it produced an
Americanism -- "The Dead End Kids."

5.　ROBERT SHERWOOD (1896-1955): HUMANIST

Playwright, screenwriter, essayist, historian and propagandist, Sherwood was a man of strong emotions and good will
who preached simplistic solutions to the complicated human
problems that concerned him. After serving in France in World
War I, he developed a hatred of war that became the theme of
several of his plays: *The Road to Rome, Acropolis, Idiot's
Delight*. Scattered among these plays are frivolous and
sentimental comedies such as *Waterloo Bridge* (1930) and
Reunion in Vienna (1931). As the Thirties moved on, however,
and war became a definite threat to civilization once more,
Sherwood's attitude changed. His concern for the individual
remained as strong as ever, but he began to understand a concept
of humanity and freedom greater than the mere fulfillment of
the individual. Sherwood's persistent moralism, however,
helped him become a major propagandist for FDR.

(a)　War Condemned: "The Human Equation"
The Road to Rome (1927), a potent satire, reflects Sherwood's
wartime service and his resulting aversion to war. The scene is
Rome: Fabius has just been made dictator when Hannibal's
army appears outside the gates. Feigning a return to her family
home, Amytis, Fabius' Greek-born wife, goes to Hannibal's
camp, is captured and then saved by Hannibal, whom she
beguiles. Amytis then interprets the force which led to war as
"the voice of the shopkeepers in Carthage," and tells Hannibal
of the "human equation" which is "so much more beautiful than
war." Next morning, Hannibal decides to retreat, and Amytis
is returned to Fabius, who pompously and ironically states that
Hannibal has been overcome by the moral force of Rome. The
play is slight, with a great deal of farce and burlesque about it.

In *Idiot's Delight* (1936) Sherwood restated his belief that war
is completely irrational. The action takes place in an Italian

resort hotel where a song-and-dance troupe and various guests are stranded when war breaks out. The horror of the war is expressed with force, as the German scientist rages against the "obscene maniacs" whom he must join, while the Frenchman attacks the munition makers of the world, "Krupp, Skoda, and Vickers and DuPont. The league of death." In counterpoint to Sherwood's anti-war intensity and his concern for Democracy and Christianity is a romantic plot line which reaches a theatrically brilliant climax as bombs fall at the final curtain.

(b) The Question of War: A Time to Fight

There Shall Be No Night (1940) was Sherwood's violent reaction to Russia's invasion of Finland. A renouned Finnish scientist, Dr. Kaarlo Valkonen, cannot understand the reasons for war until Russia attacks, his son is killed and destruction seems imminent. Throwing aside his experiments, Dr. Valkonen joins the medical corps. In his neurological research he had been trying to defeat the "degeneration of the human race," but, he now concludes, "This is a war for everybody." His death in the war makes Sherwood's point clear in emotional, melodramatic terms, and the play was a great success.

6.   "THE TROUBLES I'VE SEEN"

In the typical modern play the chief cause of conflict is not man, nor Fate, nor universal law but a social condition in which the dramatist sees some possibility of adjustment. The number of topics on which playwrights had opinions and suggestions for change were legion. The following plays indicate some of the activity in theatres between the two World Wars and the diversity of human interest.

(a) Economic and Political Issues

These issues were persistent in the plays of Anderson and Behrman. Also relevant are *Beggar on Horseback* (1924) by George S. Kaufman and Marc Connelly, *Holiday* (1928) by Philip Barry, *Having Wonderful Time* (1937) by Arthur Kober and *The Land Is Bright* (1941) by Kaufman and Edna Ferber.

(b) Social and Personal Issues

Social and personal problems are the basis of most plays by Behrman, Barry, George Kelly and Rachel Crothers. Plays on these issues include *Expressing Willie* (1924) by Crothers, *In a Garden* (1925) by Barry, *Brief Moment* (1931) by Behrman, *Wednesday's Child* (1934) by Leopold Atlas, *Reflected Glory* (1936) by Kelly, *The Women* (1936) by Clare Boothe and *Claudia* (1941) by Rose Franken.

(c)   War and Crime
Several of Robert Sherwood's plays might be included under this heading.   Other war plays are Irwin Shaw's *Bury the Dead* (1936), Paul Green's *Johnny Johnson* (1936) and Clare Boothe's anti-Nazi play, *Margin for Error* (1939). Crime plays include Elmer Rice's *Counsellor-at-Law* (1931) and Shaw's *The Gentle People* (1938).

(d)   Religious and Moral Issues
Plays inviting moral comment include such diverse issues as prohibition (*The Old Soak,* 1922, by Don Marquis), free love (*The Vinegar Tree,* 1930, by Paul Osborn) and academic freedom (*The Male Animal,* 1940, by James Thurber and Elliott Nugent). The extensive part that religion plays in numerous dramas suggests an unfailing interest of American playwrights: *The Fool* (1923), in which a Christian minister practices Christ-like living and loses his job and the respect of his fellow men, and *The Enemy* (1925) by Channing Pollock; *Bride of the Lamb* (1926) by William Hurlburt; *The Criminal Code* (1929) by Martin Flavin; *The Green Pastures* (1930) by Marc Connelly; *Shroud My Body Down* (1934) by Paul Green; *Hotel Universe* (1930) and *Here Come the Clowns* (1938) by Philip Barry; *Susan and God* (1937) by Rachel Crothers; and numerous plays by Eugene O'Neill and Maxwell Anderson.

(e)   Race and Prejudice
Folk drama and the protest plays frequently deal with race prejudice.   Prejudice toward Orientals appears in John Colton's *The Shanghai Gesture* (1926) and *The Color Line* (1928) by Irene Taylor MacNair.   Prejudice is frequent in *Judge Lynch* (1924) by William R. Rogers, Jr.; DuBose Heyward's *Brass Ankle* (1931), which tells of those who pass for white but have enough "colored blood" to bear "colored children"; and plays by Paul Green.   Maxwell Anderson's *The Wingless Victory* (1936) shows New Englanders' prejudice toward a Malayan woman.

C. The Heightened Problem

The socio-political condition of America provided the conflicts for most of the plays written during the Twenties and the Thirties. Many dramatists were sufficiently talented to express their emotional concerns in the kind of popular melodrama that made Broadway "angels" happy. A few playwrights had the imagination and the skill to raise a particular issue to a suggestion of universal significance, while still not involving themselves in any profound search for meaning in life. Essentially, they were moralists, all careful analysts of society, all realists who were not interested in experimentation in form.

Reflecting the attitudes of some American novelists and following a trend started by Susan Glaspell's *The Verge* and John Howard Lawson's *Roger Bloomer*, they showed certain psychological insight into both character and situation -- Robert Sherwood, George Kelly and Lillian Hellman. Neither concerned specifically with satire or social commentary nor interested in the spiritual or psychological struggle, they saw people as social animals and dramatized their reactions to society. Historically, their work shows a dependence upon the writings of Auguste Comte, the Father of Modern Sociology, and William James, the psychologist.

1.   ROBERT SHERWOOD: PERSISTENT MORALIST

As Sherwood once bitterly complained, he started out with a "big message and ended up with nothing but good entertainment." He wanted to be taken seriously and was always unhappy when critics did not see the "human equation" that haunted him. With *Reunion in Vienna,* for example, Sherwood thought that he had satirized modern science in the guise of a presumably intellectual psychologist who is cuckolded, but audiences failed to see the conflict of humanity versus science and, instead, thoroughly enjoyed the rollicking, bed-rolling farce written for two exceptional actors, Alfred Lunt and Lynn Fontanne. In only one play, in fact, *Acropolis* (1933), did Sherwood try to express his thoughts unadorned by any glittering wit; and this play, pitting practical men of war against thoughtful men concerned with life and beauty during the Age of Pericles, failed on stage and was never published. In *The Petrified Forest* Sherwood tried to explain the despair of the vanishing intellectual -- "Homo-Semi-Americanus -- a specimen of the in-between age," but again he produced first-rate entertainment in a romantic melodrama linking the gunman and the poet.

The Petrified Forest (1935)

(Plot) The Black Mesa Filling Station and Bar-B-Q in eastern Arizona is run by the Maples -- old Gramp, Jason and his daughter, Gabby -- and Boze, a dull football player interested in Gabby. All complain about their lives, even Squier, a traveller who had potential as an artist until he married a rich woman and forgot his ambitions. Before Squier travels on, he shares Gabby's romantic dreams of going to France and her taste for Villon's poetry. Then, Duke Mantee, a hunted criminal, arrives with part of his gang to wait in this appointed place for his girl. Squier returns, and the desperate situation of the people becomes as revealing as it is uncomfortable. In a romantic gesture, Squier, drawing an analogy between himself and Mantee as frustrated individuals, makes out his insurance policy to Gabby so that she can go to France and then arranges for Duke to kill him. When the manhunt closes in, Duke kills Squier as he promised. Perhaps in Gabby some of Squier's ambitions and dreams will be realized.

(Discussion) Sherwood presented a group of individuals who have become dissatisfied with life because they have lost their ideals and given up their illusions. As a consequence, their world has changed. Humanity now lives in a petrified forest, a "world of outmoded ideas." Squier suffers the "lostness" of the sensitive individual, and both he and Mantee are condemned in this world as romantic idealists. In making the point that people must keep their illusions and escape from the petrified forest, Sherwood and Squier find hope in Gabby -- clearly yet another romantic illusion.

2.   GEORGE KELLY (1887-1974): MORAL LESSONS

George Kelly's career in the theatre started in 1916, when he began to write vaudeville skits such as "Finders Keepers" and

"The Flattering Word." When he expanded other sketches -- "The Show Off" and "Mrs. Ritter Appears" -- into full-length comedies, he was taken more seriously by critics, and during the 1920s his reputation soared with such plays as *Craig's Wife* (1925), which received a Pulitzer Prize. Always, however, he had strong detractors: too formulistic a writer, too severe in his moral judgments, too limited in his character development. Heywood Broun wrote that Kelly "must regiment his folk and Prussianize them." Mary McCarthy complained that his stage properties assume the qualities of characters, that argument surpasses action; she called a Kelly play "a long ad-lib." After the failure of *Philip Goes Forth* (1931), Kelly wrote mainly for the movies and returned to the theatre with only four dramas, none successful.

Essentially a severe and moral man, he was concerned with the self-condemning weakness of the individual. Montrose J. Moses, a historian of drama, called Kelly "a simple moralist using the theatre for simple moral purposes." Although such a criticism is an over-simplification, Kelly did base his judgments on a few essential moral principles: be honest, be pure, be truthful. He believed that people controlled their own lives, and he judged them for their failures, blaming neither heredity nor social forces. His insistence upon judging, however, sometimes detracts from the dramatic value of his plays, although it was his purpose to make the lesson more universally applicable than the situation he dramatized.

Kelly believed that "art is the form per se," that "if one is sufficiently convinced of the vitality of his observations, . . . he is driven to formalize it." His mastery of form, however, and his conscious interest in the details of straightforward realism brought the criticism that he created puppet characters and a photographic exactness which led to caricature. Kelly, however, did not stray from his formula, and the authenticity of his scene and dialogue and the force of his characterization are often memorable. Consequently, his format is both his strength and his weakness, as it allows his determined logic to appear at the same time that it limits and detracts from the more universal quality of his plays.

(a) Social Problems and Individual Weaknesses
Although he attacked various social ills, Kelly was mainly
concerned with human weaknesses. Not society itself but the
reactions of the individuals in a society which makes
happiness impossible interested him. In *The Torchbearers*
(1932) Kelly attacked the absurdities of the Little Theater
Movement and the ridiculous affectations of the people
involved, but he did it through a revelation of individual
weaknesses. The plot of *Philip Goes Forth* (1931) concerns a
man who is persuaded to go to New York to write when it is
obvious that he belongs where he is as a businessman. Kelly
soft-pedaled a criticism of the society which made the choice
so appealing and emphasized the weakness of the man who
allows himself to be persuaded when he knows what his
position in life should be. Although he treated social
disorders, Kelly let his judgments fall upon the individual.
Only in *The Show-Off* (1924), in which a braggart and liar is
blessed far beyond his desserts, did he dramatize a conflict
between an individual and society, but the play is situation
farce and cannot be taken seriously as social criticism.

(b) The Damned
Those people whom Kelly found willfully corrupt among a
weak and vacillating humanity, he damned with a Puritan
conviction. *Craig's Wife* (1925) tells of Mrs. Craig's
determination not only to be independent but to control. She is a
cold and quarrelsome person, who alienates her neighbors,
accuses her aunt of snooping, tries to ruin a niece's life and
distrusts her husband. She wants independent security. At the
end of the play, Kelly gives her just that -- with the loss of
friends and husband -- because he believes that she acts
willfully. Likewise, in *Behold the Bridegroom* (1927), he
allows a "wanton woman" to be condemned for her choices.
When Antoinette Lyle finally meets someone she loves, the
guilt she feels makes her reveal her past, but she is too late in
her discovery: she is rejected, and there will be no marriage. In
Daisy Mayme (1926) a well-made plot brings a happy ending
for the hero and Daisy Mayme, while her antagonist, a
conniving and vicious woman, loses everything. Throughout
these plays Kelly showed a discriminating insight into
character, an attention to truthful detail and a conviction

which distinguish him among contemporary writers of the social problem play.

3.   LILLIAN HELLMAN (1906-1984): "I AM A MORAL WRITER"

During the period between the wars, Lillian Hellman wrote only four plays, but they were enough to bring her a reputation for vigorous and unyielding confrontation in whatever she wrote or did. In a preface to a collection of four of her plays, she wrote: "I am a moral writer, often too moral a writer, and I cannot avoid, it seems, that last summing up." This determination, plus her reliance upon violent action, brought charges from critics of "melodrama" and "sensationalism," to which Hellman characteristically responded with an argument about the effectiveness in the theatre of violent action with a purpose. With all her might she attacked what she found distasteful in society, from strikebreaking to fascism and unnatural greed to human degeneracy, and the morals she drew are obvious. Do not fool around with human lives; do something about degenerate greed. Using both comedic and melodramatic techniques, Hellman exposes the selfishness and the cruelty of humanity with a penetrating clarity and a highly theatrical effectiveness. Generally, her objectives were no different from those of her contemporaries, but with superior artistry and more intense and controlled imagination, she succeeded in attaining a universality.

(a) Social Anger: *The Children's Hour* (1934)

Victorian writers extolled the moral strength of woman, which the moral view of an enthusiastic and talented woman playwright could create, but they did not understand the influence it could exert on a theatre audience. Hellman's first Broadway play, *The Children's Hour,* ironically taking its title from Longfellow's poem, dramatizes the evil quality of children. To satisfy a perverse need for excitement, Mary Tilford, a young student in a girls' school run by Martha Dobie and Karen Wright, invents a story suggesting an unnatural affection between the two teachers and gleefully tells it to her grandmother when she is disciplined for her unacceptable conduct at school. The grandmother is incensed; the story is spread around; and although the teachers try to defend themselves, they are ostracized by the community and forced to close their school. Later, Martha, fearing that she may be preventing Karen's happiness in her approaching marriage to a young doctor, commits suicide. When the grandmother learns and reveals the truth, it is too late for Martha, but Karen can try to find a future. Brooks Atkinson called the play a story of "two people . . . defeated by the malignance of an aroused public opinion."

(b)   The Degeneracy of Greed: *The Little Foxes* **(1939)**
(Plot)   To increase their fortunes, the southern Hubbards are negotiating a partnership with a Chicago industrialist. Ben, the older brother in the Hubbard family, is crafty, unscrupulous, with pretentions toward aristocracy. It is he who forced his cruel and cowardly brother, Oscar, to marry Birdie, a naive but tender woman, cruelly used, whose family estate the Hubbards now control. Regina, the greedy sister, unloving and unloved, is married to Horace Giddens, who is recuperating from a heart condition at Johns Hopkins. To get her third of the money necessary for the proposed partnership, Regina sends her daughter, Alexandra, to bring Horace home. Meanwhile, Leo, Birdie and Oscar's weak son who works in Horace's bank, has revealed that Horace's safe deposit box contains bonds worth $88,000. When Ben realizes that Horace will not give Regina any money, he has Oscar "borrow" the bonds and go to Chicago. Horace discovers the theft when he remakes his will in favor of Alexandra, but, without stopping the thieves, he wills the bonds to Regina. Furious, Regina causes Horace to have a heart attack and then coldly watches him panic and die in an attempt to get his medicine. Regina then forces Ben to give her the greater part of the new business, but he suspects that she is implicated in Horace's death. Her greedy satisfaction is also marred by Alexandra's new understanding of the family degeneracy.

(Discussion)   This realistic study of "the little foxes that spoil the vines" is a horror melodrama and a social warning. Very carefully controlled, the action rises and falls with excellent suspense and sensation. There are the bonds, the medicine and the overwhelming cruelty set against well-drawn characters. The Hubbard family, in its greed and suggestion of incestual idocy, presents a dramatic contrast to Birdie. As usual in a Hellman play, the moral which is both the horror and the warning is clear. In the words of the Negro Addie: "There are people who eat the earth and eat all the people on it like in the Bible with the locusts. Then there are people who stand around and watch them eat it. Sometimes I think it ain't right to stand and watch them do it."

D. Satire on the Stage

Satire in American drama dates back to Governor Hunter's *Androboros,* the plays of Mercy Warren during the Revolution and Royall Tyler's *The Contrast* (1787). Mainly as a part of farce-comedy, it continued in the Yankee plays, the social comedies about New York City and the works of Charles Hoyt and George Ade. Between the World Wars, the bitter protests against aspects of society were almost always satiric. O'Neill, Anderson, Sherwood, Sidney Howard, Kelly, Rice -- all were satirists, and most serious plays of the period are satires. Particular emphasis, however, should be given to the plays of George S. Kaufman and his numerous collaborators.

The means of satire is the ridiculing of institutions or aspects of human behavior. Its objective is to reform, although the degree of seriousness involved varies with the playwright. There is also a variation in the degree of detachment which the dramatist exercises. In satire, however, the dramatist has a preconceived end, and whether one laughs or winces, the final appeal, stimulated through emotion or intellect, is for the audience's positive response.

1.   CAPITALISM AND MATERIALISM

A representative list of plays satirizing capitalism and materialism would include the following: *Dulcy* (1921) by George S. Kaufman and Marc Connelly; *The Adding Machine* (1923) by Elmer Rice; *Beggar on Horseback* (1924) by Kaufman and Connelly; *Marco Millions* (1927) by Eugene O'Neill, "the sourest and most magnificent poke in the jaw that American business and the American businessman have ever got," according to George J. Nathan, the drama critic; *Meteor* (1929) by S. N. Behrman; *Dodsworth* (1934) by Sidney Howard, a dramatization of Sinclair Lewis' satire of the American businessman; *High Tor* (1937) by Maxwell Anderson; and *The Little Foxes* (1939) by Lillian Hellman.

2.   POLITICS AND POLITICIANS

Politics and politicians have always been popular with satirists: Maxwell Anderson's biting satire on justice in the Sacco-Vanzetti trial in *Gods of the Lightning* (1928) and his picture of the corruption and pork-barreling in Congress in *Both Your Houses* (1933); the riotous musical-drama, *Of Thee I Sing* (1931) by Kaufman and Morrie Ryskind, which ridicules the manner in which a President is nominated, his platform ("love"), his campaigning and the way he and his wife view the affairs of the nation; Kaufman and Katharine Dayton's *First Lady* (1935), a satire on such a "politically-minded somebody as Alice Longworth Roosevelt might have been"; another satire on the FDR administration, *I'd Rather Be Right* (1937) by Kaufman and Moss Hart; Maxwell Anderson's satire on tyrannical government, *Knickerbocker Holiday* (1938); *Washington Jitters* (1938) by John Boruff and Walter Hart, a satire on Congressional hijinks and the jargon of government.

3.   THE MOTION PICTURE INDUSTRY

Once the movie industry got underway, its idiosyncrasies provided excellent material for the satirist: *Merton of the Movies* (1922) by Kaufman and Connelly, a spoof of the movie-struck clerk who cannot act; *Once in a Lifetime* (1930) by Kaufman and Moss Hart, a hilarious burlesque of movie making through the activities of three vaudeville performers who decide to teach the silent movie stars how to talk; Lawrence Riley's *Personal Appearance* (1934), on the problems of a star and her public; *Boy Meets Girl* (1935) by Bella and Samuel Spewack, a satire on writing and casting a movie; *Kiss the Boys Good-bye* (1938), a satire on Hollywood's search for talent, by Clare Boothe.

4.   WAR AND VIOLENCE

Robert Sherwood's early attacks on war -- *The Road to Rome* (1927) and *Idiot's Delight* (1935) -- are satirical in nature. Other satires on war include Reginald Lawrence's *Men Must*

Fight (1931), John Haynes Holmes' *If This Be Treason* (1935), Irwin Shaw's *Bury the Dead* (1935) and Maxwell Anderson's *Feast of the Ortolans* (1937).

5. LIFE, LIVING AND SOCIETY

Patterns of human behavior have frequently been ridiculed in the theatre. Polite society has always been a target -- *Dinner at Eight* (1932) by Kaufman and Edna Ferber. Theatre life may be represented by these same authors' *The Royal Family* (1927), suggestive of the Barrymore family, and George Kelly's *The Torch-Bearers* (1922), a spoof of the Little Theatre Movement. *The Front Page* (1928) by Ben Hecht and Charles MacArthur satirizes reporters, editors, politics, police corruption, psychology and schools of journalism. Social responsibility is treated in Sinclair Lewis and John C. Moffitt's anti-fascist play, *It Can't Happen Here* (1936). Clare Boothe's *The Women* (1936) -- with its all-female cast -- is a pointed satire on women who, according to the author, "deserve to be smacked across the head with a meat axe."

Occasionally, the satiric view slips into something more serious than the play's first act suggests. *Merrily We Roll Along* (1934), by Kaufman and Hart, develops from a burlesque of Hollywood activities to a serious choice facing the artist -- the dilemma between one's idealism and the compulsion for financial reward. *The Male Animal* (1940) by James Thurber and Elliott Nugent satirizes the absurdities which can be found only in a college or university. The play becomes serious when the social and romantic problem changes to the personal problem of surrendering to "prejudice and dictation." In satire the iron fist is frequently within the minstrel's white glove, and many of America's best playwrights of this period used the genre with great skill.

E.   Light Comedy

The spirit of the Thirties was not particularly conducive to light comedy. S. N. Behrman, in fact, tried to argue this point in a play called *No Time for Comedy*. With the stock market crash, the Depression, the concern over fascism, the problems in Europe, the dissatisfaction with the "New Deal" and the

approach of World War II, few of the better playwrights of
the period easily assumed light-hearted attitudes in the
theatre.   Frequently, those plays which do approach light
comedy carry a sting of seriousness. The prime exponent of this
type of drama was George S. Kaufman, who, with various
collaborators, created some of the liveliest nights in the
theatre between the wars.   There were other good light
comedies written during this period, but the attempts were
scattered and few.

1.   OUTSTANDING LIGHT COMEDIES

Farce and light comedies tread closely to one another, but they
can be distinguished. Whereas in farce the world is irrational
or frivolous, the action coincidental or absurd and the
characters simple and manipulated, in comedy one is drawn
into the realm of meaningfulness where attention is focussed on
wit and irony by well-developed characters who determine the
action. Farce characteristics, however, are frequently found in
comedy, and critics may differ as to where the line between the
forms should be drawn.

(a) Eugene O'Neill: *Ah, Wilderness!* (1933)

Many have regretted that O'Neill wrote only one comedy.
Sean O'Casey, Irish playwright, noted: "I've one reproach
only to make of him -- that he didn't use his gift for comedy
oftener, as shown in 'Ah, Wilderness!'" Written just before the
hiatus in O'Neill's career, this play shows the romantic and
positive values that he wanted to find, while also fitting into
his search for meaning -- this time through the maturing of
Richard Miller, a typical O'Neill poet. Filled with haunting
nostalgia, as well as some acute insights into humanity, the
play has the reality and wit of comedy at its best.

(Plot) The serenity of the Miller household on the Fourth of
July is disturbed by Mr. Macomber, who has come to accuse
Richard Miller, age sixteen, of writing nasty poetry to his
daughter, Muriel. Discontented with himself and the world,
Richard denies Macomber's charges to his father (who has
recognized Swinburne's poetry) and asks to be alone. Another
lonely person is Sid, Mrs. Miller's brother, who would like to
marry Mr. Miller's sister. Pathetically, she can't marry a man

who drinks, and he can't stop drinking.   Reacting to his disappointment with Muriel, Richard goes to a bar with an older boy who has a "couple of swift babies," finally gets into a fight and is tossed out of the bar.   Disheveled and drunk, he returns home.   Next day, while Mr. and Mrs. Miller try to decide what to do, the experienced Sid nurses Richard.   A letter from Muriel restores the boy, and that night, in adolescent wonder and awe, they declare their love.   The difficulties which face maturing youth are many, but for both parents and children O'Neill's curtain falls on happiness.

(b)   Anne Nichols: *Abie's Irish Rose* (1937)

Having one of the longest runs in Broadway history, *Abie's Irish Rose* is a situation comedy which is distinguished by its witty dialogue.   When Abraham Levy falls in love with Rose Mary Murphy and secretly marries her, he expects difficulties in the family circle and therefore introduces her to his father as "Rose Mary Murpheski."   His father is so impressed with the girl that he urges Abie to propose marriage.   At the wedding Rose Mary's father is late, and Rose and Abie are married by a rabbi before he comes in with a Catholic priest and both families finally discover what is happening.   Amid the uproar, the priest marries them for the third time, but a year later the fathers are still unreconciled.   Then there is to be a baby -- more difficulty!   Murphy will leave the baby his money if it is a girl, and Levy will do the same if it is a boy. Fortunately, the "baby" turns out to be twins -- Patrick Joseph and Rebecca -- and both sets of in-laws are finally delighted.

(c)   Arthur Kober: *Having Wonderful Time* (1937)

This is a play about young people in New York who ride to work every day on the subway, thinking of "those two weeks of vacation paradise which are accepted as handsome recompense for fifty weeks of drudgery."   The scene is an adult vacation camp which, with its penny-pinching owner and waiters who double as gigolos, is not what the heroine, "Teddy" Stern, expected.   She finds Chick, an unemployed lawyer, interesting, but he feels too poor to ask her to marry him.   Then at a party where a "wolf" tries to get Teddy drunk preparatory to seduction, Chick becomes angry and Teddy decides that perhaps he is The One.   At her instigation he says, "Yes," and she will keep her job. Satire in the play brings a gloomy if compassionate seriousness to the farce-comic episodes.

(d) Howard Lindsay and Russel Crouse:
Life With Father (1939)

This play ran for 3,216 consecutive performances (1939-1947), breaking all New York records. It gracefully combines the serio-humorous attempts of a father to run his family efficiently and a great deal of information about American upper-class life during the 1880s. Although the plot is episodic, the connecting thread is the persistent effort of Vinnie, the Mother, to get Father baptized, an event which seems imminent at the end of the play. A reviewer called it "a series of tableaux rather than an orthodox dramatic work." During a hilarious evening in the theatre, however, the audience learns of Father's response to all exigencies ("Damn!"), the effect that Father's suit has upon young Clarence (it will not let him kneel in church), young John's success in selling "Bartlett's Beneficient Balm" and Vinnie's conniving to get Father baptized.

(e) James Thurber and Elliott Nugent:
The Male Animal (1940)

This is the story of a professor's decision to read Vanzetti's declaration of faith to his English class. The reactions of the college trustees and all alumni-conscious people, however, turn a simple class exercise into a serious issue. Unfortunately, the uproar takes place on the day of the *big* football game. To further complicate matters, the professor's self-centered wife provokes him into defending his manhood against her former football-playing sweetheart, one of many alums returning for the game. Such action is obviously comic, but as one critic commented: "There is more than meets the funny bone in this scrawled lampoon on the civilized male at bay."

2.   GEORGE S. KAUFMAN (1889-1961) AND COMPANY

George Freedley, historian of modern drama, described Kaufman as "one of the best representatives of the highly competent craftsman in playwriting in America." Kaufman's thorough knowledge of the theatre, in fact, earned him the title of "play doctor." But he was more than this. Although early critics tended to regard him mainly as an irrepressible spoofer, he provided a depth of insight into the sanity beneath his mirth that exposed much of the absurdity and pretense in life. Essentially, he gave audiences what they wanted and at the same time stung them in ways that his pervasive wit made bearable. A born collaborator, he demanded much of those who worked with him, while contributing an imagination and originality which made his light, satiric comedies distinctive in American theatre. With a number of collaborators -- Morrie Ryskind (*Of Thee I Sing,* 1932), Ring Lardner (*June Moon,* 1929), Katharine Dayton (*First Lady,* 1935), Marc Connelly, Edna Ferber and Moss Hart -- Kaufman managed to provoke comedy from many aspects of life: the movies, the theatre, politics, high society, business and love.

(a) With Marc Connelly
After early unsuccessful attempts at solo playwriting, Kaufman teamed up with Marc Connelly, author of *The Green Pastures,* to the delight of thousands. Their first attempt, *Dulcy* (1921), based on a Franklin P. Adams character, celebrates the small-brained but well-meaning wife whose stupidity seems to ruin but actually helps her husband's business career. Next came *To the Ladies* (1922), a view of the bright wife who saves the job of the dull husband. As the heroine says, "Nearly all of the great men have been married; it can't be merely a coincidence." *Merton of the Movies* (1922) burlesques the Hollywood actor. Their most successful collaboration, however, was *Beggar on Horseback* (1924), attacking that society which attempts to merchandise its artistry.

(b) With Edna Ferber
The author of the memorable *Show Boat* and Kaufman were successful in three of their playwriting ventures: *The Royal Family* (1927), *Dinner at Eight* (1932) and *Stage Door* (1936), which toys with the young actress breaking into Broadway big time and gives her the additional problem of choosing between the movies and the stage.

(c) And with Moss Hart
From this team America got some of its best lighthearted farce-comedies. Hart was an intense but warm and emotional man

whose wit and sense of humanity is clear in his autobiography, *Act I* (1959). Starting his career with one of the touring companies of Augustus Pitou, Jr., "King of the One Night Stands," Hart first joined Kaufman with *Once in a Lifetime* and later wrote several successful plays by himself, of which *Lady in the Dark* (1941) is a fine example.

Once in a Lifetime (1930) remains the quintessential burlesque of Hollywood absurdity. Another joint venture, *You Can't Take It With You,* was a Pulitzer winner in 1936. The team was less successful in other plays -- one about the theatre, *The Fabulous Invalid* (1938); a highly patriotic play called *The American Way* (1939); and *George Washington Slept Here* (1940), built on their own adventures in restoring an old house. They made their most enduring contribution to American drama in *The Man Who Came to Dinner* (1939), based on the acerbic personality of the lecturing drama critic Alexander Woollcott, who, according to Kaufman, would "disport himself" in the play.

The Man Who Came to Dinner (1939)
A lecturer, Sheridan Whiteside, supposedly breaks a hip during a visit to a small town and is forced to stay with a family whom he happily, and bitterly, torments by means of the guests he receives, the advice he gives to his hosts' children and his numerous taunting comments. Then he discovers that his prize secretary is falling in love with the town's newspaperman. What has once been fun for "Sherry," now becomes serious. To break up their happiness, he does everything in his power -- which is considerable.

The play is episodic and cluttered but witty and fast moving. In true farce style, embarrassment is used for its own sake and for the pleasure of Whiteside and the audience. Each device is exploited for humor: telegraph, telephone, letters, some penguins, an incompetent village doctor, a Christmas radio program, convicts, an impersonation, even a mummy case. Still, the play is not pure farce. Love is taken seriously in the final scenes, and Whiteside shows a speck of humanity. A problem in this kind of play is the ending. Having written at a tremendous speed for three acts, what does a dramatist do? In this play a broken hip is an effective answer.

F.   High Comedy

Whereas "drama as a weapon" involves the utmost commitment to a cause on the part of the dramatist, high comedy or a sophisticated comedy of manners demands the author's sense of detachment. As might be expected detachment was far from a keynote of American drama during the Twenties and Thirties. Writers of propaganda, social commentary and satire could not be detached. The point is well made in S. N. Behrman's *Biography*. Having lived an irregular life of enjoyment and satisfaction, Marion infuriates Richard, the committed young radical. "God, how I hate detachment," he responds. A corollary to the necessary detachment in a high comedy is the characters' dependence on expedience as a basis for decisions. The writer of high comedy, therefore, should have a worldly attitude toward life and be able to portray a fashionable society with wit and imagination.

Predictably, America has produced very little high comedy. Restoration and eighteenth-century England, with the works of Congreve and Sheridan, was a more natural place for such drama to flourish. Those in America who most nearly approximated high comedy were S. N. Behrman and Philip Barry, and neither could fully concentrate his efforts in this genre. Behrman found himself protesting with the other dramatists of the Thirties, and Barry became involved in a philosophical search for truth. It is a difficult genre, and critics have either employed the term indiscriminately or, refusing to be put on the defensive, have purposefully used it in a vague manner.

Barrett Clark's criticism of Paul Osborn's *The Vinegar Tree* as a "high comedy, bordering on both farce and tragedy," indicates the vague use of the term ("Some Broadway Plays Pass in Review," *Drama Magazine*, 1931, p. 14). As a drama in which a man is pressured first by a girl who wants "experience in life" and second by the girl's mother, who is feeling the pangs of middle age, this play has high comedy potential.   Its conventional ending, however, lacks both expediency and detachment. Another near miss is Mark Reed's *Yes, My Darling Daughter* (1937). The daughter of a free-thinking mother and a conservative father, Ellen forces her mother to agree to her spending a weekend with her boyfriend, who is leaving for Europe. Afterwards, the father is furious and wants to force a marriage, which the boy will accept but which Ellen refuses as old fashioned moral coercion. Finally, she agrees when she sees how silly it is to refuse on principle the man she loves.

1.   S. N. BEHRMAN (1893-1973): SOPHISTICATED WIT

Behrman studied with George Pierce Baker and worked as a book reviewer, press agent and playreader before writing a successful play for Broadway. In *No Time for Comedy* (1939) a character advises the playwright-protagonist: "Your genius is for comedy; stand with it." In life, however, Behrman was unable to do this consistently. In most of his plays, even those which show his fine wit, talent for clever dialogue and particular skill in dramatizing a sophisticated situation, he allowed his emotions to influence his writing. It is abundantly clear, for example, that he was opposed to political totalitarianism, that he believed in the civilized individual, that he distrusted fanaticism and hated fascism. Such feelings, however, cannot be allowed to control the action and thought in high comedy.

When Behrman managed to avoid emotional involvement, he approached high comedy. Leonie Frothingham in *End of Summer* (1936) is a fine character for high comedy; so is Lady Wyngate in *Rain from Heaven* (1934). As complete plays, however, only *The Second Man* and *Biography* may be termed high comedy.

(a) *The Second Man* (1927)
(Plot) Clark Storey, a cynical, fourth-rate writer, lives in reasonable happiness with Mrs. Kendall Frayne, a widow who enjoys supporting him. His comfortable existance, however, is interrupted by the eager pursuit of Monica Grey, who is in turn jealously adored by Austin Lowe, a brilliant chemist but a bumbling lover. When it seems that Storey may finally marry Kendall, Monica desperately tries to stop the marriage, even with the invented news that she carries Storey's baby. Storey is interested, and Austin is infuriated, but the question remains: Can Storey exchange comfort for love? The answer: He cannot.

(Discussion) There, of course, is the "second man" in Storey, who explains his position: "For, together with, and as it were behind, so much pleasurable emotion, there is always that other strange second man in me, calm, critical, observant, unmoved, blasé, odious." The play is marred by some melodramatic heroics, but the clever dialogue, the detachment by which the hero lives and the expediency of his final decision provide the characteristics of high comedy.

(b) *Biography* (1932)

(Plot) Marion Froude is a third-rate artist who has received a great deal of publicity for her paintings of and affairs with notable people. Newly arrived in New York, she is visited by the staid and naive Leander Nolan, presumably her first lover. When Marion tells him that Richard Kurt, a sensitive young man who hides behind a cynical attitude, has asked her to write her biography for his magazine, Nolan, a candidate for the U.S. Senate, fears that his political life will suffer from her revelations. Immediately, he appeals to his backer, Orin Kinnicott, father of his fiancée, Slade. But when Marion charms Kinnicott and Slade is fascinated both by Kurt and by "the woman" from Nolan's past, Nolan leaves in disgust. Marion and Kurt realize that they are in love, but when Marion decides not to write the biography, Kurt becomes furious. His fanaticism makes it impossible for him to understand a tolerant person, and Marion realizes their true incompatibility. When she is called to paint the portrait of a Hollywood celebrity, she cheerfully departs.

(Discussion) The dominance of Marion makes this play high comedy. Her detachment and sense of expediency illustrate the author's complete control of his materials. Marion has an inescapable wit and an ability to throw people off balance, while she remains in perfect command of her emotions. In this instance Behrman's use of sophisticated action, dialogue and characters reveals the correct relationship between emotion and intellect and results in high comedy.

2.   PHILIP BARRY (1896-1949): "THE LIGHTNING BUG"

A critic described Philip Barry as "the lightning bug -- now he lights up, now he doesn't." In terms of Broadway, where

Barry's plays achieved erratic success from 1923 to 1949, the metaphor was as apt as it was clever. A serious-minded man with a quick wit and a talent for sophisticated comedy, Barry wanted to write profoundly about life. When he tried to plumb the depths of meaning (*Hotel Universe, Here Come the Clowns*), he failed in the theatre; when he employed his comic touch (*Paris Bound, The Animal Kingdom*), he was very successful -- the lightning bug!

Like many of his characters, Barry was a worldly person who lived on Park Avenue, on the French Riviéra, in London and in Paris. Even the bright life of his comedies, however, was colored by the restlessness and stuffiness of the society that concerned and saddened him. As a playwright who was a meticulous craftsman and stylist, he ignored his critics and continued to satisfy his audiences with sparkling comedies and himself with his determined search for meaning in life. His comedies are in the tradition of Clyde Fitch, Rachel Crothers and Sidney Howard, yet superior to all in wit, intellect and imagination. Like his predecessors, he was occasionally given to preaching, but mainly he showed the necessary disciplined detachment. This control of viewpoint, plus polished dialogue and the sense of unity of effect, distinguishes Barry as America's foremost writer of high comedy.

(a) Discovery -- Intelligently Used

In a lecture on high comedy, April 4, 1904, George Pierce Baker, the Harvard professor who taught Barry the art of play-writing, said: "You see a certain number of people, and you see the difference between what each of these persons is and what he thinks he is. Now, if you can represent that for your particular public, you can write high comedy." Barry did this and more. Introducing appropriate sophistication, he allowed a character to see the difference and to act upon this knowledge with the proper mixture of emotion and intelligence. In *You and I* (1923) he posed a question: Should the hero get married or go to Paris and study architecture? The father of the hero once chose marriage. When the hero does the same, the father gives up his business in order to paint, only to discover that he lacks talent. He has, however, realized something else and decides to send both his son and future daughter-in-law to Paris after they are married. The hero in *Holiday* (1928) makes a thoroughly expedient decision after making the discovery that Baker described. Tracy Lord in *The Philadelphia Story* (1939) sees the truth about herself after being accused of lacking love and understanding for her first husband. Expediently, she begins again. Generally dealing with problems of marriage, Barry's comedies have that quality of sophisticated discovery from which truthful and expedient choices are made -- the whole producing excellent high comedy.

(b) *Paris Bound* (1929)

(Plot) On Jim and Mary Hutton's wedding day, the only sour note is the presence of Jim's divorced parents -- divorced because the father was unfaithful and the mother could not see that the spiritual side of marriage was more important than the physical. Mary shares her father-in-law's views, but her real test comes six years later, when she learns that Jim has been seen with an old girlfriend on his business trips to Europe. Immediately jumping toward divorce, she discovers to her own surprise that her friendship with a young ballet composer could easily develop into an affair, and she accepts her husband without question upon his return from Europe.

(Discussion) The elder Mr. Hutton's lines may be preachy, but there is a sustaining wit in the dialogue, excellent change of pace and a remarkable unity throughout. A ballet cleverly accentuates the idea in the play.

(c) *The Animal Kingdom* (1932)

(Plot) Tom Collier is a rebel. A bachelor, he publishes good books which do not make money and has an artist, Daisy, as his mistress. Then, he marries the ambitious Cecelia Henry, who immediately campaigns for changes -- abandonment of his friends, merger with a big publisher and reconciliation with his father, who frowns on Tom's way of life. Whenever Tom does what she wants, Cecelia rewards him; otherwise, she locks the bedroom door. Finally, he leaves the locked door to go to Daisy, who is truly his soul mate.

(Discussion)   In this play Barry presented the socially improper but expedient and honest conclusion. Understanding the true nature of his characters, he allowed them to act freely and sincerely, ignoring socially imposed boundaries.

V. "TOWN HALL TONIGHT"
MELODRAMA AND FARCE

The theatre could not exist without melodrama and farce, and a good part of American drama written between the World Wars fits into one or the other of these categories or has some of its characteristics. The terms melodrama and farce are frequently used in a derogatory fashion to suggest that a playwright has attempted to write tragedy or comedy and failed. Although in certain instances the criticism may be just, the condescending tone is damaging to two perfectly acceptable dramatic forms. Eugene O'Neill, for example, has been dealt with disparagingly as a writer of first-rate melodrama, while Lillian Hellman has sometimes been criticized for her use of melodramatic techniques to achieve thrilling climaxes. Most of the protest and social commentary plays employ some characteristics of melodrama, and many comedies have the contrived action and controlled confusion of farce. This does not mean that the dramatists lacked insight or dramatic skills, although it does suggest the great difficulty of writing tragedy or fine comedy. Because the terms melodrama and farce describe forms of drama, they may be accurately employed to suggest dramatic techniques and a dramatist's objective.

Melodrama and farce as genres make definite demands upon the dramatist. Melodrama lacks psychological insight and well-rounded character development but depends upon fast-moving and suspenseful action to fulfill its objective, which is to thrill. The concept of time, which the dramatist must unabashedly manipulate, is also of prime importance in melodrama. Farce uses one-dimensional characters whose actions are determined by cleverly contrived plot movements, and it reaches its objective of laughter by the creation of confusing and embarrassing situations through an abundance of incongruous misunderstandings. Few American dramatists have mastered the requirements with notable success.

A. Modern Melodrama

The melodrama of Augustin Day and Owen Davis is dead. Frank Rahill, writing in *Theatre Arts* ["Melodrama," XVI (April 1932), 293], complained that "what passes for melodrama today is really a degenerate offspring"; the "sacred dogmas have become a joke," and instead of being thrilled, people simply laugh. Although this criticism is severe, it is true that, by and large, sensational melodrama has been replaced by other kinds of melodrama. The most successful is probably the mystery or crime melodrama that movies and television now so expediently control. Other melodrama is difficult to classify. Its aim is, as always, to thrill -- and it does this through an exciting adventure, a heroic act or a heart-touching ordeal. It differs from the older form of American melodrama in that modern dramatists attempt to be more subtle, more realistic and perhaps more truthful.

1.   MELODRAMA OF MYSTERY AND CRIME

Mystery and melodrama go hand-in-hand in many plays, but the few outstanding mystery melodramas are easy to list: *The Bat* by Mary Roberts Rinehart and Avery Hopwood; *Broadway* by Philip Dunning and George Abbott; and the comic melodrama, *Arsenic and Old Lace* by Joseph O. Kesselring. Others are Sidney Howard's *Ned McCobb's Daughter* (1926); Bartlett Cormack's *The Racket* (1927); and Howard Lindsay and Damon Runyon's *A Slight Case of Murder* (1935). Of all dramas, the inherently complicated plot of the melodrama is the most difficult to summarize.

(a) *The Bat* (1920)
Miss Cornelia Van Gorder has leased an old country house, where she lives with her maid and a young woman named Dale Odgen. Recently, the local bank has failed and a cashier named Jack Bailey has disappeared; also, someone has tried to enter Cornelia's house, and people have been warned over the radio that a criminal called The Bat is at large in the area. The action begins as Brooks (actually Bailey, who is engaged to Dale) is hired as a gardener; and a detective is employed by the women for protection. Dr. Wells drops by and arouses suspicion by trying to persuade Cornelia to leave. As Jack and

Dale secretly discuss their difficulties, Jack remembers that the old house has a secret room and, expecting to find the missing bank money in that room, he calls Dick Fleming, son of the bank president who owns the house, to come over that night. The house blueprints are found, but Dick is mysteriously shot and killed.   Immediately, Dr. Wells tries to get the blueprints from Dale, who is suspected of Dick's murder by the detective. There is more mystery and more suspense when the detective is found tied up, an unknown man faints at the door of the room in which the women stay -- and a black bat is tacked onto the door. In the final act, the secret room is discovered, along with the bank president's body. The doctor is exposed as being part of the conspiracy, and the unknown man is identified as a detective. When the Bat, who has been masquerading as the hired detective throughout the action, sets the garage on fire to get the people out of the house, where the money is hidden, the real detective captures him -- ending a fast-moving and exciting drama.

(b) *Broadway* (1926)
Barrett Clark called *Broadway* "a first-rate specimen of the peppy melodrama, jazzed up with girls, a couple of murders, wisecracks, light repartee and music."   Brooks Atkinson commented on it as "exhilarating, madly colored melodrama, a kaleidoscope, spattered with the bright pigments of local color." The scene is the Paradise Night Club in New York. Roy, a poor but kindly performer, loves a very naïve and sweet chorine named Billie. But Billie is being courted by Steve, a liquor-peddling gangster who shoots his chief competitor in the back. Justice is served, however, as the dead gangster's girlfriend -- and a very nice girl at that -- shoots Steve, leaving Billie with second thoughts which eventually turn her toward Roy and marriage.

(c) *Arsenic and Old Lace* (1941)
The two sweet old Brewster sisters, Martha and Abby, are really sentimental and senile murderers, who give poisoned wine to lonely old men whom they wish only to make happy. They have killed twelve men, whom their insane nephew, who thinks he is Teddy Roosevelt, has buried in the basement, under the delusion that he is digging locks for the Panama Canal and

burying yellow fever victims. Mortimer Brewster is horrified when he discovers this particular idiosyncrasy of his aunts, and his understandably disturbed activities irritate his girlfriend, Elaine. He has been trying to get "Teddy" committed to an institution; now he sees other obligations as well. To complicate matters, Jonathan, a brother of Martha and Abby, having escaped from a Prison from the Criminal Insane, arrives with a friend and a dead body of their own to dispose of, a Mr. Spenalzo. After an evening full of well-timed suspense, the police finally arrest Jonathan, and Mr. Witherspoon from the rest home arrives to take not only "Teddy" but Martha and Abby, who have decided that they will commit themselves, having told Mortimer that he actually cannot sign for them because he is not really a Brewster. Everyone thrills to Mortimer's joyous shout, "I'm a bastard!" and Elaine "leaps into his illegitimate arms," as the old ladies, having decided that Mr. Witherspoon is lonely, serve him some of their infamous elderberry wine.

2.   MORE SUBTLE MELODRAMA

The material for melodrama is unlimited. It is necessary only that the dramatist find excitement and thrills in the life portrayed. That life can be almost anything, but the writer of modern melodrama is less dependent upon the achievements of the stage carpenter than his predecessor in the late nineteenth century. Owen Davis, a master of the old melodrama, accepted the change in style in *The Nervous Wreck* (1923) and numerous other plays. Don Marquis, best known for his poetry-writing cockroach in *archie and mehitabel*, wrote a sentimental melodrama about an old drunkard who takes the blame for his son's misdoings and finally brings happiness to everyone in *The Old Soak* (1922). A fine writer of melodrama, Sidney Howard bent the form toward social drama. His play about Walter Reed's discovery of the yellow fever mosquito, *Yellow Jack* (1934), is a good example of adventure melodrama. More successful in the theatre were Preston Sturges' melodramatic farce, *Strictly Dishonorable* (1929), and the sophisticated musical melodrama *Lady in the Dark* by Moss Hart with lyrics by Ira Gershwin and music by Kurt Weill.

Lady in the Dark **(1941)**

At the pinnacle of her success as editor of *Allure* fashion magazine, Liza Elliott is having a nervous breakdown. Depressed, filled with terror, unable to sleep, she goes to a psychiatrist who discovers, through a song that Liza sings and the dream she tells him, that she is afraid to be herself. She lives with Mr. Nesbitt, publisher of the magazine, whose wife has thus far not given him a divorce. Slowly, Liza's character is revealed through well-designed and suspenseful action. She wants to be beautiful, but she dresses in a severe manner. She apparently dislikes one of the men in her office, named Charlie, who, in one of Liza's dreams, tells her that she is afraid to be the woman she wants to be. When Nesbitt tells her that he is getting a divorce, she becomes frantic with fear. Having gradually learned about herself, Liza discovers that she can find happiness -- with Charlie.

B.   Same Old Farce

The professed writers of farce during the period between the wars were far fewer than those who actually wrote farce. Not only do the protest plays exist on contrived situations and unmotivated embarrassments, but writers of comedy and social drama more than occasionally inadvertently forced a point, a character or an effect. Most of the plays about Hollywood are farces -- Kaufman and Hart's *Once in a Lifetime,* the Spewack's *Boy Meets Girl.* Kaufman, in fact, dealt liberally in farce in his early play about theatrical life, *The Butter and Egg Man* (1925). Another good farce involving theatre people is John Emerson and Anita Loos' *The Whole Town's Talking* (1924). To make his daughter, Ethel, interested in marrying his business partner, Chester, Mr. Simons invents the tale of Chester's affair with Letty Lythe, a movie star. The scheme works, until Letty comes to town with a very jealous boyfriend. Eventually, both Chester and the truth triumph. Many farces were written and have been well forgotten, but a few good examples of the genre still appeal to audiences.

Beginning about the middle of the Thirties and extending into the war years, farce became quite popular. In 1933, Howard Lindsay's *She Loves Me Not* explored the problems that two

Princeton boys would have if they tried to hide a chorus girl in their rooms. *Room Service* (1937) by J. Murray and A. Boretz deals with a man's attempt to produce a play. Frances Swann's *Out of the Frying Pan* (1941) tells how a group of young theatre enthusiasts try to work their way into a director's heart by way of his stomach. Two frequently produced farces of youthful absurdities are J. Monk and F. J. Finklehoffe's *Brother Rat* (1936), which describes life in a military prep school, and *What a Life!* (1938) by Clifford Goldsmith, which dramatizes the exploits of Henry Aldrich. By 1940 war conditions changed attitudes. In *My Sister Eileen*, written that year, Joseph Fields and Jerome Chodorov showed small-town girls living in New York -- their troubles with their friends and their apartment (recently vacated by a prostitute) and additional episodes involving jobs, jail and the Brazilian navy.

Three Men on a Horse (1935)

George Abbott as a director of plays and musicals has consistently shown a magic touch in production. In this play, written with John Cecil Holm, he created a successful farce about an erstwhile poet named Erwin who writes ditties for a greeting card company but entertains himself while commuting on a bus with his uncanny ability to pick winners in horse races. He never bets, but he also never misses. Consequently, he is kidnapped by gamblers, who hold him in a hotel room while he supplies them with the names of winners. Absurd situations and incongruous disagreements among the gamblers spark the action of the play. Finally, a four-horse parley becomes the Big Bet, and Erwin is forced to bet, too. The gamblers think they have lost everything, until a disqualification shows Erwin to be right. Now, however, having bet, Erwin has lost his touch-- he can no longer name the winner.

VI. SEARCHERS AND FINDERS

The major figure in American drama between World War I and World War II was Eugene O'Neill, much of whose reputation rests upon his intellectual and imaginative search through both dramatic theme and form for an understanding of life -- his search for meaning. The "haunted heroes" of his plays -- who propelled him on his mystical search -- suggest the psychological and philosophical probings in which he indulged. Because O'Neill overwhelmed audiences and critics, a general impression remains that he was the only playwright of the period interested in ideas, but this is not true.

Although not as esoteric in their approaches, four other dramatists were similarly concerned, trying to present in their plays a meaningful interpretation of life: Maxwell Anderson, Philip Barry, Thornton Wilder and William Saroyan.

Maxwell Anderson, in both essays and dramas, attempted to play the philosopher -- and had a measure of success. Lacking a psychoanalytical interest in humanity, he was still haunted by the presence of evil, mainly as a day-to-day reality rather than as a philosophical concept; but he arrived at a satisfactory conclusion in which he combined a strong individualism with Aristotelian views of tragedy.   Philip Barry did not suffer personal agonies as did O'Neill, but he, too, carried out an investigation of mysticism and the life illusion. He ended his career, however, not on a note of despair but with an emphasis on love. Thornton Wilder, on the other hand, met no daunting obstacles in his search for meaning.   His solid Christian background provided an answer in which he found peace and security rather than agony and frustration. Another "finder," or perhaps one who did not need to search very far, was William Saroyan.   Like Wilder, he wrote fables which suggest epic proportions. Like Barry, Anderson and O'Neill, he tried to discover basic truths, but he was perfectly satisfied to disappear into a cloud of fantasy and simple faith, which was both disconcerting and enjoyable to his audiences. All of these dramatists seriously experimented with dramatic form; all were searchers for truth.

A.   Maxwell Anderson (1888-1959): Prophet, Dreamer, Interpreter

During his lifetime, Maxwell Anderson was called a historical dramatist, a romantic and a protest playwright -- all labels equally distasteful to him. Although not the best of poets nor the deepest of thinkers, he seemed interested in becoming a philosopher-poet-dramatist. In an essay entitled "Whatever

Hope We Have," he concerned himself with ideas, and the force with which he attacked aspects of society shows him to have been a man of conviction.   An idealist, he was a thoughtful writer who saw the potential of a humanity seemingly marred beyond redemption by its baser instincts. Yet Anderson found a faith in which his idealism could attain satisfaction. A searcher, less demanding of answers than some, he made a reconciling discovery. Concerning the direction of his search, he had this to say: "It is encumbent on the dramatist to be a poet, and encumbent on the poet to be prophet, dreamer, and interpreter of the racial dream."

1.   A CONCERNED IDEALIST

As an idealist who believed in individual freedom, Anderson was forced to see as part of that freedom, and frequently triumphing over good, an evil which he repeatedly represented in an image featuring rats.   In *Elizabeth the Queen* he complained that "the rats inherit the earth."   In *Key Largo* a character bitterly refers to "the rats that ate my country to the bone."   By the time he wrote *Anne of the Thousand Days* in 1948, Anderson had become reconciled to the "mask and tongue" of people, "the hog behind the eyes, the rat behind the tongue, . . . Man, woman, and child, you have obeyed them always, and I have."   (II, 4)   People are not perfect and never will be; corruption makes absolutes impossible. As Esdras says in *Winterset:* "You're young enough to see the truth, and there is no truth." Justice on earth is man made and therefore relative: "The truth is what the judges will find, what the king will decide." (*Anne of the Thousand Days,* III, 2)

2.   "NONE BUT THE LONELY . . . . "

Anderson's most significant early plays are about strong and searching individuals who suffer from loneliness and feelings of lostness.   Their fate is that of the sensitive person in modern society -- a loneliness which approaches the agony of O'Neill or the lostness of Thomas Wolfe's Eugene Gant and Albert Camus' Stranger.   Mio (*Winterset*) feels himself an "outcast of the world, snake in the streets"; Oparre (*The Wingless Victory*) says, "I've never known you, and I'm alone"; Mary Stuart (*Mary of Scotland*), "We are alone, always alone";

Pablo Montoya (*Night Over Taos*) remembers that "always I've known too late that I was alone"; Elizabeth (*Elizabeth the Queen*), "The years are long living among strangers." This recognition of the lonely state of every human being in a society in which evil is a dominant force propelled Anderson toward his final philosophical step.

3.   "A FAITH IN THE HUMAN RACE"

In an essay entitled "Poetry in the Theater," Anderson expressed a belief "that the theater is essentially a cathedral of the spirit, devoted to the exaltation of men." "The artist's faith," he wrote in another essay ("Whatever Hope We Have"), "is simply a faith in the human race and its gradual acquisition of wisdom." Without "a personal, a national, and a racial faith," people become "dry bones in a death valley, waiting for the word that will bring us life." The search exists, and it is the artist with a faith -- even if it is "only a faith that men will have a faith" -- expressing living emotions in the language of poetry, who may be able to bring that wisdom and exaltation. This faith, though a vaguely conceived cornerstone of Anderson's philosophy, formed the basis of a search in which meaning could be discovered. The rats may inherit the earth, individuals may suffer loneliness and justice may not exist, but people can find their souls. They have that freedom. This belief or faith in humanity is the basis of Anderson's "Essence of Tragedy," which gives individuals a strength and a dignity seldom accorded them since Shakespeare's time.

B.   Philip Barry (1896-1949): "Looking for an Answer"

The serious side of Philip Barry's drama is seldom discussed. Mainly, those plays failed in the theatre and have not attracted thoughtful criticism. Although the bright comedies of manners brought him both a reputation and financial reward, it was in the serious plays that he sought personal satisfaction and carried on his philosophical probings. Clearly, he was troubled by some of the same basic problems that disturbed O'Neill, but although he took some of the steps that O'Neill had found meaningful, he was far removed from this play-wright at the end of his career. Both were Irish Catholics. Barry kept his faith.

Alternating between successful high comedies and the heavier, less dramatic thematic plays, Barry started asking questions about the nature of humanity in *In a Garden* (1925). Probing an individual's experimentation with human life, he discovered that people understand very little. In *White Wings* (1926), a satire on the changing world, he dramatized a romance between Archie Inch, the son of a street cleaner who depended upon horses as a necessity of his profession, and Mary Todd, whose father invented the automobile. Here again, Barry examined the nature of people and their conflicts -- their struggles toward progress and their inability to absorb change. *Hotel Universe* (1930) shows Barry's attempt to use a mystical approach to solve his problems, as O'Neill had done in *Desire Under the Elms* and *Mourning Becomes Electra*. In *Here Come the Clowns* (1938), he seems to have rested upon the necessity of illusion in life, a concept which suggests O'Neill's *The Iceman Cometh*. Whereas O'Neill became pessimistic and more concerned with illusion in later plays, Barry returned to an answer that O'Neill had already dismissed (*Days Without End*). The answer that Barry looked for in *Hotel Universe,* he found in *Second Threshold* (1949-51) -- Christian love. Unfortunately, it is not convincingly portrayed.

1.   *HOTEL UNIVERSE* (1930): INCONCLUSIVE BUT HOPEFUL

(Plot) A group of Ann Field's friends are visiting at her French Riviéra home. All are unhappy and torture themselves over a recent suicide who simply jumped off a cliff into the Mediterranean shouting, "I'm off for Africa." Pat Farley, for example, cannot return Ann's love because of the suicide of a girl he once loved. Norman Rose, a Jew, is afraid to declare his love for Alice Kendall, whose emotional aimlessness is a key to her unhappiness. Pat plans suicide; Lily Malone, a repressed actress bothered by an Electra complex, has already tried it; none of the group would avoid death. Then Ann's father, Stephen, a scientist who seems to have strange powers, makes each person relive his or her past and become purged of emotional problems.   Stephen finally dies, but with this suggestion of hope: "Wherever there is an end -- from it the beginning springs."

(Discussion)   Dismissed by critics as "hackneyed," "sentimental" and filled with "second-rate mysticism," the play nonetheless depicts Barry's sense of despair.   Typical of the Lost Generation, it combines a Fitzgerald scene with a Hemingway regret: "It's a rotten feeling, knowing your youth is gone -- knowing that all the brave things you once dreamed of doing somehow just won't get done"; "Nothing matters a damn anyway."   Unfortunately, Barry's reliance upon Freud was heavy-handed and his mysticism artificially imposed.   The play also lacks action. The concluding note of hope, however, is characteristic of Barry's philosophy.

2.   *HERE COME THE CLOWNS* (1938):   ILLUSION AND TRUTH

(Plot)   In the back room of Ma Speedy's cafe, where theatre performers gather, the talk is of Clancy, an actor who wandered on the stage that evening after a year's absence, apparently looking for someone.   When Clancy enters, Max Pabst, another performer, asks if Clancy had been looking for him: "I am interested only in truth.   But truth is so often an illusion I must, you see, in truth call myself an illusionist." Clancy then reveals that he is searching for God, and Pabst ("Truth would prepare the way for Him, would it not?") proceeds to tell some of those present the truth about themselves in order to sweep away their illusions.   Clancy discovers that his wife, Nora, became pregnant by another man when she left him, and he questions Mr. Concannon, the owner of the Globe Theater, about evil and suffering.   Concannon's answer is a question: "There must be persecution, must there not -- to fortify man's faith in heaven?"   When one of the actors tries to shoot Pabst for telling the truth, he kills Clancy, who dies without regret, but not before giving Barry's hopeful answer to the confusion of truth and lies: "The free will of man . . . can as easily be turned to Good as to Bad. . . . It can rise over anything, anything!"

(Discussion) A confusing play and not well unified, *Here Come the Clowns* reveals Barry's hopeful search for meaning in life.

In *Hotel Universe* he had no answer, only hope. Here he suggested the agonies that people suffer because they lack truth. The "illusionist" is necessary in life, but he is badly misunderstood. Although Barry says that the free will of individuals can bring truth, only Clancy, who dies, realizes this. There must be another step, philosophically speaking.

3. *SECOND THRESHOLD* (1949): LOVE

(Plot)   Josiah Bolton, "a man of 42 at the end of his soul's rope, recovering from [an] attempt at suicide," has been a successful lawyer while making a mess of his life: his wife has divorced him; his son has disappointed him; and his daughter, Miranda, is about to marry a middle-aged bachelor. Then Miranda learns that Bolton's various accidents have been half-hearted attempts at suicide. After trying unsuccessfully to interest him in life, she opens her heart, saying that although she loves life, she will kill herself if he commits suicide. Suddenly, they both discover that genuine love was all that he needed and wanted.

(Discussion)   Given the disillusionment of *Hotel Universe* and the suffering of *Here Come the Clowns*, what makes life worth living? Barry's answer involves the threshold of the room separating life from death. Step over the first threshold into this room, which may be so long that you can't see the end of it or may be a stuffy alcove. Each person determines the position of the "second threshold." For Barry, the answer is love. In some ways, particularly in its dialogue and overall unity, *Second Threshold* is comparable to Barry's comedies in its effect, and it was much more successful on the stage than the other two plays. Although he had worked on the play off and on for eleven years, Barry did not live to see it produced, and Robert Sherwood made some revisions before its production.

C. Thornton Wilder (1897-1975): People Will Prevail

Having written a Pulitzer Prize winning novel, *The Bridge of San Luis Rey* (1927), and several one-act plays, Thornton Wilder started his Broadway career with the Pulitzer Prize winning *Our Town* (1938). Although his dramatic output has been slight in quantity, it is impressive. A humanist whose experiments in dramatic form suggest some influence from German expressionists, Wilder had a strong and substantially based approach to life. (His brother, Amos Wilder, a theologian, wrote effectively on religion and literature.) His themes reveal no agonizing search for absolutes because he had already accepted an answer which Barry worked toward for years and which O'Neill rejected -- Christian love. There is good and there is evil, but there is no frustrating dilemma: there is only life. As the Stage Manager in *Our Town* says, "The cottage, the go-cart, the Sunday afternoon drives in the Ford, the first rheumatism, the grandchildren, the second rheumatism, the deathbed, the reading of the will. -- Once in a thousand times its interesting."

1.   A THEORY OF PLAYWRITING

In an essay entitled "Some Thoughts on Playwriting," Wilder explained his experimentation in the theatre. The stage, he noted, is "fundamental pretense" which thrives on a "multiplication of additional pretenses." Rebelling from the theatre's emphasis on realism, Wilder believed that a primary objective in drama is to stimulate the spectators' imagination. Therefore, through bare stage realism, imaginary scenery and colloquial but strongly suggestive speech, he intended that the events of his plays be raised from the specific to the general. This experimental release from realistic conventions, together with his concern for a literary style and though-provoking ideas, make Wilder's work extremely attractive to both theatre and literary critics.

2.   ONE-ACT EXPERIMENTATION

The Angel That Troubled the Waters (1928) consists of sixteen three-minute sketches in which three actors discuss problems of morality and religion. Later, in 1931, Wilder published *The Long Christmas Dinner and Other Plays in One Act*. The title play shows his interest in experimental stage devices and his interpretation of the cyclical and fleeting nature of humanity. Distorting time, *The Long Christmas Dinner* condenses ninety years of Christmas dinners into a one-act play. With a long dining table, chairs and two doorways, one wreathed in flowers and the other draped in black, Wilder suggested birth and death, humor and sadness, as people enter, sit down, eat, live and leave. People are pretty much the same. On a stage, bare except for strategically placed chairs, another play shows a family taking a "happy journey to Trenton and Camden." In both idea and form these early one-act plays suggest the nature of his later work.

3.   THE CYCLE OF LIFE

Wilder's best commentary on life appears in *Our Town* and *The Skin of Our Teeth.* In a deceptively simple manner he interwove with the important events the casual day-to-day activities; but in his view of life, the seemingly inconsequential is the meaningful. People must live each day as they think best. Truth will persist; humanity with prevail. There is no cause to worry or to wonder -- this is life! In that view, in which human beings are part of that energy which comes from the Creator, the here and now is only an aspect of the larger cycle of things in which one considers -- philosophically -- time, space and motion. In this sense Wilder was one of America's most modern playwrights. Although his techniques suggest the traditional literary epic and allegory, his humanistic approach sprang from his strong Christian faith.

(a)   *Our Town* (1938): Our Living and Our Dying
(Plot) The Webbs and the Gibbses live side by side in a small town, Grover's Corners, New Hampshire. George Gibbs and Emily Webb share childhood and school, fall in love and marry. Later, Emily dies in childbirth but has an opportunity to return to earth for one day. Although warned by the dead not to return, she chooses her twelfth birthday and is horrified by the lack of perception and understanding on the part of the living. Back in the graveyard, she is content as the play ends.

(Discussion) The lack of scenery and props, except for a couple of chairs and stepladders, and the use of the Stage Manager to introduce and comment on the action of the play illustrate Wilder's expressionism. The play is disarmingly simple with its folk approach -- language, customs, superstitions and homey characters -- and sentimental idealism. But the simplicity evokes thought-provoking ideas about "man's relationship to man" -- the strangeness, the frustration. In this life, individuals never reveal themselves completely. Emily pleads: "Let's look at one another!" But the thesis is not the pessimistic idea expressed by the Stage Manager that only "Saints and poets maybe!" can appreciate life. Rather, it is that people are like that; it is acceptance, not frustration.

(b) *The Skin of Our Teeth* (1942): The Story of Civilization
(Plot) George Antrobus of Excelsior, New Jersey, lives with his wife, a daughter and two sons, one of whom, Henry (Cain), kills his brother -- "a boyish impulse," because he is only 4,000 years old. Sabina appears as a maid, temptress and camp-follower, sometimes leaving her character to comment on the play's action directly to the audience. In Act I the family anxiously awaits the return of Mr. Antrobus, who has just finished inventing the wheel and the alphabet, as a sheet of ice is beginning to cover the entire continent. The Antrobuses try to maintain their fire, and people crowd around to keep from freezing to death. Sabina finally appeals to the audience: "Pass up your chairs, everybody. Save the human race."

Act II takes place at a convention of the Ancient and Honorable Order of Mammals, Subdivision Humans, in Atlantic City. Antrobus is elected president with the help of his wife, and Sabina has become a temptress trying to seduce him. But she fails, and as the floods approach, Antrobus saves his family and Sabina by taking them into an ark along with the aminals, two by two. After a war (Act III) in which Henry has fought on the wrong side, Antrobus' conflict with him becomes so real that the play has to be stopped. There seems to be no way to change Henry, and Sabina, a maid once more, repeats lines that have opened the play and then tells the audience: "We have to go on for ages and ages yet. You go home. The end of this play isn't written yet. . . . Their [Mr. and Mrs. Antrobus'] heads are full of plans and they're as confident as the first day they began -- and they told me to tell you: good night."

(Discussion) Following the general movement of Ice Age, Flood and War, the play suggests a perpetual life cycle of progress. It ends as it begins: people recovering from chaos, seeing evil as a part of life and learning "that all the objects of my desire and fear were in themselves nothing good or bad save insofar as the mind was affected by them." They remain determined to search out "something truly good and communicable to man." It is the never ending but stubborn struggle of individuals to survive by the skin of their teeth; and with their pressing needs, their families and great books they will succeed. The theme is serious, and the comic treatment is successful only because Wilder was certain of his theological and philosophical position. In technique, Wilder admitted debts to James Joyce's *Finnegan's Wake* and *Hellzapoppin'* with vaudevillians Olson and Johnson. For him, the combination of serious and comic was a consistent and meaningful approach.

D. William Saroyan (1908-1981): "The Beautiful People"

William Saroyan had an unbounded faith in the goodness of people and their ability to overcome all evil; but unlike Wilder, he seems to have had no reason for believing as he did. In the Preface to *Don't Go Away Mad* (1949) he wrote: "I seem to insist that people are good, that living is good, that decency is right, that good is not only achievable but inevitable -- and there does not appear to be any justification for this." With a wandering and accumulative style of writing, Saroyan became a mythmaker, an epic fabler. As Wilder presented scenes which require the audience's imagination, Saroyan presented characters who, to become real, have to stimulate that imagination. For both playwrights, theatre was a cooperative experience among dramatists, actors and audiences. As a searcher, however, Saroyan made no pretense to being a philosopher. He simply believed in the "beautiful people" who are basically sweet and kind and good. Life is, he acknowledged, sadly beautiful, but in his plays he insisted that the beauty dominate the sadness. If he disturbed people with this view and made them think, he only emphasized another part of the human myth which needs retelling.

1.   VAUDEVILLE AND DREAMS

Saroyan's major plays before World War II are *My Heart's in the Highlands* (1939), *The Time of Your Life* (1939), *Love's Old*

Sweet Song (1940) and *The Beautiful People* (1941). In all of these plays there are strong suggestions of vaudeville, in both action and characters. In a typical Saroyan play, the plot is so sketchy and improbable that its insignificance becomes a basic, if false, assumption, and the characters are as strange an assortment of people as ever appeared on the RKO Keith vaudeville circuit. In *The Time of Your Life* there are a Kit Carson storyteller, a dancer, a pinball machine artist, a comic monologuist, a prostitute and a free-spending hero who does anything he can for anybody. The scene is a San Francisco honky-tonk where people come to perform, to complain and to dream. No act on the vaudeville stage was much better than Mr. MacGregor's bugle playing in *My Heart's in the Highlands,* and the poet's son, Johnny, is a master at conning Mr. Kosak out of more groceries. When a large family of Oklahoma migratory workers decides to camp on a lady's lawn in Bakersfield, California, until one of them gives birth to a child, the audience watches an extraordinaty scene (*Love's Old Sweet Song*). Both the happenings and the people in Saroyan's plays are rambling, sketch-like and unexpected, like a series of disconnected acts on a vaudeville stage.

Saroyan's people all have dreams; in fact, his plays are held together by their dreams. In *The Time of Your Life,* Joe says: "I believe in dreams sooner than statistics." Of course, Joe and the others know that there is evil in the world, just as Thornton Wilder's Stage Manager explains in *Our Town.* Johnny, the poet's son in *My Heart's in the Highlands,* comments on the situation he finds, "I'm not mentioning any names, Pa, but something's wrong somewhere." Mainly, however, Saroyan's characters let it rest at that, because "there will always be poets in the world." Sometimes they act -- Kit Carson kills the mean Blick in *The Time of Your Life,* and then the dreams begin again -- but usually Saroyan's people accept misfortune as part of life and believe that things will finally come out all right. And in Saroyan's plays dreams frequently do come true.

2.   LIVE AND LOVE

In spite of Saroyan's sense of humor and use of vaudevillian fantasy, he was a serious playwright with a feeling for experimentation and a positive approach to life. He was not concerned with most of the conflicting evils and problems that frustrated other writers. Barry worked hard to arrive at his conclusion in *Second Threshold.* Wilder had a strong faith to help him. Saroyan sang happily as he walked along and believed. His conclusions do not seem profound because they are so simply revealed, but they are stiumlating in the theatre.

Saroyan wrote about living and loving. Love was not only possible, it was all. "In the time of your life," he wrote, "live -- so that in that good time there shall be no ugliness or death for yourself or for any life your life touches, so that in that wondrous time you shall not add to the misery and sorrow of the world, but shall smile to the infinite delight and mystery of it." Now is "the time of your life"! As Joe tells Tom: "Go ahead. Correct the errors of the world." And Tom is capable of the attempt because he is capable of love. In *My Heart's in the Highlands,* it is an impulsive love of beauty which controls people and what little plot exists. Love conquers all at the end of *Love's Old Sweet Song.*   If this approach seems overly sentimental or optimistic, it probably is.

My Heart's in the Highlands (1939)
In an old house in Fresno, California, a nine-year-old boy named Johnny lives in poverty with his father, an unsuccessful poet, and his grandmother. One day, old Jasper MacGregor, who has run away from an old folks' home, appears and plays the bugle so beautifully that neighbors bring food, but soon he is returned to the old folks' home, and Johnny must try to get food for himself and his family from Mr. Kosak, the grocer. Then the real estate man tells Johnny's father that they are being evicted. MacGregor returns, having run away again, and dies while playing King Lear. New tenants arrive, and Johnny, his father and grandmother leave. "My heart's in the highlands, my heart is not here. My heart's in the highlands a-chasing the deer." (Robert Burns)

VII. CRITICISM: AN EMERGING TRADITION

With the creation of a more sophisticated drama after World War I, there emerged a more cosmopolitan and educated criticism. Although most of the criticism of plays remained in the hands of newspaper reporters, a new form appeared when performances in certain theatres began to be regularly reviewed by those who professed some knowledge of theatre and drama. In the period between the wars, these new critics achieved status, and their more enlightened work suggests the beginnings of a criticism competent to cope with modern drama. Academic critics, too, were beginning to awaken to the pleasures and achievements of the drama, while newspapers and magazines outside of New York were beginning to attach more significance to theatre reporting and to select their drama critics with greater emphasis on talent. Criticism, however, remained a body of theatre reviews with reference to particular per-formances, because, as William Hawkins, drama critic for the New York *Telegram and Sun,* later suggested (*Theatre Annual,* XIV, 1956), "the bulk of the Critics' readers are interested in a simple, blanket opinion which makes clear the subject of the show and its over-all quality. They do not want their limited reading time cluttered up with complex or erudite explanations or comparisons." American drama had not yet made a strong appeal to the literary scholar, and criticism remained largely journalistic. A literary tradition, however, was emerging -- yet very slowly.

A. Rise of the Educated Critic

By World War I professors were beginning to publish books on drama and theatre. Richard Burton, University of Minnesota, published *The New American Drama* in 1913, the same year that Archibald Henderson, University of North Carolina, wrote *European Dramatists.* In 1915 Thomas H. Dickinson, University of Wisconsin, wrote *The Case of American Drama,* and Ludwig Lewisohn, Ohio State University, published *The Modern Drama.* A rising young critic and a prolitic writer who served as editor of plays published by Samuel French from 1918 to 1936, Barrett H. Clark was drama editor of *Drama Magazine* during the 1920s, a biographer of Eugene O'Neill, a compiler of *America's Lost Plays* and, with George Freedley, author of *A History of Modern Drama* (1947). Two scholarly critics, Arthur Hobson Quinn and Montrose J. Moses, established reputations as historians of American drama.

B.   Guidelines Set by the Journalists

As the American theatre became a more creative and imaginative institution and American drama became intellectually challenging as well as enjoyable, the status of the drama critic improved and their numbers increased. The following were among the better-known critics who established reputations during the Twenties and Thirties. Brooks Atkinson (1894-1984) started his long career as a drama critic for the *New York Times* in 1925. John Mason Brown (1900-1969) was drama critic for the *Theatre Arts Monthly* for four years before his 1929-1941 stint in the same job at the New York *Evening Post*. Richard Watts, Jr. (1898-1981) started working for the New York *Herald Tribune* in 1924 and became its drama editor twelve years later. Burns Mantle (1873-1948) was drama critic for the New York *Daily News* from 1922 to 1943; his volumes of *Best Plays* provide some continuity in the study of American drama. Robert Benchley (1889-45) is remembered most clearly for his writing in the *New Yorker*, whose staff he joined in 1929. For nine years previous to that move, he had been drama editor of the old *Life* magazine. Other critics whose writings were significant during this period were Walter Prichard Eaton, Gilbert Seldes, Kenneth Macgowan, John Anderson, Percy Hammond, Joseph Mersand and John Gassner.

C.   Cosmopolitan Tastes

Three outstanding columnists and theatre critics during the Twenties and Thirties were George Jean Nathan, Alexander Woollcott and Stark Young. Edith J. R. Isaacs (1878-1956), a fine critic in her own right and editor of the *Theatre Arts Monthly* labeled them as follows: Nathan, "Critic as Showman"; Woollcott, "Critic as Actor"; and Young, "Critic as Critic." [*Theatre Arts Monthly*, XXVI (February, March, April 1942)]

1.   GEORGE JEAN NATHAN (1882-1958): FORTHRIGHT CRITIC

A person of considerable mind and wit and only a modicum of heart, Nathan served as drama critic or drama editor for several magazines and newspapers, in particular *Smart Set*,

Vanity Fair, the *American Mercury* and the New York *Journal American.* During the early years of his career, he enjoyed shocking his readers with irreverent attacks on American character and institutions -- attacks which gained him a reputation as an incisive critic and iconoclast. He was one of the first to recognize the stature of O'Neill and Saroyan, and his books on the theatre appeared with remarkable regularity after *Another Book on the Theatre* (1916).

2.   ALEXANDER WOOLLCOTT (1887-1943): "THE MAN WHO CAME TO DINNER"

The source for Kaufman and Hart's *The Man Who Came to Dinner,* Woollcott assumed an attitude toward this play which was characteristic of his criticism -- self promotion. He toured with the play, acting himself as Sheridan Whiteside -- but without the success achieved by Monty Woolley. As a critic who loved the theatre and fitted well into the F. Scott Fitzgerald circle, he reported for the *New York Times,* the *Herald* and the *World.* His published volumes, such as *Enchanted Aisles* (1924), gained him a popular audience, but he contributed mainly his personality, his wit and his enjoyment of theatre gossip. Unlike Nathan, who could criticize with perspective and art as well as wit, Woollcott added nothing but a little glitter to American dramatic criticism, but he did that very well.

3.   STARK YOUNG (1881-1963): ACADEMIC CRITIC

Tending to be more intellectual than emotional in his criticism, Young taught English on the university level before becoming an associate editor of *Theatre Arts Monthly.* He had an appreciation of art and literature which gave his criticisms a distinctive tone. Although among such contemporaries as Nathan and Woollcott he was a somber companion, his opinions -- *The Flower in Drama* (1923); *The Theatre* (1927) -- are more valuable to the historian of American drama.

D.   Marxist Criticism

During the 1930s the Communist attempt to create and control theatres was pursued not only by committed playwrights but by committed critics. *New Masses* and the *Daily Worker* could be relied upon to promote Marxist causes; Mike Gold (1894-1967) was the major spokesman for the Party line. *New Theatre* was another magazine with a Marxist slant; its editor was Ben Blake. Certain playwrights of the Left-Wing theatre also wrote vigorous dramatic criticism; John Howard Lawson is an excellent example. A Left-leaning critic of sufficient seriousness to present her criticisms in book form, Eleanor Flexner wrote *American Playwrights, 1918-1938* (1938).

E.   Critical Books and Magazines

One criterion for determining a developing and serious criticism of the drama is the number of publications dealing with the subject. Some of the books published during the decades between the wars still remain primary sources for American drama and theatre research: *The American Dramatist* (rev. 1925) by Montrose J. Moses, *A Short History of the American Drama* (1932) by Margaret Mayorga and *A History of the American Drama from the Beginning to the Civil War* (1923, rev. 1943) and *A History of American Drama from the Civil War to the Present Day* (1927, rev. 1936) by Arthur H. Quinn.

Other books include *The American Theatre* (1938) by John Anderson, *An Hour of American Drama* (1930) by Barrett H. Clark, *Playwrights of the New American Theater* (1925) by Thomas H. Dickinson, *American Playwrights, 1918-1938* (1938) by Eleanor Flexner, *The American Drama Since 1918* (rev. 1957) by Joseph Wood Krutch, *Our Amercan Theatre* (1923) by Oliver M. Sayler and the yearly volumes of Burns Mantle and George Jean Nathan.

Among theatre magazines the *Theatre Arts Monthly*, founded in 1916 by Sheldon Cheney, stands supreme. From 1922 to 1946 it was edited by Edith Isaacs, assisted by Rosamond Gilder, who edited the magazine until 1948 when it combined with *The Stage* and, essentially, ceased to exist. *Theatre Magazine* ran from 1900 to 1931. The *Little Theatre Monthly* merged with *The Drama*, which, starting before World War I and continuing under various names until 1931, was particularly effective during the Twenties with Barrett H. Clark as editor. Indicative of mazazine activity in the 1930s is the *New*

Theatre magazine, which started in 1931 as *Workers Theatre,* became *New Theatre* in 1934 and appeared for two issues in 1937 as *New Theatre and Film.* Among other magazines were *The Playgoer* (1926-1954) and *Players Magazine* (1924-).

VIII. ACHIEVEMENT IN THEATRE

This history of American theatre from 1915 to 1941 is a story of change and achievement. During the second decade of the century, several influences brought distinct innovations in theatre production which were translated into mature achievements in the Twenties. Then, two events -- the talking movie and the stock market crash -- had their effect upon theatre attendance. New producing organizations, however, stimulated theatre activity during the Thirties; and by the beginning of World War II, the quality of American theatre productions, helped by new and imaginative playwrights and designers, reached a new height.

A. Approaching Maturity

Spurred on by influences from Europe and imaginative Americans, the theatre during the second decade of the twentieth century assessed and organized itself in ways that had never before been attempted. Such activity had its consequences.   Foreign influence was clearly healthy for American theatre.   An illustration of German expressionism appeared in New York in Max Reinhardt's *Sumurûm* in 1912. In 1915, the English producer-drama critic, Granville Barker, showed English stage techniques in a series of plays he produced at Wallack's Theatre in New York. Two years later, Jacques Copeau and his Vieux Colombier brought the French version of the new staging to New York. This "New Stagecraft" (inspired by the work of Edward Gordon Craig, Adolphe Appia and Reinhardt) aimed to synthesize in the theatre the artistry of design, sculpture, music, light and movement.   Baker's teaching at Harvard's 47 Workshop affected the theatre through several of the prominent dramatists of the Twenties. Little Theatres also produced significant results.   The Provincetown Players supported the talent of Eugene O'Neill; the Neighborhood Players (1915-1927) was a pioneering experimental theatre connected with the Henry Street Settlement House on New York's Lower East Side; and the Theatre Guild, founded in December of 1918, grew from the ambitions of the Washington Square Players (1915-1918). Other organizations established about this time were the Drama League of America (1910), which with its magazine, the *Drama Quarterly*, aspired to support good drama, and the Dramatists Guild, which started in 1912 as a division of the Authors League of America.

One particular incident during this second decade showed the actor's growth in maturity and power. For 150 years actors had been notoriously disorganized and had sunk to an absurd position of indignity under the Theatrical Syndicate. The arch individualism and the self-importance exhibited by actors had always fostered problems, but in 1919 a new era began. For six years, Actors Equity Association had tried to work out with managers a contract involving fair wages, travel compensation, an eight-performance week and other benefits. The effort failed. In the summer of 1919, the actors -- or most of them -- went on a strike and four weeks later won their cause. After this first actors' strike in American theatre history, the first Equity contract was signed on September 6, 1919.

By 1920, American theatres and actors enjoyed a strong position. Realism on stage prevailed, although it was being challenged. There was some threat posed by the movies and the popularity of the radio, but otherwise the outlook was bright.

B. Theatre During the Twenties: Prosperity

In 1920 there were 150 plays produced in New York's eighty theatres; in 1927-28 there were 280. There was also significant theatre activity throughout the country, as Kenneth Macgowan reported in *Footlights Across America* (1929). The Theatre Guild was very active, bringing many foreign plays to America as well as stimulating work by American-born playwrights. Even repertory was revived with a modicum of success, when in 1926 Eva LeGallienne opened the Civic Repertory Theatre in New York for six seasons. It was a period of prosperity for American Theatre.

O'Neill dominated the decade, and expressionism was the innovation in theatre staging. Besides introducing an impressive number of new American playwrights, this decade showed the developing artistry of several stage designers -- Joseph Urban, Robert Edmund Jones, Lee Simonson and Norman Bel Geddes. Unfortunately, the Twenties ended on a low note. The first full-length talking movie, *The Jazz Singer*, was released in 1927; and in 1929, *Variety* magazine reported the stock market crash -- "Wall St. Lays an Egg." The Depression had begun.

C. Theatre in the Thirties: Struggle

Across the country in 1920 theatres numbered nearly 1,500; ten years later that number had been reduced to about 500. In New York during the 1930-31 season there were about 190 plays produced; by the 1939-40 season, there were only eighty. The struggle in this decade was also marked by the activity of various producing organizations. One bright development for the theatre was the increased delight in musicals. By 1940 the movies had become more than a threat to the live theatre, but, although fewer plays were being produced, high quality was sustained. Soon war would bring drastic changes.

1. PRODUCING ORGANIZATIONS

The best-known experiments in theatre production were the Group Theatre, the Federal Theatre and the Playwrights' Company. With Communist theatres, the Mercury Theatre of John Houseman and Orson Welles and the Theatre Guild, which had been producing plays since its formation in 1918 and had subsidized the Group Theatre, these varied producing organizations made the Thirties one of the more interesting decades in American Theatre history.

(a) The Group Theatre
Three employees of the Theatre Guild -- Harold Clurman, Cheryl Crawford and Lee Strasberg -- were responsible for starting the Group Theatre in 1931. Their objective was to produce plays concerned with contemporary moral and social problems and to develop serious playwrights for a permanent acting company. They were also united in their approach to

acting -- a training method involving improvisation and the Stanislavsky system. Before the Group Theatre was dissolved in 1941, it offered twenty-three productions, of which thirteen emphasized social and economic problems. Although it was clearly not Communist controlled, the Group Theatre is often remembered for its Left-Wing productions. Its significance, however, can also be measured in terms of the more serious playwriting that it stimulated and for its influence on the development of American acting -- ideas later carried on in Strasberg's Actors' Studio. Finally, a number of difficulties brought about the demise of the Group Theatre -- little money, weak plays and temperamental actors.

(b) The Federal Theatre
William Dunlap called for a government-supported theatre early in the nineteenth century, but it took the remainder of the century for the first major movement toward a national theatre (1892-1911) to become organized. By the turn of the twentieth century, dozens of articles by distinguished theatre people -- Henry A. Clapp, Norman Hapgood, Brander Matthews, Helena Modjeska, Robert Stodart, among others -- supported the idea of an endowed national theatre. Not until the Works Progress Administration's Federal Theatre Project, however, did America attempt a nationally sponsored theatre. Initiated to ease unemployment among theatre artists during the Depression, the Federal Theatre enjoyed an appropriation of over six million dollars and the effective leadership of Hallie Flanagan, its national director. Starting in 1935, Mrs. Flanagan determined to provide relief for the unemployed, incentives for developing new plays and theatrical skills and opportunities for experimentation in a variety of theatre forms. Until this project of the WPA was killed by Congress on June 30, 1939, many of her objectives were fulfilled, while she ran the project with an efficiency and patience which have rarely been seen among government workers.

During its four years of existence, the Federal Theatre Project promoted many careers and provided children's theatre, puppet theatre, Negro theatre and "free, adult, uncensored theatre" for millions of people across the country. Among its memorable accomplishments were the Living Newspaper productions and its simultaneous presentation at twenty-one theatres across the nation of *It Can't Happen Here*, October 27, 1936, by Sinclair Lewis and John C. Moffitt. Like the Group Theatre, the Federal Theatre was accused of Communist infiltration. Although it did produce a few Marxist plays, it was never Communist controlled, and its social plays were (according to Flanagan, *Arena*, 1940, p. 183-84) to depict "the struggle of many different kinds of people to understand the natural, social and economic forces around them and to achieve through these forces a better life for more people." Generally, the scope of the Federal Theatre productions in both theme and form is to be admired.

(c)   The Playwrights' Company

During the spring of 1938 five dramatists -- Maxwell Anderson, S. N. Behrman, Sidney Howard, Elmer Rice and Robert Sherwood -- rebelling against the strictures of the Theatre Guild, decided that the best way to produce their plays was to form an organization, the Playwrights' Company.   For dramatists who wanted an independence which they had failed to achieve in the Dramatists Guild, this was a step forward.   All of the original members were established dramatists whose productions had been among the most successful in the American theatre.   The first play produced by the Playwrights' Company was Sherwood's *Abe Lincoln in Illinois* (1939).   In 1953 Robert Anderson joined the Company, which, between October 1938 and July 1961, produced thirty-nine plays and co-produced twenty-nine others. In June 1960 the Playwrights' Company was formally dissolved.

2.   THE MUSICAL THEATRE

American musical comedy is not modern.   William Dunlap, the Father of American Drama, wrote a musical play called *The Archers; or, Mountaineers of Switzerland* in 1796, and his was not the first.   Many nineteenth-century playwrights made use of music and song; and frequently an actor with a good voice would insert a song into a play.

For most critics *The Black Crook* (1866) by Charles M. Barrass is recognized as the ancestor of modern musical comedy.   When a youth in love with a peasant maid falls into the hands of the

Alchymist (the Black Crook), who would sell his soul or anybody else's to the Devil, the Devil smiles. But the Alchymist is foiled by the pretty maid who sings, dances and shows her ankles to the audience. In a grand ballet pitting fairies against demons, the fairies win; the young couple is reunited and the Alchymist disappears. *The Black Crook* played for sixteen months at Niblo's Garden in New York.

Eventually, the display of legs replaced the legitimate aspects of musicals, and burlesque became popular. Musical drama, however, continued in many guises: *Evangeline* (1874), an American opera-bouffe by Edward E. Rice; *The Brook* (1879) by Nate Salsbury; the popular farces (with music) of Edward Harrigan and Tony Hart; *A Trip to Chinatown* (1890) by Charles Hoyt, which combined music and farce for a record of 657 performances.

(a) Successful Experimentation Between the Wars
Before World War I two major writers of musical drama -- Victor Herbert with *Babes in Toyland* (1903) and *Sweethearts* (1913) and George M. Cohan with numerous musicals, such as *Forty-Five Minutes from Broadway* (1906) -- suggested the two trends that modern musicals would follow: the romantic operetta and the fast-moving comedy. Later writers who experimented between the wars included Rudolf Friml (*Rose Marie,* 1924; *The Vagabond King,* 1925), Sigmund Romberg (*Blossom Time,* 1921; *The Student Prince,* 1924) and Vincent Youmans (*No, No, Nanette,* 1925; *Hit the Deck,* 1927). Jerome Kern gave Marilyn Miller a memorable role in *Sunny* (1925) and, with Oscar Hammerstein II, created the very successful *Show Boat* (1927), which, in pointing the way for future serious musical plays, is a significant landmark in the progress of the American musical.

In general, the Thirties are recognized as the period of great songwriters rather than of great musicals. George and Ira Gershwin started writing together in 1918 and became particularly successful with *Lady, Be Good!* (1924) and *Strike Up the Band* (1930). They joined the Heywards for *Porgy and Bess* (1935), providing such songs as "Summertime" and "I Got Plenty O' Nuttin'." In *Anything Goes* (1934) by Cole Porter the trumpet-voiced Ethel Merman sang "You're the Top" and "Blow, Gabriel, Blow." Richard Rodgers and Lorenz Hart were at their best in song, and could also write good satires, such as *I'd Rather Be Right* (1937), a spoof on presidential campaigns. Other musical political satires include *Of Thee I Sing* (1931) by Kaufman and Ryskind and Maxwell Anderson and Kurt Weill's *Knickerbocker Holiday* (1938). The musical revue of the 1930s is well represented by Arthur Schwartz, Howard Dietz and Kaufman's *The Band Wagon* (1931) with its songs ("A Pretty Girl Is Like a Melody") and the revues (*As Thousands Cheer*, 1933) of Irving Berlin.

(b) Approaching Maturity
The stage was set. The music and songs of Irving Berlin, Jerome Kern, George Gershwin and Cole Porter had established a popular entertainment which could only grow. The deaths of Gershwin in 1937 and Kern in 1945 thinned the ranks which were quickly filled by Rodgers and Hart (*The Boys from Syracuse*, 1938; *Pal Joey*, 1940) and Oscar Hammerstein II. George Abbott became a director with a magical touch for musical comedy, which was beginning to reach a form in which the score and the lyrics were unified into an artistic whole. When, in 1943, Rodgers and Hammerstein teamed up to write *Oklahoma!*, the artistry of modern American musical comedy was unquestioned and its superior position in world theatre assured.

IX. SUMMARY

The period between the World Wars began in confusion and ended with a sense of achievement and distinction that had never before been experienced in America. Recently emerging from a commercial theatre monolopy which produced few plays that were more than mediocre, dramatists and theatre artists alike reacted enthusiastically to foreign influences. These stimulating forces for the drama appeared before World War I, but America needed creative and rebellious spirits in both the drama and the theatre. With Eugene O'Neill, the Little Theater Movement, the Theatre Guild and the strength that these forces supplied to others, the nation began to build a significant modern drama. Various threads of its own past were happily cut, while others were woven into a tapestry in ways once thought impossible.

The Twenties were a period of hopefulness and prosperity in the theatre. The sense of freedom and individuality which pervaded the decade also characterized the drama. As a consequence of the increased emphasis on the drama in universities and communities, the optimism of the stage in general and the heightened status of the playwright among literary people and critics, a new breed of dramatists appeared -- including Sidney Howard, Susan Glaspell, Maxwell Anderson, Philip Barry, Paul Green, Robert Sherwood and Elmer Rice. Their training was generally quite different from that of the dramatists at the turn of the century, and the result was a refreshing variety in theme and form. The experimentation in form (particularly in expressionism), the wide range of ideas and the high quality of the plays distinguish the drama of Twenties from that of the past.

The Thirties were a difficult but vital and moving period. The range of play themes continued to expand, but a majority of the plays might be called social drama, contributing to the dominant social consciousness of this decade. From Left to Right serves as a guiding principle for studying many of the plays written during these years -- from the propaganda drama of the Left-Wing theatre through social thesis plays, social melodramas and social satires to light or domestic comedies and comedies of manners. It was a period of growth and turmoil in the theatre, and the playwrights whose reputations had developed during the previous decade were joined by those primarily interested in social issues. At the close of this decade World War II had begun, and a different atmosphere surrounded both playwrights and the theatre.

Perhaps the most significant aspect of American drama between the World Wars was the concern of playwrights for ideas of spiritual or universal import. Although it is true that a social consciousness dominated or was infused into most of the plays of this period, it is also true that an awareness of the spiritual side of life and a questioning of people and their values absorbed the interests of the best playwrights. Their plays show in both craftsmanship and depth of thought that American playwriting from its early imitation through its growth to a profession and an art, had finally reached a position of challenging importance in world drama.

SELECTED BIBLIOGRAPHY

Bernheim, Alfred. *The Business of the Theatre*. 1932; New York: Benjamin Blom, 1964.
Deutch, Helen and Stella Hannau. *The Provincetown*. New York: Farrar & Rinehart, 1931.
Dickinson, Thomas H. *Playwrights of the New American Theater*. New York: The Macmillan Co., 1925.
Downer, Alan S. *Fifty Years of American Drama 1900-1950*. Chicago: Henry Regnery Co., 1951.
Falk, Doris. *Eugene O'Neill and the Tragic Tension*. New Brunswick: Rutgers Univ. Press, 1958.
Flanagan, Hallie. *Arena*. New York: Duell, Sloan, and Pearce, 1940.
Goldstein, Malcolm. *The Political Stage: American Drama and Theater of the Great Depression*. New York: Oxford Univ. Press, 1974.
Hewitt, Barnard. *Theatre U.S.A. 1665-1957*. New York: McGraw-Hill Book Co., 1959.
Himelstein, Morgan Y. *Drama Was a Weapon*. New Brunswick: Rutgers Univ. Press, 1963.
Kinne, Wisner P. *George Pierce Baker and the American Theatre*. Cambridge: Harvard Univ. Press, 1954.
Krutch, Joseph Wood. *The American Drama Since 1918*. New York: George Braziller, rev. 1957.
Macgowan, Kenneth. *Footlights Across America*. New York: Harcourt, Brace and Co., 1929.
Mathews, Jane. *The Federal Theatre, 1935-1939*. Princeton: Princeton Univ. Press, 1967.
Quinn, Arthur H. *A History of the American Drama from the Civil War to the Present Day*. New York: Appleton-Century-Crofts, rev. 1936.
Rabkin, Gerald. *Drama and Commitment*. Bloomington: Indiana Univ. Press, 1964.
Sarlos, Robbie. *Jig Cook and the Provincetown Players*. Amherst: Univ. of Massachusetts Press, 1982.
Valgemae, Mardi. *Accelerated Grimace: Expressionism in the American Drama of the 1920s*. Carbondale: Southern Illinois Univ. Press, 1972.

Chapter Five

The Post-War Generation of Playwrights
1945-1965

In *Mid-Century Drama* (1960) the English drama critic
Laurence Kitchen entitled his essay on drama in the United
States "The Potent Intruder." The intrusion, of course, had
begun 150 years earlier, but its potency was seriously questioned
during most of the intervening years. By the 1930s, however,
American drama had assumed a position of stature in world
drama. At mid-century it became a recognized force.

During the war years, American plays reflected the agony and
anger of an aroused people; the major distinguishing feature
was a psychological interest in the emotional reaction to war.
The high quality of the earlier plays by O'Neill, Anderson,
Wilder, Hellman, Saroyan and Barry which had attracted
international interest was continued mainly in the later dramas
of O'Neill and in the work of two newcomers: Arthur Miller
and Tennessee Williams. In a manner unequalled by past
performance in American drama, Miller and Williams captured
the attention of an international audience. For many of the
dramatists writing before World War II, the gap provided by
the war years marked an end to their most creative artistry,
and over the next score of years newspapers recorded the
artistic decline and/or the deaths of the active playwrights of
the Thirties.

For the generation after World War II the theatre provided
more of the social drama, satire, comedy and melodrama that
had been popular between the wars, although attempts to
write poetic drama were more numerous and, in a few instances,
gained both commercial and artistic success. A traditional
American love of sentiment was bonded with a post-war
fascination with violence and sex to produce a distinctly
commercial form with roots that reached back into the
nineteenth century.

On May 22, 1893, the American Theatre opened on West 42nd
Street in New York City with a production of *The Prodigal*

Daughter, and at that moment Broadway was born. During the early years of the twentieth century Broadway grew and flourished, coldly controlled by big business, its only goal being "SRO."   For the post-war generation of playwrights, alternative productions in Off Broadway theatres, regional playhouses, university stages and summer stock had a growing appeal, but no success was comparable to a Broadway production. When the Vivian Beaumont Theatre at Lincoln Center opened in 1965, Herbert Blau and Jules Irvine quickly abandoned the San Francisco Actors Workshop, which they had founded in 1952, to co-direct the new theatre. The central conflict in the American theatre world, therefore, remained a more intensified New York versus All Others. Meanwhile, commerce would be served, and critics would slowly increase their influence.

Lady Gregory, the Irish playwright and director of the Abbey Theatre, once noted that the Abbey directors had early in the life of the theatre made the mistake of confusing theatrics with literary values. The difficulties consequent to such a confusion will probably always exist in all theatres. Certainly, the exception is noticeably rare. One way to avoid confusing literature and theatre, is to avoid the question -- an effort remarkably illustrated by the commercial success of American musical comedy. Throughout the period from 1945 to 1965 the strength of American drama as a "potent intruder" was found in the plays of O'Neill, Miller and Williams, while Broadway and Off Broadway existed mainly on light comedy and musicals, a few challenges to social traditions and, in the early 1960s, the beginnings of a reactionary drama.

I. AMERICAN DRAMA AND WORLD WAR II

In the past the theatre responded with varying degrees of vigor to wars in which America was involved. During the Revolution, Mrs. Mercy Warren's partisan satires were a vital part of the War of the Belle Lettres. The naval battles of the War of 1812 stimulated spectacular stage entertainment. The mid-nineteenth-century war with Mexico and the Spanish-American War sparked only minor interest among playwrights, but numerous writers dramatized romantic and exciting adventures which they associated with both the Blue and the Gray during the Civil War. Few of these plays, however, present a serious war issue: the object was entertainment. Plays concerned with World War I did little to change this characteristic of wartime drama. Vaudeville and musical comedy were interspersed with such plays as James Forbes' *The Famous Mrs. Fair* (1919), Gilbert Emery's *The Hero* (1921) and the popular *What Price Glory?* (1924) by Anderson and Stallings. World War II, however, was different. Entertainment was still important, but amid the light comedies, the musicals and the heroic melodramas, plays appeared which dealt seriously with the problems that war creates.

A. Melodrama and Propaganda

Wartime adventures easily conform to the demands of melodrama, and wartime emotions encourage prejudices that are grist for the propagandist. For a few writers, the Spanish Civil War had already aroused both principles and passions. Ernest Hemingway had written a slight play about counter espionage and girls in *The Fifth Column* (1940), and Maxwell Anderson had posed a serious question in *Key Largo* (1939). John Steinbeck described the heroism of the Norwegians against Nazi occupation in *The Moon Is Down* (1942). As the prominent dramatists of the Thirties directed their thoughts toward the war, they were joined by others.

1. STRONG OPINIONS: HELLMAN AND SHERWOOD

Both Lillian Hellman and Robert Sherwood reacted vigorously to the fighting in Europe. With her superior control of melodramatic action, Hellman took a powerful anti-fascist stand in *Watch on the Rhine* (1941). She assumed an even stronger position as she ridiculed the previous twenty years of American foreign policy in *The Searching Wind* (1944). By 1940 Sherwood had abandoned his satiric approach to war with *There Shall Be No Night*, a bitter denunciation of totalitarianism. In *The Rugged Path* (1945), he presented a noble if biased argument in favor of intervention. Even with Spencer Tracy in the lead, however, the play had only a brief run in New York.

2.   *COMMAND DECISION* (1945) BY WILLIAM W. HAINES

Command Decision is a model of the highly adventurous, suspenseful and carefully controlled war drama. Focussing on an air base commander's order for long-range bombing, the play incorporates all the right ingredients for a successful melodrama. There is suspense in the waiting for the planes to return, sentiment in a pilot's death contrasted with the birth of his son, satire on congressmen and stupid legislative pressure, humor to ease the tension, propaganda for the patriotic and the overall impression that war creates no heroes -- only the brave people who win the peace for a grateful country despite incomprehensible blunders by its government officials.

B.   A More Serious Tone

The best dramas during World War II reveal psychological concern for the individual and the social problems which war creates. Maxwell Anderson's *The Eve of Saint Mark* (1942) suggests the change in a soldier's life as the challenge of battle and his thoughts of home give him power to find meaning in his own death. *Tomorrow the World* (1943) by James Gow and Arnaud d'Usseau pictures a Nazi war orphan in America and the seemingly impossible task of reshaping people once controlled by Nazi ideals.

As fighting stopped, dramatists became interested in the results of war. Philip Barry's *Foolish Notion* (1945) contrasts the homecoming of a soldier with the expectations of those intimately concerned with him. *Home of the Brave* (1945) by Arthur Laurents is a penetrating dramatization of the shock treatment used to release a Jewish soldier from the ethnic sensitivity and guilt which have left him paralyzed after his initial ecstacy when a companion was killed in battle. Arnaud d'Usseau's *Deep Are the Roots* (1945) shows a Southern white girl, grateful for a Negro friend's efforts in the war, offering to marry him when he returns a hero.

C.   War, Farce and Comedy

Some dramatists appealed to a broader view in numerous farces and sentimental comedies. Conditions in Washington prompted

Joseph Fields to write *The Doughgirls* (1942), as military and civilian personality bumped heads and rubbed shoulders. *Dear Ruth* (1944) by Norman Krasna is a sentimental comedy of a young girl who involves her older sister with a soldier by writing amorous letters to him over her sister's name. John Patrick's sentimental story of *The Hasty Heart* (1945) tells of a Scottish soldier dying in a hospital in a hostile atmosphere. Perhaps the most popular of war comedies is Joshua Logan's *Mr. Roberts* (1948), an adaptation of Thomas Heggen's novel. By this time the war was over and everyone could laugh more easily at the GI's complaints and his rebellion against an unbending authority.

II. INTERNATIONAL AMERICAN DRAMATISTS

Although American drama at mid-century was a recognized force in world theatre, it is unfortunately true that American dramatists with international reputations were but a small handful. The few plays of Thornton Wilder were popular on the Continent; O'Neill's work was regarded with respect; a number of musicals and certain plays by the major pre-war dramatists were being produced in London, but the only post-war playwrights receiving continuous attention were Arthur Miller and Tennessee Williams, both showing distinctive views of humanity in the tradition of the best dramatists throughout history. The one upheld the dignity of the individual; the other condemned a world of corruption and desperation where people must fight for or accept the dream of mere survival. One concerned himself with a person's soul in a realistic world; the other was compassionately absorbed with the individual's physical and emotional survival in a world where "humankind cannot bear very much reality." One searched for meaning in a world of contradictions; the other idealistically understood a world inhabited by dreamers and survivors who "can bring down kingdoms on earth." The enthusiastic reception of Miller and Williams as America's foremost playwrights for the post-war generation suggests the scope of the American mind, the growing liberalism of the American theatre and a maturing disposition among American theatre critics.

A.   Arthur Miller (1915-) and Human Dignity

In the tradition of the great playwrights of the past, Miller was concerned with truth and the individual's unrelenting yet doomed search for recognition as a human being. Although his success as a writer of tragic drama was seriously questioned, Miller wrote a number of essays between 1945 and 1965 outlining his views on tragic theory and on "social drama," which he defined as "the drama of the whole man." He also created a handful of plays which, with varying effect, illustrate his ideas. Despite the limited number of plays -- five from 1945 to 1963 -- he aroused considerably enthusiasm, popular and critical, for both his ideas and his techniques. During this early period, Miller's concern for dramatic theory, his combination of the realistic and the expressionistic in his plays and his basic interest in human dignity link him with the best traditions of the past. Upon his return to Broadway in 1964 with *After the Fall*, having been inactive in theatre since 1956, Miller, the playwright of ideas, exhibited some new ideas.

1.   A THEORY OF THE DRAMA

The most significant of Miller's essays are his Introduction to his *Collected Plays* (1957), "The Family in Modern Drama" (*Atlantic Monthly*, April 1956) and "On Social Plays," an Introduction to *A View From the Bridge* (1955). With Ibsen, whose play, *An Enemy of the People*, he adapted in 1950, Miller believed that idea was important in a play; like Robert Frost, he believed that his purpose was to state a truth that was known but not really known. In discussing the possibility of tragedy, Miller contended that, Aristotle notwithstanding, the common man was a fit hero, and that more important than social status were the intensity of the passion dramatized and the discovery of a conflict or challenge that a human being could neither resist nor deny.   With this intellectual preparation Miller approached the writing of tragedy.

A major hypothesis in Miller's writing is that the dramatist must concern himself with people and the nature of humankind. Until the dramatist accounts for the total condition of human beings, Miller argued, he or she will not produce great art. With an almost Emersonian emphasis, he believed in dramatizing "the whole man" as part of a family and society. To do this it was necessary to combine theatrical techniques of realism and expressionism which Miller representationally equated with family and society. An idealist whose theories reflected his own efforts, he challenged himself to create a body of work that would extend itself to "ultimate causes," engaging its "relevancy for the race" and emphasizing a balance which is "all" in great drama.

2.   PERSONAL DIGNITY: NAME VERSUS ANIMAL

"The tragic feeling," Miller wrote, "is evoked in us when we are in the presence of a character who is ready to lay down his life, if need be, to secure one thing -- his sense of personal dignity." Miller's concern for the dignity of the individual sets him apart from his contemporaries -- a concern which he dramatized as a man's respect for his name. Without this identity, a man becomes an animal; and it is the choice of retaining one's name or being called an animal that is the culminating crisis in which Miller's heroes must always fight for their names. In *All My Sons* (1947), Chris condemns his father at the end of Act II for being "not even an animal," and the last act dramatizes the father's vain attempt to salvage some dignity from his life. Biff in *Death of a Salesman* (1949), having complained that "we're all animals," remarks that his father, Willy Loman, did not know who he was. The point is made more explicitly in *The Crucible* (1953), as Proctor refuses to let his confession be used to influence others: "How may I live without my name? I have given you my soul; leave me my name!" The climax of *A View from the Bridge* (1956) occurs when the informer, Eddie Carbone, encounters the vengeful Marco. As Eddie half pleads and half demands to be given his "name," Marco can utter only the word "animal." In *After the Fall* (1964), the question, "In whose name?" is asked, but the answer -- "Always in your own blood-covered name you turn your back" -- is different. There is no longer the pleading of the doomed and defeated; Quentin in *After the Fall* learns to live.

3.   LIMITED PRODUCTIVITY, SIGNIFICANT ACHIEVEMENT

Miller's reputation in the theatre of the early 1960s rested upon very few plays. His first play for the New York stage, *The*

Man Who Had All the Luck (1944), failed.   Three years later, *All My Sons* won three awards, and *Death of a Salesman* (1949) received a Pulitzer Prize.   *The Crucible* (1953) was followed in 1955 by two short plays: *A View from the Bridge* (later expanded to two acts) and *A Memory of Two Mondays*.   His success was as a playwright of ideas, a realistic playwright in the American tradition who could create psychologically valid characters with whom his audiences could identify.   That he could do this equally well in such diversely conceived plays as *The Crucible* and *A View from the Bridge* only confirms his position as one of America's best modern playwrights.

(a)   *All My Sons* (1947)
During World War II Joe Keller was a businessman who not only caused soldiers to die by shipping out faulty cylinder heads for the airplanes they flew but allowed his partner to go to prison for the deed.   Misguided by his desire to make money for his family and not wholly aware of the falseness of his position, he is finally driven to suicide when his son forces upon him a larger consciousness of responsibility.

(b)   *Death of a Salesman* (1949)
Illustrating Miller's theory of the tragedy of the common man as well as his technique of mixing realism and expressionism, this play is one of the most controversial in the modern American theatre.   Intended to dramatize "the process of Willy Loman's way of mind," *Death of a Salesman* portrays a man with "the wrong dreams," who is never able to see the truth or accept the world as it is.   Frustrated by his own weaknesses, desperately disappointed in his sons, victimized by twisted values, Willy is a misplaced man, without "a thing in the ground," who will give up his life before giving up his false ideas.   He is both victim and hero, and his suicide is an ironic comment on a man's obsession with personal dignity.

(c)   *The Crucible* (1953)
Stimulated by the "witch-hunt" tactics of Senator Joseph McCarthy, Miller drew his scene from the Salem witch trials. The accusations of witchcraft against John and Elizabeth Proctor and the subsequent trial showing John's personal integrity and strength are set, first, against the mass hysteria

of a village overwhelmed by superstition and fear; and, second, against the impassioned change in the Reverend Hale, who, sent to help exorcise the Devil, finally denounces the proceedings of the court. Proctor, in the face of death, confesses witchcraft. When he refuses to allow his name to be used to influence others to make a confession which he knows is false, he becomes ennobled and finds a personal dignity which, with death, evokes the sense of tragedy.

B.   Tennessee Williams (1911-1983): Master of Compassion

Raised in a family in which his father's strong and violent attitude was in dramatic contrast to the gentler, protective view of his mother, Thomas Lanier (Tennessee) Williams fused two seemingly paradoxical approaches to life. A lover of beauty, he was frighteningly aware of the ugliness of humanity. The questions he asked in his art propelled him toward an overwhelming compassion for people. He did this most successfully in the plays that he wrote during the 1940s and 1950s. From his first success in 1945, *The Glass Menagerie,* to *The Night of the Iguana* in 1961, his style was a brilliant "poetic naturalism," while his major concern was with dreamers and survivors. In the mid-1960s he suffered a mental and physical collapse. After that, he lost the large audiences who had enjoyed his earlier work and a decade later complained that he was "widely regarded as the ghost of a writer."

1.   CHAMPION OF THE LONELY AND DESPERATE

When *A Streetcar Named Desire* (1947) was produced in Austria, it was called *Loneliness, the Last Step.* Loneliness and its consequent fears dominate *The Glass Menagerie* (1945); and in *Camino Real* (1953) the word "lonely" is repeated as a prelude to death, while the word "brother" may not be spoken. Williams instinctively understood loneliness, perhaps because of his own constant and desperate yet failed attempts to escape the reality of his loneliness.

Writing about Tennessee Williams, critics and historians have concentrated upon the strong characters in his plays, his repeated themes of loneliness, surviving and dreaming, his shocking exploitation of sex and violence and the beautifully romantic and lyrical quality of his writing. It is true that sensationalism and violence fill his plays after *The Glass Menagerie*: rape in *A Streetcar Named Desire*; homosexuality in *Cat on a Hot Tin Roof* (1955); a man torn apart by dogs in *Orpheus Descending* (1957); castration in *Sweet Bird of Youth* (1958); cannibalism in *Suddenly Last Summer* (1958). These were means to an end, however, for Williams. Clive Barnes, theatre critic, explained in a 1974 review of a performance of *Cat on a Hot Tin Roof*: "People used to think that Tennessee Williams' plays were about sex and violence. How wrong they were -- they are about love and survival."

As he wrote about people in their desperate searches for happiness or escape, Williams showed overwhelming compassion -- for Laura in *The Glass Menagerie*, Lady in *Orpheus Descending*, Alma in *Summer and Smoke* (1948), Shannon in *The Night of the Iguana*, Blanche in *A Streetcar Named Desire*. Mixing loving sentiment and sexual violence, Williams suggested the escape for dreamers that leads to survival. In a memorable image from *Orpheus Descending*, he portrayed their plight: "You know," Val Xavior tells Lady, "they's a kind of bird that don't have legs so it can't light on nothing but has to stay all its life on its wings in the sky?" Both Val and Lady want to be "one of those birds and never be -- corrupted." In this fashion Williams revealed the feelings of the "weak, beautiful people" that disturb Maggie in *Cat on a Hot Tin Roof*, "those being of a golden kind," described in Grandpa's last poem in *The Night of the Iguana*, who to survive must escape "the earth's obscene, corrupting love."

2.   THE DREAMER'S ROAD TO SURVIVAL

Many critics consider *The Glass Menagerie*, Williams' strongly autobiographical memory play, his best. Tom lives with his mother, Amanda, and his sister, Laura. Sensitive, unhappy, something of a poet, Tom rebels against his job in a shoe factory and the sympathetic insistence of his romantic mother that he invite for dinner some young man who might be interested in Laura, who is crippled, excessively shy and reclusive. When it turns out that the young man he finally brings home is engaged to be married, Amanda's indignant anger drives Tom away, although he never forgets his sister.

Williams saw the world through compassionate eyes but as neither unthinking idealist nor lofty romantic. Nowhere did he express his belief in the acceptance of reality as a basis for survival more forcefully and poetically than in *Camino Real*, his "testament" and a 1953 failure on Broadway. In sixteen blocks or scenes on the Camino Real, Don Quixote dreams a pageant of old and new meanings in which Kilroy, the all-American boy with a solid gold heart, meets the various corruptors of life, is seduced by fraud, becomes a patsy and finally is chosen the fit companion of Don Quixote, dreamer. "Desperation" is the price of admission to the Camino Real, where "a dream is nothing to live in," where "you've got to be realistic." The Survivor makes Williams' discovery: "When Peeto, my pony, was born he stood on his four legs at once and accepted the world! He was wiser than I. . . ."

III. PRE-WAR DRAMATISTS

For its post-war entertainment, America looked toward her new dramatists. Those who had been actively writing during the Twenties and Thirties were generally less effective in the theatre in the Fifties. Some died, some wrote fewer plays, others simply faded from the scene. Although O'Neill's plays continued to appear, all had been written before the war. Few of the pre-war playwrights enhanced their reputations, although Elmer Rice, Maxwell Anderson, S. N. Behrman, George S. Kaufman and William Saroyan continued to write plays with some of the characteristics which had made their earlier efforts successful. Thornton Wilder added to the body of his work but could not top his pre-war achievements. Only Lillian Hellman advanced a reputation that had established her among America's best pre-war dramatists.

A.   The Posthumous Eugene O'Neill (1888-1953)

O'Neill died in 1953, but he had written his last play in 1941-43. This play, *A Moon for the Misbegotten*, and *The*

Iceman   Cometh were first produced in 1946 and 1947 respectively, but without much success. It was not until the late Fifties that O'Neill enthusiasts began again to gather in the wings. In 1956 a successful revival of *The Iceman Cometh* was followed by *Long Day's Journey into Night* (1939-41), a play concerned with the terrible agonies suffered by O'Neill's family -- the four haunted Tyrones -- his mother, his father, his brother, himself. It is generally acclaimed as one of O'Neill's best works in spite of its burdensome effect upon audiences and the author's obvious self-flagelation. *A Moon for the Misbegotten* appeared again in 1957, the same year that *A Touch of the Poet* was produced in Sweden before being brought to America. Critics observed that O'Neill's faults were as damning as ever, but they still hailed him as America's major playwright. As the winner of four Pulitzer Prizes for his plays and the Nobel Prize for Literature, the only American dramatist to date so honored, O'Neill will be remembered as America's premier dramatist of the twentieth century.

1.   THE CONTINUING IDEA OF ILLUSION

A Moon for the Misbegotten (written in 1941-43, published in 1952) reveals O'Neill's continued fascination with illusion which had appeared in *The Iceman Cometh* and *A Touch of the Poet*. This play dramatizes a familiar thesis, with the characters living behind pretense and psychic masks -- without success. For O'Neill, there was in a life of illusion reason for both praise and condemnation.

2.   THE CYCLE: A TALE OF POSSESSORS SELF-DISPOSSESSED

Never quite sure of the number of plays that his cycle would include, O'Neill wrote drafts of the first four plays of this cycle which would trace the fortunes of the Harford family and the corrupting effect of material things upon it. On February 21, 1943, in despair over world conditions, he burned the first two plays -- *Greed of the Meek* and *Give Me Death*. The third play was *A Touch of the Poet* (1935-42). *More Stately Mansions*, the fourth play, was published (after being produced in Sweden) in 1964 in a version less than one-half the length of O'Neill's manuscript.

More Stately Mansions (begun in 1936, never completed)
O'Neill's later plays turn desperately upon himself. As he saw
greed and corruption engulf humanity, his natural despair
allowed him to understand his fellow beings only in terms of
illusion or insanity. Once the illusion has been stripped away,
there are only corruption and cruelty. Simon Harford (the hero
of *A Touch of the Poet*), now married to Sara, once wanted to be
a poet, but has now, as a rich merchant, become obsessed with
"the possession of power as the only freedom." Oliver Wendell
Holmes' poem from which the title of the play was taken is
quoted by Simon with "a mocking irony tinged with a bitter,
tragic sadness." His life is consumed by his desire to dominate
in business and to be dominated by his wife and his mother,
whose fight for control of Simon is the central action of the
play. His cruelty toward them is climaxed by his suggestion
that they murder each other. Yet he thinks often of escape into
insanity, which finally comes to him, leaving him as a child to
Sara, who swears with "a fierce, passionate, possessive
tenderness" to be all he will "ever need in life." As always,
O'Neill's sensitive poet is defeated.

B.   Philip Barry (1896-1949)

Barry's immediate reaction to the war was a protest play
called *Liberty Jones* (1941), which dramatizes a fascism versus
democracy theme. *Without Love* (1942), a romantic comedy,
makes use of Ireland's role in the war. After *Foolish Notion*
(1945), a psychological study of a soldier's homecoming, Barry
returned to the problem of "man's search for meaning" in *Second
Threshold* (1949) and found his answer in "love." This play
was revised slightly by Robert Sherwood before a posthumous
production in 1951 on Broadway, where, like Barry's other
post-Thirties plays, it was only moderately successful.

C.   Robert Sherwood (1896-1955)

With the advent of war in Europe, Sherwood changed his
thinking about the purpose of drama, as his play *There Shall
Be No Night* (1940) triumphantly shows. Having thus
revealed his ability to write brilliant propaganda, he was

hired as a speech writer for President Roosevelt, who appointed him director of the Overseas Branch of the Office of War Information. None of his post-war plays was successful in the theatre. *The Rugged Path* (1945) is a propaganda play for victory in the war. After collaborating with Irving Berlin and Moss Hart on the musical *Miss Liberty* (1949), he wrote a final play, *Small War on Murray Hill* (performed posthumously, 1957), in which he used the flirtatious wife of a Tory sympathizer to ridicule the efforts of the British during the New York battles of the American Revolution. Throughout his career, he won three Pulitzer Prizes for drama and one for biography, *Roosevelt and Hopkins* (1948).

D.   Maxwell Anderson (1888-1959)

During the final twenty years of his life, Anderson wrote a dozen plays, most showing a decline in his dramatic powers. *Candle in the Wind* (1941), concerned with an American actress' efforts to get her fiancé released from a Nazi prison, was followed by two mediocre war plays -- *The Eve of St. Mark* (1942) and *Storm Operation* (1944). Several of his last plays are adaptations of novels -- *Lost in the Stars* (1949), a musical dramatization of Alan Paton's *Cry the Beloved Country; The Bad Seed* (1954), the story of a child criminal by William March; *The Day the Money Stopped* (1958), a co-authored adaptation of Brendan Gill's novel.

Three of Anderson's post-war plays maintain the serious thought and dramaturgy of his earlier work. In *Joan of Lorraine* (1946) he presented a rehearsal of a Joan of Arc play in which the leading actress and the director argue about interpretation -- whether beliefs should be compromised. Joan's, and Anderson's, answer is that one cannot live without belief. *Anne of the Thousand Days* (1948) about one of the wives of Henry VIII, is a weak return to the theme of *Elizabeth the Queen* and *Mary of Scotland,* reasserting Anderson's bitter attitude toward mankind's lust for power. *Barefoot in Athens* (1951) serves as a fitting climax to Anderson's writing. Dramatizing Socrates' trial, Anderson answered two questions that had always plagued him: democracy is the only acceptable form of government; truth is the only guide for freedom.

E.   George S. Kaufman (1889-1961)

After spectacular success during the Thirties, Kaufman had great difficulty catching the comic spirit after the war. With Edna Ferber, he wrote *Bravo!* (1948). For *The Small Hours* (1951) and *Fancy Meeting You Again* (1952), he worked with Leueen McGrath, whom he had married in 1949. Neither play was a success, but his career ended on a high note. With Howard Teichmann in *The Solid Gold Cadillac* (1953), a play which exploits the comic situation of a "little old lady" taking over the leadership of a large corporation, he rediscovered his old form. In a final musical written with his wife and Abe Burrows with music by Cole Porter, *Silk Stockings* (1955), he once again struck the right chord for American audiences. Concerned with communism and U.S.-Soviet relations, the play allows audiences to watch and sympathize with a budding romance between a Russian Commissar and an American agent. Over a period of thirty-seven years Kaufman had forty-five plays produced. Of these, twenty-seven were considered "hits"; eighteen were failures.

F.   Moss Hart (1904-1961)

Having established his playwriting career during the Thirties as a collaborator with George S. Kaufman, Hart wrote three plays after World War II. *Christopher Blake* (1946) is a drama about a divorce hearing; *Light up the Sky* (1948) toys with types of theatre people, but without success. In *The Climate of Eden* (1952) Hart tried unsuccessfully to dramatize Edgar Mittelhölzer's *Shadows Move among Them,* a strange tale of guilt set in British Guiana. Mainly, Hart devoted himself to directing during these years and won a Tony Award for his work on *My Fair Lady* (1956).

G.   Clifford Odets (1906-1963)

Odets never returned to Broadway with the force of his initial debut in the Thirties. *Clash By Night* (1941) was a failure in spite of Odets' intensity in treating love and social forces. After the war he wrote only three plays -- *The Big Knife* (1949), the story of a successful actor who bargains his soul for

fame and finally commits suicide; *The Country Girl* (1949), a
dramatization of the psychological problems of an aging,
alcoholic and insecure actor and his wife, who are redeemed by
his success in a play; *The Flowering Peach* (1954), an interesting
retelling of Noah and the Ark in which the symbol of
regeneration for a corrupt world is the family. Of these, only
The Country Girl was well received -- revised in 1968 as *Winter
Journey*. Odets seems destined, as he bitterly complained, to be
remembered as a playwright of the American Thirties.

H.   Elmer Rice (1892-1967)

Starting his career before World War I, Rice wrote several
plays after World War II, although with little success. Only
Dream Girl (1945), an expressionistic comedy which dramatizes a girl's many dreams, suggests anything of his pre-war
popularity. A musical version of *Street Scene*, written with
Kurt Weill and Langston Hughes in 1947, did not last in the
theatre. Three later plays also did nothing for his reputation
-- *The Grand Tour* (1951), in which a schoolteacher and an
embezzler find romance in Europe; *The Winner* (1954), a crime
melodrama which once more makes use of Rice's early legal
training; and *Cue for Passion* (1958), a weak story of a
California Hamlet whose Horatio is a criminal psychologist.
Rice recounted his experiences in *The Living Theatre* (1959) and
Minority Report (1963), in which, always the liberal idealist,
he preached individual freedom from all tyranny.

I.   S. N. Behrman (1893-1973)

Although during the post-war years Behrman was the most
consistently active of those dramatists who made their
reputations before the war, his works were mainly adapted or
derived from existing stories or plays. He never returned to
high comedy. Instead, he plucked the strong, egotistical
character types from his early plays and placed them in
sentimental comedies. Occasionally, the old Behrman wit is
recognizable, but his reputation in the history of American
drama rests upon the plays he wrote between the two World
Wars.

Behrman's best post-war plays are *Dunnigan's Daughter* (1945), the story of a determined woman who controls her circumstances; *Jane* (1952), about another eccentric, capable woman, borrowed from a Somerset Maugham story; and *Lord Pengo* (1962), the story of an art dealer (from Behrman's story, "The Days of Duveen") who is typical of Behrman's characters of the Thirties in his eccentricity, egotism, charm and single-minded concern for material things.

Other post-World War II plays include *Jacobowksy and the Colonel* (1944), a farce adapted from a play by Franz Werfel; *I Know My Love* (1949), a comedy adapted from Marcel Achard's *Aupres de Ma Blonde; Fanny* (1954), a musical co-authored with Joshua Logan and adapted from a Marcel Pagnol trilogy; *The Cold Wind and the Warm* (1958), an account of Jewish life in Massachusetts, based on Behrman's memoir, *The Worcester Account* (1954); and *But for Whom Charlie* (1964), about a man trying to free himself from a domineering father -- a weak climax to a long and productive life in the theatre.

J.   George Kelly (1887-1974)

Coming to Broadway via the vaudeville circuit, where he produced his own skits, Kelly had forged his reputation in the Twenties. In *The Deep Mrs. Sykes* (1945), Kelly portrayed a blindly egotistical woman who is damned by her own suspicious and crafty nature and thereby joins the Kelly gallery of unpleasant women. *The Fatal Weakness* (1946) comments in an outdated fashion on marriage. Neither play was successful, although they preserve the hallmarks of Kelly's dramatic talent -- an interest in "the satanic female race" and a lack of detachment in picturing it. His later work was unpublished and unproduced: *Can Two Walk Together?* (1949), concerned with "the tragic rushing into marriage," and *When All Else Fails* (1951), a satiric comedy about a recent and reluctant widow. By the 1960s Kelly was a rare visitor to the theatre.

K.   Thornton Wilder (1897-1975)

As one of America's playwrights best-known around the world, Wilder established a reputation from three full-length plays and a handful of one-acts. As both playwright and theorist, he deserves his position among America's best writers. After World War II he wrote a surprising number of plays: *Our Century* (1947); *The Victors* (1948), based on a play by Jean-Paul Sartre; *A Life in the Sun* (1955), based on the Alcestis legend and, with music by Louise Talma, produced in 1962 as *The Alcestiad; The Drunken Sisters* (1957), a brief portrayal of a time when Apollo got the Fates drunk; *Bernice* and *The Wreck of the 5:25,* both produced unsuccessfully in 1957; and *Plays for Bleecker Street* (1962), including *Infancy, Childhood* a n d *Someone from Assisi.* His best work during these years was *The Matchmaker* (1954), a version of his earlier play, *T h e Merchant of Yonkers* (1939), which became *Hello, Dolly!* (1964) in the hands of Jerry Herman and Michael Stewart.

L.   William Saroyan (1908-1981)

Saroyan was an honest eccentric whose view of life was at once exciting, exasperating and penetrating in its abrupt simplicity. At a time when optimism and innocence were suspect in society, he created a brave new world without much else. As he continued to write plays and to philosophize in an unorthodox but frequently amusing manner, his plays reflect modern confusions in society as simply and straightforwardly as his wandering thoughts and erratic style could present them.

From 1944 through 1980 Saroyan produced or published twenty-eight stage plays, as well as a number of television and radio plays. All show his buoyant optimism and sentimentality, but none reach the quality of his pre-war efforts. His interest in the comedy-tragedy of life, however, remained undiminished throughout his playwriting career. *Sam's Ego House* (1947) illustrates Saroyan's view of life in the United States; *Don't Go Away Mad* (1949) is a play of Saroyan optimism set in a hospital for incurable diseases; *The Slaughter of the Innocents* (1952) dramatizes the idea that individuals are victims of their own acts. Saroyan's one Broadway play, *The Cave Dwellers* (1957), tells of people with virtues of royal proportion who live in an old theatre building (that represents the world) and find that all is good. Other plays include *The Dogs; or, The Paris Comedy, or The Secret of Life* (1960), *T h e*

London Comedy; or, Sam the Highest Jumper of Them All (1960) and *The Rebirth Celebration of the Human Race at Artie Zabala's Off Broadway Theatre* (1975).

M. Lillian Hellman (1906-1984)

After *My Mother, My Father and Me* (1963), a box-office failure based on Burt Blechman's novel *How Much?*, and her adaptation of Emanuel Roblès' *Montserrat* (1949), Hellman stopped writing for the theatre. She had also adapted *The Lark* (1955) from Anouilh's *L'Alouette,* and worked on *Candide* (1956), a "comic operetta" with music by Leonard Bernstein and lyrics by Richard Wilbur and others, which is remembered as a famous Broadway failure. (The 1973 successful version of *Candide* had a completely new book by Hugh Wheeler.)

In spite of her weak post-war box office record, Hellman added to her reputation as one of the leading dramatists of the contemporary theatre with three strong plays. *Another Part of the Forest* (1946) shows the Hubbard family during a period before *The Little Foxes* and dramatizes Ben Hubbard's unscrupulous way of gaining control of the clan. The South is also the scene of *The Autumn Garden* (1951), which, in a Chekovian tradition, portrays some of the cruelties of man as well as the agony of age: "At any given moment you're only the sum of your life up to then." In *Toys in the Attic* (1960), Hellman created a penetrating picture of life, warning against the innocent who falls in love with truth.

IV. ART AND ENTERTAINMENT

"The purpose of Art is to raise doubt; the purpose of entertainment is to reassure," wrote John Whiting, a modern English dramatist. ["From My Diary," *The Twentieth Century,* CLXIX (February 1961), 200] The distinction drawn is an interesting one, even if the critic assumes that in the best entertainment there is evidence of art. In Broadway theatres there is no doubt that audiences want to be reassured and that light entertainment is the best means to this end. For the most part, plays that have stayed on Broadway -- that is, those that have made money for the owners of the theatres -- have

been melodramas, comedies or musicals. "Broadway's angels,"
playwrights understand, "are mainly on the side of the cynics
who cater to the matinee ladies and the tired businessmen"
(Murray Schumach, *Kansas City Star*, October 4, 1964).

In the post-war theatre, as in all theatres, money controlled;
audiences decided what they wanted to see. Other than Miller
and Williams, few playwrights attempted to "raise doubts."
Among those who showed serious potential were William Inge,
Arthur Laurents and Paddy Chayefsky. Most playwrights
concentrated on "entertainment" in two or three plays without
being able to maintain their momentum. Certain experimenters
asserted themselves, but their work lacked maturity. Poetic
dramatists were still learning that poetry "must serve the
theater before it can again rule there," as the Irish
playwright, Lady Gregory, once warned. By the 1960s there
were also new dramatists appearing -- William Hanley, Neil
Simon, Lorraine Hansberry, Edward Albee, Arthur Kopit and
Lewis John Carlino.

A.   Seriousness and Entertainment

A number of plays suggest the serious ambitions of the new
dramatists. Some wrote what may be called psychological
dramas; others used comedy effectively to touch upon social
conditions; still others -- such as William Archibald in *The
Innocents* (1950), an adaptation of Henry James' *The Turn of the
Screw*, and Louis O. Coxe and Robert Chapman's 1951
adaptation of Herman Melville's short story, *Billy Budd* --
brought to the stage some of the serious thoughts of American
literary figures. The only dramatists who presented a body of
work in which they attempted to deal seriously with life were
Inge, Laurents and Chayefsky.

1.   THREE DRAMATISTS OF SKILL AND AMBITION

(a)   William Inge (1913-1973)

When Inge first came to Broadway with *Come Back, Little
Sheba* (1950), he seemed destined to compete with Miller and
Williams. Quite different from these writers, however, he
found no potential for tragedy in the drab lives of the ordinary
people who appear in his plays. Instead, he emphasized their

pathetic and sometimes comic natures in surroundings and situations to which he brought a suggestion of universality. Nor was he an experimenter with dramatic form. A straightforward, realistic setting in middle America, presented in a straightforward, realistic manner, was his trademark. His appeal rested firmly upon his ability to fascinate audiences with the basic human and important truths he found in the common activities of unimportant people.

Unfortunately, Inge never fulfilled his early promise. Depression and alcoholism overwhelmed him. In the history books his reputation is determined by only four plays: *Come Back, Little Sheba*, the story of a slovenly romantic woman and her alcoholic husband as they are made to face the reality of their life; *Picnic* (1953), a portrayal of women revealed by passion and driven to a bleak future; *Bus Stop* (1955), a sketchy presentation of various people in a bus stop and their attitudes toward love; and *The Dark at the Top of the Stairs* (1957), a psychological study of the need for love and understanding within a family and among all people.

Inge managed successfully to mingle sex and sentiment and to present lonely people whose problems are solved -- for good or for ill -- by love. The formulaic quality of his work suggests a subservience to both Broadway and Hollywood commercialism. Although his characters are conceived with insight and skill, his psychologically oriented solutions frequently seem superficial. Among his late plays are *A Loss of Roses* (1960), concerning the growth from youth to maturity; *Natural Affections* (1963), a poorly constructed melodrama of unnatural affection between mother and son; and *Where's Daddy?* (1966), a mild satire on contemporary manners and morals.

(b) Arthur Laurents (1918-)

A promising dramatist appearing immediately after World War II, Laurents continued to show his potential with his honest concern for the dignity of the individual in society, his insight in revealing character, his use of music and his imaginative experimentation in theatrical techniques. *The Bird Cage* (1950) describes a world of tyranny as it is mirrored in the activity of a night club owner who is defied by a heroic chorus girl. In *The Time of the Cuckoo* (1952) a sentimental spinster learns a good deal about life and herself during a vacation in Venice. The theme of loneliness is imaginatively portrayed in *A Clearing in the Woods* (1957), in which three characters are used to show aspects of the heroine's past and to help her reconcile herself to a world where she can find love. *Invitation to a March* (1960) is a comic fantasy dramatizing the individual's choice either to follow his own bent or the desires of others. During the 1940s Laurents had written for radio and the movies, and in the 1950s he became particularly successful in writing the book for musicals such as *West Side Story* (1957) and *Gypsy* (1959). Whether in musical comedy or in straight drama, Laurents attempted to express his optimistic view of humanity, but he essentially abandoned his interest in serious drama in the mid-1950s.

(c)   Paddy Chayefsky (1923-1981)
A determined idealist who believed the messages in his plays, Chayefsky once explained that he wrote "out of social necessity." Throughout his writing career, he moved easily back and forth as he created plays for radio, television, the screen and the stage. His first post-war Broadway play, *Middle of the Night* (1956), is, in fact, a revision of a television play, and the popularity of *Marty* as a television play (1953) and screenplay (1955) probably brought him greater recognition than any of his stage plays.

By the mid-1960s Chayefsky's reputation as a Broadway dramatist was well established. *Middle of the Night,* about a fifty-three year old widower and a twenty-four year old girl who decide that "even a few years of happiness you don't throw away," was well received. In *The Tenth Man* (1959) Chayefsky showed a group of Jews exorcising a dybbuk from a demented girl who is finally taken from the synagogue by the "tenth man." The presumption that she will be cured by this man's love may be considered sentimental and romantic, but the humor is delightful. A more thoughtful play, also marked by clever humor, is *Gideon* (1961). Chosen by God to deliver his people, a reluctant Gideon becomes prideful and tests God until God admits love for Gideon -- but with a cosmic sense of mocking humor: let a man try to be God if he will. In *The Passion of*

Josef D (1964) Chayefsky suggests, through Lenin, that God is no longer possible, that "nothing is real." Unfortunately, Chayefsky wrote only one more play for Broadway, preferring to answer "a call to disaster," as he expressed himself later in life, through screenwriting.

2.   SOCIAL DRAMA

This vague category is intended to include plays of more serious than comic purpose which build, sometimes in a melodramatic fashion, upon a social issue. Entertainment with a message! Throughout the history of American theatre, a significant percentage of dramatists have had this objective. Robert Sherwood may have complained that he always started with a big idea and ended up with nothing but good entertainment, but he was fortunate to be able to do this -- and well rewarded with three Pulitzer Prizes for drama, second only to O'Neill, who received four.

(a) Comedy/Melodrama

Mixing comedy and melodrama, a number of playwrights of the 1950s attempted to intrude a social issue into an entertaining dramatic structure. *The Girl on the Via Flaminia* (1954) by Alfred Hayes is such a play, as it portrays the wartime love of an American soldier for an Italian girl, their desire for independence as well as their dependence upon one another and the attitudes of society. So is Ketti Frings' dramatization of Thomas Wolfe's *Look Homeward, Angel* (1957), Carson McCullers' Broadway version of *The Member of the Wedding* (1950) and William Gibson's *The Miracle Worker* (1959). Dore Schary (1905-1980) dramatized Franklin Delano Roosevelt's private life in *Sunrise at Campobello* (1958). None of his later plays proved attractive to audiences, but in each Schary examined serious issues: *The Highest Tree* (1959), about an atomic scientist who opposes nuclear testing after he is stricken with leukemia; *The Devil's Advocate* (1961), an adaptation of Morris West's novel about a man killed in World War II who is considered for Beatification.

(b) A More Particular Social Issue

The Civil Rights movement began to gain attention in New York during the 1950s with a number of plays: Louis Peterson's

Take a Giant Step (1953); *Trouble in Mind* (1955), a play of black-white relations by Alice Childress (1920-); and *A Land Beyond the River* (1957) by Loften Mitchell (1919-). The outstanding writer of plays dealing with black issues was Lorraine Hansberry (1930-1965), whose *A Raisin in the Sun* (1959) dramatizes the decision of a Negro family to move into a white neighborhood. Her dramatic virtues of humor, intellectual insight and compassion for humanity are also evident in *The Sign in Sidney Brustein's Window* (1964), which she wrote shortly before her untimely death from cancer.

3.   PSYCHOLOGICAL MELODRAMA

A number of dramatists emphasized the psychological aspects of their material. Joseph Kramm's *The Shrike* (1952) is a good illustration. Waking up in the psychological ward of a city hospital, an attempted suicide learns that in the eyes of the authorities he is a criminal and that he can be released only if he places himself under the control of his wife, from whom he is estranged. *All the Way Home* (1960), Tad Mosel's adaptation of James Agee's novel, *A Death in the Family*, treats the reaction of a young boy and his mother to the sudden death of the father. Michael V. Gazzo's *A Hatful of Rain* (1955) deals with the problems of a drug addict. Herman Wouk created a fine courtroom psychological melodrama from his own novel in *The Caine Mutiny Court Martial* (1954). *The Diary of Anne Frank* (1955) by Frances Goodrich and Albert Hackett shows a young girl's perceptive reactions to the cruelties of war. One of the best psychological dramas, Morton Wishengrad's *The Rope Dancers* (1959) tells of a woman who conceives by her drunken husband, and their child has six fingers on one hand. Fearful and guilty, the mother calls the hand evil, a curse, and makes the child wear a mitten until a doctor convinces her that "we all wear a glove over something." When the doctor removes the extra finger, however, the child dies. Reminiscent of Nathaniel Hawthorne's "The Birthmark," Wishengrad's play deals with the forces of good and evil.

4.   CRIME MELODRAMA AS ENTERTAINMENT

Crime melodramas have attracted American theatre audiences since the flood of New York crime plays during the 1850s. In one of the best, Joseph Hayes' *The Desperate Hours* (1955), an escaped convict returns to kill the sheriff who put him away. Waiting for his chance, the killer and his two pals invade a family's home and, after great excitement and suspense, are finally killed. *A Shot in the Dark* (1961), Harry Kurnitz's adaptation of a French novel, focuses on the question of whether a person should be tried for murder. *A Case of Libel* (1963), a play by Henry Denker based on Louis Nizer's *My Life in Court,* made its point for an honest lawyer, while revealing all the crudities and niceties of a libel suit.

B.   Contemporary Comedy

All too frequently on Broadway, the only alternative to giving audiences a thrill has been giving them a laugh. In comedy the range has always been great, and numerous post-war playwrights found success with sentimental, light or satirical comedy.

1.   SENTIMENTAL COMEDY

Sentiment has long been a marketable commodity on Broadway, although some playwrights have manifested particular finesse in its dissemination. Jerome Chodorov and Joseph Fields were successful with their treatments of sex and marriage problems in both *Anniversary Waltz* (1954) and *The Ponder Heart* (1956). William Gibson's *Two for the Seesaw* (1958) effectively infuses it in a modern psychological comedy. Joshua Logan's version of *The Cherry Orchard,* called *The Wisteria Trees* (1950), capitalizes on the traditional sentimentality of audiences; John Patrick's *The Teahouse of the August Moon* (1953), an adaptation of Vern Sneider's novel, creates a sentimental comedy on the island of Okinawa.

Robert Anderson (1917-)
The most successful writer of sentimental comedy and melodrama during this period, Anderson built his plays largely on a theme of loneliness. The slow movement in his plays and his unrelenting emphasis upon sweetness, sentiment and illicit sex as a solution to human problems, however, detract from his overall effectiveness. After several plays that never got to New York, Anderson wrote *Tea and Sympathy* (1953), treating

a lonely student at a New England boy's school, whose problems in trying to prove his manhood are solved by his headmaster's wife, whose sympathy knows no limits. Having the "right" amount of sex and sentiment, the play was a Broadway hit. *All Summer Long* (1954), dramatizing the flooding of a family house by a river and the symbolic erosion of the family foundations, was less successful. *Silent Night, Lonely Night* (1959) describes a sad Christmas Eve vigil by a couple, married, but not to each other, who find strength and understanding during a brief time together.

2.   LIGHT COMEDY

A commonplace observation among theatre people is that tired businessmen and ladies who attend matinees enjoy a bright, witty, fast-moving comedy that requires little or no thought. The subject matter is not important. Among those whose plays say something about American tastes and attitudes for the generation after World War II is George Axelrod (1922-), whose success rests upon his ability to write clever, simply structured comedy that seems at first outrageous and naughty but is generally acceptable and comforting. *The Seven Year Itch* (1952) and *Will Success Spoil Rock Hunter?* (1955), the best of Axelrod's polished and tailored plays, were the most imaginative among the slim pieces of professionally manufactured theatre of the time. Norman Krasna (1909-1984) was a successful playwright in the Thirties before bringing his comic skills to post-war audiences with *John Loves Mary* (1947), *Kind Sir* (1953) and *Who Was That Lady I Saw You With?* (1958). Hollywood took most of his energy after the war. Samuel Taylor (1912-), another writer of light-hearted comedy, started during the 1930s and entertained the post-war crowds with such popular romances as *The Happy Time* (1950), *Sabrina Fair* (1953) and *The Pleasure of His Company* (1958). Taylor also spent a lot of time in Hollywood -- *Topaz* with Alfred Hitchcock -- and writing for radio and television.

For those who wanted excellent light comedy and had no preference concerning theme, there was Mary Ellen Chase's play about Elwood P. Dowd's six-foot rabbit, *Harvey* (1944). *Auntie Mame* (1956), an adaptation of Patrick Dennis' novel by

Jerome Lawrence and Robert E. Lee, dramatizes another fantastic character. Other light comedies include Anita Loos' *Happy Birthday* (1946), Harry Kurnitz's *Reclining Figure* (1954), Ira Levin's *No Time for Sergeants* (1955), Jean Kerr's *Mary, Mary* (1961) and Murray Schisgal's *Luv* (1963). All of these plays reassured the tired businessman and the matinee ladies.

A new name among Broadway playwrights in the 1960s was Neil Simon (1927-), whose first full-length comedy, *Come Blow Your Horn* (1961), exploits the antics of two girl-crazy sons of a Jewish businessman. Fast repartee and well structured situations are a trademark for Simon, who became extremely productive and the most successful playwright of the decade: *Barefoot in the Park* (1963) and *The Odd Couple* (1965).

3.   SATIRIC COMEDY

Almost all American comedy attempts to satirize or ridicule something or somebody -- from suburbia in *Auntie Mame* to the army in *The Teahouse of the August Moon*. Known more as a director of stage and screen than as a playwright, Garson Kanin (1912-) found just the right combination of hokum and sentiment in *Born Yesterday* (1946), which satirizes business and politics while exploring the comic possibilities of a millionaire junkman and the ex-chorus girl who lives with him. Howard Lindsay and Russel Crouse's *State of the Union* (1945) ridicules both the personal and public problems of a Presidential candidate. Gore Vidal (1925-) satirized war in *Visit to a Small Planet* (1956) and politics in *The Best Man* (1960).

C.   Drama in Poetry

Without becoming involved in an argument over terms -- poetic drama, verse drama or mood drama -- it is possible to note a slowly increasing post-war interest in plays written in poetry. The challenge of uniting good poetry and good drama -- or creating poetry which serves the theatre -- was more frequently accepted by those who were aware of the importance of poetic language on the stage. This concern is illustrated most clearly in the plays of Tennessee Williams and the early work of Edward Albee, but there were others who felt the same needs. In general, however, attempts to write plays in poetry came from poets rather than dramatists -- Robert Frost, Robinson Jeffers, William Carlos Williams, e. e. cummings, Archibald MacLeish, Robert Lowell, Richard Wilbur, Langston Hughes and Richard Eberhart.

Scholars rarely agree on any definition of poetry. The generalization that "poetry is nothing more than perfect speech" resolves very few arguments, while allowing for a diversity in expression which may be termed "poetry."

1.   DRAMATISTS WRITING IN POETRY

Among the dramatists who used poetic form, Maxwell Anderson is the best known. After World War II, however, he continued his writing of poetic drama only with *Anne of the Thousand Days* (1949). N. Richard Nash was markedly unsuccessful with a pretentious romantic tragedy, *See the Jaguar* (1952). Equally weak was Arch Oboler's *Night of the Auk* (1956), a space-age melodrama. One of the more stageworthy poetic dramas produced in New York is *Hogan's Goat* (1965) by William Alfred (1922-), a play in blank verse, dealing with a mayoralty campaign in Irish Brooklyn in the 1890s.

2.   POETS WRITING PLAYS

Practicing poets might write much better "poetry" than playwrights, but their plays have frequently been marred by poorly created and motivated characters and by a serious lack of dramatic conflict and action. Although *Him* (1927), an esoteric play by e. e. cummings (1894-1962), was produced in 1928, the author was less ambitious with *Santa Claus* (1946), a discursive thesis play pitting Death (knowledge) against Santa Claus (understanding). Robinson Jeffers (1887-1962) wrote a modern version of *Medea* (1947) that starred Judith Anderson on Broadway. Other plays by Jeffers include *The Tower Beyond Tragedy* (1950) and *The Cretan Woman* (1954), a forceful and stageworthy play on the Phaedra-Hippolytus myth. *Many Loves* (1958), one of two produced plays by William Carlos Williams (1883-1963), concerned with the writing of a verse play, showed in production the difficulties that an abstract poet must overcome to write an actable play.

In *The Visionary Farms* (1951) Richard Eberhart (1904-), dramatized the modern paradox of progress and commercial corruption. Eberhart's other plays include *The Apparition* (1951), *Triptych* (1955), *Devils and Angels* (1956) and *The Mad Musician* (1962).

Langston Hughes (1902-1967) had his first Broadway success with *Mulatto* in the 1930s and had a number of interracial plays -- *Little Ham* (1936), *Joy to My Soul* (1937) and *Front Porch* (1938) -- produced in Cleveland. After World War II, he wrote the book and lyrics for Kurt Weill's musical version of *Street Scene* (1947) and had good reviews with *Simply Heavenly* (1957), in which he dramatized the philosophy of his folk hero from *Simple Takes a Wife,* and with *Tambourines to Glory* (1963), another folk musical.

The outstanding poetic dramatist after World War II was Archibald MacLeish (1892-1982). Most of his dramatic work was written for radio or television, including *The Trojan Horse* (1952); *This Music Crept by Me Upon the Waters* (1953), which illustrates his theory of "word-excited imagination," as two sophisticated people believe they have found happiness and fulfillment on an island in the Antibes; *The Secret of Freedom* (1959); and *The American Bell* (1962). With *J. B.* (1958), a modern version of the Job story, MacLeish proved that he could write drama that was both good as poetry and effective as theatre. *J. B.* ran for 364 performances in New York, received the Pulitzer Prize and inspired Brooks Atkinson to write that it portrayed "the spiritual dilemma of the twentieth century." *Heracles* (1965) was not successful in the theatre.

D. Musical Theatre

Having gained considerable momentum during the Thirties, after World War II American musical comedy attained a popularity and artistic achievement worthy of its superior position in the world of musical theatre. Although some musicals were clearly commercially prepared patchwork products, the period from World War II through the mid-1960s was dominated by happy operettas and light-hearted musical comedies. Richard Rodgers and Oscar Hammerstein II created some of their most memorable works: *Carousel* (1945), *South Pacific* (1949), *The King and I* (1951) and *The Sound of Music* (1959). Alan Jay Lerner and Frederick Loewe's *My Fair Lady* (1956) was based on G. B. Shaw's *Pygmalion*, and Frank Loesser's *The Most Happy Fella* (1956) was modeled on Sidney Howard's *They Knew What They Wanted*. Both musicals present well-developed characters and plot conflicts which are supported by the music as well as the lyrics. Most of the musicals are not on serious topics, but occasionally, as in *West Side Story* (1957) by Leonard Bernstein, Arthur Laurents and Stephen Sondheim, the appeal is to emotions of sorrow and despair. Love, however, was invariably the issue which the composer, the lyricist and the librettist surrounded with sweetness and sentiment, fast-moving comedy, perhaps some light ridiculing or a bit of moralizing and a good story.

Among other popular post-war musicals are *Kiss Me, Kate* (1948) by Cole Porter, *Guys and Dolls* (1950) by Frank Loesser, *Annie Get Your Gun* (1946) and *Call Me Madam* (1950) by Irving Berlin, *Gentlemen Prefer Blonds* (1949) and *Gypsy* (1959) by Jule Styne, *The Pajama Game* (1954) and *Damn Yankees* (1955) by Richard Adler and Jerry Ross, *The Music Man* (1957) by Meredith Willson, *Fiorello!* (1959) and *Fiddler on the Roof* (1964) by Jerry Bock and *Man of La Mancha* (1965) by Mitch Leigh. *The Fantasticks* (1960) by Tom Jones and Harvey Schmidt became America's longest-running musical.

Revues, such as Harold Rome's *Call Me Mister* (1946), and spectacles like *New Faces* (1952, 1956) tended to disappear, but another kind of musical play exemplified by Gian-Carlo Menotti's *The Medium* (1947), *The Consul* (1950), *The Saint of Bleecker Street* (1954) and *Maria Golovin* (1958), was created. The form of musical theatre varied considerably for this generation and would change even more during the 1960s.

E.   The Popularity of the Pageant

Numerous pageants were performed yearly for summer visitors to historic places or were written for particular celebrations. For the Mountainside Theatre in Cherokee, North Carolina, Kermit Hunter wrote the story of Conquistador De Soto and the

Cherokee Indians in *Unto These Hills* (1950). *Forever This Land* (1952) presents Lincoln's life in New Salem from 1831 to 1837. Pageants were performed every year from Plymouth in New England to Paul Bunyan Land and to the southern shores of California. Among the most popular pageants and festivals are *Wilderness Road* (1955, Berea, Kentucky) and *The Stephen Foster Story* (1959, Bardstown, Kentucky). The Institute for Outdoor Drama was established in 1963 at the University of North Carolina at Chapel Hill.

F.   New Voices in the 1960s

The social and political upheavals that would disturb Americans by the mid-1960s and challenge dramatists to follow new directions were beginning to be felt in the earliest years of the decade. In terms of theatrical achievement, however, the decade seemed to have little to offer. No Pulitzer prizes were given for drama in 1963, 1964, 1966 or 1968; in 1960 and 1962 the musical theatre was given the award. But during the early 1960's there were suggestions that presaged a change, a different persuasion in the writing of American plays: in the work of William Hanley and Lewis John Carlino, in the ethnic plays of James Baldwin and LeRoi Jones, in the hopeful attempts of Herb Gardner and Frank Gilroy and in the avant garde experiments of Edward Albee, Jack Gelber, Arthur Kopit and Jack Richardson. There was a new era approaching.

1.   A NEW VITALITY -- SHORT-LIVED:
WILLIAM HANLEY (1931-), LEWIS JOHN CARLINO (1932-)

One of the few new playwrights who infused some vitality into the American drama of the early 1960s, Hanley satisfied his playwriting aspirations rather quickly and concentrated on writing for television after 1968. Among a trio of one-act plays, *Whisper into My Good Ear* (1962), *Mrs. Dally Has a Lover* (1962) and *Today is Independence Day* (1963), the second play was the most popular: a conversation between the middle-aged Mrs. Dally and her eighteen-year-old lover. Hanley's only full-length Broadway success, *Slow Dance on the Killing Ground* (1964), foreshadows the new era. A young black genius, a middle-class white girl and a Jew who has denied his heritage are unmasked and found guilty in a mock trial that dramatizes the idea that no one can escape the violence of the world, "the killing ground."

Between June 1963 and May 1964, Carlino had four one-act plays and one full-length play produced in Off Broadway theatres. With *Epiphany* (1963), concerned with a ornithologist who is discovered by his wife in a homosexual act and turns into a rooster, Carlino seemed to establish himself. *Telemachus Clay* (1963), showing the artist as a young man through dreams, memories and flashbacks, support that optimistic view. *Double Talk* (1964), however, showed no advance in Carlino's artistry, and he has since bent his efforts toward fiction, television and screenplays.

2. ETHNIC THEATRE: JAMES BALDWIN (1924-1987), AMIRI BARAKA (NEE LEROI JONES (1934-)

As the Civil Rights movement progressed slowly, the search for a black identity stimulated more aggressive work by black dramatists and experimentation with dramatic form. James Baldwin's major theme in both his fiction and his plays was "identity" or its denial, race and racism. Early in his life he wrote, "If I am to be a playwright, I should try to improve a troubled world, and try to be numbered among the great artists of my race." *The Amen Corner* (1954) did not receive professional production until 1964, the same year that *Blues for Mr. Charlie* was staged. Both plays present eloquently preached theses and controlled views of black society, and both exhibit an experimental theatricalism. Critics reacted cautiously, but Baldwin's message is nonetheless clear in *Blues for Mr. Charlie*, which examines black-white reactions to the murder of an angry black youth by a white bigot.

Baraka had always tried to be a revolutionary and by the early 1960s was disturbing audiences with exposés of raw social tension on a very naturalistic level. Exploiting social and racial problems with a "blatant anti-white" posture, according to Errol G. Hill, black historian, Baraka burst upon the early Sixties scene with *The Toilet* (1962), *Dutchman* (1964), *The Slave* (1964), *The Baptism* (1964) and *Experimental Death Unit No. 1* (1965).

3.   SOCIAL COMMENTARY: HERB GARDNER (1934-), FRANK GILROY (1925 -)

Gardner and Gilroy are representative of those thoughtful playwrights who, during the 1960s, gained attention with one popular play each -- *A Thousand Clowns* (1962) by Gardner and *The Subject Was Roses* (1964) by Gilroy. Neither dramatist has produced a substantial body of work, although Gardner continues to have occasional successes in New York, while Gilroy has turned his hand to television.

4.   THE AVANT GARDE

At the beginning of the 1960s, four young playwrights -- Edward Albee, Jack Richardson, Arthur Kopit and Jack Gelber -- attracted the attention of theatre audiences and critics as the best prospects for claiming the title Major American Dramatist.

(a) Jack Richardson (1935-)

A dramatist of penetrating intellect, Richardson was concerned with the victimization of the individual by various social forces. In *The Prodigal* (1960) he retold the story of Orestes, making the hero a modern cynic. *Gallows Humor* (1961) contrasts a condemned man with his executioner, showing the greater "freedom" of the former, a theme he repeated in *Xmas in Las Vegas* (1965). *Lorenzo* (1963) uses a group of players in Renaissance Italy to suggest the value of illusion over reality. In 1968 he returned to New York with *As Happy as Kings* and then stopped writing for the stage.

(b)   Arthur Kopit (1937-)

Fresh from Harvard, Kopit was quickly decreed an "undergraduate playwright" with the fashionable success of *Oh Dad, Poor Dad, Mama's Hung You in the Closet and I'm Feeling So Sad* (1961). This hilarious burlesque of absurdist drama ends with the question which may have stimulated Kopit in the beginning: "What is the meaning of this?" Prior to this production, Kopit had a number of plays produced in Cambridge, such as *On the Runway of Life, You Never Know What's Coming Off Next* (1957), and he continued to pour out an avalanche of plays dedicated to the proposition that "comedy is a very powerful tool" to treat very serious subjects: *Asylum;*

or, What the Gentlemen Are Up To, and *As for the Ladies* (1963), *The Conquest of Everest* (1964) and *The Day the Whores Came Out to Play Tennis* (1965). It would be four more years before the "undergraduate" label would be lifted.

(c)   Jack Gelber (1932-)

Gelber is important for his influence upon improvisational and group drama. By denying the illusion of the stage and merging actors and audience, he presumably created a reality in which pretense is not necessary. *The Connection* (1959), the audience is told, presents real dope addicts who ad lib a plotless evening for which their payment will be a "fix." This artificially inspired "realism" is supported by a jazz accompaniment and by panhandlers working the theatre lobby between acts. In *The Apple* (1961), Gelber made theatre in a coffee shop where he introduced his characters -- the Negro, the Jew, the homosexual, the whore, the spastic and the drunk -- and presented a series of improvised scenes inviting the audience to make whatever it would of the symbol of "The Apple."

(d)   Edward Albee (1928-)

After the 1960 performance in New York of *The Zoo Story* (1959), newspaper critics began to consider Edward Albee a major dramatist. At this early stage, he was vitriolic in his attacks upon the human condition. With wit and skill in creating dialogue he dramatized his contempt for social and personal complacency, false values and the "American Dream." Although Albee enjoyed a cynically intellectual approach, his plays lacked the compassion and the concern for human dignity which distinguish the works of most major playwrights.

Like his peers, Albee started with one-act plays. *The Zoo Story* dramatizes the meeting of two strangers, one of whom tells the other his life problems, goads him to anger and, finally, forces him to be the means of his suicide. *The Death of Bessie Smith* (1960) focusses upon the auto accident of the blues singer and the refusal of two white hospitals to admit her.

With the Broadway production of *Who's Afraid of Virginia Woolf?* (1962), Albee distinguished himself among American dramatists. Employing lacerating wit and characters who perform with ingenius malice and speak in a dialogue almost poetic in rhythm and tone, Albee wrote about "love" between a man and a woman which reflects his own view of illusion as "the American weakness." Always experimenting with form, Albee adapted *The Ballad of the Sad Café* (1963), Carson McCullers' story, and then three years later *Malcolm* (1966), the novel by James Purdy. To further confound the critics, and audiences as well, Albee presented them with a mystery play, *Tiny Alice* (1964). Audacious, belligerent and distasteful to many, this metaphysical toy with its experimental technique and abundant opportunity for interpretation also emphasizes Albee's interest in truth and illusion.

V. THEATRES AND CRITICS

After a UNESCO conference in Paris in 1947 and another in Prague the following year, the International Theatre Institute was founded, with Rosamond Gilder as the head of the American delegation.   The International Federation for Theatre Research was founded in 1955. In 1951 Circle in the Square, New York's oldest theatre company, had been formed, and two years later Norris Houghton and Edward T. Hambleton organized the Phoenix Theatre, a repertory theatre, also in New York City.

The term "Off Broadway" was coined in the mid-1950s for theatre outside the Times Square area in New York. "Off Off Broadway" was first used in the 1960s to distinguish professional commercial theatre from professional non-commercial theatre, but the term soon embraced a wide range of theatrical activity, including an alternative theatre grounded in unlimited experimentation that soon tested an audience's patience, taste and endurance. By 1965 there were several small producing organizations: Cafe Cino in 1958; Judson's Poet's Theatre in 1961; Cafe La Mama with Ellen Stewart in command in 1962; and Theatre Genesis in 1964. By mid-decade there were nearly forty coffee houses, churches and lofts producing the plays of fifty or sixty unknown playwrights.

Meanwhile, the writing of more challenging dramatic criticism indicated a distinct advance in the history of American drama.

Some respected older journalistic critics continued to write -- John Mason Brown, Walter Kerr, Brooks Atkinson, Richard Watts, Jr. -- and their numbers were swelled by Henry Hewes, William Glover, Robert Brustein and Gerald Weales. The establishment of scholarly journals -- *Tulane Drama Review, Modern Drama, Drama Survey* -- and the interest of university presses began to stimulate an atmosphere conducive to a tradition of literary criticism. In essence, criticism, although progressing slowly from the turn of the century, had by now reached a level of significant achievement.

VI. SUMMARY

During the three hundred years since *Ye Bare and Ye Cubb* was performed in Virginia, the advance of American drama to its position of world significance was slow and painful. By World War II, however, American dramatists had established a place for themselves. After mid-century, only two newcomers seemed to possess the imagination and talent to press the case for American drama. The great majority of plays on Broadway were psychological or sentimental melodramas, while the demands of commercial interests gave over more and more theatres to the increasingly popular musical comedies. Consequently, Americans began to look beyond Broadway for more stimulating theatre artistry.

Beyond Broadway, the Vivian Beaumont Theatre at Lincoln Center was opened in 1965. Across the country, audiences witnessed the greatest expansion of theatres since the nineteenth century: the Alley Theatre in Houston (1945), the Arena Stage in Washington (1950), the San Francisco Mime Troupe (1959), the Guthrie Theatre in Minneapolis (1963), the Free Southern Theatre based in New Orleans (1963-64), El Teatro Campesino in California (1965) and an impressive number of workshop theatres and summer stock companies, among many others.

SELECTED BIBLIOGRAPHY

Abramson, Doris E. *Negro Playwrights in the American Theatre, 1925-1959.* New York: Columbia Univ. Press, 1969.

Bigsby, C. W. E. *Modern American Drama, 1945-1990.* New York: Cambridge Univ. Press, 1992.

Donoghue, Denis. *The Third Voice: Modern British and American Verse Drama.* Princeton Univ. Press, 1959.

Downer, Alan S. *Recent American Drama.* Minneapolis: Univ. of Minnesota Press, 1961.

Gassner, John. *Theatre at the Crossroads.* New York: Holt, Rinehart and Winston, 1960.

Kitchin, Laurence. *Mid-Century Drama.* London: Faber and Faber, 1960.

Lewis, Allan. *American Plays and Playwrights of the Contemporary Theatre.* New York: Crown Publishers, 1965.

Nelson, Benjamin. *Tennessee Williams, The Man and His Work.* New York: Obolensky, 1961.

Novick, Julius. *Beyond Broadway: The Quest for Permanent Theatres.* New York: Hill and Wang, 1968.

Taubman, Howard. *The Making of the American Theatre.* New York: Coward-McCann, 1965.

Weales, Gerald. *American Drama Since World War II.* New York: Harcourt, Brace & World, 1962.

_____. *The Jumping-Off Place: American Drama in the 1960s, From Broadway to Off Off Broadway to Happenings.* New York: Macmillan, 1969.

Welland, Dennis. *Arthur Miller.* Edinburgh: Oliver and Boyd, 1961.

Chapter Six

From Protest Drama to Politically Correct Theatre
The Last Thirty Years

The social upheaval that changed America during the 1960s and 1970s reverberated throughout the theatre with rippling effects that both limit and expand the theatre of the 1990s. The Civil Rights movement that pushed into the national spotlight with the 1954 decision regarding Brown vs. the Board of Education of Topeka culminated in the Civil Rights legislation of June 29, 1964, stimulating reactions -- blacks rioting in Newark and Detroit, 1967; the assassination of Dr. Martin Luther King, Jr., 1968 -- that a quarter of a century later continue to show an ambivalent unrest. Disorder spread across America with anti-war demonstrations in Washington, the assassination of Robert Kennedy, the Kent State University incident, the experimentation with illegal drugs, the mass celebration of rebellion at Woodstock, the passage of Roe vs. Wade and the climax of political corruption symbolized by the Watergate break-in and President Nixon's resignation.

Increased violent crime and the growing drug sub-culture on America's streets showed that "One nation indivisible" was becoming more than a "teeming nation of nations" -- a nation openly "divisible." The guarantee of liberty was being interpreted as an endorsement of license, and rights of individuals seemed destined to supercede the common good. By the mid-1980s, when the space ship Challenger exploded in flight (1986), AIDS was being recognized as a disaster of unknown dimensions. In 1987 Wall Street crashed (October 19), and the Iran Contra Hearings revealed more government exploitation. Individual and national prestige suffered. The sexual revolution joined with the hedonistic call of the uncommitted to create a society which dramatists were quick to capture for theatre audiences.

The Roman critic Horace saw in art a means "to teach and to delight." As contemporary playwrights reacted to a new society which seemed blatantly committed to remaining uncommitted, they were unable to attain Horace's balance -- so necessary for successful theatre -- and asserted their limited views: to "enlighten" and to propagandize. With far greater intensity than the reform-oriented theatre of the Thirties ever achieved, the theatre of the 1970s and 1980s became an "agenda" theatre: sexual freedom, black empowerment, homosexual aggrandizement, feminist objectives. There were also, as ever, playwrights who toyed with light comedy and emphasized traditional themes and virtues, but the emphasis of most plays during these years was politically avant garde. Society in general was "doing it"; why not the theatre? Stretch the boundaries, test the limits, take risks! In society at large, prevalent attitudes suggested to some an explosion of anarchy, to others, high adventure. Such attitudes, however, produced neither dramatists of intellectual stature nor a theatre of distinction -- only a penchant for experimentation, which must be judged by future critics and historians.

I. DISTINCTIVE VOICES: PAST AND PRESENT

Despite Tennessee Williams' death in 1983 and Miller's recent lack of an impressive victory in the theatre, these two remain distinctive voices, America's greatest playwrights of the last half of the twentieth century.   There have been few challengers. Edward Albee's plays sparkled with promise during the 1960s, but twenty years later that promise seems only a memory. From the mid-1960s to the mid-1980s, Sam Shepard appeared to some critics to carry the hope of the American theatre on his shoulders, but he has apparently tired of writing for the stage. Only Neil Simon has consistently written plays for more than thirty years with an outstanding success rate.

A.   Arthur Miller (1915-)

In recent decades Miller has been more appreciated on the international stage -- particularly in Great Britain -- than in the United States. Of his plays written since 1965, only *The Price* (1968) has been successful in New York. Featuring two brothers, poles apart in ideas as well as actions, the play harks back to the familiar 1930s and explores the terrible "price" that rivalry and selfishness exact, but not without a touch of comedy. *The Creation of the World and Other Business* (1972), concerned with the nature of individual responsibility; *The Archbishop's Ceiling* (1977), revised in 1984 but never staged in the United States; and *The American Clock* (1979), showing scenes from the Depression years and based on Studs Terkel's *Hard Times*, were failures on stage, although each focussed, if sometimes without the clearest vision, upon the ideas which have become the hallmarks of Miller plays.

Although Miller has continued to raise moral and psychological issues in short dramas -- *Playing for Time* (1980), *Two Way Mirror* (1982) and *Danger! Memory!* (1987) -- his full-length play, *The Ride Down Mount Morgan* (1991), premiered in London. *Broken Glass* (1994) opened on Broadway fifty years to the month after the opening of his first Broadway play, *The Man Who Had All the Luck*. Taking its name from the anti-Semiticism of Kristalnach in 1938 but dealing with modern problems of denial, blame and guilt through the story of a woman's sudden hysterical paralysis, *Broken Glass* is a kind of melodramatic thriller in which Miller speaks his mind on moral issues. Once again, New York critics, as they had with Tennessee Williams' later work, seemed to resent the intrusion of ideas of a serious nature which do not reflect the current popular agenda.

B. Tennessee Williams (1911-1983)

From 1966 until his death, nineteen of Williams' plays premiered in New York or in London's West End theatres, where they frequently received better notices. During these years he also rewrote, revised, turned short stories into plays and short plays into longer plays. He wrote daily, traveled a good deal, endured personal illness, confinements and addictions. If his style of playwriting did not appear as gripping to American audiences as it once had, it had not changed very much, either. *The Gnädiges Fraulein* (1966) and *Small Craft Warnings* (1972), a revision of *Confessional* (1970), illustrate his repeated return to earlier techniques. Nor did his themes change, or the characters through whom he expressed his strong humanitarian feelings. The fugitive kind, male or female, the outsiders, reappear in *The Two Character Play* (1967; revised as *Outcry*, 1971, and again in 1974), *I Can't Imagine Tomorrow* (1976) and *Vieux Carré* (1977).

Williams always remained interested in people and in living, and his late plays continue to reflect that interest, even if some of them lack evidence of his earlier vigor: *A Lovely Summer for Creve Coeur* (1978), *Clothes for a Summer Hotel* (1980), *Something Cloudy, Something Clear* (1981). Survival was instinctive with Williams and acceptance a virtue, as Chris explains to Mrs. Goforth in *The Milk Train Doesn't Stop Here Anymore* (1962; revised and produced in 1963, 1964 and 1968). In *Kingdom of Earth* (produced as *The Seven Descents of Myrtle*, 1968), Myrtle clearly restates the message of the Survivor from *Camino Real* as he tells of "Peeto my pony."

C. Edward Albee (1928-)

A 1968 essay concluded that Albee's "Then, Now, and Nowhere Generation" showed a movement toward "an amoral and emasculated society." Albee's position, popular as his approach was in the 1960s with *A Delicate Balance* (1966), which explores some of the themes in *Who's Afraid of Virginia Woolf,* has suffered from changes occurring in the dramatist and the audiences he has chosen to address. After stylistic experimentation in *Box-Mao-Box* (1968), Albee returned to his characteristic carping on upper-middle-class American life in *All Over* (1971). In *Seascape* (1975), a winner of the Pulitzer Prize, Albee again confronted American complacency with probing questions concerning identity and individual values. Both *Counting the Ways* (1976) and *Listening* (1977) are experimental plays dealing with attitudes toward life and death. *The Lady from Dubuque* (1980) shows a return to his earlier successful techniques. His last Broadway production, *The Man Who Had Three Arms* (1983), was a critical disaster, and later plays, such as *Marriage Play* (1987) and *Three Tall Women* (1991), premiered abroad.

In recent years, Albee has served as a university professor and relegated his time to directing his own works, a task which illustrates his expressed vehemence against directorial excesses. Throughout his career, Albee has confused critics and scholars interested in identifying his motives and categorizing his dramatic techniques. His best efforts, however, are marked by a facility with language, skillful dialogue and a concern for substantial and provocative themes.

D. Sam Shepard (1943-)

Shepard appears to be that rebel in American drama who confounds the critics by his energy (more than forty plays) and his inventiveness. Lacking a commercial Broadway success, he has defied the conventional approach to popularity and become a spokesman for the post-Sixties generation of playgoers, many of whom acknowledge him as a living symbol of what it means to be an American at this time. More than any other contemporary dramatist, Shepard shows the influences of his generation (the rock and roll culture, the drugs). Among his early plays are *Cowboys* (1964); *La Turista* (1966), his first full-length play, strongly suggestive of Beckett's *Waiting for Godot; Operation Sidewinder* (1970), a comic journey worthy of the Marx Brothers into a serious social problem; and *Mad Dog Blues* (1971), a camp rendition of the rock and drug world.

In 1971 Shepard escaped to London, where he produced four plays, including *The Tooth of Crime* (1972), the tragedy of a man named Hoss and Shepard's most impressive work to date. During the late 1970s he wrote his "family trilogy" -- *Curse of the Starving Class* (1976), *Buried Child* (1978) and *True West* (1980) -- as well as *Fool for Love* (1979) and *A Lie of the Mind* (1985). After a hiatus of six years in which he became interested in screenwriting and movie acting, Shepard wrote *The States of Shock* (1991), a look at post-Vietnam America.

E.   Neil Simon (1927-)

With a hit on the New York stage almost every year since *Come Blow Your Horn* in 1961, Simon still has a difficult time convincing serious critics and historians of American drama that he deserves more thoughtful consideration than as a writer of funny gags and transcient comic successes. With such hilarious comedies as *Barefoot in the Park* (1963), *The Odd*

Couple (1965), *The Star-Spangled Girl* (1966) and the musical *Sweet Charity* (1966), he was the most successful playwright of the 1960s, with four shows running simultaneously on Broadway. He continued the trend with *Plaza Suite* (1968), *Promises, Promises* (1968) and *The Last of the Red Hot Lovers* (1969) and then changed to a more serious focus with *The Gingerbread Lady* (1970), which deals with alcoholism, and two bittersweet comedies -- *The Prisoner of Second Avenue* (1972) and *The Sunshine Boys* (1972). With the strongly autobiographical *Chapter Two* (1977), projecting his own problems upon the stage, he wrote what some consider his finest play. His success continued with a trilogy of autobiographical plays: *Brighton Beach Memoirs* (1983), *Biloxi Blues* (1985) and *Broadway Bound* (1986), in all of which Simon maintained a balance of thought and good humor. *Jake's Women* (1988) did not last long in New York, but for *Lost in Yonkers* (1991), again a play in which Simon's serious views emerge, he finally received the critical acclaim that he worked for -- a Pulitzer Prize and the Tony Award.

II. OBSERVERS OF SOCIETY

To catch the latest fad, to question disturbing actions, to comment on a current problem: these are objectives for play-wrights seeking quick success. The resulting play exposes the playwright as a thoughtful observer, a light-hearted sentimentalist, a satirist or a reformer taking an opportunity to "correct the errors of the world," as Saroyan might say.

A.   A Serious Bent

Paddy Chayefsky (1923-1981) was a self-styled social critic who, late in his life, concentrated his efforts on screenplays -- *The Hospital* (1971), *Network* (1975) and *Altered States* (1979). His last stage play, *The Latent Heterosexual* (1968), was an undeniably serious play showing the wretched horror of the times. William Saroyan (1908-1981) remained interested in the comedy-tragedy of life until the end of his career but produced nothing of great dramatic value during his last years. Bernard Pomerance (1940-) challenged the concept of physical "normality" in *The Elephant Man* (1977).

1.   ROMULUS LINNEY (1930-)

Linney has been described by Martin Gottfried of the New York *Post* as "a playwright of true literacy, a writer in the grand tradition," but even with seventeen plays produced on and off Broadway, in regional theatres and on stages around the world, Linney's work is not well known. Historical subjects and his own experiences provide the bases for his plots. His best known play, *The Love Suicide at Schofield Barracks* (1972), revives thoughts of Chikamatsu's Kabuki plays.   Among his other plays are *Democracy and Esther* (1974), a dramatization of Henry Adams' two novels of society in late nineteenth-century Washington, D.C.; *Holy Ghosts* (1974), about snake worshipers in the South; and *The Captivity of Pixie Shedman* (1981), a gothic tale. A self-described "poet of America's heartland," Linney is a playwright of substance and variety whose imaginative craftsmanship and rich use of language identify him as a major writer for future scholars to discover.

2.   RONALD RIBMAN (1932-)

Ribman first attracted attention in 1965 with *Harry, Noon and Night,* a play about losers, as his next play would also be -- *The Journey of the Fifth Horse* (1966).   Concerned with people "caught between aspiration and possibility," Ribman has written a substantial number of plays -- including *The Ceremony of Innocence* (1967), *Cold Storage* (1977) and *Sweet Table at the Richelieu* (1987) -- which reveal the playwright's facility with language and his interest in writing for a thoughtful audience.

3.   ARTHUR KOPIT (1937-)

Having found success in the 1950s by making fun of everything, Kopit took life more seriously in *Indians* (1968), a study of the white man's destruction of the Indian and a response to America's involvement in Vietnam.   In *Wings* (1978) he employed various techniques to explore a woman's recovery from a stroke. *The End of the World* (1984) also makes use of devices to mumble some painful and funny comments about the possiblity of nuclear destruction. He continued his sporadic record on Broadway with *The Road to Nirvana* (1990), a bizarre comedy about Hollywood antics. He has also written the books for musicals: *Nine* (1981) and a version of *Phantom of the Opera* (1991).

4.   MARSHA NORMAN (1947-)

Norman tends to be regarded as the author of two plays: *Getting Out* (1978), in which she looked closely at the choices open to a young woman "getting out" of prison, and *'night, Mother* (1983), a tense dramatization of a woman's preparing her mother and herself for her suicide. *Traveler in the Dark* (1984), which describes the conflict between a thoughtful doctor/scientist and his minister father, was not well received. Her other plays include *Winter Shakers* (1987) and *Sarah and Abraham* (1988) and *The Secret Garden* (1991), both musicals. Norman's recent weak showing with legitimate plays has provoked her to question Broadway's interest in serious drama.

5.   BETH HENLEY (1952-)

Henley has shown a compassion for human frailties which she combines with a balanced appreciation of mankind's comic and pathetic progress through life. *Crimes of the Heart* (1981) exudes an aura of ingenuousness that brought it an epic quality -- and a Pulitzer Prize. Maintaining that level of creativity, however, has been a constant challenge for Henley. Set in Mississippi, both *The Wake of Jamey Foster* (1982) and *The Miss Firecracker Contest* (1984) employ death as a natural event stimulating responses of humor, pathos and irritation. More recent plays include *The Debutante Ball* (1985), *The Lucky Spot* (1986) and *Abundance* (1990). Henley is at her best in scenes with women who long for freedom, love to remember the past and tend toward sentiment and gossip.

6.   DAVID HENRY HWANG (1957-)

M. Butterfly (1988), with its traditional theme and contemporary fascination, introduced Hwang to national audiences. Throughout the 1980s he wrote plays showing the problems associated with identity in a multicultural age. His early plays include *FOB* (1980), the tale of a Chinese man "Fresh Off the Boat"; *The Dance and the Railroad* (1981), in which Hwang incorporated ideas and techniques from traditional Chinese Opera; and *Family Devotions* (1981), a presentation of conflicting ideologies. *Rich Relations* (1986) satirizes upper-middle class America.

B.   The Light-Hearted and Sentimental

During the 1960s and 1970s, Neil Simon was the most popular writer of light comedy. Despite his change to a more serious view, he has kept that reputation. Only a few dramatists have challenged his position. Jean Kerr (1923-) has written ten popular comedies, including *Poor Richard* (1964), *Finishing Touches* (1973) and *Lunch Hour* (1980). Popular in the 1960s with *Luv* (1964), Murray Schisgal (1926-) has contributed little since then: *Jimmy Shine* (1968), a comic vaudeville piece, and *All Over Town* (1974), a successful farce of confused identity. With *Solitaire/Double Solitaire* (1971), Robert Anderson (1917-) returned to his theme of loneliness. His attempt to combine four slight comedies into an evening's entertainment -- *You Know I Can't Hear You When the Water's Running* (1967) -- was very successful but shows little of his earlier wit or sensitivity. The autobiographical *I Never Sang for My Father* (1968) proved far too introspective for critics and audiences.

Herb Gardner (1934-) creates successful comedies combining a lavishly encumbered stage, a love story and a gift for the monologue, the quick repartee and the one-line gag. *Thieves* (1974) tells about a group of apartment dwellers, each with a problem to which no one listens, each a thief and each being robbed by passing time. *I'm Not Rappaport* (1985) dramatizes the efforts of an old and irascible Jew, who refuses to be intimidated by either the establishment or the criminal underworld, to maintain his independence. *Conversations with My Father* (1991) explores the tensions within a Jewish immigrant family as they become assimilated into American society. Insisting that he writes to entertain audiences, Gardner might be a "role model" for aspiring dramatists.

C.   In the Tradition of American Satire

Nothing of life's absurdity has ever escaped the American satirist, a fact revealed in such works as *Rip Van Winkle*

(1981) and *Some Americans Abroad* (1989) by Richard Nelson (1950-); the trashy satire of Ronald Tavel (1941-), who set out to "catch the attention of critics" in such plays as *The Ovens of Anita Orangejuice* (1978); the Vietnam satire, *How I Got That Story* (1979) by Amlin Gray (1946-); and the cartoonist's approach of Jules Feiffer (1929-) in *Little Murders* (1967) and *Grown Ups* (1981).

1.   DAVID RABE (1940-)

Rabe apparently owes his playwriting success to the fact that he was drafted to serve in Vietnam and to Joseph Papp, who produced five of his early plays at the New York Shakespeare Festival. A dramatist of limited output, he seems destined to be identified with his popular trilogy about the Vietnam War -- *The Basic Training of Pavlo Hummel* (1971), *Sticks and Bones* (1971) and *Streamers* (1976) -- which present a bitterly satiric and sometimes comic view of its senseless horror. *In the Boom Boom Room* (1973), concerned with the plight of a go-go dancer, was less successful. In *Hurlyburly* (1984) Rabe reemphasized the violent and pointless Age of Anxiety that he assumes to be exclusively American.

2.   CHRISTOPHER DURANG (1949-)

Durang has been criticized for his self-absorbed glibness and praised for formidable skills as a satirist of conventional American institutions and values. Impatient and fearless, he confronts the absurdities of Catholicism, the American family and psychiatrists with a defiantly presumptious impunity. Among his best-known works are *Sister Mary Ignatius Explains It All for You* (1979), an attack on dogmatic parochial education, *The Marriage of Bette and Boo* (1973) and *Baby with the Bathwater* (1983).

D.   Agenda Playwriting: A Popular Approach

It may be argued that every playwright has an "agenda." Some, however, show clearer focus in their themes, have stronger and more confining views and reveal a consistent determination to say whatever they think about the society they have observed. Tina Howe (1937-) has acknowledged that all of her plays are about art: *Museum* (1976) examines the real and presumed relationships among creators and their viewers; *The Art of Dining* (1979) focusses, with comic delight, on Howe's obsessions for art and food, and *Painting Churches* (1983) uses a background of artistry to show the necessity of acceptance in a family. Albert Innaurato (1948-) started out during the 1970s as a restless critic of excesses, frequently using food as a motif in his plays: *The Transfiguration of Benno Blimpie* (1963), a bizarre story of a fat man eating himself to death, and *Gemini* (1976), the tale of another excess, which ran for four years in New York.

1. A. R. GURNERY, JR. (1930-)

Gurney revealed his concern for WASP manners and mores in his first full-length play, *Scenes from American Life* (1970), which presents WASP life in its various phases, starting in the 1930s. *Children* (1974) studies tensions within a WASP family. *Who Killed Richard Cory?* (1976) explores the middle-age crisis of a WASP lawyer. Gurney further combined his literary interests with his conservative and genteel tastes in *The Golden Age* (1981), suggested by "The Aspern Papers" by Henry James; *The Dining Room* (1981) and *Another Antigone* (1986). He has been called "encouraging prolific" as he promotes his solid beliefs in well-balanced comedies -- *Love Letters* (1989), *The Snow Ball* (1991), *The Old Boy* (1991) -- that set his work apart from and well above the usual Broadway fare.

2. LANFORD WILSON (1937-)

Wilson frequently shows his interest in the human conflicts which separate the past from the present and traditional values from the pressures of modern living. His best-known work is a trilogy about the Talley family: *The Fifth of July* (1978), which identifies the present scattered remnants of the family and their lost roots; *Talley and Son* (1985), written last but set during World War II and second in the scheme of family events; *Talley's Folly* (1982), concurrent in time with *Talley and Son* but dealing with business conflicts between father and grandfather. Among earlier successful plays, *The Rimers of Eldrich* (1965) ridicules small town bigotries and *The Hot l Baltimore* (1976) dramatizes a call girl's struggle to recover her past. Among more recent plays, *Burn This* (1987) dramatizes the grief of a dancer for her dead lover through past and present reactions.

3.   DAVID MAMET (1947-)

Mamet deals with the sham of American life, particularly the society of capitalists, with a directness of Anglo-Saxon speech that defines the level of sophistication he sees.   The significance of the argument in his plays, however, should not be underestimated, nor should the value of his essays on authenticity, truth and responsibility.   Mamet's early one-act plays, such as *Duck Variations* (1972) and *Sexual Perversity in Chicago* (1974), in which abusive language stimulates abusive actions, brought his work to national attention.   His full-length plays, such as *American Buffalo* (1975), are also concerned with the destructive power of language.   *Glen Garry Glen Ross* (1983), about shady real estate dealings, won a Pulitzer Prize. *Speed-the-Plow* (1989) was a success at New York's Lincoln Center.   Mamet's productivity is remarkable, even as he spends more time directing plays and writing for the movies.

III. POLITICALLY CORRECT DRAMA

To the advent over the past thirty years of increasingly liberal tendencies in America's political, judicial and social institutions, playwrights have responded in traditional fashion.   As new terms and phrases express the idiosyncrasies of contemporary fads, fashions and human behavior, new plays mirror them in language, action and theme.   For a generation for whom polite manners and common courtesy have been lost or disregarded as irrelevant, the guiding phrase for appropriate behavior has become "politically correct."   In particular, it has been applied to approaches toward groups regarded as socially or politically "disenfranchised." Although "P.C." approaches have recently fallen into disfavor and the term itself has become an object of ridicule, regional and professional not-for-profit theatres have continued to call for politically correct themes as they vie for grant money, either from the National Endowment for the Arts or liberal private foundations.

A. Beginnings

The 1960s were exciting years for proponents of revolt, reformation, the destruction of preconceptions and traditions and the inventions of new ways to present new truths. The 1970s were a time for retrenchment. So wrote Jean-Claude Van Itallie (1936-), who made his reputation during the 1960s with *America Hurrah* (1966) and *The Serpent* (1968), which satirize or question concepts around which attitudes of political correctness would later be established. His other plays include *King of the U.S.* (1972) and *Mystery Play* (1973). Howard Sackler (1929-1982) approached the situation differently in *The Great White Hope* (1967), a fictionalized account of Jack Johnson, an African-American boxer who became the world heavyweight champion. One critic described Sackler's viewpoint as "undigested late-1960s white liberal guilt," an assessment which helps clarify the politically correct position.

B. Black Dramatists

The contributions of African-American dramatists were neither outstanding nor well received until the Civil Rights movement was well underway in the late 1950s. A decade later, black playwrights were a force on Broadway. Supported by a liberal white establishment, including scholars writing scores of books and articles on "Black Drama," African-American playwrights were soon faced with a dilemma which has been discussed -- Geneviève Fabre, *Drumbeats, Masks, and Metaphor,* 1983 -- but never satisfactorily resolved: Should black dramatists write for general American audiences and promote integration of the races or write for black audiences and create an exclusively black body of work?

1.   SPEAKING OUT

Alice Childress (1920-) has been a continuing voice for black women in *Wine in the Wilderness* (1969) and *Moms* (1987), on the life of comedienne Jackie "Moms" Mabley. After his successful critique of black-white relations in *Blues for Mr. Charlie* (1964), James Baldwin (1924-1987) found his approach lacking the militancy required of black drama in the 1970s.

Lonnie Elder III (1931-) wrote exclusively for a black audience and is known for one play, *Ceremonies in Dark Old Men* (1965). Charles Gordone (1925-) also wrote only one successful play, *No Place to Be Somebody* (1969), but nonetheless became the first black playwright to win a Pulitzer Prize. Fitting a category of drama once defined by W. E. B. DuBois as a "play of the contact of black and white," Gordone's play dramatizes "Charlie fever," a metaphor for black rage against white power.

2. A GATHERING OF FORCES

Douglas Turner Ward (1930-), defiant in his belief that black dramatists must write for predominantly black audiences, has worked as a playwright, actor and director to achieve the ideal black-oriented theatre. *Happy Ending* and *Day of Absence,* both written in 1965, exhibit his favorite devices of "satire, exaggeration and mordant humor." Adrienne Kennedy (1931-) calls her plays "states of mind." Scattered throughout her technically fascinating but dramaturgically confusing works are the issues which haunt her characters -- prejudice, racial heritage and sexual identity: *A Rat's Mass* (1966), *The Lennon Play: In His Own Rite* (1967) and *The Owl Answers* (1969). Ronald Milner (1938-) is a major spokesman for black theatre in America. *Who's Got His Own* (1966) shows the agony of a black family in a white racist society. In other "morality dramas," he studies constructive and destructive behavior. *What the Wine Sellers Buy* (1973) deals with the position of black women in black society; *Checkmates* (1987) examines the "kill whitey" mentality.

3. BLACK MILITANCY

Amiri Baraka (LeRoy Jones, 1934-) became a leader of the black revolutionary movement and declared in his manifesto, *The Revolutionary Theatre,* that the theatre must be "a weapon." *A Black Mass* (1966), *Home on the Range* (1968) and *Bloodrites* (1970) are blatant agitprop plays. As Baraka's life changed (a result of a prison term), his plays also changed. By the mid-1970s he had rejected black nationalism for revolutionary socialism, as shown in *The Motion of History* (1975). In 1984 Baraka published his autobiography and stopped writing for the theatre. Ed Bullins (1935-) is probably the most prolific black dramatist in America with several dozen plays starting with *Clara's Ole Man* (1965).   In *The Theme Is Blackness* (1966), *The Electronic Nigger* (1968) and *The Duplex* (1970), Bullins sounded a rebellious voice, writing only for black audiences and refusing to cooperate with the white theatre establishment.   His confrontational style continued with *House Party* (1973) and *The Taking of Miss Janie* (1975).   Charles Fuller (1939-) works with the Negro Ensemble Company in New York, which continues to produce Fuller's violent plays depicting angry black men.   His best-known play is *A Soldier's Play* (1981), concerned with the murder of an unpopular black army sergeant.   Other plays include *The Brownsville Raid* (1975) and *Zooman and the Sign* (1980).

4.   AUGUST WILSON (1945-)

Wilson came to prominence in 1984 as a direct consequence of collaboration with a black director, Lloyd Richards, and extensive developmental work on his ideas at the O'Neill Theater Center's National Playwrights Conference and the Yale Repertory Theatre under the direction of Richards.   With this type of collaborative effort and the support of six major foundation fellowships in as many years, Wilson gained a reputation as an impressive contributor to American drama. His plays focus on "the black experience in twentieth-century America," and are meant for a mainstream audience: *Ma Rainey's Black Bottom* (1984), set in Chicago during the 1920s; *Fences* (1985), a Pulitzer Prize play set in the 1950s, which eulogizes a black baseball player; and *Joe Turner's Come and Gone* (1986), which deals with the post-Civil War generation. *The Piano Lesson* (1987), another Pulitzer Prize winner, was followed by *Two Trains Running* (1990).

C. Feminist Drama

As both a continuation of politics and a consequence of the Civil Rights movement, a liberal feminist movement was generated in the 1970s. To separate themselves from general Leftist activity, women such as Megan Terry and Roberta Sklar formed their own women's theatre groups: Omaha Magic Theatre and the Women's Experimental Theatre, respectively. By the 1980s women playwrights were receiving major awards -- Beth

Henley, Marsha Norman, Wendy Wasserstein -- and professional organizations, such as Julia Miles' Women's Project, supported women in all aspects of theatre.

1.   MEGAN TERRY (1932-)

Terry began her major theatre work with the Open Theatre during the 1960s and achieved international acclaim with *Viet Rock* (1966), a protest play about the war in Vietnam and the first rock musical. An intelligent and imaginative playwright who has employed distinctive theatrical techniques, Terry has been called the "mother of American feminist drama." Of her own work, she has written: "I design my plays to provoke laughter -- thought may follow." Within her more than sixty plays, Terry has dealt with such diverse issues as sexism, violence, women in prison, the sexist nature of language, jogging, adolescent drinking, materialistic greed in America and political confusion. Among her better known plays are *Calm Down Mother* (1965), *Comings and Goings* (1966), *Approaching Simone* (1970), *Babes in the Big House* (1979) and *Walking Through Walls* (1987). Since 1974 she has served as playwright-in-residence at the Omaha Magic Theatre, encouraging the writing of avant garde work and performance art.

2.   MARIA IRENE FORNÉS (1930-)

Fornés established her reputation in avant garde theatre with both plays and musicals -- *Tango Palace* (1964) and *Dr. Kheal* (1968). With *Fefu and Her Friends* (1977), Fornés focussed on female friendships, albeit with her experimental nature foremost and her comic pose entact. *Mud* (1983) treats an abused woman at the center of a domestic triangle; *The Conduct of Life* (1985) shows the brutal relationships of three women with the husband of one of them, a state torturer.

3.   WENDY WASSERSTEIN (1950-)

Wasserstein possesses that combination of personal traits and abilities which allows her to observe society as a sensible and witty optimist. Focussing exclusively on women, she has achieved both commercial and artistic success. *Uncommon Women and Others* (1975) reveals the innermost thoughts of five women at a college reunion.   *The Heidi Chronicles* (1988) traces the history of the women's movement through the life of one woman.   Among her other plays are *Any Woman Can* (1973) and *The Sisters Rosensweig* (1992).

D.   Gay and Lesbian Drama

Homosexuals appeared in plays long before the "sexual revolution of the 1960s" provided opportunities which new liberal approaches to "freedom" encouraged. *The Boys in the Band* (1968) by Matt Crowley reflects a change in attitude which was quickly exploited in the 1970s, first Off Broadway with plays by Terrence McNally (*The City*, 1975) and Harvey Fierstein (*Torch Song Trilogy*, 1981) and on Broadway with Martin Sherman's *Bent* (1978) and the musical *La Cage Aux Folles* (1983) by Fierstein and Jerry Herman.   Charles Ludlum's work illustrates the extremes of homosexual theatre in such plays as *Bluebeard* (1970) and *The Mystery of Irma Vep* (1984). Gay producing companies also appeared, such as The Glines and Meridian Gay Theatre in New York and Theatre Rhinoceros in San Francisco.

Lesbian feminist theatre groups of the 1970s included the Lavender Cellar in Minneapolis and the Red Dyke Theatre in Atlanta.   By the 1980s the troupe known as Split Britches in New York's East Village and the WOW Café in the West Village were producing plays by Holly Hughes, called "the quintessential Dyke Noir" playwright and performer. Karen Malpede combined feminism and pacifism in *Making Peace* (1979) and *Us* (1988).

Terrence McNally (1939-)
McNally began his career at the Guthrie Theater in the 1960s with *And Things That Go Bunp in the Night* (1964), using a comic-satiric approach and a command of language that have gained him an impressive reputation over the years.   His subject matter covers the usual gamut of events from the Vietnam War to the sexual revolution.   As does the hero in *Where Has Tommy Flowers Gone?* (1971), McNally came to New York, where he has focussed his plays on the homosexual in society with a witty and commercially successful positive

approach. His recent plays include *Frankie and Johnny in the Clair de Lune* (1987), *The Lisbon Traviata* (1985, 1989) and *Lips Together, Teeth Apart* (1991).

E.   AIDS: A New Issue for Playwrights

During the mid-1980s a few plays dealing with AIDS appeared across the country: Larry Kramer's *The Normal Heart* (1985), William M. Hoffman's *As Is* (1985). As the virus spread and the political pressure to control the disease intensified, the number of plays increased to reflect the varied responses and attitudes toward the epidemic. A founding member of the Gay Men's Health Crisis, Kramer built his career on AIDS: *Reports from the Holocaust: The Making of an AIDS Activist* (1989). Homosexuality dominates Harry Kondoleon's plays, such as *Christmas on Mars* (1983). Tony Kushner had written few plays -- *A Bright Room Called Day* (1986); *L'Illusion* (1988), adapted from Corneille -- until *Angels in America* opened in New York in 1993, captured the public interest and received a Pulitzer Prize. A long time in preparation, *Angels in America: A Gay Fantasia on National Themes*, consists of two long plays, subtitled *Millennium Approaches* and *Perestroika*.

IV. THE AVANT GARDE

Popular in current theatre jargon are phrases such as "Stretch the Boundaries" and "Take Risks." In reality, these phrases mean new plays and new ideas that will sell tickets and capture grant funding.

A.   Theatre of Self Indulgence

In the contemporary American theatre, personal aggrandize-ment, reflecting current social trends and rebelling against the strictures of traditional forms and ideas, attracts audiences and is often supported by grant monies. Beginning with such works as *Oh! Calcutta!* (1969), a musical revue -- resulting from the collaborative efforts of numerous people -- which ran for 5,959 performances in New York, playwrights began to capitalize upon the public's newly admitted appetite for erotica.

Extremely "narcissistic and reflective," Spalding Gray (1941-)
seems interested only in his own progress through life --
Rumstick Road (1977), *Nayatt School* (1978) and *Point Judith*
(1979), all written with Elizabeth LeCompte; and *Swimming to
Cambodia* (1984) and *Terrors of Pleasure* (1985).   Rochelle
Owens (1936) calls attention to herself with tales of eroticism,
sexual perversion and violence in such plays as *Futz* (1965),
featuring the love of a man for a pig and the pleasures of
sodomy, and *Beclch* (1968), a savage play about grotesque
primitive rituals and rites.   Charles Busch (1955-), a female
impersonator fascinated with Hollywood "glamour," exploits
himself for the purpose of satire.   The success of *The Vampire
Lesbians of Sodom* (1985) helped create a "Busch" cult.

B.   Experimenters

As people of vision whose innovations become traditions or as
self-serving glory seekers, experimenters introduce new and
often controversial devices and subject matter which must be
evaluated by future generations.

1.   PLAYWRIGHTS: JACK GELBER (1932-),
RICHARD SCHECHNER (1934-), JOHN GUARE (1938-)

With such plays as *Square in the Eye* (1965), *Sleep* (1972) and
Rehearsal (1976), Gelber continued his contributions to the
improvisational and group drama.   Schechner founded the
Performance Group (1967-1980) and began to explore audience
participation in plays and the use of theatrical language:
Dionysus in 69 (1969), *Commune* (1970).   Critics scarcely know
how to react to Guare's frequently outrageous and unexpected
dramatic conceptions which audiences, nevertheless, find
entertaining.   His belief that "avoiding humiliation is the core
of tragedy and comedy and probably of our lives," forms the
basis of such plays as *The House of Blue Leaves* (1971), *Marco
Polo Sings a Solo* (1976) and *Six Degrees of Separation* (1990).

2.   ACTOR-DIRECTOR-PLAYWRIGHTS:
LEE BREWER (1937-), RICHARD FOREMAN (1937-),
ROBERT WILSON (1941-)

Associated with Mabou Mines, an experimental theatre
company known for mixing acting styles, narrative techniques

and multimedia staging, Brewer prepared an animation trilogy -- *The Red Horse* (1970), *The B. Beaver* (1974) and *The Shaggy Dog* (1978) -- in which monologues address human problems through beast fables. In 1988, he created and directed a gender-reversed *King Lear*, which features Queen Lear and her three sons. In 1968 Foreman decided that he wanted a theatre which would be radically different from anything that he had ever seen. His plays, he writes, attempt to capture "the buzz of consciousness," and they have proved remarkably popular. Among his works are *Total Recall* (1970), *Pandering to the Masses* (1975), *Film Is Evil; Radio Is Good* (1987) -- all of which make distinct demands upon his audiences. Wilson eschews plot, characters and playscripts. The term "theatre composition" may best describe his interest in visual and aural communication set against a background of momentous scenic effects. Among his titles are *The Life and Times of Joseph Stalin* (1973) which runs for twelve hours; *the CIVIL warS* (1983) and *The Black Rider: the casting of magic bullets* (1990).

V. AMERICAN TRADITIONS

From the earliest of times, Americans have associated poetry, music and spectacle with the theatre. Although those early characteristics of drama are still very much in evidence on the American stage, there have been changes of emphasis consistent with cultural and social changes, new scientific discoveries and industrial innovations.

A. Poetry in the Theatre

Many dramatists, from Tennessee Williams to August Wilson, might consider themselves, or be regarded by others, as poets, but few poets of repute find any degree of success in the theatre. Robert Lowell (1917-1977) built upon his earlier success with *Endecott and the Red Cross* (1968) and an adaptation from Aeschylus, *Prometheus Bound* (1967). Archibald MacLeish (1892-1982) wrote four plays after 1965 -- *An Evening's Journey to Conway, Massachusetts* (1967), *The Play of Herod* (1968), *Scratch* (1971) and *The Great American Fourth of July* (1975) -- but none achieved the success of his earlier work. Richard Wilbur (1921-) continues to enhance his reputation as a translator and adaptor of Molière (*The School for Wives*, 1971) and Racine (*Phaedra*, 1985). Ntozake Shange (1948-) created a long-running Broadway show in *for colored girls who have considered suicide/when the rainbow is enuf* (1976). A poet with a strong feminist approach, she incorporates words, music and dance into what she calls "choreopoems," such as *Boogie Woogie Landscapes* (1980) and *from okra to greens* (1986).

B. Musical Theatre

By the mid-1960s, it had become clear that the musical theatre's brilliant comic traditions would soon be gone. A few followed the traditional mode: *Mame* (1966), book by Jerome Lawrence and Robert E. Lee, music by Jerry Herman; *Cabaret* (1966), book by Joe Masteroff, music and lyrics by John Kander and Fred Ebb, respectively; *You're a Good Man, Charlie Brown* (1967), by Clark Gesner; *Zorbá* (1968), book by Joseph Stein, music and lyrics by Kander and Ebb; *Promises, Promises* (1968), book by Neil Simon, music by Burt Bacharach, lyrics by Hal David. The new approach to musical theatre came with Megan Terry's *Viet Rock* (1966); the first "American tribal love-rock musical," *Hair* (1967), by Gerome Ragni, James Rado and Galt MacDermot; and experimental musicals such as *Promenade* (1969) by Maria Irene Fornés.

The concept musical emerged in the 1970s, and the popularity of musicals created by choreographer-directors dominated that decade and the next. Some of the most successful were Bob Fosse's *Pippin* (1972) and *Chicago* (1975), Michael Bennett's *A Chorus Line* (1975) and Tommy Tune's *Nine* (1982) and *The Will Rogers Follies* (1991). These years also produced some memorable musical comedies -- *Applause* (1970) by Betty Comden and Adolph Green; *Grease* (1972) by Jim Jacobs and Warren Casey; *Sugar Babies* (1979) book by Ralph G. Allen, music by Johnny McHugh, lyrics by Dorothy Fields and Al Dubin; *Nunsense* (1985) by Dan Goggin.

Stephen Sondheim (1930-)
The most significant figure in musical theatre during the last twenty-five years, Sondheim established a reputation as a composer and lyricist for *A Funny Thing Happened on the Way*

to the Forum (1962). He has dominated the American musical theatre scene ever since: *Company* (1970), *Follies* (1971), *A Little Night Music* (1973), *Pacific Overtures* (1976), *Sweeney Todd* (1979), *Sunday in the Park With George* (1984), *Into the Woods* (1987), *Assassins* (1991), *Passion* (1994). His popularity is such that a journal, entitled *The Sondheim Review,* now exists for "those who love Stephen Sondheim's work."

C. Spectacles on Stage

Early American playwrights created spectacles with water and smoke and moving diaramas. Throughout the nineteenth century, playwrights used animals and the mechanical inventions of stage carpenters. Pageants moved outdoors during the twentieth century, and crowds of people played against massive scenery from North Carolina to Texas to Minnesota. In recent years the sense of spectacle has been elaborately accomplished in the hands of computer technicians and in the minds of energetic experimenters.

D. Critics and Scholars

The tradition of reviewing New York theatre productions was well established by World War II, but the commercial nature of New York theatre had also, by this time, thrust upon the reviewer a new obligation. The reviewer had to be a competent predictor of audience reactions and a source of information. As financial stakes rose and ticket prices soared, the good review became tantamount to success. Tensions between reviewers and producers made headlines (i.e., John Simon vs. Joseph Papp), and the power of the reviewer became a source of acrimony.

Since the early 1960s, the art of the reviewer or critic has changed as Off Broadway theatre has become more important, and the number of newspapers in New York has dwindled. Off Broadway developed its own critics in the *Village Voice*. By 1967, the only New York newspapers regularly reviewing plays were the *New York Times,* the *Post* and the *Daily News.* Consequently, the power of such critics as Clive Barnes and Frank Rich skyrocketed; reviews appearing in weekly or monthly magazines in New York became more influencial, and the voices of academic/professional critics such as Robert Brustein and Eric Bentley assumed more importance.

With the greater emphasis in colleges and universities upon contemporary trends and issues, journals devoted to drama and theatre scholarship were started (*Modern Drama,* 1958); research organizations were founded (American Society for Theatre Research, 1957); courses of study were created. Soon scholarship reflected social and political demands, and the number of books and articles on black drama, women in theatre and gender studies increased. Mistaking their obligations, scholars began to search for a playwright of substance at a time when few writers showed distinctive qualities. The *Cambridge Guide to American Theatre,* 1993, indeed a substantial undertaking, reflects a post-modern revisionism through its emphasis on contemporary fascinations, while omitting events and people whose historical significance has long been proven.

VI. SUMMARY

Historians argue, properly, that the passage of time is necessary to an accurate evaluation of events and people. About the thirty-year period starting in the mid-1960s, few conclusions may be drawn with any degree of certainty. A more liberal drama and theatre reflecting momentary public thinking may be one result, but that in itself only follows the fashion of earlier times when one day's news was on the stage the next. That playwrights protest and propagandize is also not new. The purpose of theatre, however, remains constant, and as "one nation indivisible" becomes determinedly "divisible," society will be portrayed in a currently acceptable manner. If there are meaningful voices to protest, they are being heard in America's numerous and substantial regional theatres. Each year, more theatres show discomfort with the coarseness of many post-modern plays and reflect the demands of their audiences by calling for "traditional values" on stage.

One final note on change and continuity: George Abbott, 107 years old in 1994, who first appeared as a Broadway actor in 1913, directed a workshop production of a new musical in 1989 and is still a presence on Broadway.

SELECTED BIBLIOGRAPHY

Berkowitz, Gerald M. *New Broadways: Theatre Across America 1950-1980.* Totowa: Rowan and Littlefield, 1982.

Bigsby, C. W. E. *Modern American Drama, 1945-1990.* Cambridge: Cambridge Univ. Press, 1992.

Bogard, Travis, Richard Moody and Walter J. Meserve. *The Revels History of Drama in English, Vol. VIII: American Drama.* London: Methuen, 1977.

Fabre, Geneviève. *Drumbeats, Masks and Metaphor: Contemporary Afro-American Theatre.* Cambridge: Harvard Univ. Press, 1983.

Hart, Linda, ed. *Making a Spectacle: Feminine Essays on Contemporary Women's Theatre.* Ann Arbor: Univ. of Michigan Press, 1989.

Miller, Arthur. *The Theatre Essays of Arthur Miller.* Ed. Robert A. Martin. New York: Viking Press, 1978.

Parker, Dorothy, ed. *Essays on Modern American Drama: Williams, Miller, Albee, and Shepard.* Toronto: Univ. of Toronto Press, 1987.

Rogoff, Gordon. *Theatre Is Not Safe: Theatre Criticism 1962-1986.* Evanston: Northwestern Univ. Press, 1987.

Syilassy, Zoltán. *American Theatre of the 1960s.* Carbondale: Southern Illinois Univ. Press, 1986.

Index

INDEX TO PLAYS